Helen —

Thanks for having "faith" in me!

Karen Kruse

7-22-04

Living By Faith

Real Life Stories That
Will Touch Your Heart & Soul

Compiled by
Tina L. Miller

Obadiah Press

607 North Cleveland Street
Merrill, Wisconsin 54452

Living By Faith
Real Life Stories That Will Touch Your Heart & Soul

Published by Obadiah Press
Edited by Tina L. Miller
Final Proofreading by Sallie Bachar

Cover photo and design by Tina L. Miller

Page layout and design by Tina L. Miller

ISBN: 0-9713266-2-2

Printed and published in the United States of America
by Obadiah Press

Dedicated to the memory of
Endyll Princeton McDaniels
February 22, 1982 - February 25, 2003

Table of Contents

Foreword

In 2002 my then partner and I wanted to do something to help new and aspiring writers get recognized and published. We knew we couldn't publish *all* of them—not on our budget! But we wondered how we might help at least a few. Obadiah Press had by then published a number of books, several of which were anthologies—collections of short stories or essays—and in doing so had enjoyed the opportunity to work with many new writers.

We decided to hold an annual writing contest to help discover more new and aspiring writers and help them fulfill their dream of publication, as well! And so the Obadiah Press Annual Writer's Contest was born, providing the opportunity for many writers to become published authors in a collection of stories we hope will inspire all who read them.

This book is the first in a series of books featuring the winning essays from each of our annual contests. Each book is focused on a specific theme. Our first contest in 2002 was appropriately on the theme of "Faith" and you are holding the results of that contest—and the fulfillment of a lifetime of dreams for some of our authors—in your hands now.

Happy reading! Oh, and you *may* want to have a box of tissues handy for some of these. I'm a sucker for a tearjerker, and some of these definitely fall into that category.

Blessings!

Tina L. Miller
Compiling Author, Editor, and Publisher

P.S. To learn more about *this year's* annual writing contest, log on to our website at www.obadiahpress.com

1

Faith In Miracles

Miracles And Mustard Seeds

By Vicki Goodfellow Duke
Calgary, Alberta, Canada

Miracles—those extraordinary moments when God's hand reaches into time to transform a life irrevocably—make our faith shine. His merciful love and awesome power are gloriously visible in the sudden conversion of a wayward heart or in the healing of a sick child.

Miracles are very real, for who can deny God's intervention in the inexplicable recovery of a terminally ill newborn?

Nicholas was still in utero when he was first diagnosed with serious heart defects; his parents were told that he would require open heart surgery in the first week of his life. Subsequent ultrasounds revealed a worsening condition as the time of his birth approached. In the first few days of Nicholas' life, his vital signs gave scanty hope to his parents and doctors, and plans to transport him to a children's hospital for surgery were cancelled. He was much too ill. Family and friends began to prepare emotionally for his death.

When Nicholas was four days old, his parents were told that he was going to die. In their grief, they turned to their church community for support. A lady named Anna heard the story of the sick little boy and began to pray for him. As she prayed, Anna felt more and more strongly that she needed to go to the hospital to pray with the family. She was surprised at her own resolve to go visit a family that she hardly knew.

Two days later, with the family's permission, Anna did something she had never done before—she laid her hands upon the child. In that moment, Anna knew that God was using her as a conduit. As she prayed, the three machines keeping Nicholas alive beeped and flashed simultaneously. It was as if something had told them they were no longer necessary. Heat rushed through Anna's hands and she knew in her heart, without a doubt, that Nicholas was healed.

Tests later in the day revealed what a faith-filled woman already knew: Nicholas was a perfectly healthy six-day-old baby boy.

Doctors and technicians, loathe to call something a miracle, admitted the impossibility of Nicholas' unaided recovery and deemed the phenomenon a "mystery." Yet the faithful know, it is no mystery other than the mystery of God's love.

The miraculous affirms to us that God is ever watchful and ever present, and it is easy to have faith when its results are visible and concrete. Miracles are gifts of a distinct and supernatural kind, and we are grateful for them as we journey through this "vale of tears."

In the course of an ordinary life, however, the presence of miracles is rare. Many lives have been completed with no wonders observed, no marvels experienced.

It is in the ordinariness of daily living that faith is tested, nourished, and fortified.

In the countless details that comprise a life, it takes true faith to believe what we cannot see.

It is 7:30 on a Thursday morning, and I have been up for over an hour. I need extra time this morning to do all of my regular tasks and then get myself and the baby ready to be somewhere by 9:00 a.m. I have had this particular morning planned for six weeks. It's been a long time since I spent a quiet morning in prayerful reflection, and I am hopeful that this morning's mothers' retreat will afford me the opportunity to do just that.

I rush to cook breakfast, iron uniforms, make lunches, feed the baby, and resolve sibling conflicts. By 8:10 a.m. I am thrown together, yet ready to leave the house. It is only as we are leaving the house that I realize that my six-year-old is missing her school tie—again. I have already replaced the tie once this year, at a cost of $25, and we have had long discussions about keeping things in their proper place. My patience is thin. I yell at my daughter, criticizing her and her habits, and she is reduced to tears. We leave the house 15 minutes late, angry, and tie-less.

After dropping the kids at school—late—I realize I have forgotten the baby's bottle, race back home, grab the bottle, and am just about to leave when the doorbell rings. It is my friend from across the street. Frustrated, I desperately, half-rudely try to brush her off, but she "needs" to talk to me right this minute about her long-standing marriage problems. By the time I am able to usher her out the door, it is already past 9:00 a.m.

When I arrive at the retreat, stressed and irritated, I am greeted by an apologetic woman who informs me that the retreat is full. She cannot make an exception because of "fire regulations," and I am turned away, almost in tears.

With my great plans unfulfilled, I return home and spend the day doing the usual mundane daily duties. But I brood in bitter disappointment. There is not peace, but anxiety, in my heart and I cannot believe that God is anywhere near.

I cry out to Him in complaint; surely He knows how very much I wanted to go to this retreat today. Surely He sees how busy and hectic my life has become. Surely He knows that I am only attempting to be a better servant, to get closer to Him. Surely He could have pulled off a small miracle for me this morning. Why then, as my loving Father, did He not do so?

I am reminded of Isaiah 55:8: *"For my thoughts are not your thoughts, neither are your ways my ways..."* and I remember; I remember that faith means trusting when I do not understand. Our Father sees all, and I, only *"through a glass, darkly."* I recall that in the shadow of Nicholas' miracle, there was a boy in the same hospital wing who didn't have a miracle and who died in his mommy's arms just three days after Nicholas was healed. I know that God loved that baby just as much as He loved Nicholas and could have saved him, but He did not. Why? I don't know the answer, but I am assured that the One who created me, who sustains me in life, knows the answer. And I remember to trust. And that is my faith.

In failing to accept what My Father sends me in any given day, I am missing His whispers and His gentle nudges. Truly, He ordains all of the moments in my life. He is there not only in the momentous events, but in each dreary, seemingly unimportant little happening. He is there not as an unconcerned onlooker, but as a loving Father. He says to me, in my moments of dryness, boredom, and disappointment, "Do not be afraid, it is I."

It is in these little moments that He gives me the greatest opportunity to love Him. I am not motivated by lofty inspirations or warm feelings, but by bare faith: hoping and believing in what I cannot see. He is calling me to deny my own preferences and to prefer His will, even when it involves suffering. In doing so I may unite myself most intimately to Him and His own great sacrifice, His suffering and death on the cross.

Our Lord invites me, in every hour and at every juncture, to become Christ-like. He is looking for my patience in dealing with my child's faults, as He is ever so patient with me in my continuous failings. He is asking me to go beyond myself and my own desires in the face of someone else's need. He is nudging me to become more generous and more compassionate. He calls me to serve Him and to love Him in the ordinariness of daily life and to trust beyond measure in His providence.

There is an existence that I cannot see, a supernatural reality which transcends the natural world. God in His mercy has promised to transform me, to transform each of us to make us *"holy in His sight."* All that is required is a little faith: faith the size of a mustard seed. And that, in its ordinariness, is a miracle.

A Mother's Intuition

By Diana L. Smith
Geneva, New York

She looked so small and frail as she lay quietly sleeping in her bouncy, her tiny hands closed around a corner of that fuzzy knit blanket she came home from the hospital in when she was born 10 weeks ago. I lay beside her on the floor just watching her, wondering if she knew how much I loved her, wondering how this beautiful angel could be a part of me. I could sit beside her for a lifetime and never tire of her precious face.

This had been a most difficult week—one that new mothers fear most. My little girl was unusually fussy and would not drink her bottle at all. Normally eating was more than just survival for her, it was a passion. Already I knew that she was a true connoisseur of food—her eyes lit up every time I said the words "ba ba." If I were remiss in remembering that it was mealtime, she would remind me with her rendition of a 12-piece orchestra! She was also a very active child. Right from the very beginning, she would do somersaults and aerobic exercises in utero until the inside of my large belly was black and blue.

But these last few days she was not herself. She was extremely quiet, almost lethargic. She had this persistent cough and a high-pitched wheeze, one that seemed to get progressively worse. I knew it was time for a trip to the pediatrician's office. To my dismay, she was diagnosed with bronchiolitis, a complication of respiratory syncytical virus – RSV for short. The doctor gave her a nebulizer treatment of albuterol and said not to worry; many children under two years old contract this virus each year, some with no more serious side effects than a bad cold. The doctor recommended I treat her at home with a nebulizer machine that would give her medicine to open up her airways. Because some cases did turn into serious respiratory infections, we set up a follow-up appointment for the following day.

Now as I watched her sleep, I felt so helpless. I had just spent the weekend hovering over her, praying she would shake this virus. My little Hannah. She was so little and defenseless. How could I rest easy when she was struggling just to take a breath? I wanted to protect her and take away any pain or hardship she had to endure. My son, Joshua, at two and a half and already wise beyond his years, looked upon his new baby sister as a playmate and partner in crime. I had to be clear-headed and strong for both of my children. I lay beside her and touched her sweet face. Was she even aware of what was happening to her? I hoped not. Her face was so pale and transparent that I could see the veins in her temple. Her lips were a grayish hue, not the bright red they had been a few days ago. I pulled back the warm blanket to check her breathing. Her ribs tightened every time she took a breath.

I suddenly felt a sick feeling rush over me. She was getting worse, not better. I knew I could not wait until tomorrow to bring her back for her scheduled appointment. I needed to call now.

The nurse on the other end of the phone was calm and very supportive. How was her color? How fast was she breathing? I put my head close to Hannah's and counted how many times her chest rose. I counted 75 times in one minute. *That can't be right.* I try again. This time I count 80. The nurse calmly tells me I need to bring her in, NOW. I hung up the phone and sat for a minute. *Okay. Don't panic. Just think. What do I need to do first?* I dialed my sister who said she'd be right over to watch Joshua. Then I called my husband at work. I got the answering machine and left a message. I packed the diaper bag, dressed Hannah in her snowsuit, and loaded up the car.

Thank goodness we only lived a couple of minutes from the doctor's office. I tried to think good thoughts. *She'll be okay. The doctor will give her something to make her better.* As we hurried into the office, the nurse recognized me and told me to come right back.

I undressed Hannah and watched as the nurses hovered around her getting vitals and recording information. She seemed unaware of all the commotion going on around her. I held her little hand in mine, rubbed her head, and whispered, "It'll be okay, little one. Mommy loves you." The nurses hooked her up to some machine that checked her oxygen level.

They kept doing it over, seemingly not satisfied with the reading they were getting. The doctor walked in, along with another nurse carrying an oxygen tank. Now I began to panic. *What was happening? Oh God, something is really wrong.* As they hooked my tiny little baby up to that huge, cold oxygen tank, the doctor explained that Hannah wasn't getting enough oxygen and needed some help. An ambulance was on the way to take us to the hospital.

"Please don't worry. It will be better if the ambulance drives you than if you went yourself," the doctor calmly told me. " I am glad you brought her in right away. Do you need to call anyone?"

My mind was a blank. *Oh, right. I need to call my husband!* My hand shook as I dialed his work number. When he answered, I almost burst into tears. "I had to bring her back to the doctor's—she wasn't breathing right. They have this big oxygen tank hooked to her and she's just lying here…and they called an ambulance to take us to the hospital. I'm scared, Rog. She looks really sick!" As I blurted out what the doctor told me, I heard the sound of the ambulance sirens in the distance.

"Oh, geez. I hear the sirens. I'll be right over. Hang in there, Sweetie. She'll be okay, I promise." The sound of his voice was a great comfort.

A few minutes later the ambulance pulled in and paramedics pushed a stretcher through the halls of the doctor's office. As I held Hannah tightly in my arms, the paramedics lifted us up onto the stretcher, oxygen tank and all. They wrapped us up with blankets, tight like mummies, as the cold wind of March was upon us and snow was falling outside. Riding out into the corridor, my baby snuggled deep in my arms with a mask over her little face to help her breathe, I felt the inquisitive stares of the other parents in the waiting room. For one quick second, I had a vision of being the main character in a movie where the audience knows what is about to happen but the star does not. A gust of cold outside air quickly brought me back to my senses.

I'd never seen the inside of an ambulance, much less ridden in one. This whole scenario was surreal—a big blur. *Is this really happening?* Whizzing through town and picking up speed, the sound of the sirens kept me rooted in the present. I tightened my hold on Hannah, as if to let her know she was safe from all harm in my arms. Before I knew it, the ambulance doors swung open, and we were rolling into the hospital elevators up to the pediatric floor.

A room was ready for her, abuzz with nurses and staff hooking up machines and hustling to complete all the tests the doctor ordered. They placed her little body in a large, metal crib surrounded by an oxygen tent. I have never seen so many different people come together as a team. As long as I live, I will always remember how devoted these people were to the care of my daughter.

I watched on the sidelines in a daze until my husband, Roger, arrived. Then we huddled together helplessly—two parents at the mercy of an illness that threatened the life of our precious little girl. What can you do in a situation like this? When everything is out of your control? You pray. A lot. And we did.

The tests confirmed what the doctor had thought: bilateral pneumonia. Such a big illness for such a little person. Hannah needed to stay in the tent for at least a few days, maybe more, depending on how quickly her immune system could fight off the infection.

I looked at my precious child through the clear, plastic tent. She was just lying there, a small bundle in the middle of this big, cold bed—eyes closed, little feet sticking out through her terry nightshirt, her little toe hooked to a machine that read her vitals. If there was ever a moment in my life that I felt completely helpless and small, this was it. I could not do a thing to make her better. It was out of my hands. She was in God's hands now. And He would take care of her. Funny how these things happen just when you think you are getting the hang of it. Life, that is.

Over the course of the next few days, I learned a lot about my husband and my daughter. God had given them their own special bond. Not only did I have a new respect for the love of fathers and daughters, I also learned how couples come together and become stronger in the face of disaster. Hannah was a fighter. I should have figured that one out from the start. That quality probably helped save her life, along with the many prayers from family, friends, and fellow church members.

I spent many hours huddled under that tent rocking her, praying, talking to her, letting her know she was not alone. It wasn't long before the news of a two and a half-month old with pneumonia had doctors and nurses from all over the hospital peaking in to check on this little bundle of joy, as well.

After five days of sleepless nights, curled up on the single cushioned chair next to my daughter's bed, wondering when and if this crisis would pass, I was relieved to hear the doctor say she was finally getting better. Her color had returned, her fever was down and appetite up, and her oxygen level was back to within normal range at 98 percent. Hannah could finally come home. I suddenly felt overwhelmed and drained of all energy. Our precious child had made it!

As I packed up our personal belongings and waited for Roger to pick us up, the doctor came in to check on Hannah one last time. She was a *very* lucky little girl, he said. When I had first brought her in to the doctor's office, her oxygen level had dropped to 80 percent, which was *extremely* low and very life threatening. She had been teetering on the brink of life, but by the grace of God, she had been returned to us. Had I waited any longer, she might not have made it.

When I realized how close we came to losing our baby girl, I broke down. All those days of being strong and holding it together were suddenly a thing of the past. At that moment, I realized Hannah was sent as a special gift from God. He had given us the gift of forever being a part of each other's souls. He had also given us faith—faith in Him and in the bond between mother and daughter. That bond helped save her life. It could never be broken.

On Easter Sunday, March 30, 1997, Hannah left the hospital with a renewed spirit. Isn't that a perfect ending? Actually, it is just the beginning for Hannah—the beginning of the rest of her life.

Faith—Just A Simple Belief?

By Heide AW Kaminski
Tecumseh, Michigan

Faith…what is faith? According to my Merriam-Webster Thesaurus, it means "belief."

But can faith really be defined in one word?

"I believe in Santa Claus."

"I believe he said 10:00 a.m."

"I believe I am coming down with the flu."

Does the word "believe" in these sentences do the word "faith" any justice?

I have faith in a higher power. A lot of people call this higher power "God." Others call the power "Allah," "Great Spirit In The Sky," "Jehovah," and many other names. Regardless of the name, we all have the same core *faith*—the undeniable, unshatterable, indisputable trust that someone out there is responsible for this phenomenal creation we call our earth and all the wonders on it. And we all trust that this Someone is constantly looking out for us.

Let me give you an example from my life that illustrates what I think *faith* means:

Several years ago I was driving down a dirt road on a sunny July afternoon. With me were my then 1½-year-old son and a mildly retarded young woman. The weather was gorgeous, the landscape was beautiful, and our minds were still drawing wonderful energy from the church service we had just left. The last thing on our minds was the possibility of impending doom.

All of a sudden I spotted a huge pothole up ahead of me.

I slammed on my brakes and tried to veer out of the path of the hole but did not succeed. The road was very narrow and a small bridge with metal rails on either side was just past the pothole. Ditches about eight feet deep bordered both sides of the road. My chances of avoiding this pothole were pretty slim.

The right rear tire of my SUV hit the hole, and with a loud bang, the tire blew.

My son, innocent enough, thought this was all fun. He was squealing with delight as our vehicle teetered back and forth. Desperately, I tried to steer it away from the rails. With a swift slide, I made it across the bridge safely but then there were the deep ditches.

By now my friend was panicking and screaming with fear.

I tried to stay calm, so as not to feed her fear, but it took a lot of energy. I was scared to death myself!

It all happened so fast, but in an instant it occurred to me that I had absolutely no control over my vehicle.

I looked over my shoulder at my bouncing, squealing baby and prayed. "God, please do not let anything bad happen to my baby."

Then I let go of the stirring wheel.

"God it's Yours. I can't drive this thing to safety. You do it!"

As I am writing this, years later, I am almost about to cry. Chills are racing through my entire body.

That day in 1999 I consider the day when I encountered a few moments of pure faith—faith so strong that it allowed a miracle to happen.

You've probably read stories about parents who develop unbelievable powers in a moment of despair when they have to save their baby's life. Their powers are momentarily created by the ultimate faith. At that instant they are allowing God's arms to reach out through them to perform a miracle.

This is pretty awesome. But it can also be quite scary. *I should let someone else reach out through me?* Doubt can creep into the way. *Can a miracle really happen?* It is this fear and doubt that may stop many of us from experiencing true miracles.

On that day in July of 1999 I let completely go of that fear and doubt. I infinitely trusted in God. I had *faith* that God could not possibly ignore my prayer.

With a loud and hefty thud my SUV plunged straight down into the ditch on the right side of the road. I can only think of the "Demon Drop" at the Cedar Point Amusement Park as an illustration for our fall. Shaking and screaming, we scrambled out of the vehicle. Climbing out of the ditch was hard. It was narrow, full of brush, and quite steep.

When we stood on the road, I was amazed to see that, not only were we alive and well, aside from a few bruises and scratches, but my SUV was not even visible from where we stood. The roof was flush with the road. Yet no one was hurt.

We walked to a nearby house to call for help, my husband was soon on his way with a tow truck to pick up the totaled vehicle, and a police officer was dispatched to the scene.

The officer walked around, measured tire marks, and examined their direction. After he was done with his investigation, he shook his head.

"Judging by these tire marks, I cannot believe you guys are standing here. Your vehicle was obviously headed for rolling. I doubt that you all would have survived. Can't figure out what made it slide into the ditch instead…"

Though the officer was bewildered, I knew…

God sent an army of angels that swooped down when He heard my call. They couldn't stop an accident from happening anymore, but they pushed with all their might to modifying the roll into a slide and changed a potentially disasterous situation into a much less serious accident.

With no walls of doubt and fear to push through, those angels arrived in time to save what was most important in this situation: Our lives.

Three years later, as I turned onto the miracle road for the first time since that wondrous event, my little boy perked up: "Mommy, I don't want to get into an accident!"

I was in awe. *He remembered!*

We stopped at the place of the phenomenon. The crushed branches had long given in to weather and time conditions. It didn't look strange at all. It was just a ditch filled with grass and brush.

We stood there for a moment of silence. Serendipity embalmed us. "This is where we met God a few years ago," I explained to my little boy. And through the soft breeze I could hear angels singing…

Faith Sustains

By Nadine Coretta White
Hinesville, Georgia

When we were children, my mother always talked to us about faith in God and faith in ourselves. As an adult and a mother, my faith in God was put to the test. On January 14, 2002, I gave birth to my daughter at 27 weeks of gestation. She was only 1 pound and 14 ounces. She was a miracle baby in every sense of the word. Even though the situation made me sad, I never doubted that my baby would be okay eventually.

The events preceding my spontaneous labor were, in my opinion, handled poorly by my attending physicians/physician assistants. I remember going to the hospital about three or four days before my delivery with complaints of abdominal cramping. I was told that my uterus was expanding and that I should not worry. A few days passed and the cramping increased, but not enough to make me worry due to the absence of pain consistent with expected labor.

On the afternoon of January 14, 2002, my husband and I were at the hospital for an unrelated appointment, and fortunately, I decided to check with the labor section of the obstetrics and gynecology clinic just to be sure that there was nothing wrong. I thank God for that insight, because who knows what complications I would have had if I didn't go for a checkup at the precise time I did. The physician assistant decided to give me a thorough checkup and discovered I was already six centimeters dilated. The physician assistant on duty got a second and third opinion from the head nurse and the obstetrician who all confirmed that I was indeed six centimeters dilated.

The obstetrician decided that I needed immediate surgery since the baby was in the breach position. I was devestated and scared because I was only 27 weeks pregnant. He immediately started making preparations for me to go to another hospital that was better equipped to handle premature babies. But when I dilated quickly to eight centimeters, plans to transport me were canceled. I was prepped for surgery immediately.

I was scared because I was worried about everything the baby would have to contend with. I knew she was going to be all right, because I was confident the doctors knew what they were doing and that God was still in control of the entire situation.

Before the delivery the pediatrician told us that most times premature babies do not cry at birth, so we should not be despondent if she did not cry. When my baby came out of the womb, she weighed only 1 pound and 14 ounces, but she was kicking and screaming, and we were delighted. We named her Crystal Niaomi. The baby was transported to another hospital about an hour away that was better equipped to handle premature babies. I was not able to see her until three days later when I was discharged.

The entire experience was stunning, and I was in shock for quite a few days. I remember the second day I was in the hospital, I cried for about three hours because I felt so overwhelmed. The experience was not what I had in mind for my first pregnancy, but I received lots of reassurance from the doctors and nurses during my stay at the hospital.

I was discharged January 17, 2002, but I did not go to the hospital immediately to see the baby because I was still in such dreadful pain from my caesarean section. I called the neonatal unit at the hospital, and they advised me to stay at home and get some rest. They gave me a toll free number to reach the neonatal intensive care unit and get information on the baby at any time.

I persevered and went to the hospital on January 18, but I was simply disheartened to see the tubes and bandages that seemed to engulf my baby's tiny body in the incubator. This was not the picture I had imagined I would see after giving birth to my first child, but I figured the Lord must have had me deal with this for a special reason.

Crystal spent more than two months in the hospital. During that time she received two transfusions. She was monitored primarily for weight gain and signs of problems associated with prematurity. Fortunately, she never had any major problems that threatened her life. She had a few episodes of bradycardia, which I was told is typical of premature babies. The nurses also had the difficult task of teaching her how to take a bottle before she was even ready to suck naturally. This process required a great deal of patience and understanding, and for that I thanked the nurses very much. They were entrusted with caring for my baby in the early stages of her life.

About five to six weeks after being at the hospital, when Crystal was big enough, my husband and I were allowed to participate in feeding, changing, and bathing her. The first time I had to change her in her incubator, I was very nervous because she was so delicate, and I was scared I was going to hurt her. As much as I wanted to hold her, I was terrified the first time because she was barely a handful. However, the time that we spent with the baby in the hospital was a welcomed learning experience for my husband and me. We were educated on everything and anything that was important to the well being of our baby upon her release from the hospital. My daughter's out-of-body gestational completion, as I like to call it, was a long and tedious process that finally came to an end on March 23, 2002. Our baby was finally able to come home with us.

It has been nine months since Crystal has been home, and she is doing splendidly. She is growing well and has had no genuine setbacks from her prematurity. She is almost walking and is as happy and healthy as a baby can be. We look at her every day in amazement, and we give thanks to God. This experience has been the most difficult in my life, but it has also helped to reinforce my faith in God. This was a period in my life during which I could trust no one else but Him. He was the one that sustained my daughter's life and at the same time renewed my faith in Him. For a moment, I think I had forgotten how miraculous God could be.

For My Son: Faith...

By Tina Pinson
Grand Junction, Colorado

Hmmm. Do I know what faith is all about? The Bible talks about faith: by faith you are saved through grace... these three remain, faith, hope and love... There's a whole chapter in Hebrews devoted to that one little word. Faith.

What does it mean?

The Scriptures say: *Now faith is being sure of what we hope for and certain of what we do not see.* Hebrews 11:1

Maybe that's why it's so hard to comprehend, because we want to see and want to be certain.

Sometimes we get to see. But most times, we don't get that luxury. Most times, we can only hope; we can only trust. Most times, we can only have faith.

I think at times I am a faithful and trusting sort. Funny though, when I start believing I've arrived at some spiritual plane, something happens to remind me just how far away I truly am.

September 11, 2001 was a hard time for my family and me. The dark cloud that descended on our home, however, was not from the tragedies of the day. It did not descend from the destruction that filled our television screen. Oh, I cried, and followed the story as it unfolded on the news. But that wasn't what kept me up at night. That wasn't what held my soul so firmly in its grip.

There was something else I grieved and wept for. Something else that a nation would never know.

You see, just a couple days before the attack on September 11, I learned that my son—my 20-year-old son, my baby—was diagnosed with cancer.

Cancer, what a word. Doctors will tell you that there is a phenomenal recovery rate these days. I heard the word and thought...*death sentence*. My husband, who'd just gone through months of dealing with his father having cancer, was devastated. All he could think about was how he wanted his children to outlive him. I thought about that, as well. About the hopes and dreams I had for my son. The dreams I knew he must have for himself.

While the world hungrily digested each newscast, I waited for telephone calls. I waited for a new diagnosis.

It never came.

So I went to the Lord. I prayed. I wept. I prayed some more. And with each call from my son, I became further frustrated with God and myself. My son wasn't being healed. Was my faith too shallow? Didn't I love God enough? Was God holding something against me? Didn't God love me? Didn't He love my son?

If so, why did my son have cancer? Why did he have to have an operation? And why were there tumors in his pelvic area?

"God," I cried. "I'm Your child. My son is Your child. Why aren't You answering my prayers? Are You even listening to me? Are You there?"

Then word came that my son would have to go through chemotherapy. Having heard the worst of stories concerning radiation therapy, my husband and I fell into each other's arms in tears.

"No, God!" I cried. Or did I yell? "Not that. Please not that."

After I'd cried for a time, I begged God to remember, *as if He would forget*, that my son was nearly a thousand miles away from me. He would need a shoulder. He would need love.

I didn't have the means to get there. So I asked God to watch over him and protect him. And maybe, just maybe, send someone along to comfort my precious child.

God heard that prayer. (As He heard them all.) And by the end of the week, He was sending me to my son.

While I didn't have the money for a ticket, God provided it through a friend. Our Christian family gathered funds to support my trip and promised to support us in prayer, as well.

I saw the hand of the Lord so clearly.

While I didn't know what the morrow would bring, I had a strange sense of peace—of calm assurance.

Thirty minutes before I was to fly out on October 11 on a United flight, the government issued its first security warning. I cried. It shook me up so much that my knees trembled when I walked to the plane. But when I remembered where I was headed and Who had secured the means and plotted the course, I was again overcome with peace.

When I met my son at the airport, I refrained from kissing the Tarmac, but I cried when I saw the tubes hanging out his chest from the catheter they had surgically placed in his heart. I cringed each time he asked me to help him clean it.

I asked God for strength. I asked Him, the Great Physician, to guard and guide the procedures that were to come.

The following Monday we arose to go to the hospital so my son could begin his chemo series. I knew that no matter what, God was in control. A billboard we passed along the way even flashed a like sentiment. "Jesus holds the future," it said. I grasped that promise, that truth, and claimed it for my own. When I began to doubt, I claimed it again.

Did I find the hospital daunting? You bet. Was I chilled and trembling when I sat in the waiting room? Uh huh.

Then they called my son's name. And I can't remember what happened exactly. My heart either dropped to my toes or became lodged in my throat.

Here it was, the moment we'd been dreading. My son was going to start his chemo.

"Oh, God, give my son strength. Give me strength." Because about that time I was ready to run.

My son came back out from a side room not long after. He looked stymied. Which clearly bewildered me. I knew chemo couldn't be given so fast. It was supposed to take a couple hours or more. So why was he out in the waiting room now when he needed to start his series?

"The doctor wants to see me," my son said.

"About what?" I asked, certain that, whatever the reason, it could not be good.

He shrugged. "I'm not sure."

When we were led into the doctor's office, all I could think was that my son's cancer had gotten worse, which didn't make a lot of sense, because if that were the case, then they surely needed to start chemo. Maybe they needed to operate again? I prepared for the worst and again prayed for God to give the doctor wisdom and me peace.

Oh, and Lord, heal my son. I prayed silently, wondering if I truly believed He would.

Then I took a seat across from the doctor and stoically waited for the news.

"I've decided not to give you chemo," he addressed my son.

My son was a picture of shock, as I'm sure I was.

"I'm going to recommend testing for now," the doctor continued. "But I don't want to put you through chemo. I don't feel it's necessary."

Necessary? I nearly yelled. Thankfully, for the doctor's sake, my son spoke first. "But what about the cancer? The tumors they found in the last ultrasound?"

"There was nothing on the last scan," the doctor replied. "Maybe some swelling, which we'll keep an eye on, but nothing to warrant chemo right now. I think we got it all."

I sat there with my mouth gaping, and it sank in. It finally sank in. They'd gotten it all. All the cancer. I wanted to yell, to jump up and cheer. *God healed my son.* My heart sang as I tried to hold back the tears. God had revealed Himself to me again. I'd flown out to sit with my son as he took chemo and convalesced. I was determined to do everything humanly possible for my son. God did everything heavenly possible. He'd healed him.

Healed him...what a miracle.

My son has continued with his testing, and nothing has resurfaced. I know it won't.

I have since come to realize that while I could love my son with all of me, I could never love him or protect him the way God can. He's God's precious child, too. While I have hopes and dreams for him, they can never match God's ultimate, loving plan. And it's not my faith that makes God faithful.

He just is.

Tears Of Mary

By Karen Kruse
Glenview, Illinois

May 7, 1994, started much the same as any other Saturday in the suburbs of Chicago, but this Saturday would change my life profoundly. My friend, Patty, and I had plans to go exploring in the neighborhood bookstores for the day, but the night before Patty called to suggest we change our plans slightly and meet at my apartment, then go visit the Gothic church in Techny, Illinois. I love the beautiful architecture of the church in all its serene beauty, and at this time of day we would be the only visitors, so I thought it was a great idea.

A cold rain fell gently that Saturday morning as we headed over to Techny. I was looking forward to our visit, as I wanted to light a candle for Saint Lucy, the patron saint of eyes. I recently had corrective eye surgery and had prayed for Saint Lucy's intercession on my behalf. I promised her through prayer that I would light a candle for her in tribute and thanks. The eye operations were very successful, and I thank her to this day.

We scampered through the bone-chilling drizzle into the church, and it was an absolutely beautiful sight. Many of the saints were represented in full-size, white marble statues. Stained glass windows surrounded us. Everywhere emanated a feeling of peace and love. There were no candles available for lighting, as it was not the custom of this church, so I simply walked quietly to the front pew and prayed, silently thanking all who helped in one way or another.

I drank in the beauty and felt God's presence. After a few minutes, Patty and I departed. In the huge vestibule of the church we saw more lifelike statues and more colorful stained glass windows. I paused to admire the inspiring window of Daniel in the den of lions. It was simply breathtaking!

I even knelt on the cold, hard, bare marble floor and prayed a prayer of thanks to my guardian angel, Daniel. In a moment of meditation one day, my guardian angel's name had come to me as Daniel. Since I know he is always with me and watches over me, I wanted to let him know I appreciate his efforts. That silent union made me feel at peace with the world. I arose ready to enjoy our day.

Back in the car we decided to head north to continue wandering through bookstores as planned. Then Patty abruptly asked if I would have been game to go to Cicero to see the weeping icon of the Virgin Mary that was reported recently to be actually crying at St. George Antiochian Orthodox Church. Of course, I would have loved to see and witness such a wonderful event and wished out loud that she had suggested it earlier. It was already late morning and we had more or less talked ourselves out of going today when suddenly I blurted out that if I had a map, I could get us there.

As quickly as we had talked ourselves out of going, we were on our way! Heading south, we planned to ask for specific directions when we arrived in the area. Luckily Patty had a map, so I played navigator. The rain was still falling, but lighter now. I mused, "Even if we wait an hour in the cold rain to see a miracle, it will be worth it." Patty agreed.

Without thinking, I added. "We will park right in front and there will be no real line."

Patty wanted to know how I knew that. I didn't know how. I just *knew*. Then I added, "Our guardian angels are taking care of us. It's raining, and that's always been a good omen for me. You'll see." It was just a matter of faith.

We arrived in Cicero and asked for directions in a realtor's office. Sure enough, we were only blocks from the church, and we found it located across the street from a car wash as directed. Our hearts raced. What would we witness? This was the scene of a modern day miracle taking place, and we were about to get a glimpse!

As I predicted, there was a tiny lot directly across from the small Greek church, and we parked about four cars in from the street without a problem. Hmmm. No lines outside either. My feeling of divine guidance was right on target. The rain had subsided, too.

Our palms began to sweat as we tried to grasp what we were about to experience. Shaking, we walked up the stairs to the church, our anticipation mounting with each step. The line ended just inside the door. It only looked like a short wait.

Candles burned everywhere. A Greek Orthodox hymn played softly in the background, lending an even holier atmosphere to the surroundings. Unlit candles were available for a donation if you wished to light one. I certainly did. Remember, my original purpose when we visited Techny earlier that day was to light a candle in honor of Saint Lucy. I picked up a long white taper and reverently left a dollar for the privilege.

On the altar of the church eight icons beckoned to us. Each was a religious painting done on tapestry or wood, not canvas as is more common in an oil painting. There were four on the left and four on the right of center in the front of the church, mounted on a lattice-like wall similar to a room divider.

The icon of the Virgin Mary with the Christ Child had been crying since the Greek Orthodox Palm Sunday. It was now two weeks later and the phenomenon was still happening. This particular icon was located on the left side, the first portrait next to the center opening. It was surrounded by a garland of flowers and hundreds of burning candles. There were banks of candles immediately before the Lady and several more further away. It was beautiful to see, but at this point I didn't feel anything different.

Earlier in the week the weeping icon had been pronounced a miracle by the Greek Church. Forever she will be known as "Our Lady of Cicero." To see a miracle would be incredible to say the least, but we couldn't see anything yet.

A Greek priest stood at the head of our slow moving line and an elderly lady stationed in the first pew handed everyone a little plastic bag as they passed. She explained the tears of the icon were being collected and then mixed with holy oil. We would be anointed with it by the priest with a cotton swab, and then he'd drop it in our little bag to keep as a precious memento of this sacred occasion.

Reaching the front of the line, Patty exclaimed, "I see it! She's crying!" I looked but didn't see anything. I was disappointed and felt a rush of fear. *What if everyone else could see it but me?* I thought. After all, I had brand new eyes from Saint Lucy, so I should be able to see very well.

But after one more step, I, too, saw it for the first time! I could see the wetness of her tears running down her face and robe. Every fiber of my being felt the miracle. I couldn't believe what I was observing.

Three more steps and we stood in front of the priest. He anointed me with the sacred oil, making a sign of the cross on my forehead while reciting a prayer to Mother Mary. "Amen," I said as I started to cross the altar toward the sacred icon. I waited patiently for those before me to pray and stare in amazement.

Then it was my turn. I stood four feet in front of her. So close. Patty was still on my left, and we both stared in amazement at the sight before us. From the inner corner of both her eyes, tears flowed freely, running the entire length of the portrait. She looked sad. The Marian message had always been to "pray for peace." That message seemed to come across loud and clear without words. She looked sad in response to the world condition. What have we done to her precious planet? Her heart ached. Her children were in turmoil. They needed help, but was it too late? She was here to bring a message of hope, but also a stern warning. We are destroying ourselves. In an instant, all that information was conveyed to me.

I've prayed all my life. With this fabulous sight before me, I forgot how. In the presence of tears from God, I could not think. These were tears from heaven; there was no doubt in my mind. Either you believe or you don't.

I had been intrigued by the possibility of witnessing an historic religious event, but I had no idea how I would react. Now tears flowed from my eyes just as they did from the painting of Mary. I was standing in the presence of God. Words are inadequate to describe the feeling. How can human words describe such a heavenly occurrence? I was overwhelmed.

All of a sudden, I was many people, many lives. Questions flooded my brain. Did I live during the time of the crucifixion? More importantly, did I believe? I believe now. God is within each one of us. This event seemed to move my vibration up a notch, making me operate on a much higher plane. I felt changed, enriched.

When knowledge of prayer returned to me, I tried again. It was futile. The prayers were jumbled and confused. It was only a few seconds of time, but somehow time stood still while I was within her divine gaze.

Reality crashed in on me once again as I lit my candle from those beneath the icon. Shaking, I managed to carry it while stepping down two steps off the altar to several large trays of sand filled with other burning candles. As I placed my candle among the others, I remembered my intent to light one for Saint Lucy. I silently thanked her and smiled as I thought, *What a wonderfully sacred place to give thanks!* I headed for the pew and sat down heavily. My knees were weak and shaking. Patty slid in next to me.

We were both still crying. We couldn't speak, nor did we want to, as words eluded us. To comprehend what we just saw was going to take some time. Again I tried to pray and was more successful this time. We were still close to this amazing sight not more than 15 feet before us. People of all denominations were in attendance, and they cried and prayed also. The spirit of God was in that small church that afternoon. I could feel it. How appropriate that it was the day before Mother's Day. What a tribute to the greatest Mother of them all! It was a blessing, and I got to be a part of it!

When our breathing returned to normal, Patty and I glanced at each other and, with a nod, we got up to leave. As our experience came to a close, we silently left the church. Our hearts filled with love, we felt connected to everyone! We walked slowly, reverently, to the car, still stunned by the magnitude of the event.

In the days to come, I was surprised to find many people scoffed at my experience. It didn't matter. I knew I had witnessed a miracle, and my faith continues to grow. It just proves what I've always believed:

To the believer, no explanation is necessary.

To the skeptic, no explanation is possible.

I am truly blessed.

Out Of The Pit Of Despair

By Nancy Arant Williams
Stover, Missouri

If I'd never believed it before, I believed it now. The enemy of my soul was out to steal, kill, and destroy; of that I was certain. I felt like I was going down for the third time, with barely enough strength to push two fingers through the surface of the water that was drowning me.

I had a new empathy for Job, bless his heart. Just like that man of God who authored one of my favorite Scriptures, Job 13:15, *"Though He slay me, yet will I hope in Him,"* I was determined to go the distance. Sometimes. At other times, I could barely muster the strength to pray.

For the first 30 years of my life I was relatively untouched by pain or sorrow. I felt deeply grateful to a sovereign God, knowing that others all around me were suffering. It was clear that there, but for the grace of God, go I.

But all that changed in an instant, and multiplied sorrows heaped themselves upon my grief—a time of loss that began when I lost my grandmother and didn't end until 15 years later.

I am not of a melancholy disposition. Just the opposite, in fact. But there is just so much stress a healthy spirit can take before it shatters. And I was reaching that point at record speed.

I sat in my car watching a train. I had parked my car in a small lot where I could watch the trains come and go. They were massive, powerful enough to stop anything, including my pain. That was all I cared about.

I had considered many ways to end life, and most of them were revolting, to say the least. A train was the most impersonal and, therefore, the method of choice.

These days it was all I could do to get up in the morning. I kept waiting for the other shoe to drop. I felt like the sun had set and a permanent darkness had overtaken me.

I had cried out to God over and over to grab hold of me and set me on a rock. I had all the promises in Psalms memorized, and I hung onto them like a lifeline. And yet here I was sitting at the train tracks. How could that be?

Why hadn't He answered my cries for help? And where was my faith?

I wept, sobbing inconsolably. The windows were tightly rolled up, fogged over with my grief. Suddenly I felt the presence of the Lord fill my car. *He was there.*

I knew Him. And He knew my name. He had etched it in the Lamb's Book of Life years before. And I had thought we were friends. But somehow the pain of life had scarred me so deeply that I could no longer feel His presence—until that moment, sitting there watching the trains go by.

I cried, "Lord, is that You? I'm sorry. I've failed You. The fact that I'm even sitting here is terrible evidence that I am not Your child. Your children don't do things like this."

He whispered to my heart, "Didn't I promise I would never leave or forsake you? Didn't I say that no one could snatch you away from Me? I never go back on My Word."

Oddly enough, it was as if we had a silent dialogue running, and I stood listening as if I were a third party, an interested but detached bystander.

He went on, "Your pain is deep, but none is so deep that I cannot touch it. Will you let Me minister to you?"

It was as if my daddy had run to me, crouched down, and held out his arms to me. And I flew into those arms as fast as my childish heart's legs could carry me. For the first time in years I could feel His presence and His touch. He bathed me in His comforting reassurance that indeed I was His own. And my heart burst with joy. In the middle of pain I realized that He was holding onto the end of my lifeline and would never let go.

He and I sat watching the trains together. And I wept. I was amazed at the depth of the fountain of tears. Would they never end?

The tears continued to fall, but they had changed. They were no longer desperate tears of anguish, but of release. Pent up emotions simply poured out without prompting.

I could feel His arms of love enfold me, and I knew I would never be the same.

He said to my spirit, "You have work to do. You will pour it out in writing so you can see your pain in black and white. And as you pour out your heart to Me, I will heal your heartache."

Three hundred pages later, I was spent and exhausted but emptied of grief. It had drained out onto the paper. In its place was hope for the future. He poured into me Scriptures I already knew but hadn't been able to realize until then. He showed me that He had miraculously transformed my scars into the soft and healthy skin of a new baby.

Psalm 28:6-9 comforted me in a way I never dreamed possible.

It says: *Praise be to the Lord, for He has heard my cry for mercy. The Lord is my strength and my shield; my heart trusts in Him, and I am helped. My heart leaps for joy and I will give thanks to Him in song. The LORD is the strength of His people, a fortress of salvation for His anointed one. Save Your people and bless Your inheritance; be their shepherd and carry them forever.*

He had raised me out of the pit of despair and set me upon a rock. Psalm 30:2-5 became my personal shout of triumph: *O Lord my God, I called to You for help and You healed me. O Lord, You brought me up from the grave; You spared me from going down into the pit. Sing to the Lord, you saints of His; praise His holy name. For His anger lasts only a moment, but His favor lasts a lifetime; weeping may remain for a night, but rejoicing comes in the morning.*

It would be wonderful if I could say that He stopped all the trials that day. But that did not happen. There were many more to come. But God made an indelible impression on my life that day, coming to my rescue, and my faith was now secure. I would no longer despair of life, for I knew He would make a way for me through any wilderness. He had promised. And He was trustworthy. His personal intervention at the lowest point of my life led me to believe, as I still do, that in Him all things are truly possible, and indeed His tender mercies never, ever fail.

Two Women, One Faith

By Julie A. Rocheleau
Dearborn Heights, Michigan

Two women, two countries, two cultures. This is a story of two women from opposite ends of the world. Two women whose only desire was to have a baby. Both have suffered, and both have known loss. Only through the strength and courage of one was the other's desire fulfilled. Ming in China and Julie in America. There is an invisible bond between these two women that will never break. Though they've never met, their lives are sewn together by a love that only a mother knows.

Ming in China

When Ming was a little girl, she dreamed of having a house full of children. She played with her dolls and pretended to be a mommy. She dressed her dolls in beautiful, satin mandarin dresses and wrapped their long black hair on top of their heads, adorning it with a hair ornament. She fed the dolls congee and made sure they were burped. Then she wrapped them in blankets and put them to bed for a nap. Ming couldn't wait to have children.

Ming grew up and fell in love with a wonderful man. They were married and lived in a small house in Beijing. When they received their marriage certificate, they also received a child certificate allowing them to have one child. They would present this to the hospital when they were ready to give birth to their baby.

China's population was growing too fast, so the government put restrictions on how many children each couple could have. Since Ming and her husband lived in the city, they were allowed to have one baby.

Ming gave birth to a handsome baby boy. In the Chinese culture it is important for the family to have a boy for many reasons. A boy can carry on the family name and business. Also, he and his wife will care for his elderly parents when they can no longer take care of themselves. The Chinese love their little girls very much, but it is not in their best interest to keep a girl, because she will not be responsible to her own parents, but to her husband's parents. Ming watched as her little boy grew and grew. He began to talk, walk, and play like the other boys in the neighborhood.

Then, despite their precautions, the young parents found themselves expecting another child. They had a decision to make. Ming could easily go to the doctor and have an abortion. These procedures are very common in China. Millions of abortions are performed each year.

Ming and her husband talked about their options, but she already felt a bond between her and the baby growing inside of her. She couldn't bring herself to end the pregnancy as many of her friends had done when faced with the same situation.

Ming and her husband decided to go ahead with the pregnancy. She had to hide herself, she wore bigger clothes, and she did not speak of the baby to anyone. Ming moved to the countryside to live with her parents for the remainder of the pregnancy.

A few months later a beautiful baby girl was born. Ming held her baby close to her. She loved her baby very much. But deep inside of her she knew she could not keep the baby. The government could fine the couple one year's salary for having two children, and Ming and her husband could lose everything.

Soon Ming knew the day had arrived—she had to give up her baby. She needed to go back to Beijing to live with her husband and little boy. Since it was illegal to give the baby up for adoption, she would have to leave her baby somewhere where she could be found and taken to the orphanage. Ming had heard of government programs where baby girls were being adopted and taken to live in other countries, such as those in America and Europe.

On a clear, summer night, Ming dressed her baby in her prettiest mandarin dress. She put a ribbon on top of her head to hold the beautiful lock of black, straight hair and fed her a big bowl of congee. She wrapped her baby up in a blanket and put her in a cardboard box filled with newspapers for warmth. Then she walked to the business center of the village. Ming took one last look at her beautiful baby girl and placed the box on the steps of the police station. Ming felt like her heart was tearing apart. She hid behind a building for hours watching over her precious package.

Soon the sun would rise and the streets would fill with vendors and people rushing about. She knew she had to go back home and have faith that someone would pick her baby up and take her to the orphanage.

Ming didn't grow up in a church, but she always knew in her heart that there was a God. She needed His help now more than ever. Looking into the night sky, she whispered a prayer: "Please take care of my little girl. Keep her safe and warm. Find her parents who will love her as much as I do. Be with her on her journey. She will be forever in my heart."

She heard the baby whimper, and before she was tempted to run and take back her baby, Ming ran back to her parents' home, crying through the streets of the village.

Ming went back to the police station the next day, and the box was no longer there. She looked toward heaven, and she somehow knew that her prayer would be answered.

Ming mourned her baby for a long time. Some days she couldn't get out of bed to make her breakfast. She felt empty inside. Sometimes she would awaken in the middle of the night and jump out of bed looking for her baby girl. Then she would remember that dreadful night and cry herself back to sleep.

One night Ming had a dream. She saw her baby flying through the sky, soaring through the clouds. Then she saw an angel take her baby and hand her to a woman. The woman and her husband looked so happy—they had tears running down their cheeks. The baby looked frightened, but when the new mother took her into her arms, the baby stopped crying. Ming felt a calmness sweep over her, and she knew that her baby was going to be safe.

Ming bowed her head and whispered a word of thanks to God. "I know my baby will have a home with two parents that love her." She knew her heart would never heal. The pain she feels will always be a reminder of the baby girl she loved.

Julie in America

Julie was the youngest and only girl in her family. She played by herself in her room most of the time. She lined up her stuffed animals and dolls and played school. Julie always dreamed of growing up and having a big family. She wanted to be just like her mom.

Julie grew up, but she didn't get married right away. She went to school to become a nurse and then met and married a wonderful man when she was in her 30's. Knowing that she was getting older, they agreed to try to have a baby after being married only one year. To their surprise, she became pregnant right away! Dreams of diapers and baby bottles filled Julie's head. She couldn't wait to buy maternity clothes and decorate the nursery. Julie's husband was excited about the baby and couldn't wait to be a daddy.

Julie made an appointment with the doctor and with anxious anticipation waited to see her baby on the ultrasound. But the doctor sighed and told her the baby was not growing. He took blood tests and confirmed the pregnancy had ended.

This broke Julie's heart, but as soon as she felt better, she tried again. Julie and her husband tried a second and a third time, but every time she became pregnant, the baby did not grow, and she miscarried. Julie felt like she was on an emotional roller coaster. Each time she miscarried, her body slowly recovered, but emotionally she wasn't sure how many more times she could get her hopes up only to have them shattered again.

Julie told her husband she didn't want to try anymore. She was tired and said, "Maybe it was meant to be this way." She told him now they could travel and see the world with no responsibilities to tie them down. Julie went back to work and dove into the paperwork and visits she made as a home care nurse. Her husband looked on, hoping this wasn't going to be a decision she would regret for the rest of her life.

A year passed, and Julie started thinking, *Is this all there is to life?* Women all around her were having babies and announcing their pregnancies, even after years of infertility. Julie was saddened. She didn't want to start infertility treatments. There was no guarantee, and the emotional highs and lows were too much for her to bear.

One night Julie was at church. There a girl told the story of how she came to have two wonderful boys through adoption. Julie's eyes began to water. Her husband saw the anguish in her eyes as they talked about the story they heard. But adoption was out of the question for them. It was too expensive, and they were too old, she thought.

One Sunday just after the New Year, Julie was praying in church. She needed direction. What was to become of her life? She felt an emptiness in her heart that her work or travel could never fill. Just then she heard a whisper through her prayers: "You *can* adopt. Trust me."

Julie pondered this for a week without telling anyone. The next weekend she and her husband went for a long drive, and she asked him what he thought about adoption. They carefully weighed the pros and cons and realized the pros far outweighed the cons, so Julie decided to go to an adoption agency informational meeting to find out if adoption was possible for them. She remembered the voice telling her to trust God and whispered a prayer to heaven: "God, if this is meant to be and You want us to adopt a baby, open the door."

Julie came home from the meeting and told her husband about it. She was very interested in the Chinese program the agency offered, so the next week they met with the social worker. The social worker said they were just the right kind of parents to adopt from China. Within weeks they had started the long, arduous task of collecting papers for the adoption process.

A few months later Julie and her husband traveled to China. Awaiting their arrival was the most beautiful baby that Julie had ever seen. The moment the nanny put the crying baby in her arms, she knew this was a gift from heaven. The baby stopped crying and clung to her.

With tears running down her cheeks, Julie whispered a word of thanks to God. She also said a prayer for the baby's birth mother, thanking God for giving her the courage, strength, and faith to give her baby up. For Julie knew that her happiness was only through someone else's suffering.

The new family returned home to America. Julie's heart was full.

Two women, two countries, two cultures.
One baby, two mothers, one God.
Two lives, two hearts slowly healing.
One God, two women, one faith.

With God, All Things Are Possible

By Faith Jaudon
Rincon, Georgia

F*aith* sees the unseen. It *is being sure of what we hope for and certain of what we do not see.* Hebrews 11:1 It is what God's righteous live by, for without it, it is impossible to please Him. Faith does not rest on man's wisdom, but on God's power—an incredible source of power! A power that has the ability to extinguish the flaming arrows of Satan and, against all hope, to supernaturally move mountains.

Faith is not about the present, but rather the future. It deals with the invisible things of God. It is planted in the believer's heart through the hearing of God's Word, and it grows deeper in adversity. Faith is a gift measured from the hands of God to each individual who, like the apostles, cried, *"Lord, increase our faith!"* Luke 17:5(b) And with loving patience, He reaches down to those reaching up and transforms their lives.

I am one of those lives.

Once a helpless soul without hope, through the eyes of faith, I have seen the God that sees me.

There is nothing too big or too small for God. I am convinced that when real faith in God arises, a certainty comes that when we call, He will answer…that when we ask, we will receive…that when we knock, the door will be opened. (Luke 11:9-10, paraphrased by the author.) Faith, the substance of things hoped for and the evidence of things unseen, is available to all those who dare to believe God for the impossible!

Having the faith to believe God for a husband did not come easy for me. For years I asked God for a husband with no evidence of getting one. Because of past hurts, I had become insecure and fearful of rejection. I concluded that I would most likely remain single because of all the emotional baggage. But then the longing of my heart would overtake me.

My heavy heart soon became evident to those around me. A co-worker, an enthusiastic matchmaker, was determined to set me up on a blind date.

I must confess this was not what I had in mind. Nonetheless, I was learning not to limit God, and I accepted the appointment.

The day arrived, and there was a knock at the door. My heart was beating so hard I could barely breathe. I opened the door and there he stood—a real life Daniel Boone!

He spoke very slowly and countrified—a major turnoff for a dignified city girl like me. It became very evident to me that this relationship would never work. We were from two totally different worlds and headed in opposite directions.

We survived the evening and agreed that there was no need in going any further. Our misery was evident to each other, and we politely said, "Goodbye and have a nice life!"

The next day God spoke to me and reminded me of a prayer that I had been praying for years—the one in which I had asked Him specifically to bring my husband to my front door. God then told me that I would see this gentleman again and that we were not to touch for seven days because He would be purifying me to be a holy bride. I could not believe my ears!

Suddenly the phone rang, and it was him. How in the world was I going to tell a man I did not even know that God was in the process of arranging his marriage, and it was to me? I dared not! However, he understood the work God was doing in my life in reference to cleansing me of my past, so he abided by the "no touching" rule.

Over the next seven days, God gave both of us a heart for one another and a greater love for Him. Upon the completion of the seven days of purification, my Daniel Boone presented me with the most beautiful marriage proposal.

Feeling overwhelmed by the sudden events, I went before the Lord in earnest prayer. I prayed specifically for a sign of confirmation by asking, "Lord, if this man is indeed to be my husband, let my house sell immediately."

I should tell you here that my house wasn't listed on the market, because it was not for sale. However, within 30 minutes, my phone rang, and it was a newlywed couple interested in buying my home. They came over that night to look at my house and purchased it the next day.

By faith in God and trust in His word, I married my husband after only knowing him four weeks. Faith saw a match made in heaven, and faith continues to see the unseen.

As of today, my husband and I have been married four years. Two years ago he incurred a serious back injury that left him disabled. Once a strong man, this injury cost him more than his health. Being reduced to having others bathe and dress him also cost him his dignity.

Suddenly the match made in heaven did not seem so heavenly. Pressures from medical expenditures and the stress from a mate who is in constant chronic pain began to take its toll on the entire family. A home that was once filled with joy, peace, and laughter was now consumed by a spirit of affliction. It seemed that no amount of praying was moving this mountain of infirmity.

We knew that God had divinely appointed us to be together to work for His kingdom, but we were bound as captives in a prison.

Then we discovered the key to our freedom. It was our faith in God—that something that had been buried under the pain, fears, and debt of spiritual bankruptcy!

Praise the Lord, O my soul; all my inmost being, praise His holy name. Praise the Lord, O my soul, and forget not all His benefits... Psalm 103:1-2 Who forgives all our sins and heals all our sicknesses! Who redeems our lives from the pit and crowns us with love and compassion. Who satisfies our heart's desires with good things so that our youth is renewed like the eagle's. (Psalm 103:3-5, paraphrased by the author.) *The Lord works righteousness and justice for all the oppressed. He made known His ways to Moses, and His deeds to the people of Israel: The Lord is compassionate and gracious, slow to anger, abounding in love.* Psalm 103:6-8 *For as high as the heavens are above the earth, so great is His love for those who fear Him.* Psalm 103:11 *From everlasting to everlasting the Lord's love is with those who fear Him, and His righteousness with their children's children, and with those who keep His covenant and remember to obey His precepts.* Psalm 103:17-18 *Praise the Lord, O my soul.* Psalm 103:22(b)

On December 23, 2002, surrounded by family and friends in our home, my husband was supernaturally ushered into the secret chamber of God's presence and healed by faith. Rejoice with us as we celebrate his physical and spiritual restoration. As of this very moment, he is hunting with his boys, something he has wanted to do for almost two years. With God all things are possible! This is the hour of healing, believe and receive…

2

Lessons In Faith

"Expert" Advice

By Marie Thomas
Framingham, Massachusetts

It had been a morning of back-to-back meetings and information-gathering phone conferences, and still we had barely scratched the surface. I was a nutritionist and technical writer at a large company where deadlines always loomed large on the horizon, and by the time lunch rolled around, I just wanted to get away.

I got in the car and headed toward a small park where I sometimes retreated, but changed my mind at the last minute and stayed on the main road. A mile further I pulled into a place I usually avoided—the local animal shelter.

The year before we had lost our beautiful orange cat to diabetes, unknown in cats until the era of cereal foods. We were busy people, and our cat ate what we gave him. My vet consoled me with the party line that dry food was good for cats, not just a convenience to owners. I knew better, but she brushed off my concerns about cats being carnivores and possibly needing better nutrition the same way she smiled patronizingly when I told her I prayed for my pets.

I felt my husband wasn't ready for a replacement, and maybe I wasn't either, but today I wanted to look. I walked in and scanned the 60 cages stacked from floor to ceiling. Then, from a cage beside my ankle, I felt something.

A small brown paw stretched to the shoulder was swiping at my leg. I knelt down to see a tortoise-shell cat trying desperately to get my attention. The tag on the cage said she was two years old and weighed six pounds. She reached through the cage to play, and her eyes begged me to take her. I fell in love, but I needed to be sure my husband was in agreement.

When I stood to leave, she almost turned inside out reaching for me with a pleading look. I reassured her that I would be back for her, but she began mewing piteously. I had never seen such a reaction from a cat, and my heart went out to her.

When I got home from work, I told my husband about my lunchtime visit to the shelter, but he was almost unmoved. He reluctantly agreed to come with me, but his affection for our previous cat left him unwilling to open up to yet another that would leave us wounded with its passing. We drove to the shelter in silence.

When we got there, my heart dropped as I looked to find the cage empty. Then I saw her. In the corner a little blonde girl about eight years old sat on the floor—with my little cat on her lap. She was in love too. Her parents looked down on them as the tiny cat played with the girl's fingers, then stood up on its back legs and put its small paws around the girl's neck and licked her face. The little girl was in ecstasy. I knew I couldn't do anything, nor did I want to, as the father said, "I guess this is the one."

My husband had no idea what I was watching and looked around in the various cages, patiently waiting for me to show him the one I wanted. After a moment he said, "Dear, look here."

My husband is over six feet tall, and in a cage opposite his face was a golden cat with a silver-tipped tail almost identical to our previous one. The cat butted his head into the cage rails as my husband reached through to scratch his neck. I wasn't tall enough to see into the top cages, so I had missed this cat earlier.

We exchanged looks, realizing what had happened. My husband would never have come with me to see a replica of our previous cat, but once there, his heart went out to it. "Well," he said, "we can't get two."

The little tortoise-shell was happily cuddled in the little girl's arms being hugged and kissed. I pointed to the scene about 10 feet away and said, "That's okay. That's the one I wanted, but I think she's going to be fine."

Our new cat was a recently neutered stray about four years old. His fur was so richly colored that I named him Buglet after a book I had read called *The Golden Bug*. His personality was considerably more energetic than our previous tenant, and it was delightful to hear him "brreep" and then rush up or down stairs or leap onto a windowsill or the back of the sofa.

But shortly there was a problem. It seemed his neutering had been less than successful. Some of the original stitches hadn't held, and something was protruding.

We rushed him to the vet, and two days later he came home, stressed and jumpy. The vet called a bit later and said that his blood test showed he was also Feline HIV-positive, and she recommended euthanasia. When I protested, she said that if we were intent on keeping him, he would have to stay inside to avoid contact with other cats.

We hadn't expected this to be anything but simple. At my weekly work prayer meeting, I asked for prayer that in spite of the test results, our cat could live a normal life.

Amazingly, that afternoon an old friend called. During our conversation, she mentioned she had had an HIV-positive cat in her home with four other cats for over six years with no sign of contagion. Apparently so little was known about Feline HIV that some vets routinely recommended euthanasia. My biochemistry background kicked in, and I realized that tests often identify antibodies, not disease. It can simply indicate previous exposure, even immunity. I breathed a sigh of relief.

Over the next several years life almost returned to normal except that I had less faith in veterinary medicine. Then came the next lesson.

That fall, in spite of regular exams, Buggy began shaking his head a lot and walking around with his ears at half-mast. We were back to the vet and discovered he had ear mites. We got antibiotics and some ointment for his ears, and we complied faithfully. But as time passed, he only got worse. He was listless and barely eating.

After several more vet appointments with no diagnosis, we were finally told, "Well, maybe he was older than you thought when you adopted him."

After seven months, Buggy had lost considerable ground. It became apparent that in spite of consistent vet care and our best efforts, we were losing him.

Even weakened, Buggy wouldn't permit much handling. But one day, while he slept on my lap, I was able to examine his ears. I was horrified to see the medication had done nothing. Inside his ears, crusted with blood, was a full-blown ear mite infestation. The vet had obviously missed this more than once in recent exams.

We embarked on a healing program with olive oil dampened cotton, hoping it was gentle enough yet thick enough to smother the parasites. It took a week for the redness and bleeding to heal. Buggy still hated being held, but each session became easier. When there were no further open wounds, we used a natural skin ointment containing pine pitch for bug bites. Pitch is antiseptic, while deadly to insects.

Within two weeks, he was almost his former self. He slept less, his appetite increased, and he became more active. After nine months, he was recovering just in time for spring.

That summer Buggy gained weight and played energetically, but on his next trip to the vet, she said he was underweight and needed a good quality dry food. She didn't even respond when I told her that ear mites had been his problem all along. I reluctantly acquiesced to giving him dry food again, and before long he wouldn't touch anything else. Soon after Thanksgiving, he again grew lethargic. We had had him for almost seven years now, and by our best estimates, he was about 10 years old.

His ears were fine, but I noticed he was spending more time in his cat box. Fearing cystitis, I made an emergency call to the vet. He was brought in, examined, and catheterized. Another three-day stay.

I blamed myself. Again the vet reassured me I had done nothing wrong feeding him dry food and there was no known cause for cystitis. She cited mineral imbalances and struvite crystals and suggested a special food.

Once again we brought Buggy home thin, tired, and frightened. The special food was a magnesium-free dry food, so we refused it. The vet had warned us that most cats that had to be catheterized would block up again in a few weeks and that she would be available for an emergency call. It would require surgery or euthanasia—our decision.

The vet had also said, "Most of the cats in our practice live to be 12 years old. After age 10, cystitis is common." I agonized in prayer for Buggy's healing and for my wisdom. Maybe 10 years *was* old for a cat. I committed him to God and agreed to do whatever He told me. I had lost faith in the experts. As I prayed, I felt that warm feeling of His presence, and I remembered back to my childhood cats that ate mice and meat scraps, living 20 years and more. Had we been sacrificing Buggy's health to our busy schedule?

I felt God had answered me. I bought family packs of raw hamburger, warmed some to room temperature, added water, and mixed in a tablespoonful of natural canned food. If cats were true carnivores, they ate meat, not cereal held together by hydrogenated transfats. Who could imagine what that could do to them over time?

Once again Buggy got off junk food, and this time onto a nearly raw diet, which he loved. It was half the cost of commercial cat food. His improvement was almost immediate. He blossomed into a lean, muscular 15-pound kitten within about four months. His fur, which had been pale and straw-like, regained its rich golden sheen. Now at almost 14 years old, he's still vital, healthy, and energetic. He climbs trees and runs about the yard when we are out and uses his kitty stairway that my husband built diagonally up the side of his outdoor workshop. At the top, about 15 feet off the ground, he lazes away warm summer days in his "California contemporary" cat house with a balcony and overhanging roof to protect him from the direct sun. In the winter he roars up the stairs, splashing soft snow in all directions, and leaps onto the top of his house to get on the roof of the workshop. His golden fur shines in the sun against the white snow as he perches on the pinnacle surveying the neighborhood.

We may lose Buggy to old age one day, but it won't be to inflicted malnutrition. His health and long life are more important than any time that convenience foods might save us. As long as I have a freezer, the raw food diet is quick and convenient.

I realize that faith can be well placed or poorly placed and "experts" can be wrong. The value of faith is what (and Who) your faith is in. Faith in false truths can be harmful. We need to reevaluate what we think we know, what we are told, and even the motives of who is telling us.

God knows what we need for life because He invented the original system. When I put my faith in Him, He answered by reminding me of that, and that not a sparrow fell to the ground that He didn't know and care, and He cared about Buggy. He made him, and He could fix him. When my heart accepted this, I was able to have faith for his healing and in what He had taught me about His system of natural health. This Expert could be trusted to provide the answer that the book of Hebrews calls: *the substance of things hoped for, and the evidence of things not seen.*

A Mustard Seed

By Rhonda Buck
Winnipeg, Manitoba, Canada

"I tell you the truth,if you have faith as small as a mustard seed, you can say to this mountain, 'Move from here to there' and it will move. Nothing will be impossible for you."
Matthew 17:20

I am the product of a strong Christian family. In my family, you had to display visible symptoms of severe sickness, preferably approaching death, before you qualified for an absentee slip from church. I married a man of a likewise background who later on decided, in great wisdom, to leave a good paying teacher's job to become a pastor. So, as a good solid Christian, I have never really contemplated my faith.

I say I have a strong faith, but how does one really know? How does one rank faith? On a scale of 1 to 10?

"Well, I feel my faith rates a seven. Not too high as to be ostentatious, but high enough to exhibit good Christian living."

No, when speaking of faith, we often use words like strong, weak, little, or no as measuring tools of faith. Jesus, the consummate teacher, taught using tangible items that both young and old alike could understand. He tells us faith as small as a mustard seed is all we need.

Being a person who likes to relate to tangible things, I retrieved a mustard seed from my spice cabinet one day and placed it in the palm of my hand. *No problem. My faith fit easily in the mustard seed category. I had it made in the shade.*

Then I became pregnant with my fourth child.

I must admit I was never one of those women that glowed when they were pregnant—unless you consider the sickly green cast due to nausea a glow. Although, as pointed out to me by a well-meaning soul, the blessing of spending the majority of your time emptying your stomach's contents meant you didn't have to fight the battle of the bulge after the arrival of your precious bundle. So I guess there are trade offs for everything.

I wasn't overly concerned at feeling tired and run down, as one child was growing inside me and three were running circles around me. So, after all, who could avoid it under the circumstances? But, never one to pass up an opportunity, I gave up housework and focused on growing a healthy, happy baby.

In the craziness only a pregnant mother possesses, I decided to use my pre-baby time wisely and potty train my youngest. After all, it would be much simpler to have only one in diapers instead of two. I had managed it with the others, so logically I figured it would work out this time, as well. All went well. Through sheer determination and constant diligence, my sixteen-month-old had me trained with three months to spare.

Then one day with feet tired, back aching, and ankles swollen, I went to bed before my husband, Rod, returned from an evening Bible study. I awoke from a deep sleep with the pressing need for a trip to the bathroom. Now it wasn't uncommon for me to make two or three such junkets during the wee hours of the night, but to my embarrassment, I seemed to have missed the target. Slowly maneuvering myself out of bed, I made my way quietly to the bathroom. But halfway there alarm bells sounded in my head as a gush of warm liquid cascaded down my legs. A block of ice formed in the pit of my stomach.

The bathroom light confirmed my worst fears. At only six months into this pregnancy, my water had broke.

Too soon.

Clutching the sink, I steadied myself and looked into the mirror at the pale, worried face staring back at me. I must have cried out because Rod suddenly appeared at my side, gently lowering me onto the side of the tub.

I laid my hand on the swollen mound of my stomach and said an anguished prayer for the protection of my baby. As if in answer, a solid kick landed on my already very bruised rib from an earlier assault that evening.

I took a deep breath, gathered my courage, and looked into my husband's eyes. I saw what I feared, but I also saw what I needed. Shining through the concern was love. A warm comforting love that whispered promises of God's protecting hand. No matter what came about in the next few hours, I wasn't alone.

The time following turned into a blur as Rod bundled up the kids and me, loaded the car, and drove us all to the hospital 45 minutes away. I don't know if I've ever been as scared as I was that day, but when I think of the car ride into the city, I don't remember so much the fear as I do the peace that came over me.

My husband is an amazing man, and I thank God for giving him to me. He quietly told the children—strapped into their car seats like three peas in a pod—that the baby didn't want to wait three more months to meet us all. Silent tears streamed down my cheeks as I clasped my husband's hand tightly in mine, drawing comfort from his warmth and strength.

Kai, my eldest, even at age five, has always been very aware of my moods. He asked, in a voice shaking with the threat of tears, why I was sad. Choked up, I replied that I was scared because the baby needed more time in Mommy's tummy to get strong and healthy. With the unpretentious honesty only a child possesses, he asked the question we were all wondering. "Is the baby going to die?"

My husband, a man with a strong faith and a great deal of wisdom, answered the question head on. Denials and avoidance weren't his way and weren't going to change the situation, so he calmly explained to the children and to me that God is with us all the time, especially when we're scared and hurting.

With a gentle squeeze of my hand, he spoke of God's love and the gift of family. If the baby died, he or she would be in heaven, because God had sent His only Son, Jesus, to die on the cross for us so we could live in heaven forever and ever.

God made sure that no matter what happened, we would be granted the gift of a new family member. We didn't need to worry because God keeps us protected, cradled in the palms of His hands. With us now or in heaven, the baby would always be a part of our family.

As the buildings of the city came into view, I felt a peaceful calm wash over me. I turned, smiled at my husband, and told my family that Mommy loved them very much.

My eldest smiled and said with confidence that he loved me, too, but God loved me more, so I'd be okay.

Yes, no matter what happened in the hours to come, I'd be okay because I was cradled in the reassurance of my Savior's love.

I discovered my faith was indeed as small as a mustard seed, but as God promised, it was enough to move mountains.

My mustard seed is now starting kindergarten, after starting off at a tiny 2 pounds, 13 ounces. He possesses a faith as strong and unwavering as only children, in their childlike faith, can manage. Daily he continues to remind me of the gift of faith God grants to each of His children.

My Father's Hand

By Julie Bonn Heath
Port Orchard, Washington

The Oregon coast was a stunning place. The waves were high and mighty, and the foam coming in on the waves was pure white and carried beautiful shells and treasures. The sand was golden and the sun warm. The rocks in the far distance jetting up from the water managed to look rather serene in spite of their height and sharp edges. Circling overhead, gulls swooped and called out to each other as they made their way to and from their nests. I knew the Oregon coast was the most beautiful place in the entire world. No one could convince me otherwise.

But I wasn't thinking about the beauty as I perched carefully on the side of mountainous rock that also held caves we explored and secret tide pools we waded in. I was thinking about the fact that my dad had suggested climbing a nearby very large rock. And in spite of his good intentions, water had moved in below us, and we had to climb up farther, over a ways, and back down in order to get back to the sand again.

With my dad and brother quite a bit above me, I was stuck in a spot and couldn't move up, because I was unable to find a secure spot to grasp above me. I remember wondering how long I could stay there without food (I was hungry) and why my stomach always growled at the most inopportune times with some innate need to distract me from an important task at hand.

I must not have really wanted to climb in the first place. I must have been crazy. My mom's worried looks from down below weren't helping my confidence level. Worst of all, my brother was loudly whooping on and on about how great it all was from his spot four feet above me. He obviously really wanted to climb the rock. Nothing had slowed him down.

On the beach we had discussed the situation before starting out. Or rather, the majority of the group voted in favor of it. This meant that Dad said, "Let's do it," and we kids nodded our heads, and my mom shook her head with a resounding "no" and said, "Richard," in *that voice* which meant, "You will not give me a heart attack today by taking my babies up that rock."

Actually, though, it looked kind of fun, and I certainly wasn't going to let my brother get a chance at doing something like that without me. But at the time, we were just going to climb straight up a little and a tad bit to the left. It wasn't like we were going to try and tackle Mt. Everest. Now, with water lapping at my heels (or so I thought), I was convinced that the entire ocean knew that I was stuck and was going to take full advantage of my misery by grabbing me and throwing me around for a bit.

I had made it a little ways after I discovered that the tide had moved in and had pointed out to my dad (with hand and arm gestures) that we couldn't get back down to where we had started. In fact, I think I was doing okay until I looked down. What a mistake that was! Being over the waves looking down was a bit like looking at a monster's mouth waiting to gobble you up. The waves were no longer beautiful but a swirling, angry force that insisted on growling so loudly that I couldn't even hear what my dad was saying. I should have told him at the time that he couldn't have gotten a better megaphone than my brother, but of course, all my concentration was on the rising water level, the power of the waves, and the meanderings of my vivid imagination.

I knew that I couldn't go up any further. I again placed my hand above me and tried to grasp at something to no avail. I could find nothing to grab onto. Even if I could, I didn't have the upper body strength to pull myself up. Every time I felt for a ledge with my feet, there either wasn't one large enough or rocks would crumble when I tried. Even though my feet were supported and I wasn't actually hanging from the rock, I was truly petrified.

I was only about 10 feet up from the sand, and the water had risen so that it was now only about four feet below me and very loud. It was swirling in and out of the caves and roaring. The waves made fast whirlpools of water and bounced back from the rock into other waves. The result was a very cold spray that landed on me every time two or three waves collided.

I started to cry, and all the monster waves got blurry. The gulls became white blobs, and I couldn't see my dad anymore. My hands grew damp and started to slip a little from their perch. I wasn't going to be able to hang on! I remember saying, "I can't, I can't," as I looked down at my mom—who now seemed to be miles away—for reassurance.

How did the other two get so high up? What was the secret? How come they could climb up there and I couldn't? I crouched in the spot where I was like a frightened animal and contemplated the situation while I cried.

I heard my dad yell, and when I looked up, he was taking his belt off and lowering it to me. Oh, I wish I hadn't seen that! If he thought that I could possibly let go of the spot I did have a hold on to grab that belt, he was crazy. There was no way! I felt somewhat secure with where I was.

Of course, there were waves lapping at me a few feet below, the water level was rising, and every time I heard a loud boom, I looked around to see a huge log or two being smashed against the rocks. Nonetheless, I was okay right where I was. It was certainly better than hanging from a belt over those waves.

But some part of me realized that not grabbing the belt would mean staying on the rocks and not getting back down to the beach. It might even mean the very cold water getting closer and closer until it forced me to let go of the rock and try to swim. I had a choice. Could my dad's belt even hold my weight as he raised me up? How could I possibly let go of my secure holding spot to dangle over water and sharp rocks? I knew I couldn't do it, so I cried even harder, convinced that I was going to be stuck on the rocks forever.

My dad didn't get angry. He didn't even seem impatient. It took him several minutes, but he slowly made his way back down the rocks until we were about 18 inches apart, and he held out his hand. I grasped it gratefully and held on tightly as he raised me up to his level and then guided me the rest of the way.

Getting back to the beach was so much easier with my dad by my side. He had to help me a few more times as we stumbled and made our path through crumbling rock, small streams of water, and the scattered plant life amongst the rock. Going down, I discovered, was even harder than climbing up! The ledges seemed less sure, and it was harder to find secure footings with your body in the way.

I remember in particular the two additional times that he reached out his hand. I eagerly grabbed it without even thinking twice. I had faith that my dad had the strength to get both of us back to the beach. And I trusted him.

God's hand is always nearby. We only need to grab it and allow Him to lift us to a better place. When I am challenged in my adult life, I remember that day on the beach and trust my Heavenly Father as I raise my hand to His. Sometimes it takes as much faith or more as it first did on the rock ledge so long ago. But as anyone would agree, it sure is a lot better to grab a belt or a hand than to let those monster waves smash you to smithereens!

Developing Unshakable Faith

By Todd Christopher Schroeder
Ottawa, Ohio

Faith means so many wonderful things to so many people. There are approximately 5 billion people in the world today, and as such, there are probably 5 billion different perspectives on faith and its role in our lives. However, even among these different perspectives, many would agree that faith works to manifest within oneself a sense of well being and inner peace. It does so by providing one with the framework to think of life and all its sufferings with a healthy perspective and with knowledge that there is a higher order to all we see and do. Faith, then, becomes the rock of our foundation upon which we can face life's adversities with love, compassion, and peace. The goal is to discover the kind of faith that is unshakable.

The kind of faith that is unshakable does not result from blindly believing what others have told you, but rather, results from looking deeply into life's daily experiences and concluding that a higher reality must exist. This proposition must be true, because if we believe without questioning, there will remain a very real potential for doubt in the face of adversity and in the face of tragedy. However, if we first question what others believe is a spiritual truth in light of our life experiences and come to a conclusion, we will have unshaken faith in that conclusion, because it is based in experience. It is God's intention that we understand this.

We are God's creation. In our unmanifest form we are spirit; in our manifest form we have a physical body that perceives using five senses. In order to understand faith in light of who we are, we must first ask ourselves what is God's purpose in having us lead a life in physical bodies in a physical world that, on a physical level, does not allow direct perception of God and a spiritual reality. That question can only be answered in light of our experience.

Our experience tells us that we are each a totally unique individual whose experience of life is unlike anyone else's. In addition, we each have free will to make that experience whatever we want. Surely this was God's intention. God must also have intended that we develop faith through this experience. This must be true, because otherwise spiritual reality would have been revealed in a more concrete way—a way that would allow our five senses to perceive it. If God intended that we each have free will to choose our experiences along with freedom of thought to interpret those experiences, then it makes sense that it is easier to have faith in a spiritual truth not because we are told it is true, but rather, because the truth is based in experience. Therefore, one develops unshakable faith through experience and through a religious practice based on that experience.

Admittedly, there are obstacles to developing unshakable faith based on your experience. For example, many people experience life in an environment that appears to them to be an endless stream of suffering. If their life is an endless stream of suffering, then how can they develop faith in God or even faith in love based on that experience? The requirement to developing faith for those surrounded by a negative environment is the same as for those who come from a positive environment—intention. No matter who we are or where we came from, we must intend to be better and intend to discover a reality beyond this physical existence—a reality based in God. If this is our intention, then we can begin to look at our experiences from the perspective of self-discovery. At this point we can begin to see God in all there is and all we do, whether or not the situation appears to be negative or positive. This is also the beginning of true faith. God has given us the wonderful tools of self-discovery to aid in this endeavor.

Our search for God and faith must incorporate all we have at our disposal. This includes spiritual teachings as well as science. Many view science as an enemy of religion. However, God did not give us science to test our faith, but rather, we have been given the gift of science to aid in the search for truth. Therefore, science should be a friend in the development of faith.

Although a discussion of quantum physics is not appropriate here, it does serve as an example of how science can aid in the development of faith. Experiments in quantum physics prove that at a very subtle level all matter is influenced by thought. This finding helps to validate the power of prayer. For example, if someone is ill and we pray that that person recovers, according to quantum physics, our prayer has a direct positive impact on the healing process. Likewise, if we pray with a group, that effect is multiplied. Taking the opportunity during the experience of life to study science and its relation to spiritual reality can have a dramatic impact on the development of unshakable faith. This result is also true in the study and practice of spiritual teachings.

In order to develop unshakable faith in spiritual teachings, it is highly important that we test those teachings in light of experience. For example,

Jesus Christ teaches us that in living a spiritual life, we must love our enemy. He gives no exception to this rule. We must love and have compassion for our enemy no matter who that person is or what he or she has done. However, as we all know, it is very difficult to love those who hurt us, our family, or even our country. Because of this, it is difficult to have faith in the teaching and to practice it if we never take the time to examine it in the light of experience.

Experience teaches us that we cannot fully love our enemies if we judge them. Therefore, application of the teaching to our lives means we must practice non-judgment. We should not view the world and individuals in terms of right and wrong, but rather we should have understanding for all ways of life, belief systems, and different perspectives. To practice this teaching of non-judgment is to experience its effect. Experiencing the effect of the teaching has the profound impact of understanding that loving your enemy means having no enemies at all. To have no enemies fills one with a wonderful sense of inner peace and tranquility. Furthermore, it becomes clear that if everyone were to practice the teaching as Jesus intended, there would be no war or fighting, only peace and love. Therefore, experiencing the teaching leads to an unshakable faith in the truth of the teaching. Once one has that level of unshakable faith, there is nothing that could lead him or her astray from it.

Experience is the path to unshakable faith. Through a physical existence and free will, God has made possible the development of the kind of faith that could only come from such circumstances. The only requirement to developing such a faith is that we look deeply into the experience of life and objectively analyze all possibilities. If we objectively analyze all possibilities and reach conclusions in light of our experience, our faith in those conclusions will be unshakable!

Faith—The Essence Of Christianity

By Marie E. DisBrow
Klamath River, California

Many people think that being a Christian consists of going to church and doing good works. Yes, believers in Christ meet to worship Him and for fellowship with one another, and the Bible definitely encourages this. Christians also desire to do good and help their fellow man. However, there is really only one thing that is fundamental to Christianity, and that is faith. Faith is the essence of the Christian life.

Consider these "steps" of faith:

- ✝ We are saved through faith. *For it is by grace you have been saved, through faith...* Ephesians 2:8
- ✝ We receive the Spirit by faith. *I would like to learn just one thing from you: Did you receive the Spirit by observing the law, or by believing what you heard?* Galatians 3:2
- ✝ We are protected through faith. *...who through faith are shielded by God's power until the coming of the salvation that is ready to be revealed in the last time.* 1 Peter 1:5
- ✝ We live by faith. *We live by faith, not by sight.* 2 Corinthians 5:7

What is this faith? Hebrews 11:1 describes faith *as ...being sure of what we hope for and certain of what we do not see.* The first time I read this Biblical definition of faith, I was more confused than enlightened! *How can anyone be certain of something unseen? And doesn't the act of hoping in itself imply uncertainty?* I have since learned that faith is based on evidence and in a Person. The word used for faith in the above verse is the Greek *pistis* that denotes the act of giving one's trust. In the simplest of terms, faith is believing that God is willing and able to fulfill His promises.

I learned to trust God by seeing His faithfulness in my life and in the lives of others. I saw that He keeps His promises given in His Word, the Bible. He has given me strength and encouragement through a lifetime of both trials and joys, heartaches and blessings. I've felt His guidance through good times and bad.

The evidence for Christian faith is found in the Bible in the recorded teachings of Jesus and the apostles, in the witness of saints and martyrs throughout the centuries, and in the personal experience of all believers. Testimonies of God's miraculous healing and provision are faith building. As we "walk out in faith," we are able to trust God more and more, experiencing for ourselves His faithfulness to protect, provide, and prosper His people. Faith is not static. It increases when we see how God is faithful to answer prayer and as He strengthens our faith. Just as a plant puts down roots for sustenance from the soil, we need to be rooted in Jesus, who nourishes and strengthens us in faith. (See Colossians 2:6,7)

The Bible is full of stories of faith to encourage and inspire us: The Canaanite woman who persisted in pleading with Jesus for her daughter's healing, the woman who believed that simply by touching the hem of His garment she would be healed of her sickness, the centurion who realized that Jesus was even able to heal without being physically present. Many times Jesus spoke the words, *"Your faith has healed you...According to your faith will it be done unto you...Your faith has saved you...Your faith has made you well."*

George Muller (1805-1898) is famous for his faith in God to supply all the needs of his orphanage in Bristol, England. He told no one except God about his needs, yet they were always met. He obeyed Jesus' instruction in the Sermon on the Mount to avoid worry about physical needs and to *"seek first his kingdom and his righteousness, and all these things will be given to you as well."* (Matthew 6:33) God honors and blesses all who put their faith in Him and supplies every need. 2 Peter 1:3 is God's assurance that He has given us everything that we need for life and godliness. Every promise in the Scriptures must be appropriated by faith (See Hebrews 11:6), and every answered prayer increases that faith.

Although faith is a gift from God, we are instructed in 2 Peter 1:5-8 to *make every effort* to add to our faith, *in increasing measure,* the virtues of goodness, knowledge, self-control, perseverance, godliness, brotherly kindness, and love, thus making our knowledge of Jesus effective and productive. Our faith does not have to be large. Jesus said that mountains could be moved with faith "as small as a mustard seed." It is the object of our faith that is large—Almighty God Himself. Whenever I hear someone say, "Prayer works," I think, "No, it's not prayer that is powerful; it is our powerful God who is faithful to work in answer to our feeble prayers."

The first step on the Christian walk is putting faith in Jesus and accepting Him as Savior. Jesus described this event as being *born again.* (John 3:1-18) This spiritual rebirth is necessary to live in Christ. As we continue in our Christian walk, our faith may often be tested. The apostle Peter wrote that God uses the trials and sufferings in our lives to refine our faith, just as gold is refined through fire. Experiencing God's presence and guidance through hard times enables us to trust Him more and more.

My own faith has grown in response to God's constant care over my life. Looking back, I can see how He used circumstances in my life to teach me and enable me to grow spiritually. He has protected me from death several times, beginning at birth, and has seen me through illness, heartache, grief, and indecision. Many of my prayers have been answered quickly, but for some, it took years before I saw them come to pass. And yes, some of my prayers were answered with "no," because God knows best what is good for me. Trusting God's goodness and accepting His plan and purpose for my life gives me peace of mind and heart.

The key to faith is love—our love for Jesus and His love for us. His great and unconditional love for us causes us to love Him, and the Holy Spirit teaches us to love one another. Christ dwells in our hearts by faith, and being *rooted and established in love* makes us able to comprehend the love of Christ. (Ephesians 3:17-19) This love makes us want to serve the Lord by loving and serving those around us.

We can trust the Lord to guide us in our walk of faith because the Bible says that when He delights in a man's way, He makes his steps firm. (Psalm 37:23) How encouraging to know that the Lord Himself will guide our steps when we look to Him!

Faith Turns Mourning To Joy

By Lisa Landen Watkins
Mechanicsville, Virginia

As a child, you have faith in many people. You have faith in parents, siblings, friends, teachers, pastors, and others. That faith usually occurs fairly naturally. To have a deep, continual faith in God, however, does not always come so easily—particularly when times are hard. When the going gets tough, it's even tougher to keep the faith that never waivers. That was certainly the case for me as I grew into the adult I am today. We have God's promise, though, that a mustard seed of faith can move the largest mountains in one's life. That has indeed been the case along my life's journey.

I accepted Jesus as my Savior at the age of six. I can still remember sitting on the end of my bed with my mother and praying for God to come into my heart and forgive me of my sins—not that I had a great multitude of sins, being just a first grader. But having grown up in a Christian home, I recognized that I was a sinner. Before and after my profession of faith, my mom, dad, sisters, and I attended church regularly and were very involved in church activities.

When I was eight, my father felt a strong call to go into full-time ministry. So we left our family and friends, sold our business and home, and moved from Virginia to Tennessee so he could attend Bible College. The mountains of Tennessee were beautiful, and I thought to myself, *What a great adventure this is going to be.* I had no idea what lay ahead.

We settled into our new home, school, and church for what we thought would be a long haul while my father attended school. But we lived in Tennessee for only three months. During that time, my father became ill and was diagnosed with severe kidney disease. The doctors said it would be best for us to move back to Virginia where there was a large hospital that could better care for him. Before we knew it, my father, my sisters, and I were on a plane back to Virginia while our mother stayed behind to pack up the house she has just recently unpacked.

It was a tremendous blow to our family. As a nine-year-old, I asked many questions of God concerning it all. How could He allow this to happen when we had moved to fulfill His calling?

When we came back to Virginia, we learned even worse news—that both of my father's kidneys were diseased and had to be removed. He would have to go on a dialysis machine to keep him alive until an organ transplant could be arranged. For the next few years my father was in and out of hospitals undergoing countless surgeries and treatments. My mother had to go to work since my father was incapable of working much of the time. Although we had a wonderful church and family that surrounded us with love, it was total dependence on God that enabled my parents to make it through each day. My sisters and I tried to emulate their courage, but it was not easy. It took all the faith, hope, and confidence we could muster. Then on June 12, 1977, my father went home to be with the Lord. I was 14.

Once again I was struggling. I didn't understand. Where was God in all of this? I felt like my faith had hit rock bottom. But God had not been caught off guard. We were, because our prayers were not answered in the way that we wanted. Little did we know, I was being prepared for an even greater test of faith that would take place in my adulthood.

Our lives were turned upside down for quite some time. I watched my mother struggle with her grief while doing her best to raise the three of us. Since she had to work, I became like a second Mom at home, helping take care of my two younger sisters and our house. Many days it was not easy, but I knew it was the right thing to do. Two years later my mom began dating a wonderful Christian man whom we had known for many years. His wife had died a few months earlier from cancer, and he had three grown sons. In November of 1979 they were married. There was naturally some adjustment in blending the two families into one, but it was miraculous what God had done. I had a new Dad in my life, and our relationship was wonderful.

Four years later I began dating a young man whose family had been a part of our lives throughout my father's illness. Our paths had separated for a time, but God saw fit to cross them again, and in December of 1984 Steve and I were married. During the next nine years we had three wonderful sons. We had a lovely home and were very active in our church. Steve had a good job, and I was able to stay at home with my boys. He coached the boys in sports, we went camping every chance we got, and we were in church plays together. Life could not be any better. Then we hit a devastating bump in the road.

In June of 1999 Steve had a mole removed from his leg, and we were told it was melanoma cancer. We were concerned but thought that in the end, it would turn out fine. He went in for surgery, and we were relieved to learn that everything likely would be okay. But by the fall of that year, everything was not okay. The cancer had spread, and we were suddenly thrown into a horrible whirlwind of doctors, surgeries, and treatments. I began wondering, *Where is God?* I told God that He had the wrong family. Didn't He remember that I'd already traveled down this awful road before?

My faith was at a very low point during all of this. I couldn't understand how this could happen to us and felt sure God had abandoned us. I tried to pray and read the Bible, but for a long time it seemed as though nothing helped. During it all our family, friends, and church reached out to us in so many ways. Through them I started thinking that perhaps God was taking care of us after all. Slowly I started pressing in to Him. In December of 2000, after Steve had come out of another surgery, it was obvious that something terrible was happening. He was rushed to ICU, and I was told that he had several brain tumors and was hemorrhaging. They did emergency surgery, and he pulled through. But he was in a coma.

Three days later I had to make one of the most difficult decisions of my life—whether or not to have my husband taken off life support. That afternoon I signed the papers for him to be removed, knowing full well that his chances were very slim. The family came in to say their last goodbyes, and the depth of the sorrow was almost inconceivable. All the while I kept saying to myself, *This is **not** the way it is supposed to be.*

Eight hours later the nurse woke me as I slept beside Steve to tell me that Steve had opened his eyes. He had come out of the coma! A few hours later he was squeezing my hand and understanding me. It was truly a miracle! Two days later he was moved from ICU to a regular room. We celebrated Christmas in the hospital together, and he spoke his first words to me on Christmas morning. He improved enough that I was even able to bring him home.

But five days later we were back in the hospital, and he was not doing well. On January 10, 2001, my wonderful husband went home to be with the Lord.

Once again my prayers were not answered in the way I thought they should have been—only this time, instead of being one of three fatherless girls, I was a widowed mother of three fatherless boys. Although we sensed God's presence during this time, it was a tremendous struggle to get through each day. I wanted to feel at peace, and I wanted my three boys to be happy again. But instead, life with them seemed like a constant therapy session—and like it or not, I was their therapist, exhausted and suffering from the same pain—desperately missing Steve.

I cried out to God. I tried to read the Bible. I tried to pray. But I felt nothing but emptiness. In the fall of 2001 I decided to join a small group

Bible study to see if that would help me. It was very difficult, but I kept on going. All the while we somehow managed to get through birthdays, holidays, and even the anniversary of Steve's death in January. As the winter passed and spring blooms began to appear, I sensed something also blooming in my spirit. I couldn't really put my finger on it, though, for some time. Then one day after coming home from Bible study, I realized that God had slowly been doing a work in my heart. I was not grieving any longer! The hurt was gone!

He had come and performed a heart transplant. There were no circumstances in the natural to cause this change of heart. It was a supernatural act of God. Through the Bible study I had made the choice to let go and let Him be Lord of ALL! Now two and a half years later, the healing remains, and my relationship with the Lord is more intimate and sweet than it has ever been.

The Journey

You are on this journey called Life
Sometimes just walking without worry or strife
Day in and day out
You think…What's this life really about?
Then there comes a bump in the road
And all of a sudden you're carrying a heavy load
Your burdens are weighing you down
Where is the answer to be found?
You say to yourself that life seems unfair
And you wonder… "Does God really care?
Can He hear me? Can He really see my heart?
Can He touch me, in the deepest part?"
So you drop to your knees and pray
And ask God… *Please, show me the way*
All you need is to trust and believe
For He is able to do more than you can conceive
The burdens are now lifted from your heart
Stand up my child; let's make a clean start
You finally understand He really cares for you
And He's proving that *His* word is true
Thank You for Your awesome love
Thank You for sending Your Son from above
Your mercy and grace *are* more than enough
Even when the journey of life seems too hard and rough.

During this beautiful healing of my heart, God inspired me to write this poem describing this journey in my life. God came in and turned my mourning into joy. Faith does move the mountains in our lives; it just doesn't always move them in the direction we think it should.

When I am reminded of my journey in this life, both as a young girl and a woman, I can truly turn around and see God at every turn, many times carrying me over the bumps in the road. Hebrews 11:1 says that faith is being sure of what we hope for and certain of what we do not see. I can say with certainty that although I cannot see God in the flesh, I can see His hand of love, grace, and mercy in my life. And I know the day will come when I will again see both my father and my husband, and we will rejoice together in the faithfulness of an awesome God.

Faith In His Plan

By Marguerite A. Brown
Las Vegas, Nevada

Faith is the basic foundation of our belief system. With it, we can guide ourselves through the many obstacles that find their way into our lives. Without it, we walk through life unarmed, defenseless against those unforseen forces aimed at destroying the fabric of who we are and what our purpose in life is meant to be.

Though most might equate my leap in faith with sheer folly, I believe it is a testament to God's master plan. Have faith in ourselves and in Him, and eventually the answers to life's puzzles will be revealed.

My story begins 16 years ago when I met who I believed to be my soulmate.

Ours was an instant attraction, as though we were drawn together by a force greater than ourselves. The flow of our relationship was effortless, an orchestration of love and affection unlike anything either of us had ever experienced. Marriage was inevitable, and we exchanged vows nine months later in a quiet ceremony before a garden backdrop, surrounded by only our closest friends and family. On that day I made a conscious decision that I would grow old with this man, determined to respect every aspect of my promise to remain faithful, to honor and cherish in sickness and in health, for richer or for poorer, till death do us part. To this day that pledge has still stayed sacred for me, but much else has changed.

Going into the marriage, it was no secret that I was unable to conceive, and though it had always been very difficult for me to accept—I had never envisioned my life without children—I learned to live with it as God's will. I figured if my husband could still love me despite my inability to give him children, then nothing else mattered, and of course, there was always the possibility of adoption.

Though the first several years of our life together were well-intentioned, we were certainly not immune to the influences of life's daily stresses. We had our share of petty arguments and financial woes, many of which destroy even the best of marriages in the best of circumstances.

Nonetheless, we persevered, our deep love for each other the one cohesive element enabling us to stick it out. Then it suddenly hit us one day—perhaps we needed a change of environment, and without much thought, we packed up and moved west to Las Vegas, Nevada, taking with us only the basic necessities and just enough money to carry us for a month of a bare-bones existence. Neither of us were aware that this decision would ultimately test our marriage, impacting our lives in a way we could never have imagined.

Excited and hopeful, we arrived in Las Vegas with little more than our dreams of a better life. Temporarily staying with my sister, we immediately set out on a quest to secure jobs, which was our number one priority. Not much time passed before the reality of what we had done set in. Not only did we have difficulty finding work, but things were not working out between my sister and my husband, and our money was quickly dwindling. Arguments became our way of relieving stress, and we beat and badgered one another with increased frequency. It seemed as though we'd made a mistake moving cross country. Things progressively went from bad to worse, and we began spending less and less time with each other. It appeared to be the only way for us to get along.

Eventually we did find work, and we did get our own place, but not before severe damage had taken it's toll on our marriage. My husband was having an affair.

To say that I was devestated when I found out would be a gross understatement. My heart shattered, I plunged deep into an abyss of darkness, filled with indescribable pain and broken dreams. My pride prevented me from considering forgiveness, and I retaliated by banishing him from my home and from my life. For me, our marriage was over.

He moved in with her.

As the days turned into weeks and weeks into months, I began to feel I'd been hasty in deciding to give up on my husband. In time I realized I had contributed to his desire to find comfort in the arms of another woman. In my selfishness, I hadn't heard his appeals to me not to give up faith, that somehow we would make it. I had blamed him for not finding a job soon enough, for not doing everything he could to make our transition easier. In short, I had blamed him for everything that went wrong.

The problem was, we were both at fault for not carefully planning for such a drastic change in our lives, and our lack of preparation left us vunerable to life's unexpected turns. I missed him terribly, and something deep inside me never quite felt right about our separation.

I had always believed we were meant to be together, and once we met and talked, I found a way. We decided to give reconciliation a try.

Initially, things went as well as could be expected. Both of us admitted we'd made mistakes, and we were willing to do whatever was needed to mend our damaged relationship. Then, just when we thought things couldn't get worse, we got another knockdown blow: news that the other woman was now pregnant with my husband's child. I felt the blade of his words slice through the unhealed wound in my heart. An affair was one thing, but a child? I'd maintained faith throughout our ordeal, but did I have the strength to endure this? Crying uncontrollably, I told him, "She can't have this child!" He agreed and said he would ask her to terminate the pregnancy.

Of course she wouldn't hear of it. If she couldn't have the man, then she'd settle for his child, secretly hoping this would eventually lure him back into her life. She said that her Christian beliefs wouldn't allow her to have an abortion. I wanted to know where her Christian beliefs were when she was committing adultery.

The baby was due in March, and it was August. Seven unbearable months lay ahead, the intermediary months filled with accusations and blame. What hurt even more was that I wanted to be the one to give my husband a baby. It all seemed so unfair. I tried my best to remember that God never gives you more than you can bear and that if something doesn't kill you, it makes you stronger.

But each passing day proved to be a challenge, my inner voice telling me I should get out while I could. But I loved my husband, and this was testing the part of our vows that said for better or for worse. For sure this was the worse. I still hadn't met this other woman.

I will never forget the day that Samantha was born. She came into the world just before my shift at work was about to end. I got the phone call and knew that my life would never be the same. My heart was heavy, though I told myself that the well-being of this child would take precedence over my personal pain. After all, she never asked to be here. My husband and I felt that, though these were the most unusual of circumstances, as long as we stayed strong, we could get through this.

Two days later he took me to the hospital to meet my step-daughter. Born with a non-life-threatening respiratory problem, Samantha was kept in the hospital for a few days for observation, and of course, I went to see her when her mother was not there. Seeing her was more difficult than I thought it would be, and when I looked at her, I thought of how beautiful she was and how sorry I was for her having to grow up without both her mommy and daddy under one roof. I almost felt guilty for fighting for my marriage, but I knew in my heart that it was meant to be this way. I just didn't know why.

Two months passed before I set eyes on that little baby again, with my husband making periodic visits to her mother's house to check on her.

Hard as it was for me to live through that time, I continued to stay focused on the well-being of the baby, and then her mother, forced to go back to work, had no choice but to leave her in our custody during her working hours. No doubt she resented my inclusion, but as life would have it, what goes around, comes around.

I grew to love that little girl as if she were my own and treated her the same way.

I ended up being there for a lot of her firsts, many of which her mother missed out on.

It was almost as if God denied me the opportunity to bear children of my own, but selected me to help parent this child because she needed me in her life. I doted on her and spent time doing all those things for her that her mother was incapable of doing.

Financially, my husband and I were in a better position.

Today, Samantha is five years old, and she started kindergarten last fall. Although she is not yet old enough to fully comprehend her predicament, she is fully adjusted and knows that I am not her real mommy. She calls me Mama just the same, and over the years, her mother and I have learned to forgive the situation, placing our daughter before all.

I have come to realize that God has a master plan, and if you have faith in Him and can overcome the obstacles He places in your path, you will come out a stronger and wiser person. I not only learned the power of forgiveness, but also the power of faith.

I love being a mother to a bright and beautiful little girl who loves me unconditionally...and I am still married to her father. My greatest joy is knowing that I made the right decision by hanging in there, and I look forward to any future challenges that may come my way.

Gaining Ground

By Nancy M. Chapman
Norfolk, Virginia

I noticed her around mile four. She was joking with a Marine about the braces on her knees. He said if she couldn't finish the Marathon, he'd carry her on his back to her car. A few moments later she was beside me again, so I asked, "What's wrong with your knees?"

She explained about the Lymes disease and the arthritis it had inflicted on her last winter. As we jogged around the Pentagon, she reminisced about her running career and how proud she'd been to work her way up to the middle of the pack. Now she could barely run. But since she had managed to win a lottery slot for the jam-packed Marine Corps Marathon, a feat in itself, she thought she'd at least see how far she could go. Maybe halfway, she hoped.

While Carol chatted, we were doing my wimpy run/walk intervals of one minute running, three minutes walking. At 49, this was my third Marathon in six months. A year earlier I'd started training as an endurance walker, but for the last few months I'd been learning to run—and it hadn't been easy. The Marine Corps was the first marathon in which I was trying to maintain a run/walk for the entire distance. It was also the first marathon I was doing alone.

Carol asked if she could hang out with me a while, explaining that having someone to talk to might help her go farther. I'd already noticed that our pace together was slower than what I wanted to be doing, but something said I should stay with her. Probably my ego, which no doubt thought I'd be doing her a huge favor. Little did I know how much she'd do for me.

As we moved across Key Bridge into D.C.'s Georgetown District, Carol spoke of God and the lessons her arthritis was teaching her about pride and ego. She'd only started running in her 30's and had trained hard to progress. Now in her mid 40's she was sad and humbled to let go of this special ability, she said.

I tried to pay attention and show compassion, tried to ignore the voice in my head that was screaming, *Now, Nancy, you know you can go faster than this. You have a goal to meet, remember? Did you do all that training only to let a stranger hold you back?*

I wrestled with what to do. *Is my hooking up with Carol a God thing?* I wondered.

The competitor in me got even more frustrated when she stopped several times along the route to check on runners in distress, runners that my self-centered tunnel vision had kept me from even seeing.

Does she really have to stop to help everyone? my inner competitor whined. Then I saw the agony on the face of one woman who was writhing on the ground. While Carol tried to help her, I ran over to some official-looking guys to find medical help, thoroughly disgusted with myself. *What if that had been you, Nancy? Wouldn't you want someone to stop?*

Mile 13—the halfway point—came and went, and Carol was still hanging in there—and smiling. The more distance we covered, the more excited she got. She took snapshots of the mile 14 marker on Rock Creek Parkway. She talked about doing a 5K Turkey Trot at Thanksgiving with her eight-year-old daughter. She called my name, and when I turned around, she took my picture. She told me about her 24-year-old niece who not long ago hadn't been able to keep up with Carol on the trails. She tried to calculate how many miles her husband, also a marathoner, had left to go in the race. The more I learned about my marathon partner, the more I respected her and considered her my friend.

By mile 15, the medication she had taken a few miles earlier was doing little to keep her pain at bay. She thought there was an aid station at mile 16—she'd call it a race there, she said. But when we hit that mile marker and found no aid station, she decided to keep going. Nothing at mile 17 either. Her face could no longer hide the pain.

"I hope I'm not holding you back," Carol said.

"Not at all," I replied to my new friend. And by now it was the truth. It had taken more than half a marathon—not to mention 49 years—but I was finally getting my priorities straight.

Though there still wasn't an aid station at mile 18, Carol admitted she could go no further. After she announced to the Marines that she was quitting, we hugged and tried to memorize each other's email addresses.

As I waved goodbye, I checked my watch and realized that to make my goal time, I'd really have to pick up my pace. Two-thirds of the way through the 26.2 miles, speeding up seemed impossible.

But I tried anyway. With almost no confidence, I began lengthening my running intervals. Passing the Smithsonian, I became aware that my body was feeling different than it did at the same point in previous marathons. Stronger perhaps? *Hmm,* I thought. *This seems to be working.*

And so 19, 20 miles into the event I found that I was running better than I ever did in training. I pushed harder. I started passing people. And I felt great.

Just beyond mile 25 my coach appeared, as he often did, to accompany me to the finish line.

"You actually look energized," Charlie said when he saw me. God knows he hasn't seen me that way very often.

Remembering what my goal was, Charlie checked the time.

"You better run some more," he said as we headed up the final hill to the finish. In training my answer would have been, "Charlie, I just can't."

Not this time.

I crossed the finish line a minute and a half under goal.

But that wasn't the best news. Thanks to keeping Carol's pace, I ended up completing the second half of the marathon 14 minutes faster than the first half. The way experts say to do it. The way I'd never done it before. Starting slow, finishing strong. My coach was amazed.

For someone who nearly flunked tumbling in high school, it was an unbelievable accomplishment. And it's one I never would have achieved if the competitor in me hadn't been persuaded to have a little faith.

I didn't see Carol again that day, but we emailed each other later. She had looked up my time on the marathon website, she wrote, and was thrilled to know I'd made my goal. Emailing her back, I tried to explain how much she had helped me and how grateful I was, but I doubt that she fully understood.

So I sent her this.

Getting At The Innards

By Michael John Demchsak
Austin, Texas

Faith is the currency of heaven. Without it the riches of God cannot be had. This is not because God somehow wishes to deny certain people, but because He desires to exercise the soul and to transform the heart in its deepest recess. God does not want a gaggle of followers who merely obey the rules. Nor does He want a horde of souls who recline in spiritual and earthly ease. He wants disciples who have been remade from the inside out. That is the ultimate business of God, and there is nothing on earth quite so capable of accomplishing God's purpose as faith.

Faith touches the soul where it counts, and it does so in every life situation imaginable. When life smiles and the paychecks are fat or the relationships satisfying, faith sees past the bounty to its source and does not allow the soul to find its true strength and comfort in the bounty. Indeed, it frequently bids us to give away the bounty for the sake of a kingdom we cannot see. When troubles come like a blizzard and our spouse is dying of cancer or the job is bringing criticism, faith sees what seems to be the unseeable, the presence of God. It is not trite; it wrestles with real pain and does not necessarily solve every problem, but it does give a new perspective to the pain we endure. When the days march by in humdrum routine, faith prods us to the edge of a precipice out at the frontiers of life and compels us to jump. Wherever we may happen to be in our life, faith always takes us a step further.

Faith is immensely practical. It is neither shallow belief nor philosophical exercise but entails thought, emotion, will, and action. It is a holistic endeavor. When Jesus told the rich man to sell all he had, give to the poor, and follow him, He was calling the rich man to take a step of faith. The rich man had to weigh the consequences mentally, deal with his emotional reactions, deny his desires, and actually do something. That is faith. When God called Steve, a friend of mine, to give up the pursuit of a woman whom he wanted to marry, Steve agonized in his thoughts, struggled with his feelings, and ultimately had to give up his will and take some concrete steps of action. That is faith. When God came to Erin, who had just lost her husband to another woman, He bid her to seek His comfort, then to seek His forgiveness, then to give her forgiveness. At each one of those steps, Erin had to think and weep and let go and do something. And each step was progressively more difficult than the one before it. That is faith. When Dan and his wife were called to quit their jobs to go start a church, they wrestled with questions, experienced anxiety, released their securities, and submitted their resignations. That is faith.

Stories of faith are not new. Abraham left his homeland; Moses spoke to Pharaoh; Paul went to the Gentiles; and over the centuries Christians have left homelands, stood against emperors, given up comforts, and prayed for what they did not see. But always because of something they *did* see. For faith sees the person and character of God and brings it to bear in a real circumstance.

I was an ordinary man living an ordinary life. I had graduated from college and was serving out the last year of a four-year obligation in the Army. The military had opened interesting doors and enabled me to travel East Asia and the Pacific Basin, and for that I was grateful, for I had enjoyed the experience of different cultures and sights. But the military never turned out to be the sort of job that resonated with me. I never felt challenged, and my personality was not...well, military-like. All that "huuah" stuff never appealed to me. And so I was looking forward to the end of the next year when I could get out.

One day while at work, I received a note to go see the battalion executive officer, Major Thompson. The major had called me in to inform me that I had about 30 days before I would have to officially declare my intent to stay in or get out and also to find out from me which way I was leaning. I went home that night already knowing what I was going to do, but felt that, as a Christian, I should at least pray about a decision of this magnitude. And so I did. Each day during my prayer time I asked for God's leading, and slowly, as I did so, I began to sense that God was asking me to stay in. At first I ignored that feeling. But it persisted, and as it did, I could no longer ignore it. So I began to doubt it. *How do I know this is God? Surely God wouldn't call me to spend my life in a career I do not enjoy.* But that sense quietly remained, and deep down I knew what God was calling me to do, even while I expressed doubts and even though I wouldn't admit to such knowledge. The doubts and the seemingly intangible nature of this sort of communication became a kind of comfort. They provided wiggle room.

This once-simple career decision jumped from something I had merely mentioned in a prayer to something that now occupied my thoughts throughout the day. I could not shake the gentle, silent certitude that God was telling me to stay in. It was like a soft snowfall that kept piling up until it could no longer be ignored. It was like a slowly advancing puddle permeating a sponge. It was, in its own quiet way, becoming bedrock, if only I would acknowledge it as such.

As this sense came more to the forefront, so did my distress, and I was openly wrestling with God over my future. *Why? This makes no sense...I'm not a military guy...I can't do it.* But I wanted God, and side by side with the distress, I also began praying things like, "If this really is You, help me to give You my career."

Meanwhile the deadline drew nearer. It was a Saturday morning, and I was in my apartment doing laundry and dishes and sundry chores, all along, of course, thinking on this issue, when I felt I had to pray. I left the half-done dishes in the sudsy sink, went to the living room, and knelt down before a wooden chair. "Lord," I prayed slowly, "You know my heart. And You know that I do not want to stay in the military." There was a long break. "But Lord, I will trust You, and if You want me in, I will stay in." There was another break. "God, I'll stay in."

I had not prayed long and was not even sure I was done praying, but within a couple seconds, I plainly heard God speak. It was not an audible voice, and there was no smoke or blazing glory, just a living room with a man on his knees before a wooden chair. But there was a quiet, gentle, clear, inward sense of the exact sort which I had experienced for the prior several weeks. And through that small inward voice God spoke only four words, but what shocking words they were: "You can get out."

I've never been a missionary or spoken to thousands. I have no fantastic stories and will never be in the "Who's Who" for Christians. I am a regular guy who wrestled with God over his career. But I found that in the end, God wanted my heart before He would give me my career. And God knows just how to get to the heart. He simply asks for faith.

Rise & Shine!

By Susan Rose
Byron, Georgia

"Arise, shine, for your light has come, and the glory of the Lord rises upon you. See, darkness covers the earth and thick darkness is over the peoples, but the Lord rises upon you and His glory appears over you. Nations will come to your light, and kings to the brightness of your dawn."
Isaiah 60:1-3

Remember how the face of Moses glowed when he came down from the mountain? (Exodus 34:29-35) Moses had been with God, and the glory of God was seen upon him as a visible light. The children of Israel were allowed to glimpse this light—the lingering residue of God's presence.

Today God's glory is not only *on* His children, but *in* us, waiting to influence the world. Being vessels of the Holy Spirit, we have more than a residue of God. We carry around with us the fullness of His being—His love, His power, His victory, and the brightness of His glory. And by *faith*, we draw upon all that God is. Faith is the switch that activates the presence of God within.

When I read Isaiah 60:1-3 and hear God say, *"Arise, shine, for your light has come, and the glory of the Lord rises upon you,"* the Holy Spirit urges me to take the words personally. God tells me to rise up with faith to a new level—to a place of honor as His child. I'm asked to stand up and step out into my destiny. I'm asked to rise up and believe that His power and His glory will provide for all that's required of me. As long as I abide in Him, trusting and obeying, I simply cannot fail.

Since the words of Isaiah are an Old Testament prophecy to Israel, the enemy tried to convince me that I can't apply this Scripture to my life today. But the Lord intervened. These verses are important to my spiritual growth, so He sent me a message of confirmation. A few months earlier, while browsing for antiques, I purchased an embroidered scene that included a smiling sun, a birdhouse, seven flowers with button centers, and the words, "Rise and Shine," sewn in purple thread. I didn't recognize the words as being Scripture, but I liked their positive message. And I liked the simple, childlike needlework in its primitive frame. Later, when God began revealing to me the importance of Isaiah 60:1-3, I realized that the three embroidered words actually *are* Scripture. As I stood looking at the picture, God spoke to me, saying, *"I caused you to buy this. It's My assurance that the message in the book of Isaiah is for you. You'll be reminded every day that by faith, your future will be bright."*

Not just for me, the message of "rise and shine" is for every Christian who wants to rise above his past. It's for every person who longs to make a difference in this world. These words display the heart of God toward all people, young and old, wherever they may be. He wants us to reach our potential! Our Father urges us to believe. He whispers to our spirit, asking that we have faith in His love and in His strength—the love that supercedes our failures and our flaws and the strength that takes us far beyond our human limitations.

God wants every one of us to be free from dysfunction and sin. We mustn't dwell on memories of what we used to be. If Satan can convince us that we're still shameful people, that we're not worthy of what God offers, then we won't dare to claim our position of honor, authority, and blessing. We must not listen to the barrage of condemnation coming from the enemy. God's word says, *...as far as the east is from the west, so far has He removed our transgressions from us.* Psalm 103:12 Embracing God's life-giving truth will make us strong for whatever lies ahead.

Now please don't say, "But I'm just a simple person, and I can't do any better," or "Well, you don't know about my past!" These statements come from the false humility that refuses the grace of God. They come from a heart that rejects the truth. If you insist on having these mindsets, then you're living in rebellion. Don't forget the parable of the talents in Matthew 25:14-30. Jesus tells us to perform diligently, using what we've been given. When we do this, we're rewarded with promotion. But if we waste our gifts because we're lazy or even afraid, then they're taken away.

Please don't close the door on God's truth and tell Him that He can't operate in your life. Don't choose the mediocrity and failure of unbelief over the power and glory of faith.

But God chose the foolish things of the world to shame the wise; God chose the weak things of the world to shame the strong. He chose the lowly things of this world and the despised things—and the things that are not—to nullify the things that are, so that no one may boast before Him.
1 Corinthians 1:27-29 These words should make our hearts beat faster! God says He won't use human strength to do His work. He insists on using

the weak, even the *despised* people. He'll use the people who have faith.

The brightest glory of God will not be revealed when the rich or the educated take the stage. It will enter through the works of the righteous and be heard on the lips of the holy. God's brightest glory will spring from the hearts of the "unimportant." One day soon, the light of truth and hope will flood the earth—as faith flings open the gates.

Thank You, Lord, for all that You say. Thank You for every warning, every direction, every encouragement, and all revelation of Yourself. *Jesus answered: "It is written, 'Man does not live on bread alone, but on every word that comes from the mouth of God.'"* Matthew 4:4 Apart from Your Word, we'll never be able to "rise and shine." But with faith in our hearts to unlock this treasure, we'll shine like silver and gold.

And without faith it is impossible to please God, because anyone who comes to Him must believe that He exists and that He rewards those who earnestly seek Him. Hebrews 11:6

Saying Goodbye And Hello

By Annette Argabright
Corinth, Texas

"No!" my heart cried. I hung my head and sobbed. My husband had just told me that he found a job in Dallas, Texas, and we would be moving. I should have been overjoyed that he was finally able to find a job, but I wasn't. Later I would find joy in being reunited with our extended family in Texas, but at that moment my heart was broken. Steve tenderly held me and let me cry. Moving would be as hard for him as it was for our two daughters and me. I knew I was making it more difficult on him, but I couldn't help myself.

Steve had lost his job just two days after the brutal attacks upon our country on September 11. The attacks did not cause the layoff, but they certainly did affect the job market in Denver. Colorado was where we had decided to live out our lives. It was where our friends were, where our church was. It was where the mountains were. The mountains filled my soul, and Colorado was where we had learned to save our marriage and built a strong foundation for our family. We did not want to leave.

Steve left shortly after he found the job, and I stayed behind to pick up the pieces of my life and try to be strong for my children. But my strength was gone—stolen by an unknown enemy in a foreign land whose hatred had affected so many in this country. And with it went my creativity…some- thing I hold dear to my heart. Just cooking dinner was a challenge, nevermind writing, photography, or doing art projects with my daughters.

The day the realtor placed the "For Sale" sign in our yard, I felt my heart rip into tiny little pieces. With every pound of the sledgehammer that drove the sign legs into the frozen ground, I sank a little lower until I found myself sobbing uncontrollably on my knees. My daughter, too young to be offering comfort to her family, came to me and held me with all the tenderness I knew her to possess. Though I've heard we should try to shelter our children from the intensity of our pain, as it frightens them because they do not understand, I could not…they saw all my pain. I wore it like a garment.

We canceled all our activities so we could visit our favorite places in Colorado again and dropped everything to spend time with friends whenever they called. The time with our best friends was bittersweet. Now I can see that period in my life built those relationships beyond measure. I would never have known the level of friendship I shared with those few treasured people. But how would I ever tell them goodbye? How would I pull away when that moment came? I didn't think I could.

One day, as I was going through some keepsake boxes to repack them, I came across some letters my friend, Diane, had written to me. I read through some of them, remembering the friend I had lost to cancer at the age of 25 with tears and love. Then I came across some letters I had written to her. I had forgotten that after her death, her mother gave me the letters. I read through a few of those, too, and suddenly saying goodbye to Diane came rushing back to me. Diane and I had discussed her funeral many times before her death. As in my current situation, I had not known if I possessed the strength to be able to say goodbye to her when the time came.

Now I remembered the strength I found to go to her bedside and tell her goodbye just days before her death. She did not realize why I was there but went back to the days of helping me plan my wedding five years earlier. So we planned it again as tears slid down my cheeks. Finally, I could bear it no more, and I hugged and kissed her and said, "Diane, it's okay to let go now." She responded clearly, "I know. I love you." Three days later, she was gone.

At her funeral, I managed to help carry her casket to the hearse before I fell apart. My husband was unable to be with me, but an old friend was there to hold me. I cried like I never had before. Telling Diane goodbye was the hardest thing I have ever done, and my heart felt like it was breaking into tiny little pieces.

As I relived that moment in my life, I realized that I had said a heartbreaking goodbye before and had survived it. That one had been more long term; only heaven will reunite Diane and I again. But I can e-mail, write, call, and even visit my Colorado friends. After 10 years God was still using Diane as a true friend in reminding me that I can do all things through Christ who strengthens me. I had done this before, and my heart was filled with hope and became a companion to my pain. My faith was renewed.

I e-mailed Diane's mother the next morning to tell her how much I cherished her daughter's never ending friendship. It just so happened to be Diane's birthday.

When the moment to say goodbye to my treasured friends in Colorado came, it wasn't any less painful than I expected. And the last day when I said goodbye to my two best friends in the world, my heart did break into even tinier little pieces, but hope was intact. I knew I could do this as long as my faith in that hope that God gave me remained strong. So I pulled away from the home I loved through tear-filled eyes and fully relied on God's strength to propel me forward.

It has been nearly a year since the day my beloved husband told me we would need to move, and I can't say that I have flown through this with joy in my heart. It has been very challenging. I had to learn to "be still in the Lord" because that was all I could do sometimes. I am beginning to see how the Lord has blessed us, not only in our new surroundings and our new friends, but also in building our faith and knowledge of Him. I am building excitingly stronger relationships with extended family, and my friends are still my friends, only we now know each other in a deeper way.

3

A Legacy Of Faith

Red Clouds To White Whispers: Tempest In The Clear

By Jonathan Louis Kotulski
Romeoville, Illinois

Mom sat on our worn brown couch and called my brother and me to her side. She held letters in trembling hands, and tears carved white lines down her face. She looked at us lovingly as we slowly sat down. We were troubled by that face, for it is not every day that mothers look at their children with such compassion. *Why was she acting so oddly? What was the matter with us?* Sobbing, she began to speak with deliberation and told us of the past. Our past. The only thing we knew was that we were abandoned children, but then we had been adopted. However, her words now were a past laid stark before our eyes, fresh and utterly terrible, unlike the formulaic explanation we had heard before. She told us of our different identities, of strange names and places, of demons and powers, of dark nights and disillusioned women. We listened with tight throats and frowning eyes.

From 1980 to 1990, our birth mother's life was troubled water and tempest. And we were born into this time, this sea, this ocean of despair. Lily gave birth to my brother and me in 1981 and 1984, respectively. Had the storms of this decade continued in their natural course, the waves would only have carried us to water and death by water. Thankfully, nature was not the only force at work.

In the letters we traveled back to meet Lily in Margaret's basement. My spirit cringed at those words. Margaret's basement…Margaret's basement…Lily never described the place. All I knew was that she was alone there for many hours at a time. In the solitude, she began to write dark music: a stubborn, steel string accompanying a wavering angel voice. But I know only her bright music because it is all she has shared with us. I cannot imagine the wretchedness that came from that basement.

I did not understand my mother then. I was not yet a year old. But my brother, Joey, was two years older and learning the sort of person Lily was. She was often impulsive. She spoke in her letters (too ashamed to give any detail) of short incidents of calmness and rage, of kindness and abuse, her double nature often leaving Joey confused, even terrified, and causing him to grow violent, not in the manner of a normal, mischievous boy, but rather, it was a learned thing, learned from his mother. Since Joey was older, Lily left a deep impression on him, and he has endured more pain than I ever have.

The dismal basement where Lily stayed alone was also the site of Margaret's lectures. Margaret spoke silky words of spiritual power, for she was a prophetess, adorned in religion, and a manipulator, erasing and filling the minds of her subjects. I do not know what made Lily susceptible to all this, but she collapsed into Margaret's grip. And the waves rolled in her hypocrisy hell-waters. Margaret persuaded her with subtle reasoning that she was a failure, possessed by guilt and demons. Lily believed it. Margaret told Lily to abandon my brother and me and to leave us as orphans. Lily complied. The red storm clouds flew. Margaret proclaimed menacingly: "I don't see your husband or kids in the picture; I only see you and I."

Margaret's fluid ocean of words raged on, stripping Lily of all her contacts with the living.

Thousands of years ago, Abraham lifted his arm to drive a knife into Isaac, and now Margaret ordered Lily to do essentially the same to her children, as in obedience to a god. She ranted, "Now the only thing between you and your god is your attachment to your children." In the name of her god, Margaret cursed Lily with demons and imprisoned her in fear! A deathly storm flickered in the deep and prepared to thrust water around its victims. And Lily carried out Margaret's objectives, leaving us with an elderly babysitter, never to return.

Now Lily wrote of our abandonment with the image of Isaac's altar in her mind: "The night before I took the train to Chicago, Joey came out of his room to lie by me on the couch. A beautiful version of that Biblical story in song form was playing on a religious station, and there was low thunder rumbling outside. I told him I loved him *so much*. And I resigned myself to emotional death from that moment on (in the name of her god)."

My brother and I listened to the letters, our jaws tightening with each revelation. Mom lowered the letter, and we saw that her eyes held the same tension that was in our mouths. Where were the words to describe such hollow souls? And we were the children of these souls. Mom laid down the letters and began to pour out her heart to us, the words flowing as a lovely river, telling us her version of the past and how she had come to adopt us.

It was the close of winter. My parents were leading normal lives, working good jobs, and spending time with friends. Like most couples of their age, they desired to have children, and with the hope of spring also came the hope of a fruitful womb. However, they tried and hoped to no avail: infertility crushed them. Yet failure did not stop them. They stubbornly persevered, going to the doctor for tests, but were still unable to find the reason for her barrenness. The emptiness of my mother's stomach spread throughout her body, even to her soul, but the hollowness did not utterly defeat her. Instead, it became an active bitterness and turmoil, inspiring further effort.

My parents found hope in going an alternate direction and decided to pursue adoption. They delved into the busy, legal world of government agencies and began to snatch at every opportunity that appeared. Still, often they lay in bed together after facing many disappointments, mulling over the hopelessness that had filled them for so long. When they had realized the impotency of all their efforts, they had nothing left but faith.

Mom woke to the joy of abandoning her effort, as Lily had abandoned her children, yet she was comforted by David's song: "He maketh the barren woman to keep house, and to be a joyful mother of children. Praise ye the Lord!" They cried out to Him, and the mystery of adoption was revealed.

When Joey and I met our new mommy and daddy, we were wearing dirty clothes and carrying the paper bag full of belongings from our most recent foster home. The social worker said that our biological mother had cared enough to abandon us to a better place rather than to death in an alley or woods. We were alive! And we had arrived at peaceful waters. The dark waves receded, and the ocean became blue and calm. The red clouds shrunk to white whispers, and the sun rose high in the newness of life!

I look back now to the point of revelation that so frantically flooded my mind while sitting on that brown couch. That old couch was the birthplace of new understandings and new confusions. The contents of one letter spilled out a mystery that had not previously been revealed—things that were never opened before. This mystery was the true nature of faith: faith directly handed to me, before my will to choose God was of an effectual age.

Now my faith, developed over the years, meets God's grace in tearful wonder. Where is the demon-ridden life I should have lived? Where is the justice in God's grace? I am often burdened with this unearthly tension that I cannot understand. Faith is a paradox that fills me from throat to stomach with the pulse of pain and relief, the suffering and glorification of Christ, my impotency and His sufficiency. Where would I be without this home?

Faith is *looking forward to the city with foundations, whose architect and builder is God.* (Hebrews 11:10) A city with foundations…a place with foundations…a *home* with foundations. Glimpses of heaven burst in light fragments throughout my rich childhood. My brother and I would run wearing capes. We would swing our yellow baseball bats and search for apples under the apple tree. We would gather up all the sand in the sandbox in the summertime, the snow in the wintertime. We would chase the dogs and let them gnaw on our arms. We would run into the house for hot chocolate or a bandage and then back out again to the swings or bicycles. We would say our hellos to the mailman who brought us the letters of our past. Then we would open the letters, sit on the couch, and cry together.

Faith is lost in many places in time and on earth, for I have seen the despair on television and read the hopelessness in literature. I have seen voids in the eyes of the people at the grocery store who do not know where they came from. But I know where I came from, and I have also calculated the origins of my faith. First of all, it came from my parents, who acknowledged that their effort in coming to God was desolate and that Christ's merit was enough. Twice removed from me is the Original Cause of my faith, the Author of all, the God of the universe. He gave me faith before I could choose it. He led me away from the churning waters of Lily's cult to a peaceful river: my new family, grounded on the hope of glorious things unseen. And after the letters came, I knew He had chosen me before the foundations of the world. I was taken away from a bad life on earth and led to a home built on His foundations.

I would wake up on a cold Saturday morning and stumble into the kitchen. Then I would pull my oversized t-shirt over my knees, curl up, lean my tousled head against the wall, and absorb the waves of heat that came from the vent. God is that foundation.

A Scrap Of Paper

By Jenni Schoneman
Merrill, Wisconsin

It's three weeks before Christmas, and I am weary as I leave another church music rehearsal. I have reached the point in the season when I'm asking myself why I always overcommit myself this time of year.

On the way out of the rehearsal room, I hear a German carol echoing in the stairwell.

The carolers are finished practicing some Christmas concert music, and they pause to sing an old favorite before going out into the cold night. "O, du froeliche, O, du selige," they sing, "Gnadenbringende Weihnachtseit!" I hurry to join them, my problems forgotten as I grab at a chance to relive a childhood tradition of Christmases long past. "Oh, how joyfully, oh, how merrily Christmas comes with its light divine!"

As we bid one another good night, I reflect upon my ancestors who never knew me, yet gave me a priceless gift by living their faith and passing it down through the generations. Unfortunately, for most of my life I had taken faith—theirs and certainly my own—completely for granted, until the Lord used a message on a torn scrap of paper to turn my eyes back to Him. That faded little scrap of paper was what my thrifty grandma used to scrawl her wishes for her own funeral service.

The last time I saw Grandma was at her 80th birthday celebration that we held at her home in northern Indiana. It was a big family reunion in Grandma's honor. My last memory of her comes from that night around the bonfire in the woods near her house. Her sister and some of her aging distant cousins sat together reminiscing. They began singing their favorite old German hymns that they'd been taught as children, their white hairdos illuminated by firelight like so many haloes. That night there was an extra measure of peace and contentment on Grandma's face. It seemed as if she knew she wouldn't be around much longer, but she wasn't going to worry about it.

Two months later, Grandma died a few days after suffering a stroke. Although it seemed to me that 80 was a good old age, I would truly miss her; she and I had always gotten on well when I was growing up. As my parents lived only 20 miles from Grandma's town, her house was like a second home to me.

Since I had not been one of those little girls who are prone to fussing or tantrums, I met with Grandma's notions of how children should behave. I enjoyed helping her pick from her various berry crops, and she put them up in jams and preserves and fed them to me with fresh bread.

In Grandma's flower gardens, I spent many happy hours playing games of make believe under a hibiscus bush or fashioning ladies out of hollyhock blossoms. She was famous in the community for her tea roses, but all those thorns kept me at a distance.

Grandma taught me how to gather eggs from her Rhode Island Reds, and I was proud to bring her fresh eggs for the morning's breakfast, although those hens' stern, beady-eyed stares gave me a cold chill.

Just as there was little discussion about any of these everyday activities at Grandma's house, neither was there much conversation about the fact of her faith. I never doubted that my Grandma was a Christian, just like my parents were. The worn Bible always sat on the little table next to her armchair, and I knew she went to church every Sunday at 8:00 unless she really wasn't feeling well. I also knew that long ago she had led Sunday school children in singing, because I have a 1950's photograph of her singing before a group of children in the church hall, wearing her wool overcoat and a round hat with a little veil. There was also a photograph of Grandma cooking in her church kitchen, so I knew that she served in Ladies' Aid.

I never gave any of it a second thought. All of that was just Grandma.

At the time of her death, I was in my 20's, and faith had become a topic buried so deep that I didn't know how to take it out and examine it. After leaving home for college, I drifted away from the church, from studying the Bible, and from praying. It wasn't that I had stopped believing in God—He just didn't seem to fit into my life after I graduated from college, went to work in a big city, and eventually married.

At Grandma's small, private visitation, I wanted to "be there" for my mother, who had been widowed for years and now felt very alone with her mother gone. I tried very hard not to ponder the mystery and the horror of seeing my beloved grandma so cold and still. "Give your grandma a kiss," my well-meaning aunt suggested, so I did, squelching the urge to cry out and run sobbing from the funeral chapel.

In the church where Grandma had been a member all her life, the pastor paused before beginning the Scripture readings for the funeral. He looked out at us sitting in the front pews. "Agatha chose these readings quite a while ago, when she was thinking about her funeral. She wrote down the Bible references on a little piece of note paper. Underneath them, she wrote, 'My grandchildren need to be reminded of these truths.'"

Something like a white hot arrow struck me in the heart. There were the 15 other grandchildren all around me, but I knew she was talking to me. Although I lived several hundred miles away at the time of her death, somehow she knew I had wandered off from the way I was raised and from the way she had raised her four children.

As the pastor proceeded to read the verses Grandma had chosen so long ago, I listened very carefully, and they were like a healing medicine for my damaged soul: *Then Jesus declared, "I am the Bread of Life. He who comes to me will never go hungry..."* John 6:35

Grandma had loved me so much, I then realized. She was wise enough not to lecture me on how I should have been going to church. She just wanted to remind me of God's promise of eternal life as told in His Word. It is the same eternal truth that my ancestors brought with them in their German Bibles when they traveled to this country more than 100 years ago. It is the same Word I memorized in grade school and sang about in the old, treasured hymns and carols. Jesus, the Living Word, came to earth to take our place on the cross so we could have eternal life. It was her final, unforgettable way, of letting her faith be known.

Because of the precious message on that little scrap of paper, my heart was changed.

Thanks, Grandma. I'll see you up there one of these days.

Fortune Was My Name, But Faith Sustained Me

By Robert L. Giron
Arlington, Virginia

I recall a cold winter morning with everyone talking and crying all at the same time, but I couldn't figure out what was going on. I got out of bed and Papa was sitting at the table with his face in his hands, and tears were rolling down into his coffee cup. I don't recall him crying before, but I was too young to remember anything before this dreadful day. I remember Papa crying. I yelled at the men who were taking Mama out of the house, because I didn't want anyone to take her away, and with this my memory begins.

Ventura, or "Fortune" in English, was my name, but as I look back at my life there were times I felt misfortune was a better fit for my name. I was but four years old when my mother died of a heart attack in her sleep, and from that day forward Papa became my father and mother. I couldn't have asked for a better father, because he nurtured me and my brothers and sister. He taught us what was needed to survive in a difficult time, and since he was educated, he found a good paying job to care for us. At the turn of the twentieth century, the difficulty for Papa was the transition from Mexico, where his family was one of privilege, to the United States and a new language, but he managed to learn English quickly.

Fortunately for me, soon after my mother's death, my eldest brother married his wife, and so we all lived together like one big family. It fell to Papa to teach my sister-in-law, who would later became my godmother, how to keep a house and cook. You see, my godmother got married when she was but 13 years old, obviously against her parents' wishes, but at the turn of the twentieth century, folks did things differently in Texas. My godmother and I did so many things together, from shopping to skipping rope, that many thought I was her younger sister. Folks said we were stuck to each other like glue because we were always together, and as far as I was concerned she had become my mother.

Between down times, Papa decided it was time for me to get some schooling. I recall winter days especially when Papa would sit and read from the Bible to my godmother and me. We would sit beside the living room fireplace, and he would read for hours, and we would ask questions about people with strange sounding names like Herod and Job. Papa was patient and would stop reading and answer our questions. Papa also taught us our prayers. I remember having to memorize many of these prayers to receive my first communion. Later we would focus on the prayers for my confirmation, and the funny thing is that my godmother had forgotten hers, so she had to relearn them along with me.

Back then those hours of reading the Bible and learning prayers seemed like a way to pass the time; later I would discover they were the foundation I would return to whenever I felt despair.

Even when I was about 10, I began to have dreams about my future life. These dreams troubled me, because I had hopes of a happy life but my nightmares seem to foretell a life of solitude and ill health. I would wake up in a cold sweat and pray that somehow my dreams would prove false and a miracle would happen to set me free.

Then when I was 11, Papa died. I liken my life at that time to a priceless crystal bowl that shattered before my very eyes. I thank God that I had my godmother and eldest brother to rely on, for without them, I don't know what I would have done.

My eldest sister hated me and my youngest bother had also married, but his wife was quite a character. Fortunately Papa had taught me how to sew, crochet, mend clothes, cook, and keep house, and so I was all too happy to help my godmother in exchange for a warm home and loving relatives to live with. Soon after my father's funeral, my relationship with my godmother shifted to something I can't quite explain. We were like sisters, mentors, godmother and godchild, and mother and child. We looked after each other and supported one another against any insult or injury that came at us from the outside world. Even in silence, through our prayers we were each other's fortress.

Soon after my 13th birthday, I began to feel the effects of crippling arthritis. At times I could barely get out of bed, and yet I still made my way about the house with a cane to do my chores and took care of my nephews and nieces. Each morning before others would get up, I would awake and repeat the prayers my father taught me, and in the evening I would repeat them, for I had nothing else to rely on. I had only aspirin and ointment for the pain, and I had no one else to rely on except myself and God.

I admit that there were days that I felt like giving up. At times I found myself crying and feeling sorry for myself, but in the back of my mind I could hear Papa telling me to focus on the "now" and to think positively and pray when I felt lonely or depressed. Then at other times when I had so much pain I could barely stand it, I felt like cursing God for giving me the life I had, but I always repented and asked for forgiveness and somehow I felt better. Then the joy I got from my nephews and nieces gave me the strength I needed to continue.

My life from this point on became a repetition of the same routine with small variations due to births, weddings, holidays, and deaths, but basically I knew I would remain an unmarried crippled woman who lived her life through the lives of family members. Yet for this I am forever thankful, because the Bible stories Papa read to me when I was young carried me through to the ripe age of sixty-seven and also provided me the knowledge I needed to be the conduit to extend this same sense of faith to my family members and to my favorite nephew who is now telling you my story. Yes, my name was Ventura, and I was very fortunate, because faith sustained me.

Not Just Noah's Faith

By Trent Lee Brandt
Ovid, Colorado

Genesis 6-8 tells us there was a worldwide flood. In the flood, all the land animals and many of the sea creatures were buried in sedimentary rock all over the earth. This worldwide flood produced an extraordinary testimony to the truth, a physical memorial in the earth, where evolutionists dig for bones and sadly, throw away the evidence. There is also the finding of Noah's Ark, to which not nearly enough attention has been devoted. What we may not realize about the flood, though, is that Yahoweh (the Hebrew name of the Creator) asked a man named Noah to do something a little odd.

Noah was a righteous man, blameless among the people of his time, and he walked with God. (Genesis 6:10, Complete Jewish Bible) Noah not only followed our Father but also walked with Him in a time when God was grieved He had made the world. Men were corrupt and full of violence with every thought of man's heart only evil all of the time. Our Father's heart was filled with pain, and so He unfolded His plan to His servant, Noah. Yahoweh asked Noah to build an ark (a large boat with many rooms) because He was going to send a world-destroying flood.

I once heard a pastor give a present day comparison to Noah's faith in building the ark by saying, "It would be as if he was called by the Lord to build an ark here in dry Colorado. By doing so, his entire town would think he was nuts. However, there has been rain and there have been floods here in Colorado before. In Noah's day there had not. *There was as yet no wild bush on the earth, and no wild plant had as yet sprung up; for Adonai, God, had not caused it to rain on the earth, and there was no one to cultivate the ground. Rather, a mist went up from the earth which watered the entire surface of the ground.* (Genesis 2:5-6, Complete Jewish Bible)

In truth, for the pastor to compare our faith to that of Noah, our Heavenly Father would have had to ask us to build an upside down mansion in order to hold every kind of plant and animal on earth because earth's gravity was going to be reversed, and then told us that when all the people were dead, the gravitation would return to normal. To the people of

Noah's time, the idea of a flood was just as bizarre since there had never seen rain before. Yet, Noah did as His Heavenly Father asked. I can't imagine what some of his friends and family said, let alone his neighbors. "You're building what! An ark to house how many animals? [Insert laughing here] Your god told you that, eh? I do believe your age has truly started to show, old man. You need some serious help here, Noah."

However, in Noah's faith we can find another faith, a stronger faith…that of Yahoweh and Yahoshuah (the Hebrew name of Messiah). Yahoweh did exactly what He said He would do for Noah, just as our loving Father has for anyone who puts his or her faith in Him. Yahoweh had a trusting faith, in Noah. While we all seem to have more faith in our past than our present, Yahoweh has more faith in our future than our past. I know this because we live, even though we have no deserving merit.

Alas, though, my friend, we do have an undeserved merit. The merit of Yahoshuah's blood! Our Creator could have destroyed Adam and Eve and been completely righteous. Our God could have destroyed the world and simply taken Noah up into His palace and been completely righteous. Our God could have destroyed us, but He did not. It would seem, then, that our Father has more faith in us…than we do in Him.

What more then can we do? We could simply do what He has trusted us in faith to do. Through worship, be a witness of His Holy Love, to all of the ones our King longs to hold as His. *We love because He first loved us.* 1 John 4:19. Likewise, He first had faith in us.

In Matthew 17 the Messiah explained that if we have faith even as small as a mustard seed, we can speak unto a mountain saying, "Get up from here and move to there," and it will, for nothing is impossible for those who have faith. Although in the same chapter we see that prayer and fasting are needed, along with other things like love, without faith none of these would be. While love is the most important, no one can truly love, without faith. We can see the love Noah had for the Yahoweh by his faith; however, even though we still try, we simply cannot fathom the love the Creator has for us, for the reason that His enduring faith is immeasurable.

What has Yahoweh called you to do? Has He called you to write, as He did me? (I never dreamed I could write a grocery list, let alone a book.)

Perhaps He has called you to tend to His creations at an animal refuge. I'm sure Noah learned that the woodpeckers inside are a bigger threat than the storm outside (as even a small leak of water, or sin, can sink an enormous ship, or a man). Perhaps Yahoweh has something similar for you to learn. Yahoweh does love animals, and therefore caring for them is a grand thing for you to do if He has called you to do so. While working there, you may encounter people who need you more than the animals do, especially if you pray in faith for this.

Perhaps Yahoweh has called you to minister in China…or perhaps to care for the old woman across the street. Don't think what He calls you to do is too strange, pointless, or something you couldn't possibly do. Saving yourself from all the ridicule in the world is not worth missing out on the play of life Yahoweh has written down in His program.

Noah did everything just as God commanded him. Genesis 6:22

Will you? Our Father wants us to do what He made us to do, but if we turn down His Will, He'll have to find someone else who will be glad to build an ark…of faith.

The Faith Factor

By Suzanne Murrell
Orlando, Florida

Today I watched a child playing by the water's edge, the ocean licking her feet as she timidly ran in and out of the foamy surf. I guessed her to be about three years old. Her mother, standing nervously to the side, kept admonishing her: "Be careful," "Don't go so close to the waves," "Come back—you could step on something."

Suddenly the child, who just a few minutes ago felt no danger, stopped.

Cowed, she ran back from the water's edge and hid behind her mother who picked her up and began to soothe her tears. I watched the scene unfolding in sadness, remembering my own childhood experiences so very different from this one.

When just a few minutes ago the child was happily playing, now she was afraid; when just a few minutes ago she felt no danger, now she felt fear; and when before she ran in and out of the surf knowing instinctively not to take herself too far from the shore, confident her mother was nearby, now she was apprehensive, doubting herself.

And what of her mother? She is a "good" mother, I can tell, but she missed an opportunity with her child. She missed the chance for her daughter to experience the "faith factor."

As I stood there watching and observing, I felt as if I was intruding but could not walk away. I wanted to help this *good* mother become a *better* mother; I wished to share with her memories of my own summers of discovery growing up in the South, but most of all I wanted her to hear about "the vines."

Deep in the woods of rural Arkansas the menacing vines of the trees surround their massive trunks, growing almost long enough to reach across the width of the mountain streams below. At the mere age of eight, I was allowed to venture alone into those woods that ran behind my grandparents' house and, on hot, no *torrid,* summer afternoons, would climb a vine in my woodland retreat and begin to swing. Propelling myself up and over the water, when high enough, I let go and on my luckiest day would drop all the way to the cold, rocky bottom.

In youthful spirit, I had no thoughts of injury or danger. Freely I would run, spirit soaring, racing across the reddish brown sun-caked earth not fit for the planting of cotton or tobacco and through the scrap woods of an Arkansas summer day. The year was 1954.

Each of my summers was spent as the one before and the ones to come until I reached the age of 15 when I deemed my woodsy adventures too "childish." But from the age of eight I spent seven glorious summers exploring "Granmother's woods" discovering, among other things, faith. Faith in the safety of the small mountain community where my grandparents lived, faith in my large extended southern family, and faith in my own strengths and abilities gained through risktaking—risktaking allowed by grandparents who had their own faith in me.

I don't ever recall parental admonishments to be careful or to be home by a certain time. Taught responsibility very young, I knew to be home by supper, not dinner. Dinner is on Sundays after church, while supper is at 4:00 p.m. on other days. Grandmother worked most of the day in preparation for supper, and it was an unspoken rule that no one missed it and no one came to the table late.

My path to the woods was always the same, through a certain patch of blackberry bushes not yet ripe to the pregnant stage. *Pregnant!* That whispered word. A word okay for adult women in the house to use but not my grandfather or uncles and never by a "fine young lady of southern quality." I uttered it only once, whispering it at the table to my cousin, Sydney, mimicking my aunt and thinking no one heard. The slap it brought across my cheek was enough to send the word into the annals of my mind as one never to use in mixed company.

Unlike my own children, I was never a part of any after school planned, "encouraged," or conducted playgroups. I did not participate in organized hikes on well-marked woodsy paths with scout leaders or have benefit of school field trips. Grandmother assigned chores, and mine was to fill the two kitchen buckets with fresh water every morning. That was not an easy task; the well was across the road in Grandfather's woodworking shop, and the "road" was actually a state highway through our small town of Mountainburg, Arkansas.

Sometimes Grandmother would offer up a hoe for me to carry when the heat of the summer was so prolonged that the copperhead snakes came out of their hiding places looking for water. Was it then, delicately toe stepping and twisting, that I learned to dance? Unlike the daughters of today, I had no benefit of dance classes, no end-of-the-year dance recital surrounded by doting parents; yet I could dance, *really* dance around an occasional copperhead snake while carefully balancing two filled water buckets and a hoe!

My other chore was porch sweeping since the porch was the hub of summer southern existence. Always dusty from the road, our porch held chairs, rockers and tables, plants, and Granddaddy's BB gun for killing mice. Grandfather never hid the gun or locked it safely away, and we never bothered it.

Southern daughters in those days lived their lives in bonnets on porches since the house has a parlor reserved for guests' use only, but the porch was always cooler and more fun anyway. Under the porch were frogs and bugs, cats and mice, and a quick "wiggle through" to another world full of scientific discoveries; I had Mason jars filled with "experiments" to prove it. Again, there were no parental admonishments to "be careful" or chastisements not to go too far under the porch. As children, we were trusted to know our limitations and keep ourselves safe, secure in the knowledge of adults close by.

The Fourth of July was cause for our annual summer family reunion. Each branch of the family attended and was almost overrun by the children, all cousins. After dinner, if the homemade ice cream wasn't yet "ice cream," the uncles would lead us into the woods to the quicksand sinkhole. With squeals mixed with fear and anticipation, each of us was allowed to sink in the quicksand as far as our chins, if we dared, anchored safely to firm ground by our uncles' strong arms, and then swung high and into the creek to swim. Throughout the years, whenever I am faced with a difficult situation, I am reminded that with childlike faith I sunk deep into a sinkhole and made it, and I can surely make it again!

And what of our own children today? Do we allow them enough risktaking in their lives to develop their own strengths? While I am never a proponent of children being purposely placed in risk situations and thus like the seatbelt laws, the helmet requirements, and the child safety initiatives in place today, I often reflect on my own childhood summers and question, how far should we go in keeping our children "safe," given the times we live in, and more importantly, how deep is our own faith?

As a lifelong educator, I love to see a child play naturally, and I like the way children learn from one another. When children are allowed to interact freely with their world and with each other, when they are allowed freedom to explore their environment as I did, through risktaking, they learn more—they learn about their worth, their strengths, and they grow in self-esteem. But most of all, they develop a sense of faith—faith in their ability to face life's challenges and faith in knowing they can always return home again, *safe.*

At the water's edge, I envision the child's mother and I sitting and talking. I tell her about the vines and the joy of having been raised in the South. I speak of snakes, well water, gardens, and wide, cool porches; also of the woods, but especially about the vines. We share a laugh at her daughter poking very delicately at a sand crab at the water's edge, and when the child turns, she sees reflected in her mother's eyes the encouragement she needs. But most of all she feels the faith of her mother trusting her to be careful. Faith that she is safe. Faith, we have discovered, the three of us by the ocean's edge, is such a fragile commodity.

Do I dare tell her? And will she *hear*?

Our Seasons Of Faith

By Hugh Chapman
Horseshoe Bend, Arkansas

Though my career as a banker was financially rewarding, I was never content with the work. Compliance regulations, qualification formulas, and credit declinations always seemed so cold and, well… calculating. It was no wonder that, after only my fourth year on the job, I began to look with envy at the teaching career my wife, Julie, had chosen. Still, to make a career move so late in my life was absolutely out of the question. To leave a secure position and return to school was something that would take more faith (and perhaps foolishness) than I possessed.

Yet God continued to speak to me through an odd feeling of longing that would often ease into my deliberation. I'd find myself watching Julie as she graded papers until late at night. In the soft lamplight, I'd see her smile with satisfaction at the progress of her students and sigh with dismay when they failed to meet her expectations. Though her salary was only about half the amount of mine, I knew she was much more gratified in her career than I had ever been. And in time, I began to realize that there must be something more to teaching than I was able to see.

Then one winter's evening I found her fretting, in typical fourth grade teacher fashion, over a student's worsening academic performance. "Baxter will never be a strong student," she said with a sigh, " But at least he *used* to try. He began the year doing so well, but now his work has dropped to nearly nothing. I just don't understand it."

Two days later the answer became very clear—to both of us.

That evening as I arrived home, exhausted from a hard day at the office, Julie met me at the doorway. "Will you drive me to Baxter's house?" she asked.

I looked at my watch in dismay. It was already getting dark. "Oh, I don't want to bother strangers this late," I whined, "and besides, it's *cold* out there." But Julie was adamant and promised she only wanted to drive by to see the house. Reluctantly, I agreed, and together we began our journey, with Julie's hopefulness being negated only slightly by my reluctance.

Baxter's home was at least 20 miles from where we lived, but more than just the distance, the place was hard to find in the dark. We turned off the highway and then rumbled down a rural Arkansas county roadway with only a vague notion as to where we were going. In time, we turned from the graveled road onto a narrow dirt path. My concern was growing by the minute. "You know, some of these folks have shotguns by the door," I said, "and they don't always welcome strangers in the middle of the night."

But my wife was determined. "It's only 6:00 p.m.," she said, "and besides, it can't be much further." Then, pointing excitedly, she said, "Look, there it is."

Before us stood an old rundown trailer house, unlit and barely visible in the mid-winter darkness. In what might have been called a front yard (which was really only a cleared spot in the woods) there were four elementary aged children. Some were bundled in jackets, others in only their shirtsleeves. Two were busily gathering firewood, one was pouring kerosene into a lantern, and another was petting a mangy old dog. As we pulled slowly forward, a chubby kid in overalls hurried toward the car and enthusiastically greeted Julie. "My mom's not home yet, Mrs. Chapman, so you can't come in. But we can visit out here."

And though my wife did happily chat with the boy for 10 minutes, there was really no need to go inside. She had seen what she had come to see—the rundown dwelling of her fourth-grade student and all his siblings—heated with a tiny wood stove and illuminated with two kerosene lamps.

On the quiet drive home, Julie batted back a tear as she softly verbalized what we both had witnessed. "His work was good in the early fall when the days were longer. But now that it gets dark so early, he *can't see* to do his homework." It was then that I began to understand what she had known all along. Within her classroom, my wife had worked to find a means to reach these children—and perhaps to even release them from a life of destitution.

As I drove through the Arkansas night, I watched her from the corner of my eye, and from deep within, I realized that I, too, had discovered what God was calling me to do. The only question remaining was whether or not I had the *faith* to make the change.

Yet what I hadn't counted on was that God had been speaking to Julie, too, and as we discussed the possibilities—tentatively at first, then later more boldly—we began to formulate a plan. By the end of the month, I had said farewell to my friends at the bank.

For two and a half years we struggled to make ends meet while I attended college. Eventually our perseverance paid off, and I was offered my first contract. I would teach junior high special education in the same district that my wife had been teaching fourth grade. After my first day, I proudly brought forth my new class roster for Julie to see. There among the list of seventh graders was a name we both recognized: My wife's former student, Baxter. He had found the strength to hang on and had finally made it into junior high—and so had I.

As we began our new adventure together, Baxter and I became fast friends. He was a big, friendly kid with a permanently fixed smile, and though his ability was well below many of his classmates, he always gave his very best. Yet it was disheartening to watch him struggle so hard to produce so little. One evening I shared my dismay with Julie.

"It seems so unfair," I said. "Baxter struggles every day, and I can't seem to help him much. I'm thinking that maybe a more experienced teacher could do a better job."

Julie softly shook her head and replied with a sympathetic smile. "God put you in that classroom with Baxter for a purpose. You might not be able to see it now, but someday you will. You just have to have faith."

Her words were encouraging, but I'm afraid her faith was greater than mine was. Then something happened.

It was nearing Christmastime of that first year, and in the excitement of the upcoming vacation, I was having a hard time keeping the attention of my class. In hopes of making the most of an unruly situation, I assigned an essay, "What Christmas Means to Me."

Baxter's composition surprised me. Though short and ill arranged, it represented, for him, a massive effort. In large, block-printed letters and with writing seasoned with a jumble of spelling and punctuation errors, the sincerity of his work shone through.

What Christmas Means to Me

> Some wise men heard that a new king would be born in Bethlehem, and they made their way through the woods to find him and they followed a star and they came to a barn where the baby was already born. And when they saw him, they knew it was Jesus, and they bowed down and worshiped Him, because they knew that the new baby lying in a manger would be king of all kings.

I looked to Baxter with a newfound respect as he stood beside my desk waiting, hopefully, for my approval. When I paused to gather my thoughts,

Baxter quickly pointed out, "There's more on the back."

Pleasantly surprised at the length and relative accuracy of his effort, I quickly turned over the page to read the conclusion of Baxter's essay.

> The wise men were amazed at all they had seen that night, and while they were walking back to their homes, they talked about all the great things they had seen. Then, when they got about halfway home, one of the wise men turned to the others and said, "Hey, do you know what? This ought to be a Holiday!" And from then on, it was.

Baxter remained at my desk with his simple, friendly smile. He was not trying to be cute, nor funny, nor insincere. He was simply reporting an important event in the way he had imagined it to be. And for his honesty, I admire him all the more.

"Baxter," I asked, "do you believe that? Do you believe that Jesus is the Son of God and that He was sent here to be our Savior?"

Baxter seemed uncomfortable and shifted his weight from one foot to another. Finally he said, "I'm not sure, Mr. Chapman. I go to church sometimes, and that's what they say. But how can you know something like that for sure?"

"You have to have *faith* that it's true, Bax," I said, pointing to my chest. "And when you have faith, you'll know, because you'll feel it deep inside your heart."

He looked solemnly toward me. "Do you believe it?" he asked.

I nodded assuredly. "I do, Baxter, and very much so."

My student then smiled happily. "Well, if you believe it, then I believe it, too, Mr. Chapman. Because you're real smart, and you know almost everything."

From deep within, I felt his sincerity, but I had to shake my head. "No, Baxter. You shouldn't believe it because I believe it; you should believe it because you feel it from deep within your own heart. That's how you'll know for sure."

As Baxter walked away that day, I experienced a new feeling of purpose—one that I had not known before that moment. And from my own heart, I knew that I was exactly where God intended for me to be.

Six weeks later, shortly after the kids returned from Christmas vacation, Baxter approached my desk. This time he held a small New Testament opened to a well-marked page with a single underlined verse: *"For God so loved the world that He gave His only begotten Son, that whosoever believes in Him, should not perish, but have everlasting life."* John 3:16, KJV

Excitedly he whispered, "They gave this to me at church, Mr. Chapman, on the day I was saved. They say I can keep it for my own."

Though I shook Baxter's hand and patted his back, there was no way I could express the happiness I felt for the decision he had made.

More than a decade has passed since Baxter entered my first classroom. As a now-seasoned teacher, I've learned that students come suddenly into our care, share a part of our lives, and then, often just as quickly, they move on to other things. Occasionally, however, through our time together, our lives are altered forever.

Two years ago at Thanksgiving, my family received word that Baxter had been in an automobile accident. Police reports indicated no drinking, no drugs, and no hazardous road conditions—just a single automobile with a single fatality on a quiet Arkansas highway.

I said a prayer that day for Baxter, but I knew that the important decision had been made long before, an arrangement born of faith within the trusting heart of a simple young man.

But sometimes even now, in the quiet of an early winter's evening, I'll find myself driving along winding country roads. And I'll recall how a boy named Baxter, through his own faith, found the courage to exchange a broken down trailer house for a Mansion on High.

And from deep within my heart, I hold to my own faith, the assurance that I will see him again one day, only this time it will be in the company of the King of Kings.

And you know what?

A day like that just ought to be a holiday.

4

Living Examples Of Faith

An Angel On Earth

By Jan Yonke
Wausau, Wisconsin

Do you believe in angels? That's a question I think a great number of people struggle with. Personally, I believe in angels—both spiritual angels and those who live among us. Whenever I get on the subject, a certain "angel" comes to mind every time—my mom. It's difficult to know where to begin explaining all the reasons I think Mom's an angel, but I'll try to touch on as many of them as I can.

As far back as I can remember, Mom has always been there for me. And I mean always. I can't remember a time when she wasn't. I've always believed that when God made my mom, He gave her all the wonderful qualities He gives all mothers, plus the ability to be the best friend any daughter could ever have. He gave her eyes to see when I wander down a path that is a particularly treacherous one. He gave her ears to listen with compassion to problems or conflicts I may run across during my journey through life. He gave her a mouth to softly speak encouraging, uplifting words when I'm feeling down. But most importantly, He gave her a kind, caring heart. This heart is one that not only cares for Mom's own family, but also for everyone else she knows.

Prayer is an important part of Mom's life. She prays every single day, and her prayers are for everyone and anyone who needs them. Mom's list of those to be prayed for is usually quite long. Sometimes when we're talking, I'll mention someone I know at work or church who may be sick, distressed, or in need of prayers in some other way. Even though Mom may not know this person, she always includes them in her daily prayers. Then she'll check back with me at a later time, asking if this person's situation has improved. Always, her prayers to our Lord have helped in some way.

Mom's strong faith in God has always been like a beacon in the night for me. I can remember watching Mom pray when I was a child. Every night before she went to bed, she'd open her Bible and read a passage or two. Sometimes I'd sit beside her and read along. As I grew older, I'd question my faith now and then, as many teens do. But because of the strength I saw in Mom's faith and her kind, caring Christian ways, I was always drawn back to God, no matter what else might have been going on in my life at the time. Her life has been testimony to me of the love of the Lord.

The path God gave Mom to follow in life has not always been a smooth one. She has endured numerous family tragedies. But through all of this, Mom's faith never faltered. She always knew God would sustain her in her time of need.

As a child, I'd ask Mom what I'd do if our Lord would come to take her to Heaven. Who would listen to my problems and help me find a solution? Who would be there to cheerfully and wholeheartedly ask how my day was every evening? How could I possibly live my life if she wasn't there? To all of this, she simply replied, "God will make sure you have a friend who will listen and be there for you." She also reminded me that God listens whenever we talk to Him. She said He is always there and, no matter what, I could always depend on Him. He will see me through life's ups and downs. Even as a child, I could feel Mom's faith in our Lord. She helped me understand how precious we are to Him and that He will never abandon us.

Mom's caring heart has gone out numerous times to those less fortunate than herself. Mom is not monetarily wealthy, but she gives what she can to anyone who is in need. Recently, she read in the local newspaper about a young boy who had cancer. The article told how friends of the boy's family set up a fund at a bank so people could make contributions to help the boy's parents pay for his extensive medical bills. Mom never met this boy or his family, but her gentle, caring heart went out to them. She prayed for them and made a contribution to the boy's fund. In addition, Mom has contributed holiday and birthday gifts to a less fortunate family in our area. She also contributed money for them to buy much needed school supplies and clothing they otherwise would not have had.

Mom extends her loving kindness to God's animals, as well, especially birds. She puts seed out for them during the long winter months so they have plenty to eat when the harshness of winter makes it difficult for them to find food on their own. Mom often sits by the window admiring the beauty of the birds' feathers and watching them take pleasure in the small feast of seed.

Spending quality time with her children, grandchildren, and great-grandchildren has always been on the top of Mom's list of priorities. She savors every moment she spends with each of us. Mom always has a smile and usually some homemade goodies to give us when we pay her a visit. And every one of us has our own special memories of time spent playing games, enjoying a meal, or just chatting with this very special lady. From the oldest child to the youngest, Mom's love covers all of us like a warm, fuzzy blanket.

The love in Mom's heart shines brightly. No one can extinguish her flame of faith. She demonstrates daily what it means to be a Christian. She has touched more people with her faith and compassion than she could ever realize.

Thanks, God, for sending this angel to earth to be my mom and my best friend, to help so many people, and to share her faith in You.

By Faith…It's But A Day

By Dorothy M. Gundlach
Hot Springs Village, Arkansas

With Vera Hinkle *a hundred years is but a day.* "We don't know what a day holds," she says. "We know Who holds each day." With God a thousand years is but a day that's just gone by. (Psalm 90:4)

The aroma of freshly brewed coffee filled the air. We sat chatting casually, enjoying the view of a rippling waterfall from a bay window of the breakfast room. "I'm so thankful for this beautiful home and the *loving care* my daughter provides for me," she said, looking at me with a smile. Vera always has a big smile!

Meticulously dressed, physically fit, and mentally alert, this lady one century old is amazing. She takes no medication, goes to the doctor for a flu shot each year, and carries a cane only for balance. Vera is quick to give God the credit for her long, happy, and healthy life. "I do my part, though," she said. She is faithful to exercise very day. From age 90 to 99 her exercise was tripping up and down the stairs of her lower level suite where she lived with her daughter, Barbara Glover. When asked what advice she would give the younger generation, her reply was, "I don't recall anyone asking my advice. They would think a 100-year-old could not compete with computers, Internet, and email." However, she added, "The Holy Bible gives advice to every generation in all situations of life."

Vera looks forward to her daily newspaper. She especially enjoys Letters to the Editor and puzzles in monthly publications. No doubt her faith in God and positive attitude have given her the grace to glide through 100 years as if it was *no big deal*. I love to sit and visit with Vera; she is always upbeat and interesting.

In the year of 1900 God blessed many of us beyond words. Vera Hinkle was born in Coleman County, Texas. Most of us were yet to be born. William McKinley was president. Then in 1901 Teddy Roosevelt was elected. Vera remembers, "He admonished everyone to speak softly and carry a big stick."

"Many changes have occurred in these 100 years, and I've witnessed many of those changes firsthand," she recalls. "I've traveled by every form of transportation from the covered wagon to the airplane," she said. "One of my fondest memories is my dad making a me a 'special place' in our buggy to ride to church.

"When I was 18 years of age, we had a Texas drought. My family sold most of our belongings and moved to Phoenix, Arizona, traveling by train," she said. Ms. Vera found fun and adventure in everything. "The train to Phoenix was a slow one. It had to stop often for water. Once it stopped near an Army base and a young soldier boy came up to the window and visited with me. Maybe he was lonesome," she recalls.

"Change comes so quickly," she said. "We left Texas in a blizzard wearing heavy winter coats. When we arrived in Phoenix two days later, it was a scorching hot day."

"One fall there was a flu epidemic. The schools closed. My sisters, nephew, and I got a job picking cotton. Phoenix cotton fields were different from those in Texas. Cotton grew head high, and we could pick the cotton standing." Laughing, she said, "We had fun! We took our lunch, and it was just like a picnic." Vera loves picnics!

In 1967 Vera and her husband, Dolph Hinkle, moved to Vicksburg, Mississippi, to be near her daughter and family. Vera remembers her mother's stories, passed down from her grandmother. During the Civil War, they lived near enough to the battle to hear cannons firing, and once General Lee came riding up to their home. Her grandmother invited him to have lunch with them, and he accepted. Ms. Vera has a rich heritage.

Advancement in communication has been incredible in her lifetime. We've come from pony express, telegraph, and telephone to Internet and email.

When asked what had given her the most pleasure in the past year, Vera quickly replied, "I just couldn't believe so many people thought enough of me to make such elaborate preparations for my 100th birthday celebration." She shook her head and smiled happily as if to say, *I'm still awestricken!* It was a celebration done in grand style. She had arrived driven by her private "chauffeur," (a well known antique car enthusiast) in his 1940 Packard, and more than 100 well wishers waved enthusiastically as she stepped out smiling broadly.

Ms. Vera's attitude is one of gratitude. She's thankful for everything and everyone God has blessed her with.

In Vera's words, "I believe spiritual health is essential to a long, healthy life. I encourage my children, grandchildren, great grandchildren, and others to know God and seek to make Christ central in their lives." Perhaps the paramount secret to her successful life is found in these words penned by her own hand:

Reservations

Some tell of their travels and places they've been. Some seek to make reservations to far off land. My reservation was made many years ago to a city with streets of pure gold, where the Lord said, "Come follow me." I accepted the invitation, for my fare was already paid, you see, on the cross of Mount Calvary.

Don't have to worry about luggage or fancy apparel. That will be taken care of by my host who will meet me there. This passage to a land so fair is a free gift from my Savior. He only asks that I trust and obey, spreading the good news along life's way!

It's but a day.

Dad And Dee—Lessons In Faith

By Nathanael Vincent Armstrong
West Lafayette, Ohio

My father struggles with Parkinson's disease, believing that his faith will take him through the fight and lead him to win the battle. He hopes to come out whole, to be able to run without losing his balance, to be able to move without falling or shaking uncontrollably, and to be able to hold the late-coming grandchildren he's been waiting for.

There is a woman in my church named Dee who was born a quadriplegic. She's confined to her motorized wheelchair and believes that there is a God who cares more for the beauty of her faith in Him than the physical beauty of her body lying motionless in the mechanical crutch.

Then there is me—23 years old with a beautiful wife and a promising life and future—I who struggle in seemingly pitiful ways compared to these. I am all but totally ashamed to appear with them in a story along with the word "faith."

I pray, or rather fling a wish toward heaven sometimes, when I see Dad trying to accomplish something menial. I usually think about myself whenever I watch him struggle and fail at everyday tasks like walking or getting out of bed. I'm ashamed to say I pray not for him, but for myself. *God, don't let me go through a challenge like that. Would my faith survive?*

There was an instance I'll never forget. My brother and I went to take Dad to a movie. He wasn't as bad off then, so we didn't feel quite the need to go visit him as much as we do now. While we were growing up, my brother and I always enjoyed watching the *Star Wars* series on videos that Dad provided. With a new one coming out, I thought it could be like old times to take Dad to see it. He bought Skittles®, and we bought popcorn and drinks. Emaciated and frail from his medications and jerking everywhere from the Parkinson's disease, he went for the bag of Skittles® during the movie and grasped it firmly in each hand close to his chest.

I watched out of the corner of my eye. Somehow I knew I'd see something I wasn't going to forget. He pulled the bag open carefully but then an uncontrollable jerking tore it apart, spilling the Skittles® everywhere. It wasn't the mess I watched, but his face, embarrassed, sheepish.

For an instant, I glimpsed a mire of despair sinking down, deep in his eyes, that he tried to mask with a comical half-grin. He couldn't hide it for that split second, however, and in that moment, I realized his faith was fighting off the enemy that would rather have him despair than hope. I watched him make a desperate effort and refuse to give in.

I realized Dad lives on that edge, facing every day with hope and fighting every day to never give up his faith. He can either face the battles that come once, twice, or three times a day or give up and fall off the precarious edge his faith keeps him balanced on. When he can't move to wipe the dry-mouth saliva that hangs like spider webs between his lips that's caused by his medication, or when he's moving too much and he's got to stand outside the church in the parking lot during the service, holding on to a car for dear life to keep his body from knocking him down, I picture myself in his position.

I broke my leg once when I was 14. It was winter at our church denomination's youth camp, Camp McPherson. The last trip I took down "Cardiac Hill" on a sled that year was a real doozy. It earned me the wild and crazy cheers of my peers as I soared out of control off a high snowy ramp and also the total devastation of a broken leg at the bottom.

It didn't really hurt until I was trying to sleep that night. It was in those endless lonely hours that I fought Dad's battle, when I struggled with my faith more than my pain. My broken foot, propped up on an uncomfortable steel bar, constantly bugged me to the point where I began questioning things I had always held to be true. I kept turning it and moving it, trying to make the pain stop so I could sleep. It felt like hours, but knowing me, it was more like minutes.

In my mind the battle raged on: *I'm not going to do it. It's not His fault!* I thought, *I know He knew it was going to happen. All things come together for good for those who love God and are called according to His purpose.* (Romans 8:28 paraphrased by author.) *Come on, stupid! Sleep! I hate this leg.* My mind was racing in agony. The pain was making me tired but filled me with a frustrated crazy energy.

I felt like I was losing control. Then I faltered and started the slide to defeat. I called out in my mind: *Why me, God? God, why do I have to go through this? Why can't You make it stop? I thought you were all-powerful, all-knowing. You're supposed to love me! What's the deal with this? It HURTS!*

Somehow I fell asleep through the throbbing, maddening pain and exhaustion, but I'll never forget how ashamed and angry I was at God and myself. I lost that little one-night skirmish for my faith. I gave up ground when I should have believed. I'm pitiful compared to these.

I've known Dee for as long as I've gone to the Solid Rock Church. Both she and I have been very loyal attendees, but for different reasons. Her relationship with God brought her to church, while my relationship with my parents brought me.

Unable to move anything from the neck down from birth, Dee has always directed her chair with a metal stick that wobbles from her mouth to her controls. I'm not sure how old she is; honestly, I've never taken the time or had the guts to sit with her and say more than "Hi" or meekly get the door for her.

Last Sunday I noticed her hair was braided in a thousand little black braids. We were stuck in the foyer together, so I spoke to her to break the uncomfortable silence and told her it looked great. It shames me to say that that is as personal as I've ever been with Dee. I know why those words are so hard for me to say. It's because my faith is too weak to see Dee beyond what she is on the surface. I don't want to face her, to talk to her. I don't want to stare. I don't want to think about anything when I'm around her, but I can't avoid it when she dances.

Our dance team puts on little shows every holiday and for special events at the church. Not once has Dee missed out on showing her talent: driving her wheelchair. Dressed up just like one of the other graceful dance members, she looks absolutely the opposite. She dresses in the same matching outfits as the others but wears them without the others' beautiful curves and thin limbs. She spins in her chair, but not to the swift rustling of crinoline cloth, but to the electric hum of battery driven motors. She can't swing the dance banners in unison with her team, so the banners she carries fly from the back of her chair, stuck there by her dancing companions and a bit of duct tape. None of this seems to matter to her when she's dancing before God. She just spins her chair as well as she can.

I can't even relate to this; I'm too afraid to even think about it. I'll see her and put on my church face, just smilin' and God-blessin' and wondering—would my weekly war ever turn into a crescendo for God's glory?

She's a trooper. She smiles. She laughs. She lets people open the door and help her. She goes after opportunities to help others; she types the church bulletin with her mouth. I, on the other hand, grunt and complain about aches and pains, wonder if I can get up early enough on Sunday morning to get to worship practice on time, and avoid people because I don't want them to see any of my struggles. I, who am too proud to ask for a helping hand. I sink when I'm tossed in life's storm to swim.

I've also realized something: Dee's faith is strong, but her health is not. She's going to either die in her wheelchair or in a hospital bed. Dad's the same way. Parkinson's disease is terminal. The kids I plan on having soon might never see Grandpa move—ever. But Dad still believes. Even when I, his own son, do not support him, he still believes. He tells me sometimes, "I'm believing God will heal me so I can start a healing ministry and heal others."

I just nod my head. Inside I don't have half that much faith. I think of Dad spilling juice on himself when he's shaking. I think of how my little brother, Christopher, has to help him get to the bathroom when he can't move. I don't believe, I don't have the faith—not like he does. I believe he'll die and I'll be at his funeral, and I can't shake my doubt. All I can do is keep wondering what I'll say.

I know what will happen at Dee's funeral. We live in a small town. Everyone has seen her traveling the streets in her wheelchair, zipping along the cracked concrete sidewalks. Everyone saw her at the countywide evangelistic crusade when the dance team did a performance and her picture was in the paper along with the others. I'm certain there will be even more people at her funeral than at the crusade. They'll talk about the wonder of her life, her strength, her faith, and the way she danced before God. I'm sure God will be there, tugging on our hearts, encouraging us to follow her example, forcing us to look at the beautiful thing He did in Dee. Something so beautiful, rewarding, and difficult He rarely lets anyone else have the challenge of working with Him to overcome it.

At Dad's funeral I think I'll cry first and then try to think of him running in heaven, finally healed and whole, and I'll cry some more. I think I'll look at my kids who never saw Dad move and hope that when my test comes, they'll see the man of faith that I saw in my Dad. I don't know if I'll get there. My past trials have shown only how horribly I've failed. But I'm getting better. Each time I see Dad, I'm learning to never give up.

Dad continues to fight his mind game for his faith. Will he press on and believe what he reads in the Bible about God, or will he believe what he sees: hopelessness, despair, and daily torture that God could have prevented? I know what he'll say if I go and see him. He'll say to me, "One day at a time. God's grace is sufficient. Someday I'll be healed. Someday." Oh, God, help me have more faith.

Faces Of Faith

By Rochelle Griffis Lyon
Franklin, Texas

Faces. I see them in my mind's eye. I carry them in my heart. They're the faces of the people who've inspired me in my journey toward faith. Each has contributed to my growth, for each represents a different quality of faith.

Appropriately, the first of these remarkable people is the first face I remember. My mother, Dorothy McDowell Griffis, was a pretty little woman with prematurely gray hair, dark brown eyes, and a beautiful smile. Her daddy was a Baptist preacher, and she grew up in South Carolina surrounded by a lively family who valued education and music. Mama was feisty, with a quick temper and a sharp mind. She was a Sunday School teacher, and she wrestled with really heavy theological questions. Unlike me, she was never satisfied with easy answers. Two of her brothers were PhD's, and one of them told me, "Dorothy is the smart one in the family." So it was especially tragic when Mama developed Alzheimer's disease.

As her illness progressed, she changed completely. Gone was the confident, efficient woman who'd been such a formative influence in my life. Instead, a timid, frail person who followed me around like a puppy took her place. I would walk behind her, seeing the dowager's hump that had developed between her once proud shoulders, and I wondered, *Where is my mother?*

But one thing was unchangeable about my mother—her faith. Even though she had witnessed some terrible tragedies, her faith never wavered. And for me, nothing she ever said or did, no intellectual discussion, and no work of charity ever spoke so much about her faith as the sight of her, her little body bent by arthritis, kneeling beside her bed every night. Despite her illness, the habit of faith was so much a part of her spirit that she kept right on doing it as long as she was mobile.

In my mother's example, I learned the endurance of faith.

The next face of faith that influenced me was a young woman I barely knew. Mary Jordan came into my life when I was in college in Danville, Virginia. As young girls will, I idolized her. She was in her mid-20's, with a sweet, calm face, shiny brown hair that she wore in a pageboy, and a trim figure. She sang in the choir of the church I attended, and she sometimes visited my college.

There were several reasons why I felt a kinship with this woman. She loved music. I loved music. She was a medical technologist. I was studying to become a medical technologist. She had a heart condition. I had a congenital heart defect. But this young woman was a twin, and one February her twin sister came to visit Mary before she had heart surgery. The twin said that sleeping beside her, she felt the whole bed shake with the force of Mary's struggling heart.

On February 13, the night before her operation at the University of Virginia Medical Center, Mary went around giving out Valentine candies to the other patients on her floor. But open-heart surgery was a new procedure in 1960, and she didn't survive. Mary died on Valentine's Day.

It's been 42 years now, but I've never forgotten that beautiful young woman who spent her last night on earth thinking of others. She continues to inspire me with the unselfishness of her faith.

Gladys Welch was one of my all time favorite people. She was born somewhere in the frozen North, and she had a direct, down-to-earth Yankee friendliness and heartiness about her. With a halo of fluffy white hair and bright blue eyes, Gladys looked like a saint. But she was always laughing. She never took herself seriously.

"When I start getting proud of my humility, that's when I know I'm in trouble," she would say and laugh.

For many of us, Gladys was the rock we clung to amid the stormy seas of church politics and dissension. She never lost sight of the real purpose and nature of the church, and she kept us grounded.

In her late 60's, Gladys decided she wanted to write, and she and I took a writing course at the local junior college, but she never had time to work on her stories because she was too busy helping people. Gladys was a great cook, and I imagine she prepared nearly 100 tons of food for her Methodist church. One of the stories she wrote, and she giggled as she read it, was about a woman who lost a fingernail when she was making coleslaw for a church supper. I'm sure that was something Gladys had done. True to form, when my mother died, Gladys was the first person at my door, bringing our supper. "I'm here representing the church," she said.

Gladys' hands showed the results of her labors. They were big-knuckled, bent with age and arthritis—just worn out by loving acts. One day I was bemoaning the fact that my friend never had time to write when I realized that her hands were her books.

Long past retirement, Gladys opened a Western Union office. One day two young men came into the office, beat her savagely, and stole her cash. She survived and was put in ICU. The whole city was outraged.

At church the following Sunday the pastor asked for prayers for Gladys. A little voice rang out from the back of the church. "I'm here!" There was Gladys, a white wig covering her dozens of stitches, sitting in a back pew. The church erupted in applause for Gladys the indomitable. Later she wrote an account of her experience. She said that while she was being beaten, God spoke to her and told her how to survive. My friend is gone now, but I think of her often. I will never forget the magnificent courage of her faith.

And then there is another. I never actually knew Clarence Jordan, so I have only a photograph of his face. It's a nice face, not remarkable in any way. But from the record of Clarence's life, I do have a clear picture of his soul.

Clarence was a Southerner. He came from a prominent family, but he felt a spiritual calling, so he earned a PhD in New Testament Greek from Southern Baptist Theological Seminary in Louisville, Kentucky. He wrote *The Cotton Patch Version of Paul's Epistles,* among other books, and he recorded some parables. Amazingly, he also had a BS in Agriculture. He was a brilliant scholar.

In the '40s, '50s, and '60s, when racial tensions were at their peak in the South, Clarence Jordan put his faith on the line. Seeing the need to provide an example of an interracial Christian community, he established a farm, Koinonia (a Greek word that means community), in Americus, Georgia. Through sweat and determination he created a place where blacks and whites could work side by side in harmony and faith.

The Christians of that day gathered their self-righteous robes about them and shunned him as they would a leper. His own church turned its back on him. The townspeople boycotted the farm and slashed the tires of the workers' trucks when they went to town.

Even members of Clarence's own family refused to help. In 1954, after 14 years of harassment, the Ku Klux Klan rode on the farm, burned down every building, and riddled Clarence's house with bullets.

The next day, amid the ashes, Clarence walked out to the field and started replanting. When a reporter, whose voice he recognized as being one of the Klan members, came to report on the closing down of the farm, Clarence told him, "You don't understand. This place is not about success. It's about faithfulness."

Clarence Jordan was unmoved in his belief that God meant for Koinonia to remain a shining light to a nation lost in the darkness of racial prejudice. His persistence paid off. Eventually, Millard Fuller and his wife joined him. The Fullers were wealthy, and they were so impressed by Clarence's vision that they abandoned their life of wealth and ease and moved onto the farm to help.

By the time Clarence died, he had become a truly humble servant of God. As he had requested, he was buried in a pine box in an unmarked grave on the farm. I often think about his humility when I see millionaire ministers with their Mercedes, mansions, and great cathedrals. I wonder if they understand the meaning of sacrifice. To me, Clarence will always inspire by the unwavering confidence of his faith.

Irene Peterson was a neighbor for 19 years. There was something eternally young about Irene. She had long curly hair, streaked with gray, and her figure was slim and girlish. Irene was very thrifty, and she loved garage sales. She was a devoted wife, and her three lovely daughters gave her a bunch of grandchildren in whom she delighted.

To know Irene was to recognize that the cornerstone of her personality was her love of the Lord. She talked about the Lord as if He was her best friend, and indeed, He was. Irene served Him by taking care of old people.

Irene was naturally shy and modest, but I've never seen a more gifted person around older people. For more than 20 years she went every week to a nursing home and held parties and services for the residents. Many times she brought them gifts—little trinkets she had found at garage sales. She would seat them all in a circle, and then she'd work her way around it, bringing out each individual, encouraging him or her to sing or say a poem or prayer. With her praise, those old people blossomed. It was beautiful to see.

Sadly, Irene developed cancer, and her condition was grave. By then we'd moved, but my daughter, Missie, went to visit Irene. While they were talking, Missie noticed that Irene's husband had tears in his eyes.

Irene saw it, too, and she said, "Now, Charles, you must stop worrying.

The Lord will either heal me, or He'll take me home."

She had exactly the kind of faith Jesus told us we should develop—the simple faith of a child. I'm sure that when Irene died, she entered into the presence of her Lord with great joy. After all, He was someone she had known well for a long time. Irene will always be an example to me through the simplicity of her faith.

I have a favorite picture of Jesus. He is laughing. I've spent a lifetime seeking the face of Jesus. Now I see it.

The faith of Jesus was not merely a comfort or an escape from the terrible realities of a physical life. Jesus' faith in His Father was as much a part of Him as His mind and His body. His certainty of the love of God was as natural as His breath. It wasn't an intellectual decision or a creed He formulated. His faith was a living faith, and He practiced it by loving service, prayer and worship, and constant communication with His Father. Jesus lived His faith every moment He was on this earth.

The faith of Jesus began a chain reaction. It continues today in acts of loving kindness. Motivated by a seminary teacher, Clarence Jordan established Koinonia Farm. Inspired by Clarence, the Fullers started Habitat for Humanity. The chain never ends. It passes through me. Those who have gone before me lead me forward in my faith journey. I see their faces. I have only to follow them.

Faith, Fear, And The Daily Bread Of Kindness

By Niambi Walker
Louisville, Kentucky

Okay, I'm ready to write. The candles are lit, and I've pulled down my favorite writing journal from the bookshelf. You see, it's time to sit with my grandmother, and I want it to be just so. Perhaps for many that simply means driving across town and opening the door with the hidden key. Yet, as someone who has lived abroad for five years, for me spending time with family members is a time where I quiet down the daily stresses of my young ambitions and wrap myself in a patchwork quilt of memories.

I'm surprised that I've chosen to think about my grandmother. She's not someone who stands out in a crowd—never the first to hold a newborn, to make church announcements, or even to dispense the legendary wisdom of elders. Even when my grandfather was deacon, Nana sat in the back pew discreetly passing peppermint candies to her best friend, Miss Sarah, and me. Yet, like those childhood sweets, I sit here now savoring her gentle spirit because of a lesson she recently taught me about faith in the kindness of others.

In August I returned to Kentucky for a short stay with my family. Like so many others have experienced, the past year had fractured the thin wall of naiveté that kept me believing the world was not as turbulent as newspapers reported. After months of bomb scares in Europe and at home, I was feeling whipped by worldliness—feeling cheated, I suppose, that we were still expected to live meaningful lives in the face of such meaningless tragedies. Filled with cynicism and fear, I had left Paris to take a vacation from 21st century adulthood. And so, when Nana peeked through my parents' front window clutching her leather purse, I smiled my fullest smile and opened the screen door.

"Come on, Punkin'," she said. "Thought we might go ridin' down to Miss Sarah's and then go shoppin'."

On our way into the old neighborhood Nana pointed out her favorite spots. Even using side roads, it's only a 20-minute drive between Nana's house and her former streets. Yet her nostalgic tour through the area took me into a faraway and seemingly impossible world of segregated Louisville.

"This is where all the brown people lived," she explained. There is no self-pity or sense of betrayal in her voice. Her finger points left as she calls out the old "colored-only" school because this was her school. Her hand sweeps past the weary line of shops and drugstores because those were her meeting places. Still, as she calls out the names of the formerly black-only buildings and offices, I feel a sharp anger rise in me. When I followed Nana's index finger pointing to that old school building, it was as though she were signaling that hate and ignorance has long existed. Unaware of my chain of thoughts, she continued her story.

"Me and Papa moved over to the other side of town, and we've got such nice neighbors. All different kinds," sings Nana, twirling her hand as though to scoop up all the colors in the spectrum. "You know—black and white. My neighbor, Chuck—he came to Papa's funeral and gave me that plant now sitting in the kitchen. I'm not usually good with plants, but that one keeps growing."

This was a typical story ending for Nana—one that rings of her faith that hard times come and then they pass, leaving us with the business of being kind to one another. My mind buzzed with the question: *What preserved her faith in the kindness of others in spite of such intolerance?* I remained quiet pondering this question until we pulled into Miss Sarah's driveway.

On each visit back to my hometown my grandmother and I stop in to visit her longtime church sister, Miss Sarah. Her house is a place where time seems to have passed over, although the walking cane at the door tells otherwise. I amuse them with my store of anecdotes while they give me news of old friends and church members. This time while listening to them my mind drifted back to childhood summer days chasing Quinton, Miss Sarah's grandson, on my tricycle. When I ask about him, I let out a laugh. "He was so skinny!"

"Oh, girl. He's fat now," mused Ms. Sarah. "Yeah, a big boy. Got a steady job for a while now. Yeah, he's all right. Out of the woods, praise God."

A silence lay between us for a few moments. Nana reminisced about times with my grandfather who had passed several years before. After a little while she smiled and looked over at Miss Sarah. "When Papa died," she said," Miss Sarah said that I could be her sister. My brothers and sister are gone, but now I call her Sister Sarah, and her children and grandchildren call me Aunt Susie."

I had heard this before, yet for the first time I understood that Miss Sarah's kind gesture of sisterhood had helped to guide my grandmother out of grief and into thankfulness.

As my grandmother continued to list off her daily blessings, I leaned back into the chair's cushion. I flicked through my past conversations with friends in my memory, trying to find a time when we had sat 'round a table chatting about our blessings. We talk of young adult things—how to fill out self-employment tax forms, tyrannical bosses, or the latest threat of war. But here in front of me were two wrinkled women at the edge of their lives who were woven together by 70 years of sisterhood. I sighed as I thought, *If only I could download this type of contentment from a website.*

As I sit here now an ocean away from that day, I recall my awe at my grandmother's faith in the benevolence of others. When I think of the word *faith,* it seems to have the ring of something solid—impermeable—like the solid rock sung about in those old spirituals. Yet when my mind reaches out to define it, "faith" dodges my grasp. Hoping to find some reference to the meaning of faith, I look in the dictionary: /fa'th/ n. unquestioning belief that does not require proof or evidence. There it was in black and white—the solidity, the unflappability of this one syllable catchall for peace of mind. As I study the word and its meanings, my gaze slips down to "faithless," and I am surprised to find that it is not faith's antonym or "without faith," but rather it is defined as "disloyal," "unreliable," even "treacherous." I think to myself, *If "faith" were etched onto a coin that I flipped in the air, what would I find etched on the other side when it landed? Skepticism? Denial? Fear? Perhaps fear.* The events of the past year had left me smirking at notions of kindness. In the absence of faith, I feared that the real meaning of humanity was not "kindness and generosity" as my dictionary insisted, but the display of hatred and despair reported in the nightly news.

Back in Kentucky my grandmother taught me that we had a choice in the lessons that we learned from our experiences and our surroundings. She had plenty of proof that the world was unkind. Yet in place of intolerance of others, she chose friendship; in place of sadness from loss, she chose gratitude. She lives her life assured by her faith that there will be someone with a kind word or an offering of a kind act to help carry her on to the next day. In essence, Nana had chosen—and passed on the choice to me—to have faith in human kindness.

Faith Of A Father

By Carolyn R. Scheidies
Kearney, Nebraska

When I was a toddler, I thought Dad was a giant in every way. Though I squealed when he tossed me up in the air, I knew he'd always catch me. He'd chuckle as he'd lift me up in his strong arms, raise me over his head, and launch me into the air. I felt the air swish through my hair as I fell, straight into his waiting arms. Dad gained my trust.

I cannot count the times we snuggled together in a deep cushioned chair as he read one book or another to me, though in those early years I insisted on *Alice In Wonderland* over and over and over. His deep pastor's voice brought the story alive for me. Not until I grew up did he confess how he came to hate that book. He never let on, never spoiled the magic for his young daughter—the daughter who already spun stories in her head. Dad encouraged my imagination.

In his youth, Dad was a checker champion, yet when we played, he held back until I understood the game. As I got older, we played cutthroat games with no mercy given, the way I wanted it. He helped me become confident in my own reasoning abilities and would show me how I could do better—next time.

Once, out of pure jealousy, I swung a blanket at the horse my sister rode, causing the horse to rear and Karin to fall—right into a cactus patch. Dad punished me. It wasn't the first time. He wasn't afraid to spank if he thought it appropriate. (And he wasn't fooled by a book stuck down my pants.)

Afterward, he'd hold me close as he'd carry me up the stairs while explaining how he loved me and how what I did caused harm to myself or others. He was fair and always made sure I understood why he disciplined me, and I was a real trial for a parent! Dad taught me that love requires responsibility.

At 13 I contracted a severe case of Juvenile Rheumatoid Arthritis and became wheelchair bound within months. It was heartbreaking for my parents to watch me, their tomboy, never-ever-sick daughter, lose weight until my bones stuck out, my eyes protruded from shrunken sockets, and I appeared nothing more than skin and bones. Within months, my knees bent and refused to straighten; my hands drew up into claws. Worst of all, they watched the laughter fade from my eyes as day after day I screamed out in pain.

Mom and Dad prayed. Oh, how they prayed, but they did so much more—caring for me, taking me from one doctor and medical facility to another seeking help. But most comforting was simply Dad's presence, a presence I felt most strongly in his study.

In a wheelchair I pushed forward with my feet, since I couldn't use my hands, I'd inch up to his closed study door. Yes, I knew he was inside preparing his sermon for Sunday.

Tap. Tap. I doubted he heard my weak knock. "Dad." As I waited, I shivered in the slight breeze wafting in from a half-open door. I was often cold those days.

Biting my lip, I called a little louder, "Dad. Dad, may I come in?"

His hesitation broke my heart, and I felt tears gather in my eyes. Since the onset of my disease, my emotions were all akilter. Did I hear a long sigh? "Umm. Come on in, Carolyn." I knew he wouldn't say no.

With both hands, I twisted the knob and edged the door open with my foot. Slowly, I inched my wheelchair into the room. Sunlight shining into the room from the west window drew me into its warmth. With pain-filled movements, I turned the chair to face my dad.

Surrounded by bookshelves that went from floor to ceiling, Dad sat behind his desk watching me. He rifled a thin hand through even thinner dark hair and adjusted his glasses askew on his nose. He no longer seemed like a giant to me, at least physically. In fact, he wasn't all that tall, though he was strong—in so many ways.

I sensed he wanted to help me but kept himself seated to permit me to do as much as possible for myself. "I'm working, Carolyn, but what can I do for you?"

I surveyed the small office. The smell of books both old and new mingled with the tang of mimeograph ink. The books beckoned me. Though he could have been more concerned about keeping them pristine and neat, Dad put them all at my disposal.

Since I'd been ill, I'd read everything from fiction and biographies to deep theological treatises. Sometimes I pecked out stories or poems on his ancient typewriter. Dad encouraged my talents, forced me to think beyond the surface, and nurtured my dreams.

A north window overlooked the long drive to the road in rural Kansas and the wide expanse of yard. I sensed Dad waiting, sensed a mixture of impatience and a desire to please me. *What could I say?*

Finally, I raised my gaze to his solemn face. "You don't need to do anything. I just want to sit and read in here. Okay?"

After a long glance in my direction, Dad nodded, a half smile tilting his lips. For a time I watched him read his well-marked Bible, take notes, and pray. His faith was more than a Sunday affair. He lived it. My illness caused such changes in me and in my family.

My childlike faith took a beating, as did my belief that my dad could solve all my problems. He couldn't. Instead, I watched him break down and weep over my pain, over my struggle to do the simplest things.

But here, in his domain, I found a sanctuary. For while my faith wavered, Dad's did not. He put his faith in Someone higher and greater. Here in his office, I felt a certain peace. Maybe my faith in Dad wasn't misplaced after all. Maybe it was time I took up the mantle of faith he carried and found that source for myself.

My struggle was far from over physically, emotionally, and spiritually, but my faith in my father launched me to heights I never could have imagined. His faith led to my faith and gave me the assurance that I would walk again, and I would write, and the firm belief that I did have something to offer.

Dad has been gone for many years now, but he lived to see his daughter walk, lived to unite her in marriage, and lived to see her start getting published. Most of all, he lived long enough to start instilling in his grandchildren his faith—the faith of my father.

Three Strikes—You Are Not Out!
The Amazing Faith and Healing of Hattie P. Horton

By Claude Bert Victory
Inglewood, California

On November 23, 1992, at approximately 8:30 a.m., church mother Hattie P. Horton unexpectedly experienced a devastating and life-threatening aneurysm. This was one of three catastrophic maladies that would challenge the faith that had carried her through for over four decades. Before she fell into the dark abyss of unconsciousness, she had served her Lord faithfully in prayer, studied the Word of God, and lived an impeccable Christian lifestyle.

Affectionately known by all as "Mother Hattie," her unswerving faith and worship of God was admired by all, especially her local church members, her family, and the community in which she lived and served. And though miraculous healings appeared grand and mysterious to some, for those who knew her, Mother Hattie's victorious encounter with sickness and death became a never-to-be-forgotten testimony to faith in action.

The Scripture that had been read and revered so many times, *"Heal me, O Lord and I shall be healed,"* became a living reality. Mother Hattie learned that the intangibles—faith and healing—are not bound by time and distance. Wherever God is, He is there in totality in strength and power and unfragmented in His purpose.

An urgent long distance telephone call went out to Cape Town, South Africa, from Modesto, California, stating that Mother Hattie had been gravely stricken with a life-threatening aneurysm to the brain. The bleeding was internal and profuse. The doctors wanted to operate immediately. A decision had to be made; she was not expected to recover. Christian believers in faraway Cape Town, South Africa, gathered together to pray for a woman they had never seen, never heard of, and were not likely to ever meet. While Hattie was unconscious, her family opted not to allow the operation; this was to honor Hattie's unswerving faith in her God. If conscious, Hattie Horton would have approved. Her faith in God had dominated every facet of her life. Mother Hattie's son, Claude B. Victory, often reminiscenced about how she prayed early in the mornings, and he could tell the emotions stirring as she approached the throne of heaven. Those prayer recollections would haunt him throughout his life, but powerful prayers are a good thing to haunt you during your times of high anxiety.

A few days later another telephone call went out to Johannesburg, South Africa, saying that miraculously, although she was still unconscious, the internal bleeding had stopped. There would be no operation and Hattie Horton, aged 68, would recover completely in spite of her remembering an unknown physician hovering over her while she was semi-conscious stating, "Hattie, don't you know you are going to die just like your sister who died earlier of an aneurysm? I have your chart," the doctor had said.

But that doctor was proven wrong, and Mother Hattie's remarkable recovery from death's door was celebrated by all as a witness to the awesome faith that she has in God, whom she serves. The doctor only had a snapshot of Mother Hattie's life, but God had the whole Kodak picture from the beginning to the end of her life.

More importantly, Mother Hattie's faith and healing from the aneurysm was accomplished without the razzamatazz of noisy prayer lines, the loud ranting of faith healers, or even the expertise of skilled physicians. God touched her body intimately with His divine hand because Mother Hattie belonged to Him, and she was healed completely of a deadly aneurysm. *The first strike did not lessen her faith*—it only strengthened it.

While lying quietly in bed on November 22, 1993, exactly one year to the date from when she suffered the aneurysm, Mother Hattie experienced a strange heaviness in her chest area that she had never experienced before. She instinctively knew something was wrong. The heaviness grew stronger as she edged herself toward the bathroom. Mother Hattie was rushed to the Memorial Hospital in Modesto, California—the same hospital that had administered medical assistance for the aneurysm to her brain. She was given a heart scan and was surprised to learn she had suffered a heart attack. Lying in bed the following day, while praying and trusting the same God who delivered her from the aneurysm, a quiet stranger appeared at her bedside. The man introduced himself only as "The Chaplain." Gently and lovingly he took her hands and began to pray for her. She responded in prayer as tears of joy began streaming down her face. The prayers flowed sweetly like perfume from flowers. It seemed as if an alabaster box of renewed faith filled the room as she looked into this man's eyes that were filled with an angelic gleam. Not knowing her condition, he whispered softly but confidently, "I see you know the Master." The man then quickly and quietly disappeared. She was never able to find out the name of the man or his professional status at the hospital, but she knew God had sent him. She remembered the Word of God that admonishes believers to be careful in entertaining strangers, for some unawares have entertained angels.

After the heart scans, angioplasty helped unclog blocked arteries. Mother Hattie's faith once again triumphed, but she also understood that she needed to make some necessary common sense lifestyle changes—proper diet, moderate exercise, rest, and regular check-ups had to be coupled with her faith to prevent further heart problems. She determined the physical temple of God (her body) would be served with proper maintenance, honor, and respect. Mother Hattie learned a valuable lesson—faith and common sense in action work wonderfully. *The second strike did not conquer her faith*—it only strengthened it.

On December 20, 1997, Mother Hattie suffered a stroke. She was living in Hayward, California, at the time and was taken to nearby Eden Medical Center. The only visible damage was an inability to speak. While having breakfast with her husband, her speech suddenly became unintelligible and then silent. She became woozy and was laid down gently on the sofa. Immediately 911 was called. Her vital signs were normal, but her speech remained impaired. Undoubtedly she may have questioned—*Why did this happen?* She had taken every precautionary measure to strengthen her cardiovascular health through proper eating, exercise, and stress reduction.

Often we wonder, *What are the limits to which God will allow His servants' faith to be tested?* Mother Hattie learned that God always has the last word, and it is always good. Hattie's speech was miraculously restored in just a short period of time.

Doctors planned to assign her a speech therapist until one of them noticed Mother Hattie conducting a personal Bible study with another patient. She had resumed talking and praising God without ever attending a single therapy session.

Very often it seems we are all alone in our darkest moments. Abandonment and betrayal seem par for the course. Mother Hattie was speechless for a short period of time, and indeed she may have felt like John the Baptist felt in prison—all alone and abandoned. If God cared, where was He? But her faith taught her He is always there, even when you are speechless, and it doesn't seem like He cares. *This was the third strike*—but she remained firm in her faith.

On October 28, 1999, Hattie Horton received the Senior Award for outstanding service to her community at the annual awards dinner where more than 500 people gathered at Centennial Hall in Hayward, California. Hattie is now aged 77, and her faith is even deeper, richer, and more alive than ever before. Hattie lost her husband of 23 years on March 18, 2001, but she continues to teach, serve in the community, and has endeavored to become a prayer intercessor to the glory of God. When teaching younger women, she lovingly tells them, "You've got to know God for yourself." If trouble and problems never come, how can you know Him to be a deliverer? Faith untested is no faith at all.

This is the true story and remarkable saga of Hattie P. Horton, a woman who continues to walk by faith and not by sight. Hattie P. Horton can be reached at (510) 538-3639. She is there waiting to encourage you in your faith.

Unshakable Faith

By Marilyn Phillips
Bedford, Texas

All eyes watch as the petite blonde confidently walks on stage. Rebekah is the guest speaker at the Christian Cheerleaders of America National Competition (CCA) in Chattanooga, Tennessee. This dynamic young lady proclaims that her strength for today and hope for the future is in God. Rebekah receives the CCA Rianne Ellisa Scrivner Courage Award. This prestigious award is given for exhibiting outstanding courage in the face of extraordinary trials.

Rebekah shares, "I know that I have an incurable disease that may shorten my earthly existence. But I don't worry about death. I focus on eternity. As long as God has a purpose for my life, I will be on earth. I claim God's promise that, *I can do all things through Christ which strengtheneth me.* Philippians 4:13, KJV And when my purpose on earth is complete, I will go to heaven for eternity." Overwhelming emotion engulfs the audience. The audience weeps and listens to Rebekah's life story, a story that is full of adversity and unshakable faith in God. Rebekah's tremendous testimony receives a standing ovation from over 450 cheerleaders who are there to compete for the national cheerleading title.

How can this young lady focus on eternity and have unshakable faith in God when facing an incurable disease? Rebekah has an unconquerable attitude toward a life threatening disease, cystic fibrosis (CF). CF is inherited, and it is the most common fatal genetic disease. At the time of her birth in 1978, Rebekah was only expected to live until the age of 13. Now the average life span for a CF patient is mid 30's…but there is nothing average about Rebekah's life, because the hand of God is on her. Researchers claim a cure for CF is near, and we have even met CF adults who are 50 years and older. Rebekah experiences difficulty breathing daily. Although this devastating disease causes constant lung infections and frequent hospitalizations, Rebekah never lets the disease stop her from achieving goals.

As a cheerleader, this vivacious teenager's team won first place at CCA Cheerleader Camps for two years. During camps, the instructors notice her amazing attitude and leadership. Although cheerleading is physically demanding, Rebekah excels. She is accustomed to adversity. Some teens complain about a bad hair day, but Rebekah often has bad lung days and struggles just to breathe.

I know firsthand about unshakable faith. I witness it daily. This courageous young lady, my daughter, is a constant source of encouragement. She continually amazes me. Although her appearance is normal, Rebekah takes more than 100 enzyme capsules weekly to digest food and must have two hours of breathing treatments daily. Constant lung infections require additional treatments and medications and hospitalizations usually every six months.

Recently Rebekah was told she has developed diabetes as a complication of CF. Now she must take insulin to control high blood sugar levels. I was devastated and wept uncontrollably thinking how unfair it is that Rebekah must deal with two severe diseases. But my daughter refuses to allow negative feelings. She says, "Mom, diabetes is just another disease. This is no big deal! We will handle this by focusing on God." And so, that is what we do each day…focus on God.

Rebekah continues, "God has proven over and over that He has a wonderful plan for my life. Another disease will not change my faith in God."

I wonder how Rebekah can continually give praise to God when facing constant obstacles. My daughter points to a verse that helps me understand her focus: *It is a wonderful thing to be alive! If a person lives to be very old, let him rejoice in every day of life, but let him also remember that eternity is far longer, and that everything down here is futile in comparison…* Ecclesiastes 11:7-8, Living

Incurable diseases only make Rebekah more determined to live each day to the fullest. Rebekah's faith in God is unshakable and she focuses on a favorite verse, *He alone is my rock and my salvation; he is my fortress, I will not be shaken.* Psalm 62:6

You might think that Rebekah is discouraged with the physical limitations caused by CF and diabetes. On the contrary, she is an inspiration to others through her faith in God and her courage in handling the daily problems caused by two diseases. CF Specialists, Dr. Rosenblatt, Dr. Torres, Dr. Prestidge, and Dr. Brown, and Diabetes Specialist, Dana Hardin, aggressively treat the disease. They always encourage my daughter to succeed. Rebekah's family, friends and teachers believe in her. Rebekah says her brother, Bryant, has been an inspiration. He is two years older but lets his tiny sister win races and games to encourage her. Bryant is a constant companion during each hospitalization and brings her surprises.

As a cheerleader, Rebekah cheered for her brother on the football field, and Bryant cheers for his sister with each accomplishment. He is an incredible source of strength. Rebekah says her "support team" continues to help her believe she can achieve goals.

With much inner strength and faith in God, Rebekah continues to accomplish more than my mind can imagine or my heart dares to dream. She inspires her friends through her positive attitude. She always focuses on the needs of others. Many observe Rebekah's example. I have learned from my daughter that each day should be spent in celebration.

Looking at Rebekah, you would never know she has an incurable disease. She is incredible and sets high goals for her life. Goals progress from high school graduation to college. With much determination, she continually succeeds. Recently Rebekah amazed everyone again as she crossed another stage—this time as a college graduate.

My daughter achieved her dream to earn a degree in education and to become a teacher. Rebekah has always wanted to *teach*. Now she is teaching at a private Christian preschool. But Rebekah has been a *teacher* all of her life, for she has taught me about the importance of faith in God. Rebekah's faith has been instrumental in helping me to see God's hand in my daughter's life and how God uses Rebekah's testimony to help others. Her faith in God has affected others around the world because Christian Cheerleaders of America sells a book about her at cheerleading camps held in locations across the USA. Cheerleaders purchase the book and read about Rebekah's unshakable faith. Often their lives are changed forever.

Rebekah represents hope. She has shown others that the events in life, even diseases as devastating as cystic fibrosis and diabetes, cannot govern true happiness. Regardless of life's circumstance, Rebekah's unshakable faith is in God Who gives hope in every situation. *"But as for me, I will always have hope; I will praise you more and more."* Psalm 71:14

When The Sun Rose

By Abigail Susan Steidley
Virginia Beach, Virginia

The very meaning of faith is a steadfast belief, but my mother's faith goes beyond that. It is impenetrable. It has a steel lining, a granite foundation. I have felt it emanating from her core since childhood. My mother has faith in love.

When I was growing up, I felt the intensity of my parents' relationship. I longed for what they had and dreamed of my own true love. He shimmered before me, a mirage of my imagination. But what I was dreaming of was not the man himself, but the moments we would share. And those moments were patterned after the moments my parents shared each day. They laughed together; they teased each other; they were always talking. We were a family, but they were also a couple to the exclusion of all else.

When I look at my parents, I see my mother as the Rock of Gibraltar, the sun around which the planets revolve, the rock around the molten center of the earth. She loves with a strength that surpasses everything else. Without my mother, my father would be lost. She is his center, his world, and should he wonder or waver or ask if it is all worth it, she would be there to say emphatically, "Yes!"

But to understand what I am talking about, you must journey with me to my toddlerhood. I was three years old when my father's parents decided to divorce, and the ugliness that ensued cloaked our little family. My paternal grandmother haunted our house day and night, hanging onto her only son as a refuge from her husband. She disliked my mother, disliked me even. We took her son away from her, in her eyes, and so she came to him again and again with needs, with crises, with tears and storms of emotion. She began to wear him down to nothing. This is when the solid strength of my mother's faith was born.

My mother knew that the love she and her new husband had was something unshakable. I don't mean to say that she thought they would never struggle. She had worries, like anyone else. She saw her mother-in-law tearing them apart, ripping at the seams of our newborn family. But she let her faith guide her. She believed in love—and that love would triumph. She stood before my father one night, her fists clenched at her sides. You must choose, she told him. You must choose between your mother and your wife.

Now that I am married, I shiver when I imagine that scene. How terrified she must have felt in that moment. As his anger vibrated through him, she must have wanted so strongly to take those words back, to grab them from the air where they hung and throw them away. But she stood her ground, that impenetrable strength radiating from her. I can imagine it clearly. I know the look she gets in her eyes, the steely determination that she wears around herself like an aura. My dad must have looked at her and known, in that moment, that he needed her. That without her, his life would be a series of his mother's crises, his parents' fights, and his own lonely moments. He must have felt the strength of her love and her faith in him.

And so he chose his wife. He cut himself completely away from his family. For the rest of my years at home, we were free of the violent quarrels, the disturbing phone calls, the hysterical weeping, the alcoholism, and the pain. We had our own little family, and my parents had a lasting marriage. We lived in peace.

Until my father had to face his family for the last time. The news came that his father was dying. I must introduce you to his father, a man who loved alcohol, anger, and domination. I did not know him, but the pain he caused my father still cuts into my heart. But he lay on his deathbed, and so my father went to say goodbye.

He was out of town for days at a time, coming home for brief periods to work and sleep. My mother watched him spiraling downward, turning inward, and losing himself. She worried over him, prayed for him, and most of all, loved him. But she could do nothing to ease his pain. The death of a parent is never simple, never pain-free. But in my father's case, it tore a gigantic hole in his person, ripping at the threads of his world until it was completely changed. In those last few weeks of his father's life, he discovered that his sister had suffered years of sexual abuse. His father had tormented her, and his mother had pretended oblivion. His father had sought alcohol and anger, his favorite weapons, and used them against everyone he knew. His mother had blamed his sister for the incest. He was forced to see his parents for what they were. The picture terrified him, for when he looked in the mirror, he saw that the bones of his face were shaped like those of his father. He began to fear that he, too, was rotten inside.

So one night he came home to my mother, a lost man. He didn't see himself as a survivor of this terrible childhood, this tormenting father. He saw only that he was related to these people and that they had hurt others.

In his mind, the only choice was to leave everyone he loved behind, to distance himself from all those he cared for, to spare them. He felt as though he did not know what was inside himself, and he was afraid. He did not look in the mirror and see someone worth loving. He saw only the ghost of his father.

He told my mother he was leaving, and he began to pack.

I can't imagine the pain she must have felt. To hear the man you love tell you he is leaving is agonizing enough. But to know that he was hating himself so much that he didn't even feel worthy of her love—that must have felt insurmountable. It must have hurt to know that he would leave her, even though she knew that he was suffering. It would have been easy to let that hurt burrow inside; to let him go and close the door behind him, miserable and alone; hoping that he would realize his mistake—that he would see how much he was hurting her.

But my mother had faith in love. She knew without a doubt that they had the strongest love possible between man and woman. She saw my father's pain, and again that steely force flowed from her to give him strength.

"No," she told him. "You're not leaving." And she began to tell him why. They talked the entire night, through the moonlight and into the early coral-colored dawn. She listened to him, and she held him. She let him say that he was leaving, over and over again. But she never said the words he longed to hear. She never said, "Okay, fine, leave, if that's what you want." Because she knew that he was looking only for the tiniest excuse, the tiniest crack in her armor. And then he would leave, because he thought himself unworthy of her love. She fought with that iron core inside her, told him over and over again that he was worth loving and that she was not going to let him leave. She told him that he was not his father. She told him that his children loved him. She was his strength that night, and when the sun finally rose over the mountain, she had convinced him to stay.

It was a moment of crisis, a moment that comes, perhaps, to all marriages. People are human, and they break down sometimes. They fall apart. They need each other. And when one person in a marriage is lost, the other must have enough faith to be the strong one. To stand there and say, "You are not leaving. I love you." To reach out and hand that person a life preserver. To have faith in love.

With Style And Grace

By Sharon Dexter
Lake Geneva, Wisconsin

Fifteen years ago my sister, Meg*, was diagnosed with cancer. Multiple melanoma had already eaten away at her bones enough that she had fractured at least two vertebrae. The oncologist called in to treat her believed she would not live for much longer.

Two years ago Meg died. The 13 years between those two events hold the story of a growing faith.

While in the hospital that first time, her son, Joe*, came right out with it. "Mom, do you believe in God?" His belief had been strengthened through two years of AA meetings. He needed to know his mother's gut reaction to God.

"Sort of."

"Then just put yourself in His hands."

"But I've always wanted to be in control." (No surprise there!)

Joe then asked, "Do you have control of the cancer? Start with putting just that into His hands."

Meg thought on, agonized over, and conjugated that idea. So that's where she started to put herself under Authority.

The first session of chemotherapy lasted two years—two years of hell on earth. During that time she gave up her apartment and moved in with her son and his family. They worked hard at it, but Meg and Joe could not adjust to the reversed roles. She then moved in with Mother. At this time, just eating was a chore—there was no "living." But Mother's supportive faith, plus family's and friends' support, all bathed Meg in the love she needed. For the first time since childhood, she allowed herself to "take."

At the end of the two-year therapy, Meg was pronounced in remission. (There is no guaranteed *cure* in cancer.) Within two months, weak and uncertain of her own abilities, Meg determined she must move back into an apartment of her own. For six months her bedroom "curtain" was a sheet hung over the rod. She didn't want to spend the money yet—in case. Finally she decided she just might live. She bought curtains…then several new outfits.

At one agonizing point in this new life, Meg cried out to God, "But how can I *live*?" The answer came as a whisper in her ear: "You can live with style and grace."

That was indeed Meg. Style and grace had been my impression of her from childhood on. But this time "style" was dictated by her "permanent cummerbund" of skin and contracted organ. Several more vertebrae had fractured. And her "grace" was underscored by God's grace.

Meg kept her Bible, devotional book, and prayer book on the table beside her favorite chair. Daily she read and tried to understand God's Word in her life. Every visitor was, at one time or another, asked to participate in her personal search for understanding. She "grilled" the visiting pastors more than once for answers. One admitted not knowing answers, but he certainly enjoyed Meg's stimulating thinking processes.

The first remission lasted just over a year. Meg was again placed in the same two-year chemotherapy program, this time while continuing to live alone. The second remission was under nine months. Her oncologist determined a different treatment schedule was now warranted.

Each time the cancer recurred, after shorter and shorter remission times, Meg made the conscious decision to fight. Life itself was too sweet to give up. She found style and grace every step of the way. As long as she could find even moments of joy, she was willing to participate.

During the first loss of hair, Meg wore wigs. It took months before she relaxed enough to go hairless, even in front of family. One hot summer day was the clincher. But being Meg, she first had to be sure *we* were comfortable enough to try it. She was beautiful.

Next hair losses saw turbans and creatively applied scarves. Being stylish, naturally they matched her outfit. She had more scarves than skirts. That was an easy choice for birthday gifts!

Throughout it all, Meg granted God complete control of her restricted abilities. But she continued to seek some small control in her daily life. "I have to simplify," she would say each time another bout with the cancer made further inroads on her dwindling energy supply. She saw this attitude as acceptance of her lot and bent to God's will. She would take care of whatever area He gave her to work with.

One area Meg was easily able to control. Unafraid of dying, she made thorough plans for her memorial service and distribution of ashes. These she discussed with each of her four children, with Mother, and with me. Meg was determined to make the end times as comfortable for everyone else as she possibly could. Her faith was such that she knew where she was going. As she once confided, "It's not the dying that frightens me. It's how to live when it gets really bad that is scary."

Until the last few months, it never got all that "bad and scary" for her. Instead she worried, "I don't see how Joe handles that horrid flu he has" and "How do you manage to work when you have those bouts of headaches you get?" She was never without pain for the 13 remaining years of her life, yet she constantly concerned herself with others.

As long as she was able to maneuver, she volunteered as a cancer survivor to talk with other cancer patients. She knew God's grace in her life and believed His purpose in her survival might be to help other families. One woman's family so appreciated Meg's efforts that they sent a huge plant at Christmastime for several years after the woman's death. Meg never understood why they would bother to do that. After all, she did nothing more than talk and be a friend.

Friendship was as necessary as air, and Meg always knew how to be a true friend. Yet it amazed her when those friends turned around and helped her when she was in need. The "style and grace" helped her see that allowing others to reciprocate was the deepest way she could validate their friendship. She invited them for tea and fancy store-bought cookies when she could, knowing that time spent together was her contribution to the friendship. And in the quiet, these friendships deepened immeasurably.

Meg died at home as she had planned. It happened before anyone was quite "ready," but then we are never ready to lose a loved one. The memorial service went exactly as planned. Friends and relatives traveled to be with her this final time. The container of ashes was draped with a new scarf.

Mother and I had ordered the requested yellow roses, fastened into huge greens. But we added one touch to Meg's plan. Every single relative and her closest friends received one yellow rose. They were removed from the arrangements and placed in a plastic bag with a moist paper towel to keep them fresh. It was the perfect "style and grace" comment to end Meg's story. It was the last way she could give.

*Names changed.

Her Gift

By Julie Bonn Heath
Port Orchard, Washington

We were such good friends, my grandmother and I. Had we not been related, we would have found each other eventually, for we were kindred spirits, meant to share with and inspire each other, meant to laugh together, meant to cry together. When I think of the people in my life who taught me what faith is all about, she was in the top three.

As a child, I visited my grandma almost every day. She lived a mere half mile down the street, and I walked or rode my bike there frequently, often coming back after dark when the shadows jumped out and scared me as I made my way home. At the other times, I spent the night with her in the extra bedroom across the hall from her room.

She taught me most of what I know about sewing, although to this day my parents tell me that she found me "unteachable" and very strong willed during the process. Somehow she got the knowledge through my head, for when I took home economics in seventh grade, I already knew all the types of sewing stitches and how to follow a pattern.

My grandma loved to sew quilts. I did not have the patience to put a bunch of little squares together, but I was fascinated at her works of art when they were completed. Later, when I did take a small interest in it, she'd let me go through her scrap bag and pull out whatever I wanted. I never did finish a quilt, but I can tell you how to make one.

Grandma sewed some clothes for me, as well. My mom and I picked out the patterns and the material, and Grandma diligently cut, stitched, and created while I watched. Then I tried them on and complained about having to stand so still while she pinned, pinched, and measured some more. Every step of the way, she explained what she was doing and even had me cut some of the shapes from the fabric. Sewing was a skill she loved and wanted to pass on to me. She believed in the idea that we are to teach what we know to others.

At some point, when I was young, I told Grandma that I wanted a flannel nightgown. And every Christmas thereafter she apologized for not having one done, even long after I stopped wanting one.

I talked to Grandma about many things. I told her about my boyfriends ("You're too young for that," she'd say, even when I was in high school and allowed to date) and fights with my parents (she would just chuckle) and problems at school. We talked of her challenges with raising nine kids. She always asked questions, and I always answered honestly. She was so very interested in hearing about every aspect of my life. She sometimes spoke of her church and her ladies' group and how important they were to her. In late years, when she was unable to drive, someone always picked her up for church.

I read her the stories I wrote and told her about my choir and drama activities. I borrowed her encyclopedias for homework and helped her with crossword puzzles in the newspaper.

In the winter my brothers, cousins, and I slid down her steep back yard in the snow. In the summer, I picked chives from her garden and soaked her deck with water while watering her hundreds of plants. My brothers and I picked blackberries frequently from the lot next to her house.

Grandma loved to update me on the antics of my cousins and the trials of my uncles and aunts. She'd take me into her confidence saying, "Now don't tell so and so that I told you this…" as she shared. She treated me as the adult I was struggling to be.

I learned to drive in her car (she had the only automatic in the family at the time). I helped her bake for Christmas and every other holiday. We sat in the two rocking chairs at her house and read books for hours. I wrote to her if I was gone for the summer and visited her first thing after returning home.

Always when I visited, we took a break at 1:00 p.m. to watch her favorite afternoon show (she told me all about who the original characters were on the show, how things had changed, etc.). Then at 7:00 p.m. we'd watch her favorite game show. She would lean forward in her chair so that she could see it better, and I would repeat the lines when she couldn't hear it. Then I got to choose a program, and after that, we would go to bed at the same time, making me feel very much like an adult. I hugged her goodnight, and then headed off to the cozy, all-blue bedroom across the hall (where I slept with the door open and the hall light on).

Eventually, the time came when she couldn't see well enough to sew anymore. I know she missed that. She talked of sewing and asked about my projects. She watched more TV than in the past, as it helped with the loneliness. She didn't cook very much and rarely went out anywhere. It even hurt her eyes to read too much, which disappointed her, as well. Every time I visited, her Bible, a paperback book, and the week's crossword puzzle were nearby, along with a lighted magnifying glass that increased the print size when she placed it over the pages.

I was a teen and was too busy to visit as much as I used to, but we still connected as much as we could. She was getting older, and although I wouldn't admit it for the world and didn't like to think about it, I knew in my heart that I wouldn't have her forever, and it made me sad. I visited her as much as I could within the restrictions of a teen's school, church, work, and activity schedule.

When I was 18, Grandma had her last Christmas with us. As I opened my gift, chiding her for getting me anything at all on a fixed income, I was speechless when I saw a beautiful, blue (my favorite color) flannel nightgown in the box. Looking closer, I saw large, crooked stitches. She had sewn it herself, with orange thread, in a labor of love that must have taken hours.

I thought it was sweet of her. I also thought, *Grandma, I'm a teenager now. I am not going to wear a flannel nightgown.* I didn't quite understand what she was thinking, and I really wondered about her choice of orange thread with light blue flannel (she'd trained me better than that). But the nightgown was special, and I kept it folded within the tissue and box she had wrapped it in and placed it carefully in my cedar chest. I never wore it.

As an adult now, I understand more. The orange thread was because she couldn't see blue thread that matched the material. She'd sewn it all by hand because she was unable to sit at the sewing machine and see well enough to operate it. And why she did it? Because she had always meant to fulfill my request. She may have known that she didn't have a lot of time left. She certainly knew that she couldn't sew well anymore. But I had always wanted a flannel nightgown. In her mind, that is all that mattered. My grandma was faithful to the promise she felt she'd made to me, in spite of the extreme difficulty it must have been for her.

It makes me sad, yet happy, when I look at it now. That flannel nightgown is one of my most prized possessions. I'm sad because my grandma once had the most precise stitching in the world and it is stitched so crooked. It's almost as if we switched sewing skills along the way. *My* stitches were supposed to be the large, crooked ones, not hers.

I am also happy because every stitch was created with so much love in her heart for me. Did it hurt her pride to sew something like that? It must have. She was a strong, proud, and confident woman. And if so, how much more it means that she gave it to me. Fulfilling a promise to complete that nightgown for me was more important than turning out a project that was perfect in every way.

In June that year, I graduated from high school and left home to go to school in Oregon. By that fall, I had decided to participate in a summer mission trip to Alaska for the next summer and began raising funds to go. I was excited about the opportunity and threw my heart into the fundraising and planning. I talked to many people at our church to raise support, sent out letters, saved my own money, and did everything I could think of to raise the amount needed. Grandma even donated funds and scolded me two or three times as I tried to give it back to her. But in the end, I was still a few hundred short of the amount needed to go on the trip and had no hope of coming up with the remaining funds.

A few months later, my mom called me to come home to Grandma's bedside in the hospital to say goodbye. My older brother had flown home from Chicago and was there, as well. When Grandma realized that we were both there, having traveled from other states, she said that we were taking her hospital stay much too seriously.

How could I really say goodbye when she didn't even realize that she was going? Goodbyes were supposed to be mutual and understood by both people. So I hugged her and told her that I loved her. When she asked why I was there, I told her that I just wanted to see her. And then my brother and I went out into the hallway and cried. She'd been so convincing that we were being too serious that later that night I questioned what I had been told and asked my dad if the doctors were sure she was dying.

After her death, my parents sat down with my brothers and me and told us that they wanted us to have a part of the inheritance left to my dad. They would be bestowing on each of us exactly the amount of money that I was short to pay for my mission trip. This was definitely what my grandma would have wanted me to use it for, a summer spent increasing my own faith and the lessons of life and God.

My dad was surprised, when cleaning out her house, to find an extensive prayer and devotional journal that she had updated regularly. Her Bible was near her bed and had passages underlined in many places. "I didn't realize," he said, "that she was such a woman of faith."

Grandma's spiritual walk with God was quiet. But her faith was very evident. It was evident in everything she did, in everything she accomplished, and in the fulfillment of promises that she didn't have to keep.

5

With Faith, Nothing Is Impossible

A Tale Of Two Sidewalks

By Maria Garriott
Towson, Maryland

Carneal Means was dying.

Lying on the sidewalk in front of Baltimore's rundown Westport housing project, he felt his life oozing out of a massive gunshot wound in his back. His breath came out in short gasps and then hung in the bitter November air. He thrashed his head from side to side looking for help but saw nothing in the pitch dark; dealers had shot out the streetlights. He tried to move his left arm, twisted awkwardly behind his back. But he couldn't. He couldn't move his legs either.

At 1:00 that morning, the familiar compulsion to get high had driven him to the projects to buy crack cocaine. For nearly eight years crack had possessed Carneal. For more than 20 years he had been addicted to alcohol, as well.

His regular dealer had left for the night, but another dealer offered his wares. Carneal saw the drugs were tainted and refused to buy. Angry words flew between the two men. Suddenly the dealer pulled a sawed-off shotgun from his coat. Carneal looked down the dark barrel wordlessly and turned to run. At point-blank range, the dealer pulled the trigger.

"I heard the boom, an overwhelming sound. I didn't feel anything at first. My ears hurt more than my back. Then I felt an intense, cold, numbing pain, like Novocain all through my back," he said.

In the first of several divine coincidences, police in a patrol car parked around the corner heard the shots. Soon two uniformed men stood over Carneal grilling him.

"Who did it? Which way did he go?"

Carneal described his assailant. The numbness faded, replaced by a searing pain that arced through his back. Carneal begged the policemen to end his life.

"Just do it!" he cried out. "Finish me off! Get it over with!"

The police refused, and Carneal felt himself slipping away, fading out of consciousness. His thoughts turned to God.

"I knew I was dying," Carneal says. "And I knew there was no coming back. I cried out to God to forgive me, not to let it end like this. I didn't bargain with Him—it was just an honest cry. I had never done that before."

He remembered his sister, who had been talking to him about Christ, telling him that God would help him get clean. He knew his death would bring his family unrelenting pain, and this grieved him. He asked God to comfort them.

"They would know that I died a low-life addict in a dope hole," Carneal recalls. "Even in death I would be a burden—they would have to spend their money burying me, knowing I was a crackhead."

Carneal slipped into a coma. Doctors at the University of Maryland Hospital's Shock Trauma Center did not expect him to last the week and told his parents to make funeral arrangements.

But 30 days later, Carneal regained consciousness.

His prognosis was still guarded. Miraculously, the bullet had not severed his spinal cord. But it had ricocheted through his abdomen, damaging vital organs. Doctors performed numerous surgeries, finally leaving Carneal's abdomen a massive open wound.

"It seemed like every day something would fail or become infected. The doctors got tired of opening me up and closing me," Carneal recalls. "So they just decided to leave my wound open. They had my organs in a bag lying on the bed next to me and plastic covering the opening on my chest and abdomen.

Later, even when he began to heal, doctors told him he would never walk unassisted again. But Carneal refused to accept this. He kept trying to stand up without buckling, to walk the few steps to the bathroom before crumpling in a heap.

"I was a big pain to those nurses. They would find me on the floor where I'd fallen, holler at me, call me hardheaded," he says. Physical therapy was excruciating, but he refused to quit.

Finally he began standing up without falling, and eventually he could walk a few steps with a walker. Carneal persisted, graduating from a walker to a cane.

"When I got on a cane, they couldn't tell me nothing," he laughs. "That was God!"

Three months after the shooting he came home from the hospital. But old habits quickly surfaced.

"All I wanted was a cold beer," Carneal says. "I hated doing drugs. But I loved my beer. I wanted to relax with a cold beer after a day at work like a normal person."

Carneal walked to a bar, drank half a can of Colt 45, and was blindsided by an overwhelming compulsion to get high on crack.

"It hit me like a ton of bricks," he says. He hobbled down the street with his can, looking for crack. He found it.

"I got high that night. I realized I was an addict—that I had to get help." The next morning he began calling around to find a drug treatment program.

While in a short-term program, Carneal faced not only his crack addiction but also his alcoholism. He had begun drinking in high school, and alcohol had ruined his military career.

"I was a hopeless, homeless drunk and cocaine addict for 23 years. When you went downtown and saw people sleeping outside, that was me," Carneal recalls.

Terrified of using again, Carneal sought help. He entered a long-term rehab program, but the recidivism rate of many of his fellow addicts struck fear into his heart.

"Every time I turned around, one of the guys—even the counselors—was going back on drugs. I kept asking, 'What's going to keep me from using again?'"

His counselor offered no easy answers, saying only, "That's between you and God." His sister continued to pray for him and visit him, telling him that Christ would help him stay off drugs. He began to listen, to consider embracing this faith in Christ that had transformed his sister's life. Miraculously, at some point in his recovery process, God took away Carneal's compulsion to get high.

"People are always asking me what I did to get clean. I can't answer that—I did nothing," Carneal admits. "This is a God thing. It's not up to me. I know that God has taken away the compulsion for alcohol and drugs."

Carneal decided he should take his sister's advice and find a spiritual home. He visited several neighborhood churches but felt uncomfortable in each.

Then one Saturday afternoon, as he walked to the liquor store to buy a lottery ticket, he saw a strange mix of people in the neighborhood playground. Instead of the usual men drinking, loitering, and dealing drugs, people—young and old, black, white, and Asian—were serving hot dogs, grilling hamburgers, and listening to a speaker. Children lined up in little cliques to get their faces painted with stars, teddy bears, and rainbows.

A local church, Faith Christian Fellowship, had taken over the park for its annual Community Chill, an outreach event. He liked the racial mix. Not since his days in the military had he seen blacks, whites, and Asians working together. As he stood on the sidewalk and listened, one of the church members approached him and struck up a conversation. He found

Christine—a white, Vanderbilt-educated physician—easy to talk to. A few moments later the pastor strolled up and introduced himself.

"He didn't look like a pastor to me," Carneal remembers. "I was used to pastors being stern-looking and authoritative. He wasn't preaching at me—just talking about God."

Carneal listened to a speaker talk to the crowd about knowing Jesus and following Him. He wanted to hear more. In his heart, faith stirred. He wanted what his sister had. He wanted what these people had. He wanted to know Jesus.

Carneal hung around the park and even helped clean up. The next morning he attended services at the church. He found the sense of Christian community irresistible. "Like a family," he notes, "this was a for-real house of God."

The fledgling faith in Carneal's heart burst into bloom. That afternoon he returned to the church for a four-hour seminar. He joined one of Faith's small home Bible studies and met with another man weekly to pray and study the Bible.

As Carneal grew spiritually, he began to serve in the church, becoming head usher and co-leader of a home Bible study. He volunteered in the church's tutoring and sports programs for neighborhood children.

Carneal believes that God spared his life and planted the seed of faith in his heart. The only residual effect from his near-execution—a long scar stretching from below his collarbone to his groin—reminds him of God's mercy. "Every time I remove my shirt, it's a daily reminder," he says. "I'm not supposed to be here."

To help others break free from drug addiction, Carneal provides strategic leadership in the church's efforts to open a faith-based neighborhood drug treatment center—an overwhelming need in a city with over 60,000 addicts. His goal is to see lives transformed—not only by freedom from addiction—but also by a personal faith in Jesus Christ. His life shouts out the words of Jesus: *"If you hold to My teaching, you are really My disciples. Then you will know the truth, and the truth will set you free."* John 8:31(b)-32

Close Encounter Of The Spiritual Kind

By Catherine B. Laska
Wausau, Wisconsin

"I'll tell you about the safari when I get back unless I get eaten by a lion first," were words meant to be a joke to alleviate my parent's fears—but it was a joke that came all too close to becoming reality on that night of December 18, 1996—a night I will never forget!

I had volunteered in Kenya, Africa, for three months at an HIV orphanage. I was now at midpoint and knew I wanted to see something of Africa before leaving. I was told a tenting safari to Masai-Mara, a large reserve in Kenya, would be the least expensive and best way to view the wildlife of Africa. Most importantly, we would be well protected by a Masai watchman. Masai tribesmen are known to enter manhood by killing lions with their bare hands or spears.

December 17 came quickly. I met my driver, Patrick, and five traveling companions, and we loaded up our bags in the safari van with food and water essentials for the six-hour trip through the Rift Valley. It was rugged and tiring, yet adventurous and exciting.

Arriving at camp around 3:30 p.m., we were greeted by our Masai host, two cooks, and our watchman. Six small tents awaited the arrival of tenants for the next two nights and three days. My tent, furthest back and in the middle, had a makeshift shower and toilet 15 feet behind, surrounded by tall grass and bushes of different kinds with open reserve one mile away.

Settling into our tents, we rested a while before going on an evening drive that was new and fascinating. Three hours of viewing zebras, wilderbeest, and other species of wildlife in their natural habitat, combined with the fresh air and the vastness of nothing but land for miles, left me exhilarated! We arrived back at camp around 7:00 p.m. and were quickly lured in by the aroma of freshly cooked stew. We settled in under a tent for an evening of dining, relaxation, and conversation. Stars illuminating the night sky slowly vanished as rain fell upon us. David, our host, had been going to tell stories of his people and their traditions around a campfire that was now doused.

Disappointed, we ventured to our tents for a good night's sleep in the hopes that the next night would be clear and we could hear the stories then. As I was falling into a deep sleep, I clearly heard the songs of exotic native birds, and I couldn't wait to hear more sounds of the wild tomorrow!

Again morning came early. This was to be a full day of reserve driving, taking in species of wildlife not yet seen, with natural surprises of cheetah attacks on zebras and lions feasting on a large animal carcass we could no longer distinguish. The day passed, and as it did, the extreme heat turned to a cool breeze as the sun beautifully set in the distance. Time quickly passed by as we journeyed toward camp, our minds filled with peaceful, quiet reflections of the experiences of the day.

As it had the night before, the aroma of food greeted our arrival and lifted our spirits, and the campfire beckoned us to embrace its warmth under the night stars. Now in the silence and total darkness—except for the small fire and the stars above—we became attentive to the sounds of the reserve and listened to stories about the life of the Masai people and their culture. This was the night of the 18th. David spoke about his people and tradition, interrupted by sounds from the distance. His keen ears distinguished and identified various animal sounds for us.

The hour was getting late and the fire dying out. David, ending his story, put his finger against his lips, motioning for silence. With gleaming eyes, he said, "Listen! That is the sound of a leopard. That is the grunt of a lion, and I can't tell the last one." It sounded to be from an enormous animal, yet the lion's grunt sounded fiercest.

By now it was well after 10:00 p.m., and David suggested returning to our tents to sleep, since we would have a 6:00 a.m. wake-up call in the morning.

While gathering up blankets and flashlights, and blinded by the night, I asked David how close the lions were. His calm response: "Don't worry." When I asked again, he answered, "They aren't that close. When they come off the reserve at night, lions hunt for food below camp taking a cow from the Masais, so don't worry!"

Somewhat comforted, I cautiously advanced toward my tent, my small flashlight leading the way, my ears still attentive to the sounds of the wild. Entering my abode, I searched my sleeping bag for unwanted creatures resting there for the night. Satisfied that I was alone, I turned down the tent flaps and turned out the last bit of light and found myself surrounded by total darkness and the still grunting noise of a lion somewhere in the night as I drifted off to sleep.

I awoke from a shallow sleep four hours later, my body chilled by the night's breath, and I could hear the lion's grunt closer to me than ever before. I needed to use the facilities behind my tent, and my heart pumped faster and harder as I heard the grunt become louder and more consistent. As fear began to close in, I made the crucial decision to step out of the tent, risking whatever might be waiting for me.

Tuned in to my surroundings, I picked up my flashlight, unzipped the tent, and stepped into the darkness, recalling the way as an immediate right and straight ahead. Nervously walking about four feet, flashlight low, I then became totally confused and turned around. Frustrated, I returned to my tent and decided to wake up the watchman who seemed miles away. Flashing my light towards his area, I called out with a whispering, broken voice so as not to disturb the others or alert the roaming lion.

The watchman came to my tent, spear in one hand and lantern in the other, and walked me to the facility, then stood six feet back. The watchman returned me safely to my tent, and I glanced at my watch: 4:15 a.m. and still not much sleep. Cold and nervous, I crawled back into my sleeping bag that lay on a small cot within the tent. As my heart beat fast, my ears tuned to the lion's grunt, I fell into a shallow sleep.

But not for long! Suddenly what I feared most had come to pass! I awoke to the sound of a lion grunting in my right ear, nothing separating us aside from the thin tent canvas. My heart beat faster, and I became numb shivering from chest down.

As the lion encircled my tent several times with another lion not far off grunting to its companion, I knew without a doubt that I was to be its next victim!

As I lay motionless in fear and wondering when and where its jaws would grab me, a voice inside me spoke saying, "Cathy, be still and pray that God will protect you and allow you to see another day!" Praying that prayer over and over silently, I must have finally passed out. I awoke to Patrick's call for a 6:00 a.m. drive.

Relieved that I had lived to see another day, I questioned Patrick and David. David was sweating as he mumbled, "This has never happened before!" In a serious voice, Patrick added, "The watchman had seen the lion by the shower ready to attack."

Then it dawned on me. My confusion on the path had been God's first protection for me. Had I continued the few feet down the path past the shower alone, I would have been attacked. (I was told earlier that one lion will not attack two humans.)

God confirmed His protection of me a second time by placing an invisible spiritual barrier around my tent that the lion could not break through to reach me, and then allowed me to pass out.

The impact became even more powerful when a safari companion told the story of a man and woman researching at another reserve the previous week. The man had turned in early when no more than 15 minutes later a lion approached the tent, tore it to shreds, and dragged the man out by the head, killing him instantaneously.

Not only have I experienced God's protection, but I now know the power of prayer more intently. My sister in Wisconsin and a friend in Atlanta later told me they were both awakened by the Holy Spirit at the same time and date of the incident. God told them to get up and pray for me, as my life was in serious danger.

I had read the Scripture in 1 Peter 5:8 many times: *Be self-controlled and alert. Your enemy the devil prowls around like a roaring lion looking for someone to devour.*

I had always imagined and tried to feel the meaning, the intensity, and seriousness of this Scripture—but now I know from personal experience.

Love Without End

By Donna Schlachter
Denver, Colorado

"Excuse me." Hand in hand, walking along the waterfront, enjoying the crisp autumn air, we were sharing old memories and creating new ones when the woman spoke to us. Stopping dead in our tracks, we turned to face her. "You two look like newlyweds. I'm doing interviews for the Women's Television Network for a program about newlyweds and how they met. Would you mind taking a few minutes to tell me how you met?" she said.

Would we mind? Would we mind? We'd been excitedly telling our story for the past year to any and all who would listen. It was a story full of drama, excitement, romance, a broken heart, the Internet, and, of course, faith. Faith that God was able to overcome time and distance. That He was able to do what we had not been able to accomplish on our own. That He wanted to give us the desires of our heart.

"Sure," my husband, Patrick, answered quickly, ever eager to share our story and always looking for an opportunity to brag on our God. "What do you want to know?"

"Where did you meet? How long have you been married? Is this your honeymoon?" she replied, checking some notes in her hand as she held the microphone toward us.

"We met on the Internet." he said simply. I smiled, already anticipating her response.

"Really? How?" was her astonished reply.

I could see Patrick was really warming up to this now. We always wanted to share the story of our individual searches for a spouse. Patrick began with his side of the tale.

"After my divorce, I told God I wanted Him to find my next wife for me, since I had made such a mess of my first two marriages. After about 10 years, I kinda felt like God wasn't that interested in finding my wife, so I started looking again. I joined a Christian single's club on the Internet. I got a couple of replies, but they seemed to always lose interest after the second or third e-mail. Then I spent $1,200 to join a local single's club, filled out a three-page profile, and got no response. I met a few women at functions, but once we got a chance to talk, they drifted away. Although I made it clear in my profile that I was seeking a Godly wife who loved Jesus, no one seemed to take that seriously.

"Finally, I said to God, 'Lord, I want You to find me a wife like You found one for Isaac.' If you remember the story in the Bible, Isaac's father, Jacob, sent a servant to find a wife for Isaac and bring her to him. So that's what I did. I sat back for more than a year and waited for God to work it out."

I could see that Patrick had caught her attention with his part of the story, and so I picked up right where he left off.

"During this time, I went on vacation at Christmas to visit my dad and step-mom, and she asked me what kind of a man I was looking for. I told her, 'A Godly, Christian man, active in his church, who wants to teach me how to live for God.' She pressed me about other attributes like height, hair color, and so on, but I said, 'That's it. The rest doesn't matter.'

"When I came home from vacation, my computer had been fried in an electrical storm. I replaced the computer, getting one with a modem. I decided to get on the Internet to look for Christian web sites, and I found the Christian Singles Network. I signed in, paid my money, and posted my ad. I got a few responses over the next couple of weeks, but most weren't interested when they found out I lived in Eastern Canada. Still, I kept believing God had a husband for me, and that He was able to overcome time and distance to bring us together.

"I got a reply from one guy, and things seemed to be going along fine. At the same time, I decided to send out a few e-mails of my own. One ad I found wasn't like any of the others. It said one thing, 'Seeking Godly wife who loves Jesus above all else.' I thought that sounded interesting, so I e-mailed even though I knew nothing else except his occupation and city. This was really taking a big step for me. All of the other profiles went into a lot of detail, and I was avoiding divorced men who smoked or drank and were into golf, fishing, or darts. I may have been trusting God to bring me my husband, but I wasn't going to find Him a candidate who wouldn't meet my expectations!"

By this time we saw the reporter smiling, nodding her head, encouraging us to continue with the story. We were giving her way more than she really needed. Or were we?

I continued, "I got an e-mail back from Patrick. Nothing serious, just interest. So we started e-mailing. In about the third or fourth e-mail, he mentioned daughters from his second marriage. *Divorced! Twice!* I thought, *No way. This won't work. But he sounds nice, so maybe he can be a good friend.* So we continued e-mailing.

"Then this first guy I was e-mailing started calling, and we'd talk for hours. He said all sorts of nice things, leading me on. When I suggested maybe we should meet, he got feet so cold that he probably got frostbite! So I started crying on Patrick's shoulder about this guy. Can you imagine me doing that, crying about how another guy had broken my heart? To me, Patrick was still just a friend. Then he e-mailed me and said, 'I don't need to know the answers, but you need to ask yourself three questions: What do you talk about with this guy? Where does he go to church? What does he do when he isn't working?' I already knew the answers, and I realized I didn't like them: I don't talk; he talks—about himself. He doesn't go to church; he goes home every weekend to see his parents and get some home cooking. He doesn't have any friends—just works and watches TV. Then God showed me the answers to the same questions about Patrick: We talked about God. He goes to a good church (he had sent me tapes). He has friends (I talked to them on the phone), he square dances, he goes to church and church-related activities. I liked these answers a whole lot more."

"Then what?" she asked, as eager as a child to get to the happy ending she just knew had to be coming.

"I realized Patrick was the man God had picked out. It's amazing, once you make the decision to let God take control, just how easy it is to go along with the solution."

Patrick continued, "Within a month, God had provided the money for me to buy a plane ticket for her to come meet me. Since we had to wait three weeks from the time we booked the ticket until we met, we had lots of time to talk. We were on the phone up to eight hours a day. We spent a small fortune on long distance calls. But it was worth it, because it was our courtship. We talked more in that time than most dating couples would talk in a year. And I knew that I didn't want her to get on the plane to go home, so we had time to plan for her to stay. She sold everything she had."

"And he leased an apartment for me to live in until we got married. He arranged with his pastor for me to stay with them for a while. He told his daughters that he had met a woman who was coming to be his wife. He thinks I was the one who stepped out on a limb, but I think he was very brave," I added.

"The only real obstacle to us getting married was that we wanted the approval of my pastor first," Patrick said.

"I was scared to death. I mean, this pastor practically held my life in his hands. I didn't know whether I needed to study for a test or fall on my knees before him and plead for mercy!"

"What happened when you met the pastor for the first time?" the reporter asked.

"He was wonderful. Set me at ease. I was nearly drunk with relief when he said he saw no reason why we shouldn't get married," I answered.

"So we got married a month later. That was 15 months ago," Patrick said, bringing our story to an end. We could see we had given this woman much more than she had asked for, so we bid our farewells and resumed our waterfront stroll, fairly confident that this was not the kind of story the network was looking for. But somehow, we knew that it was the kind of story this woman needed to hear. And it was the kind of story we needed to hear, too, to be reminded that we serve a God Who works with our small measure of faith to bring about the completion of His plan.

We have now been married more than five years. And we still love to tell the story of our new beginning. Of a love that didn't really begin until after we were married, because we didn't have time to 'fall in love,' as the world knows it. We knew that we loved each other because God had picked us out for each other. We knew that God was in it, right from the very start. If He hadn't been, how could two people from opposite ends of the continent be brought together like this? We were both in love with God, and that love transferred to the other person.

But now for the rest of the story: When Patrick signed on with the Christian Singles Network, there was a 90-day free membership. During that time, Patrick made the commitment to God that he would leave it in God's hands to find a wife. As a result, when the 90 days were done, he refused to pay any money to keep his ad on the Internet, knowing that the ad would be removed. In fact, he thought it had been removed, since he didn't get any more responses. Until I found that unique, two-line ad: "Seeking Godly wife who loves Jesus above all else." That was over a year later! When we went to check the ad again after we were married, it was gone from the website.

Waiting On Faith

By Abigail M. Tatem
Neptune Beach, Florida

Driving to work that morning was like any other day of the week. The sun was starting to rise over the beautiful Boulder Flatirons, leaving the sky a happy lavender color. The air was cool, but not uncomfortable. There was no indication, no warning, of what was about to change my life. No bells or whistles, no thunderclap for a sign, just sudden and unadulterated change.

Driving to work that nondescript morning, the sun was extremely intense. Maybe it was the sun or maybe she was thinking of the hundreds of projects she needed to complete by the end of the week, but whatever the case, the full-sized 1989 van she was driving that morning never made it to Boulder Community Hospital where she was scheduled to work.

Three days later the remains of the van were found in a crevasse by a road crew looking for a nice shady place to have their lunch break. Inside the mangled shell of the once mighty vehicle, they found the woman trapped by the steering column.

Weeks later she told me of the ordeal and that her faith in God and her family are the only reasons she didn't die in the single vehicle collision.

The sun was extremely bright that day, and along the 30-mile stretch of wooded road to Boulder, a very large buck had run out in front of her and collided with the van, causing her to lose control. In her terror, she over corrected and rolled the van several times before it crashed to the bottom of a deep ravine where it was completely hidden by dense foliage.

She told me her first coherent thought was about her family. Unable to remember the events leading up to the crash, she began to scream for her children.

Then after hearing no response, she examined her situation more closely. Something wet and warm dripped from her hands and face—a disgusting mixture of coffee and blood. She wasn't in a great deal of pain, but she knew she needed medical attention and quickly.

After cutting her way loose from the seatbelt that was later reported to have saved her life, the reality of the accident sank in. There was no way she could escape; she was trapped in the van by the steering column. At some point during the accident, the entire front end of the vehicle had engulfed her legs, pinning her to the chair.

Exhaustion soon set in from screaming for help. No one knew where she was, and no one could see her from the road. The van was her tomb, and she was going to die unless she received a miracle.

Two cold, wet nights passed, and the woman was still alone. The dawn of the third day broke with a new hope that she would be rescued and returned to her family. But as the day grew later, her hope was fading and the shear desperateness of the situation was starting to drive her crazy. And then, just as suddenly as the accident had happened, she heard two men talking. Crying out for help in an almost inaudible voice, the woman knew her prayers had been answered and that these men were sent from God.

It took almost six hours to remove the woman from the wreckage and another three before I was contacted. When the phone rang that night, I knew someone had found my mother.

She was weak, but incredibly grateful, when I finally made it to her side at the hospital—the same hospital she was supposed to work at three days before.

My mom was always the pillar of strength in our family, and she continued to be so even through this tragic accident. She knew that if she died, the family—our family—would die, too. A devout woman, she had faith that God wouldn't let her final days be like this. She had faith that her family was searching desperately to find her.

She had faith, an indescribable belief, that she held onto so strongly that no matter how hard her body wanted to die, her spirit wouldn't allow that to happen. Her faith guided her through hell and back. Few people can claim to have been through anything more trying, both physically and emotionally, than my mother.

Her faith is guiding her still. The doctors insisted my mother would never walk again and not to hope for miracles, but she laughed, saying she was already granted one miracle and that she had faith in herself and that God wouldn't keep her in a wheelchair at her son's wedding. She was going to walk down the aisle under her own power, and there wasn't any question about that. Now, almost two years later, my mother is learning to walk again.

With the wedding less than six months away, I see my mother working toward her goal every day. She is getting stronger and more capable of the movements. Seeing her work so hard gives me faith in her. I know after what she has survived that if she wants to walk, she will learn to run. She will dance again and skip and be able to ride a bike. I have faith in that. It is something that I can't explain, but when I tell people I have faith that my mother will accomplish everything she wants to, everyone understands.

I have more faith in myself, as well. My mom is 52 years old and undaunted by the tasks that loom before her. If she can be so strong, so courageous—I can, too. My everyday problems can't compare with hers or with most of the world's, but knowing that she could survive, I know that I can.

I find myself taking more risks—good risks—and trying harder than I ever have before because she has faith that I will succeed. Faith has changed our lives forever and given my family an undeniable strength in ourselves and each other.

Faith, The Evidence Of Things Not Seen

By Nancy Arant Williams
Stover, Missouri

I woke up that day wishing I hadn't. Too many heartaches, for too long a time, had left me reeling, and even God hadn't helped me escape. Wasn't He listening anymore? If He had been, He would have let me die.

Growing up in the church wasn't hard; living life was hard. For some reason, the messages I received growing up made me think that if I did everything right—got my spiritual ducks in a row—that God would, like magic, take care of the outcome. But it hadn't worked out that way.

That day, I decided I finally had enough. If God wouldn't take me home, I'd get there myself, by hook or by crook. I already had a plan; it had germinated earlier when all I wanted was for the pain to stop.

From the beginning, I knew suicide wasn't the answer. And for most of my life, I never even considered it. For most of my life, I couldn't even identify with depression or sadness, but I could now. Its taste was bitter on my tongue.

That day I got up feeling somewhat better because relief was now in sight. I carefully dressed, put on makeup, and fixed my hair—had to go out in style, of course.

For some reason I pulled out my Bible. I had read it before, and although I had contemplated its Word for comfort, particularly the Psalms, it somehow failed to penetrate to my marrow. One last time I opened again to Psalms. David, in his heartache, so often described me when he spoke. Now there was a man I could relate to.

I opened to chapter 107, and verses 26 through 29. *They mounted up to the heavens and went down to the depths; in their peril their courage melted away. They reeled and staggered like drunken men; they were at their wits' end. Then they cried out to the Lord in their trouble, and He brought them out of their distress.*

Verse 35 continued: *He turned the desert into pools of water and the parched ground into flowing springs; there He brought the hungry to live, and they founded a city where they could settle. They sowed fields and planted vineyards that yielded a fruitful harvest; He blessed them, and their numbers greatly increased, and He did not let their herds diminish. Then their numbers decreased, and they were humbled by oppression, calamity and sorrow; He who pours contempt on nobles made them wander in a trackless waste. But He lifted the needy out of their affliction and increased their families like flocks.*

I begged you a million times to lift me up, Lord, and yet You never answered. Why should I believe You now?

I opened my mouth, and out came those very words. I said, "What makes this time any different, Lord? Why should I believe You now?"

As I walked out the door and slid into my car, I glanced around for the very last time. A lone sparrow tugged and pulled at a worm, finally yanking it from the ground and flying off. I knew just how that sparrow felt, but my tugging never ceased. I was worn out with tugging.

With my hands resting on the steering wheel, my eyes took in my surroundings. Though it was fall, the most beautiful time of year to me, I struggled, knowing it also ushered in the dismal, gray skies of winter. But if everything worked out, I wouldn't have to worry about another winter.

The massive oaks in my yard were turning a peachy pink and salmon, a most amazing hue. I could hardly tear my eyes away. They filled, suddenly, with tears. All around me I could see evidence of Your hand. If it was so clearly felt in nature, why couldn't I feel it, too?

Sick of myself and shaking my head, I started the car and pulled into traffic. Funny, though, how I ended up at my designated place with no memory of getting there.

The park where I sat was a tapestry of color as light danced with darkness among the loosening leaves. Beams of sunlight streamed through the trees and spot lit the damp earth. The smell of burning leaves tore through my consciousness and brought back memories of rakes, damp soil, and flying leaps into heaping piles of crackling leaves in the chill breeze of November. My senses overflowed at the interplay of memory, movement, textures, and colors.

It was all so beautiful. So why did I still feel so bad?

Fatigue crept between my shoulder blades, and I knew it was tension. I didn't really want to die.

I felt, before I heard, the rushing vibration of the train. Unable to see it yet, I turned on the ignition and pulled the car to where I would easily drive into its path—taking the coward's way out. Surely there had to be another way. But if so, what was it?

I thought about the engineer. I could easily put myself in another's shoes, feeling his pain, thinking his thoughts, identifying with his routines, and today I thought about that engineer—how he had taken his lunch pail in his hand, kissed his wife goodbye, and waved as he drove off to work like every other day in his life. Only today would be different, because today *I* would cause him pain. He would see my car in the distance, at the crossing, and he would assume I would be long past before he approached the intersection. But he would be wrong. And by the time he figured out what was happening, it would be too late to stop.

I could see his face contorting, feel his grief when he realized he and his behemoth would be the instrument of my death. I could feel him huff in a gasp of air as he whispered, "Hurry! Move! You still have time to get out of the way."

But he would know. He had heard it from other engineers, but until today, it had never happened to him. He had hoped to escape that specter forever. But I had singled him out. In my grief, I had chosen him to help me stop the pain. In the instant, my heart ached for him.

Once invisible, the metal monster was now on the horizon and growing in size. From a tiny pinhead in the distance, it grew rapidly as it bore down in my direction.

I was ready. I took a deep breath and put the car into gear, ready to inch forward onto the tracks.

All of a sudden, I wasn't alone. I glanced at the seat next to me and saw nothing, but I felt the presence of someone warm and caring, and I knew immediately, God, that You were there. You settled into the space, filling every inch with heat and light.

I burst into tears. I could feel You wrap Your arms around me, just in the nick of time. But where had You been all this time? Where were You when I called for help before? In my pain, I had heard only defeating silence when I called, but now, at long last, I was not alone.

Sobbing, I said, "Lord, how could You still want me? I've got nothing to offer but scars, pain, and ashes. Broken pieces. Worthless. What do You see in me?"

The voice wasn't audible, but my soul heard every word, every inflection of voice, as You whispered, "You are mine. Bought with a price. Why would I go to all that trouble if I had no intention of making You gold? Of taking every shattered piece and every bottled tear and making you a new creation, equipping you to fulfill My plan for you. And I do have a plan for you, a future and a hope, beyond your wildest dreams, if you'll just rest in Me."

The locomotive loomed over our heads, its shadow abruptly darkening the space between the sun and us. And suddenly, I didn't want to die anymore. I wanted to live, to give the engineer back his day and his hope and his life. I wanted him to go home to his wife, hug her, and smile at the end of this long day. I would give him that gift.

As I backed away from the tracks and turned my car around, I could scarcely see for the flood of tears. The sounds coming from me were groans like those from a wounded animal,close to death.

But I wasn't dying. I was being resurrected. I could feel the touch of Your hand on my soul, and I knew You had already begun to heal me, and for the first time in years, a tiny seed of hope sprang to life in my heart. And I smiled.

A tiny seed of faith sprouted up next to it, and I knew You would tenderly water and feed them both, shine the warmth of love on them, and make them bloom, fragrant and lovely, if I would just grab onto You.

That day, I knew—that I knew—that I knew. You are as alive and real as I am. You are trustworthy. You are hope and joy, peace, and life. Without You, I am empty and forlorn and hopeless. But with You, I have—like that sparrow—yanked the prize from the soil of my life, lifted my wings to soar, and turned my face toward heaven.

The Faith That First Lived In Your Grandmother

By Carolyn T Reeves
Oxford, Mississippi

I had all the symptoms of being pregnant. After months of waiting, my dream of having a baby seemed to be coming true. A trip to the doctor confirmed my self-diagnosis. Everything seemed fine, but the doctor wanted me to be aware of some possible, but unlikely, problems. I barely listened I was so eager to find my husband, Jim, and tell him the good news. *We were going to have a baby! My parents were going to have two grandchildren only months apart.*

My sister would have her first baby. A few months later there would be another addition to the family. The two children would probably grow up together and be good friends.

Mother's eyes filled with tears as I told her the good news. She knew how badly I wanted a baby. She was thrilled at the prospect of another grandchild, but she was even happier to see her oldest daughter so elated.

It was already spring, and I could easily teach until school was out in May. I needed to tell my principal to find another teacher for next year. It would be hard living on Jim's teaching salary, but we'd manage by being careful.

I ate, walked, and rested exactly as instructed. I tried to imagine my baby's appearance each week as he gained more maturity. We selected and discarded volumes of names trying to find the one name our baby would wear. A baby shower for my sister left me tingling with excitement at the prospect of the new babies.

It was the next night when I noticed light bleeding. A friend's pregnancy had been marked with several episodes of light bleeding, ending in a full-term, healthy baby, so I wasn't greatly alarmed at first, but a sickening fear replaced my confidence as the bleeding became more profuse. Mother came over and rode to the hospital with us to meet the doctor. He decided to keep me overnight since we lived 30 miles away. Our hopes were revived the next day when the bleeding subsided and the pregnancy test came back positive.

I was sent home, told to stay on bed rest, and instructed to call if anything changed. I finished the school year from my bed, grading exams and assessing final averages. Plans and dreams for a baby cautiously resumed, and my list of names began to narrow. Jim and I adjusted to my confining lifestyle. *The sacrifices would be worth it when we were able to hold our little one.*

Everything seemed to be going well until I began to notice a persistent low-grade fever. When I called the doctor, he advised me to come in as soon as possible. The tone of his voice was not reassuring.

An examination confirmed our fears. I had lost the baby weeks earlier, but part of the placenta had remained attached, giving a false positive pregnancy test. Surgery was scheduled at once to rid the uterus of any remaining tissue.

Grief for the child I had lost was intense and didn't lessen quickly. It was hard to think about starting over, but it was hard not to think about anything else. Time passed while I taught school and stayed busy, but every month was a fresh disappointment. After two years of waiting, I began going to an obstetrician who specialized in fertility problems. Kind family and friends continued to assure me I'd have another baby soon.

But it was not to be. A year later I stared in disbelief at the x-ray of my fallopian tubes. During the weeks I spent on bed rest, an infection had spread to both tubes, leaving scar tissue and fusing the tubes shut. As gently as he could, the doctor told me I would not be able to get pregnant again.

Jim and I grieved together that night. It was a bitter feeling. I had been waiting so long, and now it seemed the waiting had been in vain. This must have been how the thirsty Israelites felt when they searched for three days in the desert before finding water at Marah, only to discover it was too bitter to drink. I tried to pray, but there was no confidence God would hear or care or act.

I felt hurt and depressed when I saw Mother. I knew her faith in God was strong, somehow stronger now than before her surgery and chemotherapy. At the time of her surgery, doctors had conceded that the odds of making a full recovery were not good, but two years later, she exuded peace and vibrancy. Nevertheless, her level of faith and calmness about my situation surprised me. *She thinks this is going to be all right,* I thought bitterly. I saw no reason to be optimistic. *This faith thing is making her naïve and unrealistic.*

Mother was just one of the women of faith in our family, and her deepest desire was that all of her family would be included in the circle of those who know God though the eyes of faith. My grandmothers and my mother-in-law were also godly women who walked in and lived their faith through difficult times. Maybe the hard times makes faith stronger for some people, but it sure wasn't working for me. My attempts to have faith had not changed my situation or my attitude toward God.

"We're thinking about starting the adoption process," I told her. "The doctor suggested we not wait much longer. It will be a lengthy process."

"That's a wonderful option, but don't limit your prayers," Mother said with conviction. "Make your desires known to God in prayer without fear and with thanksgiving." I knew this was a paraphrase from Philippians 4:6-7 which had become one of Mother's life verses during the past few years. While she was in surgery I had found a slip of paper with these verses written on it with a request that God would help her family to know the peace she was experiencing.

Don't you understand? I don't have any other options, I thought. I was bordering on anger at Mother for being so naïve. I was tired of hearing about how good God is, and I was coming close to accusing God of not caring about me. *How could He care about me when I was in so much pain?* A state of depression settled in with the pain of disappointment and a yearning that wouldn't go away.

It was a few months later before I realized I had all the symptoms of being pregnant again. I hesitated to go back to the doctor so soon, but a week of nausea helped convince me to see what he thought. His initial diagnosis was what I expected. He thought this was some kind of psychosomatic reaction from a desperate desire to have a baby. He was as dumbfounded as I when he told me I was definitely pregnant and everything seemed normal.

Our first baby was a girl. Her name, Marni, means the miracle of changing the bitter to sweet. The name was derived from the Biblical account of the Israelites at the bitter waters of Marah. In the midst of a desert, they accused God of leading them into the desert to die of thirst. They had no faith that He would provide a solution to their desperate need for water. Fortunately for them, Moses didn't share their faithlessness. He placed his faith in a loving, gracious God who led His people through the desert—not to let them die, but to bring them into a land of promise. He responded in faith to what God led him to do, and the result was a miracle that changed the bitter water into sweet water.

I wish I could say I was like Moses, but I wasn't. I was like the Israelites with no faith. Sometimes other people have to have faith on behalf of those who are suffering. I know now there were at least four godly women exercising faith on my behalf. There were probably others I may not know about until I reach heaven.

Mother was granted four more years to love her precious

grandchildren. Even though she didn't live to see Matthew, whose name means "a gift from God" or Jenny, whose name means "God is gracious," she left them an infinite value. All three children are now grown, and the same kind of faith that lived in their grandmother also lives in them.

My husband and I pray that someday a discerning man of God will look at our grandchildren and commend their faith as Paul commended the faith in Timothy. *I have been reminded of your sincere faith, which first lived in your grandmother Lois and in your mother Eunice and, I am persuaded, now lives in you also.* 2 Timothy 1:5

God Has A Plan

By Tonya Aldena Townsend
Middletown, Indiana

On January 6, 2000, at 4:30 p.m. my husband, John, and I were at our 12-week prenatal appointment. This was our first child together and my husband's first time at the doctor with me. Dr. Jeffrey Blake was running late due to an emergency at the hospital, and we were given the option of rescheduling our appointment. We were both very anxious and excited about our appointment, so we decided to wait for his return. John was going to see our baby for the first time during an ultrasound instead of just the pictures I had brought home from previous ultrasounds. This day was a very important and exciting day for us, but little did we know that it would end up one of the most tragic days of our lives. Even through the tragedies of life, we must always remember to hold on to our faith.

Dr. Blake returned to the office at approximately 6:30 p.m. Marilyn, my nurse, called us back into the ultrasound room, and we were prepared for Dr. Blake to come in. As we were all laughing and talking, our excitement continued to grow. Marilyn, John, and I were discussing how it still seemed so unreal that we were actually going to have a baby. Our baby was an actual miracle and blessing to us.

When I was seventeen, I had been told I would never be able to have children. This was right after my first female surgery. Numerous others had confirmed this during my three other surgeries from 1990 to 1994. I was also diagnosed with endometriosis and ovarian cysts. In 1994, we changed doctors, and that is when I met Marilyn and Dr. Blake. They did not believe that I could never have children and began working with me to figure out exactly what was going on. From 1994 to 1999, I had two more operations to help rid my body of the endometriosis, scar tissue, and ovarian cysts. Dr. Blake then suggested that we make an appointment with Dr. Jarrett, a fertility specialist in Indianapolis.

We took his suggestion and began appointments with Dr. Jarrett in January of 1999. He continued testing and could not understand why we were not conceiving. Even though my body had not been menstruating for the past eight years, all of the tests showed I had still been ovulating. He suggested we try insemination. We agreed that we would try this once, but we made it clear we had no desire and our faith in God would not permit us to go any further. When insemination did not work, we decided our faith needed to be stronger, and we turned the whole situation over to God. Two weeks later, God gave us the sign we had asked for. My body began functioning properly for the first time in eight years, and nobody could explain it; however, we knew our prayers had been answered, and this was our sign from God. Eight months and another surgery later, we finally conceived our first child. This is why January 6, 2002, was a very important day for both of us. Our little miracle was finally becoming real to us, thanks to our faith in God.

Dr. Blake entered the room and began the ultrasound. I thought he would immediately point out the baby and show everything to John, but he didn't. A few minutes went by, and I knew something was wrong. I looked at Dr. Blake and then at Marilyn and my husband, and no one was saying anything. I finally asked if everything was okay. Dr. Blake hesitated, and then with tears in his eyes, said he could not find our baby's heartbeat. He continued with the ultrasound hoping to find something but never did. Finally he stopped the ultrasound and told us both he was sorry.

I felt like I was in a dream or he had to be mistaken. I quickly realized that I was not dreaming and there was no mistake. Our baby was dead. He went on to explain that I would need a D&C, and I began to cry. John asked how this could be when just two weeks earlier everything was okay and the pictures from the ultrasound looked great. Neither Dr. Blake nor Marilyn could give us any explanation. They both hugged us and began to cry with us. They had been there for us throughout all of our hard times and uncertainty and never gave up faith that things would work out. They were as hurt and disappointed as we were. We sat there for a long time talking and then finally got ready to leave.

The appointment for the D&C was scheduled for January 10, 2000. This was the hospital's first available surgery time, and Dr. Blake wanted to determine if my body would lose the baby on its own. I was not sure I could get through the next four days knowing the baby inside of me was dead, but I did with the help of God and John.

Dr. Blake gave us a book called "Empty Arms" and told us to go home and read it right away. He said it should help us get through this tragedy and help us understand why our baby died. After we got home and told our family of our loss, I could not sleep, so I decided to read the book. It did help a bit. I felt better and understood more about what others had gone through, and also that God was still there and He would help us through this time. I truly believe that the miscarriage was supposed to happen, not to teach us a lesson or punish us for our sins, but to save us from future heartache and loss. My faith continued to grow stronger, and I continued to remember that God has a plan for us all, and we could only pray and believe that a child was in His plan.

Our faith in God helped us to understand that the loss of our child was not a punishment from God or because of our sins. Instead, we learned we must keep our faith if we ever expect our prayers to be answered. As Matthew 21:22 states, "*If you believe, you will receive whatever you ask for in prayer.*"

Miscarriages are hard to understand and very seldom are there any real answers. We have to come to believe that miscarriages occur mainly when something is physically or mentally wrong with the baby. Pam Vredevelt says, "...Miscarriages occurring early in pregnancy are thought to be due to abnormality in the fertilized egg or in the process of its implantation in the uterus" and "the fetus may be deformed because of genetic problems inherited from the parents, but more often a chance mutation or problem has occurred during fertilization or early growth of the embryo."

WebMD states, "When pregnancy tissues from miscarriages are tested, results show that genetic abnormalities cause about 50 to 60 percent of the miscarriages."

After my D&C, we thought we had lost our one and only chance to bear our own child; however, faith that God still had a plan kept us going. Much to our surprise, in mid July 2000 we discovered we had conceived for the second time. We immediately went to the doctor, and he scheduled weekly visits, including blood work and ultrasounds. He also placed me on hormones for the first three months. There was not one moment during the first 12 weeks that we did not worry about what we would find out at the next doctors' appointment, but we still kept our faith. Finally, we turned our concerns and worry over to God and told Him we would accept whatever lay ahead of us and thanked Him for this opportunity.

On March 18, 2001, at 10:47 a.m. we delivered a healthy 5 lb., 10 oz., 19 inch baby boy. He was brought into the world with his two older stepsisters, Heather and Mandy, present in the room, along with his two grandmothers, Janice and Sue; his big cousin, Alisha; and of course, his parents, Dr. Blake, and many nurses. This room was filled with God's presence and the love He shares with all of us. We named our son Blake Edward—Blake after Dr. Blake, the only doctor who never lost faith and never gave up on us, and Edward after his father.

This little boy brought us so much joy, and we are very blessed by his presence. Our faith and trust in God helped us through our first tragedy and has since blessed us with the miracle of our son. When things feel like they are spinning out of control, our faith reminds us that God is always near. We must never forget that God has a wonderful plan for each and every one of us. If we are faithful and patient, in His time, we will have everything we need.

6

Growing In Faith

A Circle Of Chairs

By Annette Argabright
Corinth, Texas

A prayer walk. I had never heard the term before, but it fascinated me. I was at a women's retreat with my church in the beautiful Rocky Mountains. Our speaker suggested we take a prayer walk during our break and pray for whatever came to mind. She said to let Jesus lead the way.

Beth and I had been friends for a while and decided to set off on our own. The mountains had always filled my soul, so it wasn't difficult to find ways of praising God on our walk. After walking for some distance, we came upon a circle of metal chairs surrounding the remains of a campfire. First I felt hurt that someone could be so callous in the forest...God's forest. We were at a resort, and Beth and I assumed that the circle was a party place used by the employees since we found the area littered with empty beer bottles and other alcoholic beverages. We prayed over the place, but felt overwhelmed at the distaste of it all.

After lunch our speaker asked if anyone would share of her experiences. I stood up and told what we found. It sparked such an interest that approximately 12 ladies joined us to investigate.

We went to find the spot again and decided to circle it as a group, then held hands and prayed and worshipped over the area. We began, a little shyly, and then broke into song. It seemed so natural to lift my face and voice to the treetops so my praise could travel to where it needed to go. Suddenly, we were no longer at a "party" site. We were in God's cathedral surrounded by His majestic creations. With the breeze blowing the trees to and fro, the Holy Spirit flowed through the pines and us and was magnified. Through tears, we took turns praying and singing.

Suddenly a woman named Joy looked up and said, "God just told me to leave my Bible here." I, for one, was stunned, but she was serious. She laid her Bible on one of the metal chairs and left it there. She said she just had a feeling that maybe someone would find it there and be saved. We contemplated it for a while. It was a strange request, but she didn't question it.

I found myself clutching my Bible closer. My Bible had been a special birthday gift that year. I had already begun to write notes and highlight in it. "Oh God, please don't ask me to leave my Bible," I thought. He didn't, and we soon left. As we left the site, out of curiosity, I asked Joy's sister if the Bible had been just an "extra" of Joy's.

"No," she said, "it is one she carries with her always with all her notes, special bookmarks, and papers in it."

I couldn't understand that. How could Joy leave it with all those treasures inside knowing that she would never see it again? My heart ached for her, but when I asked her about it, she seemed fine. In fact, she seemed filled with joy that God would request such a thing of her.

In our room later, Beth and I talk about this incident for hours. Both of us were deeply touched by Joy's sacrifice. Then, as it began to snow, we became worried about her Bible. "Maybe we should go back out there and cover it in plastic," we contemplated. Though we were very tempted, it was dark and cold, so we didn't, but that event made us both realize how brittle our faith really was. I didn't even want to think of how I would respond had God asked me to leave my Bible.

We did not have a chance to walk back out there again before the retreat was over, but we discussed it many times over the next year. I relayed the story in awe to many people. Upon hearing it, some did not respond with the same awe-inspired confusion that I felt. I assumed they either had much stronger faith than I or they didn't think Bibles were worth pondering over. But one thing that I did ponder more than anything else that year was the strength of my own faith. How does one get to the point of following God's requests to that degree? Joy must have felt pain at leaving her treasured Bible behind, potentially to be ruined. How was she able to do that? And would it be found? Would it save someone or would it be tossed into the next party's fire? Yet Joy was content to let God do His work.

The next year our retreat was held at the same place, and Beth and I couldn't wait to walk back out to where the circle of chairs had been to see what we would find. I'm not sure if we really expected the Bible to be there, but we needed to look for some evidence. Would the chairs be gone? Would there be a piece of the Bible there? Would there be any sign at all?

We found the chairs just as they had been before, but no evidence of the Bible. What happened to it and where was it now? Was there a person somewhere now reading their way to a better life in Christ? Or did it lay in the ashes before us? We would never know.

I never found out the answers to those questions, but I did find that this year when I asked myself if I could have done what Joy did had God asked it of me, I was able to relate to what Joy did a little better. There had been many things in the past year that built and strengthened my faith, and as I revisited the circle of chairs, I could see the difference a year had made in my life and my faith. I'm not sure I could have left my Bible with as much dignity as Joy did the year prior, but I think I might have accomplished the task had God asked it of me. How had I come this far?

In the ensuing year between the retreats, my husband and I had repaired many rips in our relationship. I had begun to learn about codependency and boundaries. God had begun to heal my soul. And as I learned to trust His ways and see the miraculous results of His love, my faith in Him began to build. I learned that His way was always better and that if I trusted, I could do the seemingly impossible through Him. What I learned that year would always stay with me and help me in my future endeavors.

So who was that Bible left there for? I think quite possibly, it was for me.

A Daily Dose Of Faith

By Lisa K. Johnson
Jonesboro, Arkansas

What a day! We all have those days when we just feel like pulling our hair out, but this particular day was a real eye-opener. Not long ago, I was in a situation where I loved the people I worked with but hated my job. I prayed faithfully for six months that God would open a door. When He answered, it was more like He opened a gate. He provided me with a job that has allowed me to work out of my home. God is so faithful, and I love it when He shows off. I love my new job and being home when the kids get off the bus. I love being here so that they can get in touch with me during the day if they need me.

This particular morning, I woke up feeling really good. I got the kids off to school and my husband out the door on his way to work. I sat down with my coffee and my Bible to begin my morning quiet time. Once finished, I threw a load of laundry into the washer and sat down at the computer to check e-mail. The phone rang, and I checked the caller ID and saw that it was the school, so I knew it was one of the kids. As I picked up the phone, I heard the exasperated voice of my son telling me he had another asthma attack after running bleachers in football practice. I rushed around to get to the school to check on him. As I frantically slapped on some makeup, I began to think back over my conversations (lectures) with this child over the past couple of weeks. Most of it had been about issues regarding his hateful attitude and apathy. Now, a bit exasperated, I asked, "Lord, how do I survive these teenage years? I have faith in You, but not in my abilities to survive these trials without losing my mind." I began to remember some recent situations with my son. I thought about my discussion with him just two weeks prior about bringing home three academic referrals for poor grades. I remembered telling him that he may say that he wants to make good grades, but the fact that he does not put forth the effort shows that his true attitude reflects apathy. I told him that if he cared, he would remember to bring home his homework and his books so that he could study. I remembered implementing a new rule that books were to be brought home every night. I might as well have announced through a loudspeaker in our home, "Let the homework battles begin!" As I pondered over the details of each emotional conflict with my son, I became tired and angry. I couldn't help but think about how tiring it was to spoonfeed math problems or English sentence structure to this child. I recalled informing him just the night before that I felt like he was manipulating me so that he could find an easy way out of his homework. This particular conversation had occurred after I caught him watching television when none of his homework was done and his chores of sorting laundry and doing the dishes were still left undone. I thought about how his willful disobedience had been his choice, and since he chose not to do what was asked of him, he had essentially chosen to be punished. Yet as I recalled these conflicts, frustration and guilt began to well up inside and flood over me. How could I think such things when this child was at school and sick?

Still, as I rounded the corner at breakneck speed just a few blocks from the school, I continued to ponder over my recollections and my guilt. Then I threw myself a pity party, asking God, "Why did You give me such an emotionally difficult child to raise? He is a good boy. He is a Christian. He goes to church. He doesn't smoke, drink, or do drugs. He doesn't listen to wacko music or watch psycho movies. He doesn't hang with the wrong crowd. He is a good kid, but with his apathetic attitude and carelessness, he can be so terribly difficult and challenging at times. Why God? What did I do to deserve such a difficult child to raise? Between willful disobedience and hatefulness, I am losing faith that he will turn out to be a faithful man of Godly character. And now on top of everything, he has had another asthma attack. Lord, you know he probably forgot his inhaler again. Help me, Lord, because this child is wearing me out!"

Moments later I heard the soft, tender voice of the Holy Spirit as the Father spoke to me. "Don't you know that I blessed you with this child in order that you may learn things?" He said.

First I thought it, and then I said it aloud. "Learn? What am I supposed to learn from this child, Lord? He is literally wearing me out."

Then God hit me with a ton of bricks!

"Your son treats you just like you treat Me. You are a good person. You are a Christian. You do good things like teach Sunday School and attend Church. You are helpful. You don't do drugs, smoke, or drink. You hang with a good crowd. But you willfully disobey Me with your lack of trust, your lack of faith, and your lack of obedience to lay all of your burdens at My feet. In fact, you are a slave to simple things that hinder your relationship with Me. You say you desire to be set free and you want to be healthy and have more quiet time, but you make no efforts. Can't you see that you are just like your son in that you are also careless in certain areas and show lack of faith? You can be hateful and selfish, as well. I put this child in your life to teach you that he is a mirror image of you. You need to learn from him as well as teach him."

With tears rolling down my face and goose pimples on my arms, my only response to God was utter speechlessness (which doesn't occur very often in my life).

I made it to the school in record time, picked up my son, and drove him to the doctor. After a few medication changes, we were on our way back to school. But now I no longer felt anger toward him. Now I viewed him as an instrument—a mirror.

When I arrived back home, I got down on my knees and prayed this prayer: "Lord, forgive me for not putting all my trust and faith in You. Please help me to be obedient to Your perfect will and desire for me and my life. Lord, help me to trust You even when I don't think I can do what it takes to get through the day without stress eating or making unwise or unhealthy decisions in an attempt to nurture my soul. Lord, help me remember that You are the only One that can provide the type of nurturing my soul really desires. Lord, please forgive me for arrogant pride and selfish disobedience. Forgive me for my pity parties, for I know You work all things together for good to those who love You and are called according to Your purpose. Lord, help me to be the type of Christian mother to my children that You would have me to be. Help me, Lord, to die daily to myself and to truly put You first in all that I do. Lord, make me aware of how enslaved I am to my own faithlessness. Lord, please move me from knowing and desiring to doing what it takes. Give me strength, oh God, for I am very weak, and I need You to make me strong. Forgive me for laziness! Father, I am asking You to take control when I am out of control! Thank You for how You speak to me and how You teach me through difficult circumstances. Thank You for my wonderful family, and thank You that my son was okay today. In Jesus' name, Amen."

A Gift Of Faith

By Gloria P. Humes
Miami, Florida

There once was a man named Tony who lived an average American life. He believed that if he could survive one day at a time, he was living.

After graduating from high school, attending college for a couple of years, and serving in Uncle Sam's Air Force, he came home and settled into a "normal" life with a steady nine-to-five job. Then as day-to-day problems began to arise, this man looked for ways to relieve the pressure and the stress.

Now, even though Tony was a Christian, his faith had never been tested. He simply believed that God would do what He was supposed to do. He truly believed God and trusted things to happen as He ordained, according to His will and purpose. Tony did nothing, however, to prepare himself for the purpose God had placed on his life. And as most of us know, an unprepared person usually ends up in situations they are not strong enough to handle.

When a man is unprepared to handle life's punches, he can choose to do one of several things. He can deal with it based on his life experiences and his past, which, of course, includes the way he saw his parents deal with things. He can seek advice from outside resources like secular or religious counselors, mentors, friends, and family. He can pray, meditate on the Bible, and ask God to help him. Or he could do absolutely nothing—just wait and hope things will work out for the best. And that is just exactly what Tony decided to do! He did absolutely nothing to deal with his problems. He just kept living one day at a time hoping the problems would solve themselves and go away.

Is that faith? Is faith doing nothing but waiting and hoping for something to happen? The Bible says that faith is the substance of things hoped for and the evidence of things not seen. As time passed, Tony's problems became more and more severe. It seemed as if God had removed His hand and was allowing him to sink deeper and deeper into a downward spiral that did not seem to have an ending, a solution, or a way back up to the top. As Tony kept slipping deeper and deeper into sin and despair, he continued to believe that God would do what He was supposed to do. However, how and when God would act was now the beginning of several provocative questions. God's faith was in full operation in Tony's life. The challenge, however, was helping him see that through all the trials and tribulations, God is faithful.

Tony began to ponder in his heart questions that had never crossed his mind before. *Why am I living on the street when I have a house to live in? Where is that great job I had a few years ago? Why did my family desert me? When did I let life slip by me? When did I lose my grip on reality? On the other hand, is this as real as it is going to get? Where did I go wrong? Was there something I was supposed to do to prevent this from happening to me? Questions, questions, questions! Where are the answers?*

After sinking to the lowest of lows, Tony began to listen to the still small voice of the Holy Spirit that was speaking to his heart. Romans 10:17 reminded him *that faith comes by hearing, and hearing by the Word of God.* Soon Tony began to hear some of the answers to all those questions he was unable to answer before. The voice told him that if he would just look inside himself, he would find the answer to every one of his questions.

At first Tony did not accept this, because he thought his faith was gone and he knew for sure that he was unable to do anything about his life and what had happened to him. But as he listened more and more to this voice, he remembered the promises God had made to him. God said, *"I will never leave you nor forsake you...if you have faith the size of a mustard seed, you can speak to the mountain, and the mountain will obey...and if one in a marriage has faith and believes, I will restore the marriage..."*

As he began to meditate on those promises and realize that he must prepare himself to receive what God promised, his eyes of faith opened, and he could see light at the end of the tunnel.

The light got brighter and brighter and brighter as he studied God's word, as he prepared himself to get his family back, as he let God work in his life. He believed that God could do exceedingly, abundantly above all that he could think or ask. The light was so bright in his life now; he was able to exercise his belief of walking by faith and not by sight. And he realized that God had given him a gift that he had to share with others. This gift was the gift of faith. Ephesians 2:8 reminded him that *For by grace are ye saved through faith; and that not of yourselves: it is the gift of God.* He became extremely aware of this gift when he petitioned God to do certain things for him. He asked God to take away the desire for anything that was not pleasing in His sight, and He did. He asked God to allow him to get a job so he could begin to take care of his own needs and pay tithes, and He did. He asked God to restore his family, and He did. He remembered Hebrews 11:6: *But without faith it is impossible to please Him: for he that cometh to God must believe that He is, and that He is a rewarder of them that diligently seek Him.*

Tony's faith in God was so strong that even at his lowest point he continued to believe that God would do what He was supposed to do. This strength was not always evident, but by the grace of God, the preparation to receive worked like polish on a piece of old leather. As the trials and pressures of life kept punching, the true gift of faith that was hidden in this broken vessel came to the surface and shone like the noonday sun.

Every man (or woman) that wants to receive God's gift of faith needs to know that God is no respecter of persons—what He did for this man He can and will do for every man (or woman) that asks in faith, believing God will do what He is supposed to do—and that is to be faithful to His word.

Driving Miss Elma

By Wendy Ann Mattox
Caldwell, Idaho

One rule I learned as a kid was to never pick up strangers. Whether hitchhiking or just at the side of the road, the rule was the same. No rides to anyone we didn't know. So I find it strange that on that sunny day in August of 1990 I agreed to give a lady named Elma a ride home. Maybe it was because she was alone outside of the grocery store. Maybe it was because she seemed so frail and helpless. I believe it was fate.

Just a few months prior, my husband, Rich, and I had attended a movie at our church. The movie titled *A Man Called Norman* was inspiring. It told the story of a man that befriended a man called Norman. It told how God used Norman to teach this man to give of himself and put his selfishness aside. Moved by this movie, I remember praying that God would give me a "Norman."

A few months later and not even remembering my prayer or the movie, God introduced a lady named Elma into my life. Now I need to say, I am no saint. I usually cross the road when faced with someone like Elma. Elma was not someone who fit into my "comfort zone." But here I was giving her a ride home and making casual conversation with her. My daughter was four at the time and was not impressed with our new passenger. She sat behind Elma in her car seat plugging her nose. It was obvious that Elma had not bathed for a while.

When dropping Elma off at her house, I was struck by the poverty stricken neighborhood she lived in. As I helped Elma out of my van, I kept watch over my shoulder. I did not feel safe. Elma had a grown daughter (Gracie) who would not come out of the small cement house. She was obese and not friendly. I carried Elma's groceries to Gracie who took them inside. The smell was rancid. I was outside of my comfort level *again.*

After that first ride home, Elma asked if I could take her shopping again. The selfish side of me screamed, "No!" However, my mouth said, "Sure." And that's how it began. I drove her two times a week to a local grocery store or any other errand that she needed to accomplish. We became friends.

I wish I could say I was a perfect friend, but I wasn't. There were many times when taking Elma shopping was an inconvenience. There were times when the odor was nauseating. There were times when her chatter drove me nuts. Still, I kept driving her around. On the outside no one would know how I was feeling. However, on the inside my patience was tested as she shopped slowly. My pride was revealed since she drew attention wherever we went. My compassion was lacking, for I found her very strange and needy. However, through faith, God helped me to sincerely care for Elma. It was nothing I came up with on my own.

This arrangement continued for two years. Then our relationship took a turn. God was not finished with me yet.

Gracie called saying Elma had hurt her back. She canceled our outings for two weeks. I drove over to see Elma, but Gracie would not let me inside the house. Gracie's behavior toward me changed. Rather than indifference, she'd yell at me that she had seen me on cable television. That she knew I could read her mind. She would not let me see Elma. It was frightening, and I worried for Elma's safety, so I contacted the local authorities and Health and Welfare.

A court order was granted to allow the authorities, Health and Welfare, and the local fire department to go into the house and remove Elma on a stretcher. Gracie was taken to a mental institution in upper Idaho. At the hospital they found Elma had bedsores and maggots from lack of care. The real surprise came when they discovered four purses of Elma and Gracie's money stashed inside their house.

I went with two other ladies from Health and Welfare, and we counted the money. It totaled $56,000. This discovery made me feel betrayed and angry with Elma. Why had she acted so poor and allowed me to buy her groceries on multiple occasions? I soon realized that Elma was mentally ill and truly viewed herself as poor.

Elma went to a nursing home until her back recovered. Meanwhile, the State of Idaho wanted to assign her to a guardian/conservator. I prayed to the Lord, "No. I don't want to do this. Let her family do it. I'll remain her friend, but not her guardian." The thought was overwhelming. Unfortunately, Elma had no family willing to take this role. I groaned as my comfort zone stretched again.

A month later I was Elma's guardian and conservator and would get paid $50 a week from Elma's funds. I was scared. I was frustrated. I was confused how all this had happened so quickly. However, I continued to trust and have faith that God would help me with this new responsibility. Then the real work began.

Rich and I arranged for a dumpster to be delivered to her small home. I hired two teenagers to help us "gut" the house. The trash inside was five feet high with only a single path from the front door to the bug-infested mattress and to the bathroom. I have never seen or smelled anything like this before. After being bitten by small bugs, we wore white suits (like something out of a space movie) while throwing everything away. We had to go through everything since we were worried about more money being hidden.

After Elma's back had healed, I moved her to a retirement home nearby. When Gracie returned from the mental institute (she had been diagnosed with schizophrenia), I had them both moved to a joint room so they could be together. The new Gracie (heavily medicated) seemed much calmer. The courts decided that Gracie did not need a guardian as long as she didn't cause any problems.

The next challenge for me came when Gracie wanted to go with us on our shopping trips. "No, Lord…I don't want her in my car." I was still afraid of her. God reminded me to have faith, that He knew what was best—that He would keep my two toddlers and me safe. I relented and trusted God, and through this He helped me to grow inwardly *again.*

Through faith I learned patience, humility, and compassion for someone that I could not have sincerely loved on my own. Through faith my relationship with Elma continued for another eight years—during which time my love for Elma continued to grow.

Elma died of cancer in May of 1999. I was blessed and learned many things while caring for Elma and Gracie. I learned that sincere faith and love are from the Lord—that when we put our faith in God, all things are possible…especially things that we cannot muster on our own.

I still see Gracie and send her a card now and then. However, God closed this door in my life. Another lady is now caring for Gracie, and I'm sure God will faithfully help her just as He helped me!

Let us fix our eyes on Jesus, the author and perfecter of our faith… Hebrews 12:2a

Because I Believe

By Arthur Harley
Parkland, Florida

Faith. On the surface it's a simple and unassuming word. There's certainly nothing notable about its vital statistics: five letters, one syllable; a common diphthong framed between a pair of soft fricatives. But beneath the modest façade lies a staggering depth of meaning, if you chose to see it. Faith is a flexible concept that can be as vital or as trivial as you care to make it. You can reject it or revere it. You can see it as a blessing or a curse. The sound of it can fall on your ear as a serpent's hiss or an angel's whisper. The choice is yours.

I speak as one who has seen faith from both sides. Not long ago, when I basked in ignorance and skepticism, the very idea of faith was absurd to me. I fairly reveled in my lack of it and often glibly recited the definition of the word from my *Websters New World Dictionary* while in debate with some poor, deluded believer: *unquestioning belief that does not require proof or evidence.* "Now why," I would ask in a contrived plea for reason, "would someone believe anything without proof or evidence?" It was a question that was invariably met with uncertain mumbling or conspicuous silence. Thus did I keep true faith at bay, repeatedly trotting out the silly straw horse of "faith" I had created in my own mind and gleefully pummeling into defeat after defeat…

But that was in a previous, less enlightened life. I have since been reborn into a new life that is centered by faith. Not the wobbly caricature of it from that previous life, but real, indestructible, and everlasting faith.

My surrender to faith began some years ago when I experienced what I would describe as an awakening in my life. At the age of 31 I learned some startling truths about my family history, unsettling revelations that had the effect of shaking me loose from the long reverie I had been in. I was prompted to turn my head, take a closer look around, and find out what else I had been missing. I found that after 10 restless years in banking, I was growing disillusioned, and I began to question my career choices. Also at about this time, my wife got pregnant with our first child. I started thinking like a father before he was born, imagining what I would teach him, anticipating the questions he was bound to ask as he grew.

It was then that I began a general inquiry, a quest of comprehensive learning that opened my eyes to a world of discovery, including the realization of how little I really knew. Each revelation uncovered a new trove of questions, and I eagerly began searching for answers, beginning with the answer to the ultimate question: Is there really a God?

And in the midst of this broad inquiry, right on cue, entered an angel named Steve Brown who first whispered "faith" into my ear.

Steve is a humble Bible teacher by trade, but he is much better known as a keynote speaker and author with a national radio and book ministry called *Key Life*. I first came across Steve in 1992 when his daily radio program entertained me for 15 minutes each morning during my hour-long commute to work. It was his voice that first caught my attention: a rich, resonant baritone that rattled the cheap factory speakers in the '87 Accord I was driving at the time. But there was much more to Steve Brown than a stentorian "foghorn voice" as he called it. After listening to him for several months, I found myself increasingly intrigued by what came across as a seemingly boundless intellect. He was well-read and widely traveled. He had published several books, regularly dropped the names of celebrities and dignitaries he had met, but at the same time seemed very down-to-earth and practical. And most remarkably, he professed the same kind of faith I had recently rejected.

Starting with the Catholicism of my childhood and all the way through young adulthood, I had accepted the premise that the God we worshipped was loving and merciful. I had swallowed that idea whole and without question. I had read the Bible intermittently throughout my life, but as I read the entire Pentateuch with a critical eye for the first time, I found myself horrified by the myriad slaughters and atrocities wrought by a God who didn't seem very loving and merciful at all. In fact, he seemed incredibly cruel and capricious. Indignantly, I turned my back on that God and pronounced myself an atheist.

But I wavered.

For many reasons, but mainly because of the warmth, humor, knowledge, and authority of this man on my car radio who kept telling me that, though I may find this stuff unbelievable, he could assure me he's checked, and it's all true. He described a time when he, too, had wavered, launched an inquiry of his own, engaged in "six-years of some very hard investigation," and "a lot of hard-nosed and rational thought."

I kept thinking about this man of intellect and learning, a man with his reasonable tone and credibility who had examined the faith to see if it would hold water, put it under trial by reason—the ultimate test to my way of thinking—and came out of it a believer.

I had to find out why.

So I wrote him a letter. I took 1,000 words to ask what was essentially a seven-word question: "How can you possibly believe this nonsense?" I was pleasantly shocked when I received an inviting reply which said, in essence, "I'd be delighted to show you."

In many ways Steve and I were worlds apart: a renowned theologian and an anonymous banker; a Christian Fundamentalist and an avowed atheist; he was beyond middle-age with two grown daughters and I was in my early 30's with my firstborn still in diapers. Yet somehow within the small and silent dimensions of our letters, we formed a close friendship. Steve said we were "kindred spirits," and I think he was right. Our differences were transcended by the things we shared: a love of reading and learning, a sometimes crushing sense of our own failings, cynicism offset by wry humor, and snooty intellectualism. We became confidantes and confessors, sharing secret pains and peccadilloes.

Together we ranged far and wide. We talked about history, philosophy, music, and politics and lamented the sorry state of the society. We wrote each other book and movie reviews, editorials and mini essays. We editorialized, theorized, debated endlessly and sometimes quite heatedly about the nature of God and the implications of religious faith. Those were some of the hard places we crossed, places where we battered and bruised each other. But there were many more soft places where we made each other laugh, told funny and touching anecdotes of friends and family, and gave each other strength and encouragement during times of storm and stress.

From the beginning of our correspondence Steve made no secret of his desire to lead me to Christ. In his first letter he told me, "I am willing to spend time helping you come to some kind of resolution to your questions about the Christian faith *if* you are really interested in finding some resolution." When our relationship was at its warmest, he begged me to convert because if I wasn't going to be in heaven, he didn't want to be there either. He told me that my unbelief was rooted in anger toward God for all the suffering and injustice in the world. He said the fact that I cared enough to be angry was a good sign and was better than apathy. "Hang in there," he kept saying, "you're not as far from the Kingdom as you think."

But I resisted. Overlaying my reluctance was the same basic question I had asked in that first letter: "Why do you believe?" I had sought a totally rational answer to that question, no leap of faith required. But ultimately Steve admitted there could be no such path to belief. After exploring Christian apologetics and taking a few probes at the evidential models proposed by Thomas Aquinas, C.S. Lewis, and Francis Schaeffer, we reached a philosophical impasse. He finally had to admit that there was no bridge from reason to faith. "The older I get," he wrote, "the more I realize that my faith is not based on the intellectual arguments (as good as they are) but on the reality of the God who has chosen to reveal Himself to me. As I get older, I realize I believe because I believe because I believe…"

I was mystified and disappointed. I objected. "What about your long investigation? What about all that hard-nosed and rational thought?"

"That can only get you so far," he replied. "Apologetics will never prove the case for faith—it just clears the weeds away from around the cliff so that someone can see clearly to make the leap…and to see if one is caught by the Everlasting Arms."

I was not ready to take that leap. And so our correspondence wound down without my becoming a Christian.

Steve had done all he could with me, but thankfully God wasn't through with me yet. Even though faith remained in the cold outside of my life, my correspondence with Steve had at least opened the door. Even in my unbelief, God kept working on me. Like a thorn in my mind, He would not allow me to rest easy in my rejection of faith. He kept prompting me to continue probing, listening, reading, demanding answers to my valid questions. The Bible commands that we must always be prepared to give an answer for the faith that is in us. Implicit in that command is the fact that there *are* answers to give. At length, in His own way and in His perfect time, God channeled my mind to those answers.

And now that I have hollowed out the space that ignorance and skepticism once occupied, I have found a place for faith in my life. I have found that if faith could be likened to a tree, the root of it is trust and its fruit is hope. And a life without hope is no life at all. I have found that faith is not necessarily blind, or deaf, and it is certainly not dumb. It does not require "unquestioning belief without proof or evidence." Surely that kind of simple, involuntary faith exists, but the pathways to God are as many and as varied as the souls that travel those pathways. It is well in keeping with my analytical nature that my path to the cross was lit by logic, reason, and the overwhelming evidence in support of the Christian faith. And it is well within God's nature that once I submitted to faith, He showed me the truth of that old Augustinian adage: while the world says, "seeing is believing," God says, "believing is seeing." With reason, He has led me to a place where I now understand, somehow *without* reason, the meaning of Hebrews 11:1: *Faith is being sure of what we hope for and certain of what we do not see.*

That passage was once Greek to me. I rejoice that it now makes perfect sense. And I rejoice that Steve Brown's simple profession of faith, once a stumbling block and an irritant to me, now also makes perfect sense. In other words, as ironic and miraculous as it sounds, the essence of my faith is this: I believe because I believe because I believe…

Amen.

Faith: He Has A Plan

By Cindy Ruth Garcia
Bethany, Oklahoma

We are wounded, innocent bystanders on the byways of life. Our trust has been sabotaged; our hope has been dashed and shattered at our feet; love is a pact made on the terms of survival. We speak nicely to one another, as long as there are no irritations and no pressures to deal with. We tell the truth, mostly; mostly we ignore that we haven't always been able to measure up to the standard of perfect honesty. We are alone, and we are lonely, hungering for something better, something that fulfills our desires and satisfies our yearning.

We play a part that must be propagated; we become whom we pretend to be. We deny our pain; we deny our dreams; we deny our potential. It is a serpent that sleeps within us; we know that he exists, and we know that he would destroy us if he were to be awakened. We tiptoe silently away from that door whenever we unwittingly arrive there. To open it would be to open Pandora's box, and that must never happen, must never happen, must never happen. If I deny that it exists, it is not so. I am confident, poised, successful, and beautiful. Why not? As long as I am wishing, I'll wish for more rather than less. Mother said that if wishes were horses, we'd all ride. We are riding. Riding to nowhere, arrival imminent.

Does our life have a purpose? Do we know who we are? Do we know why we are here? Do we really believe that God exists and cares for us? Does He hear us when we cry out so desperately? We struggle; we weaken; we fall.

However our experience guides us, it is most probably guiding us wrong. Whatever our feelings dictate, they cannot be believed. In choosing our path, we must focus on a higher plane, the path of wisdom, the eternal road staked out for us by a God who loves each one of us personally and has provided for any and all contingencies in our lives.

He created us in perfect harmony with Himself, and when that closeness was broken by Adam's disobedience, a need was embedded within our very fragile souls—a need that has directed every man who has drawn breath. It is the yawning pit that hungers for a relationship, for unity, for acceptance, for understanding. It is a need that another human being cannot fulfill. Ever. Perhaps they can cloak it; perhaps they can pretend. What they cannot do is fill it.

Man broke the oneness but could not repair it. He attempted—by hiding, by getting busy, and then by ignoring it. God loved him so much that He took the initiative. He promised a solution; He prepared the way; He sent His Son to die for our sins. He walked those who sought Him through the maze of uncertainty. He gave His Word, and He gave us many examples through those who've gone before, recording their stories for all eternity.

They were saints, heroes of the faith, but we see them doubt and falter and fail. Perhaps it doesn't depend on us. Perhaps that's part of His Plan. His main instruction was to believe Him, to listen to His Words, to seek Him with all our hearts. He did mighty works through some mighty poor characters. Believe is the verb form of the Greek word for faith. *Does it mean to let Him take on the giants? Is it conceivable that He doesn't expect me to be strong? Can I stop struggling and leave all the reasoning and rhetoric to Him? Could He possibly desire for me to rest from all my effort?*

When I do fail, He promises that He will be waiting for me to draw near to Him, to 'fess up and take responsibility for that sin, and He will draw near to me. The sin was dealt with at the cross; I am the one who has turned my back on Him. The problem of broken fellowship can only be solved by turning to Him and admitting my rebellion. That's for my benefit since He sees my heart through and through, but it is often hidden to me.

Who is this Person, who loves me so much and has given me so much? I must know more about Him. If there really are over 7,000 promises, how many can we learn about and claim in a lifetime? What does His character consist of and what does He plan for the human race? What does He plan for me? Who? What? When? Where? And how? And why? The more learned, the more life bears out the learning; the more learned, the more humbled I am by the enormity of His wisdom and power and majesty.

Then a mist comes down and the thunder rolls and there is no longer any certainty, for I am lost in an ocean of endless waves and riding on a raft of doubtless make. The rain pours down; I am alone and do not know the way to shore and cannot even determine how I came to be here or why this has happened. Did I fail terribly? Did I offend You, God? Please teach me. If so, correct me and guide me, for You are my best friend. Most of all, don't let go of me. You have never failed me, and You have always provided for me in every situation of life and death. Of one thing I am certain, it is futile to choose a destination for all points promise alike and I would swim and paddle with all my might only to end up on the wrong side of the ocean, worn and exhausted by my efforts. He must carry me to His destination however long it takes. He gives me perfect peace and confidence in His doings.

Then it seems that I have learned the lessons, having understood that it has been a test of my faith in Him, and my faith has been vindicated, not acknowledged by man as I had assumed, but by the realization that continued faith is vindication enough of faith. Yes, faith itself is the prize, the means and the end and the reward all together.

However, against all reason the storm intensifies, the lightning cracks, and the waves wrestle with the craft that carries me to wheresoever He wills. It is imperative to renew my grasp on Him, to not falter my eyesight for even one moment, for it is a perilous time, and the only sanity is found in His Word. Reason demands that I renounce, that I turn to hate, to bitterness, to any action that might remove me from the unrelenting grasp of my circumstances. How is it possible for any man to bear the brunt of so much hate when he has served as the spring that has joyfully given His water?

He loves me so much that He grants me permission to seek release and escape from the unbearable torment in which I reside. It seems His love is so great that He whispers and reminds me quietly, "Yes, you are free to go. I will certainly bless you whatever you decide, but My perfect plan is for you to persevere. If you persevere, the spiritual impact of your life will spread to others; if not, it will be for your blessing alone. Choose wisely—choose the best part." I did not hear Him say these words audibly. Perhaps I was delirious. But I determined that even though I could no longer bear it, if it were His will, then He would bear it for me and He would be my shield.

He taught me to lay aside all my hopes and dreams and desires in exchange for a greater good, for without Him I am nothing, He taught me that He is good, and His plan is designed for good. I can trust Him no matter what, no matter where. Although I cannot see the outline of His plan, He is diligently bringing it about and, whether I pass or fail, He never fails. He taught me that He reveals Himself through His children, the body. It is not necessary for us to understand everything, only that it is necessary to constantly draw near to the One who does. He brought me into communion with Himself, no part of my soul off limits to His presence, so that I might intercede for others.

He has shown me that joy comes in letting go and trusting Him. It does not depend on me. My reasoning is not needed and will not affect the outcome. He is my hope and strength and song. It is very freeing to not need to be in control, to let go of my will and to trust in His. To know that He will never fail me and that, although my life appears to be destroyed, He is victorious, He has a plan, and I can trust Him that it is good, for He is good and can only do good.

He is faithful and eminently worthy of my faith in Him.

The Search For Faith

By Michelle Christine Conkey
Louisville, Colorado

"I have tried to find salvation on my own, in a search for something real. There's a guilty heart inside this flesh and bone…" These song lyrics carried through my heart and my mind as tears began to stream down my face. The consequences of all my searching for emotional fulfillment had caught up with me. Gradually, I was beginning to realize that my 11-year detour from God has caused hurt and pain to others, to myself, and to God. Why God allowed me to search, I don't fully understand. I don't seek justification for my choices. All I know is my experiences are real. My journey is one I would have never envisioned for my life. I trust it to God and humbly share it in faith.

For as long as I can remember I have always been interested in God and spiritual matters. I grew up regularly attending a traditional church with my family. As the oldest of four children, I was shy and insecure and found church to be a place of comfort. It was in high school that I asked Jesus into my life. I even vowed in my heart to remain sexually pure until marriage. I went on to college, and that is when my faith truly began to flourish. I became involved with a Christian student group. This group,, with all its fun, meaningful activities, became the focus of my life. I participated in Bible studies and various evangelism events. I found great meaning in my involvement and often felt an emotional high.

Well, emotions come and go, and shortly before graduating from college, my heart became restless. I was not feeling fulfilled and began to search outside my Christian world for something to fill my want. That's when romance stepped into the picture, and the feelings of being in love quickly brought me back to that emotional high I was craving. The feelings of being in love seemed to be all I needed, and 14 months later I was married. Again, emotions come and go, and about a year into the marriage, my feelings of being in love faded. This was just about the time I learned I was pregnant. Though scared at first, I quickly warmed to the idea of being a mother, and my emotions soared once again.

After the birth of my daughter, I became a stay-at-home mom and felt a strong love and desire to raise my daughter. I even pulled out my dormant faith and participated in women's Bible studies and taught children's classes at the church my husband and I were attending.

But gradually my restless heart began to beat louder and louder, and the simple life I was living was not enough for me. I was becoming increasingly unhappy in my marriage, and in an attempt to fill my heart with the emotion it craved, I turned to running. I poured my heart into training for various races and, within a couple of years, ran a marathon. This, too, seemed like a quick fix to my want. My accomplishment diminished with time, and my want for fulfillment and emotion returned.

Unhappiness in my marriage persisted, so I asked my husband to join me for counseling. He was reluctant and, unfortunately, little tangible change came from our efforts.

I continued to press on. I pushed my heart down and tried to keep my restlessness under control. Still, my want for emotion lingered, and about a year later I realized I was involved in an emotional affair. A battle began to play out between my heart and my mind. I shared my crisis with my husband and a couple of women in my church. Nothing seemed to help, and eventually I gave in to compromise.

I quickly realized the impact of my choices. I sought forgiveness, and my husband and I tried again to make our marriage work. Unfortunately, something just wasn't right. I moved out after seven years of marriage and faced the reality of divorce. I was scared, but ironically enough, my craving for emotion was filled again with a sense of freedom.

I allowed myself to try new things and to explore circumstances, thoughts, and relationships. I welcomed new experiences and new friends, especially people who were different than me. Some of these times were wonderful. Other times I felt a battle raging between my heart and my mind. My church attendance was sporadic, as was my prayer life. I still professed to be a Christian, even though I knew my lifestyle didn't line up with what I had once believed. Nevertheless, I let my heart's desires lead.

Eventually, logistical challenges—specifically work and living arrangements—arose. These challenges were in part due to my limited life experience. I was naïve. I wanted to give the same time and attention to my daughter as I had when I was a stay-at-home mother. I also wanted to develop a career that included meaningful work and an adequate salary. Basically, I wanted to create the ideal life, and I wanted it as soon as possible. In that search for the perfect balance, I made five job changes and relocated four times within a one-year period. I halfheartedly sought God for help, but my pride was a factor. My heart still wanted its emotional fill from life and so I continued to wander from God. I was doing things my way, and this did not help matters between my husband and me.

Emotions intensified when we could not agree on the best interests of our daughter. Matters became entrenched in the legal system when my husband sought an attorney and asked that a child advocate make recommendations for our daughter. I had hoped we could resolve matters together. However, given our degree of difficulty in communicating, I decided it was probably best to involve a professional. I never imagined our divorce would get so ugly. The child advocate made her recommendations, and they were very difficult to accept. She was critical of both of us as parents, and it caused me to spend a lot of time soul searching.

I began to realize for the first time that many of my choices over the years were based highly upon emotion. I was on a journey to please myself, and even more humiliating, my pursuit for emotional fulfillment was based in years of wandering away from God.

I was living a lie. In reality, I was not finding happiness. I was only finding more heartache. It was a difficult reality to face.

Slowly, I began to separate my emotions from everything and started to make sound choices.

Two years have passed. My search for something real has shown me that a guilty heart lives inside this flesh and bone. What is real is my daughter will grow up in a family touched by the effects of divorce. What is real is that the mistakes I made have caused pain. What is real is that I spent many years wandering from God.

My experiences of the last 11 years will journey on with me, transforming my guilty heart to more fully realize the deep love God has for me. Lamentations 3:21-23 says God offers me His love through His mercies. God is faithful to give me these mercies every day of my life. The lyrics by a popular Christian artist summarize it so well for me. "Mercy said 'no.' I'm not gonna let you go...Thank you Jesus, mercy said 'no.'"

God's faithfulness, through His daily mercies, helps me to know I can find my emotional fulfillment solely in Him. My search has grown my faith to receive God's healing touch for me and my daughter, faith to believe I was created for more than the mistakes I have made, and faith to surrender to God's perfect plan for me. His faithfulness will no doubt make it real!

Song lyrics are from *The Glory* performed by Avalon, © 1999 Jimmievision Music/BMI/Designer Music, Inc./Minnie Partners Music/McSpadden Smith Music/SESAC; and *Mercy Said No,* performed by Greg Long, composed by Dave Clark, Don Koch, and Greg Long © 1998

My Faith Walk

By Denise L. Schulz
Merrill, Wisconsin

I learned in the sixth grade that not everyone was trustworthy. It wasn't easy for me to not trust people, because I had no boundaries when it came to trusting. I learned the hard way that I had to set boundaries to keep from getting hurt. Through prayer I was able to forgive. I didn't as easily forget.

When I was nine, I had a special talk with God and told Him I realized that I needed Him to be in charge of my life—that I didn't want to control it all by myself. My Sunday school teacher had led me in prayer as she walked me to my grandma's with me and helped me to find this new strength and life in God. Having new faith in Jesus was the base for all the strength I've drawn in my life. For it is through Christ that we receive strength.

My life has not been the best or worst it could be. I am, however, somewhat of an analyst and like to ponder things like my faith walk to where I came to be now.

In my teen years I kind of forgot that Jesus was the leader of my life and that it was my responsibility to go to church, pray, read my Bible, and most importantly to seek God's counsel about my life. I did not have a mentor to help me see that church attendance and reading my Bible daily were important things. I fell away from God and church and became promiscuous. I wanted to feel loved, but I went about it the wrong way and ended up being used by others.

I didn't ask God to help me make decisions. Instead, I took it upon myself to find fulfillment, but during this time in my life, I didn't find the kind of fulfillment I thought I needed. What I found were guys who used me and lied to me to get what they wanted. I don't hold this against any of them. They were young, I was young, and that is the way things go sometimes; and since that time, I've asked for and received God's forgiveness for these things. But at the time, I still did not look to Him for the answers I sought.

I found out I was pregnant just before my 16th birthday.

Now I turned to God and repented for my choices and my actions. I realized He was my only hope. My parents were not thrilled that I was so young and that I was not married, but after everything settled down, they did get excited about being grandparents.

Again I started to get comfortable, and I forgot to include God in my daily life. I should have been in constant prayer and study of my Savior. I did start to pray more regularly, but I just called on him occasionally when I needed something or to thank Him for a blessing here and there.

I went to Sunday school and another church related Wednesday night class for a while. I memorized some Scripture. So hey, I was doing pretty well. I went to church with the family on Christmas and Easter. I still had faith, and I knew I loved Him. I just didn't have the determination, I guess, or perhaps the wisdom to realize I needed Him every minute of the day. I just called on Him when it was convenient for me.

With the help of my parents, I finished high school. My mom watched my daughter for me while I went to school the end of my junior year and my full senior year.

Then I moved to Wausau. I wanted to get a degree to interpret for the deaf. But that was easier said than done. My parents thought I should commute or else leave my daughter with them and I could see her on weekends. I just couldn't do that. Independence was important to me.

Before I could fully enroll in the program, I had to take a bunch of basic classes—sociology, psychology, basic sign language, etc.—a full semester's worth.

In the meantime, I met a guy who approached me wanting to talk. I had a weird feeling about him right away—like I just knew I would be with him forever—but instead of asking my Savior for help or guidance in how to go about dating this guy, I just let the situation run its course. And I did everything wrong again. We moved in together. He belonged to a church, but hadn't really gone much since he graduated or since he was confirmed—I'm not quite sure which. His parents got us to go sometimes, but it was mostly just here and there and on holidays.

Before long I became pregnant again and knew I should have been in prayer. But again, I forgot to include God.

I wanted badly to get engaged or married or both before anyone knew. We were engaged before anyone knew about the pregnancy and married before the baby was born. But by then I realized my husband had quite a temper at times. I started to pray about this, but it was mostly a "what can I do" kind of a prayer.

We bought a house, and my husband was often gone for a week at a time. I worked second shift. We had two small children to care for and p.m.

daycare was not easy to find. I was stressed out most of the time, and life was hard. Here I was a new wife, often functioning as a single mom of two kids, working full-time, and trying to unpack all at the same time. I didn't know which way to turn.

About that time a neighbor lady befriended me. She helped me to see that going to church was important, and reading the Bible and praying were equally important. Soon I also needed to decide where to send my daughter to school (parochial or public school). After a while of attending church, praying, and reading parts of the Bible, sending her to a parochial school became important to me. Growing up, I did not have someone to teach me to pray, go to church, and read the Bible every day. Even now, I was still learning.

I wanted my daughter to learn this from a young age, to see it taught and role modeled. Even though I planned to increase this behavior on my own, I wanted my children to have an experienced role model on a daily basis, while I learned along with them. You see, I had faith in God all along, but I just didn't know how to use or to build my relationship with Him. I wanted my children to know Him.

Even though I learned how important it is to have this relationship with God, it is very hard to discipline yourself and start a new routine of doing these things when it hasn't been a part of your upbringing. Like any new habit, it was hard to do. Another tricky thing is that you want it to become a part of your daily routine, but you don't want it to be just a routine. Having a relationship with God can't be a routine—it needs to be a real relationship where you communicate and He communicates.

I'm still working on that to this day. Some years have passed since I first sent my children to school, and I still don't have the kind of relationship with God that I want to have. I will do fine for a while, but then I slack off. I want my children to know how to have a strong relationship with God from the get go. That is why I chose parochial school for them. I have faith that this will give them a healthy, strong foundation in their own faith walk.

During my growing-up years, I learned to rely on God when I needed him. As an adult, I'm learning to realize that I need God every minute of every day, all day long. The Bible says to pray without ceasing and that with every breath I am to acknowledge my Savior. That is the relationship I long to have with Him. I have faith that someday I will have it. My faith in Him has grown, and I know it will continue to grow. Thank God!

The Bible says something about God giving us what we need when we need it, and in my experience, sometimes He doesn't give it to you a minute too soon. But it's always there the minute you need it. Prayer really can take you to great heights. Have faith and pray without ceasing!

Walking A Tightrope In High Heels

By Chave Kreger
Brooklyn, New York

Today with the corrosion of rules and regulations and an obfuscation of the roles of men and women, we are all basically walking a tightrope in high heels. Yes, men, that means *you*, too. We are teetering on the thin wire we call life with no map, navigator, or balancing bar, and we are at a distinct disadvantage because we are not properly outfitted for the journey.

Let's face it, no matter how agile we are, the tightrope is a frightening prospect. It's thin, it's slippery, and you can't get a solid footing, especially in high heels. And that's the other daunting prospect. I pride myself on my feminine demeanor, clothing, and style, and yet I am not a proponent of "elevated walking," as I refer to high heels. I see women who stride down the street on these twin towers and manage to remain upright. I don't know if they've had ballet training or simply put a drop of cement glue in their shoes, but I can't seem to follow in their lofty footsteps. I flail my arms, balance myself on the tips of my toes, and wear the acidulous "puss" of an anorectic supermodel confronted with a marbled steak.

So now that I have taken this analogy to the precipice of its elasticity, let me expound on the topic at hand. Before the 1960's life was a pretty easy-read; the lines of demarcation between men and women, between the races, between the young and old were embedded in the tapestry of our communities and comprised a visual codicil to the Constitution. People didn't veer from the normative because society's aggregate ostracism was swift and complete and brutal.

Now there is gray where black and white dominated the landscape. We're unsure of the rules, and there are few enforcers; we're tentative about our roles at home and in the workplace, and we're taking small, timid steps towards an unknown future. The technological revolution of the 80's has compounded the situation by creating myriad impositions on our attention and diverting our focus from ourselves and our personal and interpersonal lives.

There is only one constant that we have, that we have always had—something intangible yet concrete and ever present—our faith in God. Yes, there are definitely non-believers and negators in our midst, people angry at God because of personal misfortune or collective grievances for their families, ethnic groups, nations, etc. And no one can or should deprecate their pain or their right to rail against the heavens, although I have been known to counter a sullen "I don't believe in God," with an emphatic, "that's all right, because He believes in you." And I may subliminally introduce the ideology that anger is destructive, whereas true belief in God is instructive. Nevertheless, as the daughter and wife of hospital chaplains and a dedicated volunteer myself, I have seen few disbelievers in the trenches.

When tragedy strikes and medical intervention is sought, everyone needs a little spiritual upliftment, some reassurance that a Higher Power can indeed stave off morbidity, as if God is willing to challenge the angel of death to a duel for control of their destiny. And even if people don't allow themselves entirely to believe, they usually don't want to chance missing out on some anodyne for their pain or a possible precipitant to their recovery, so they approach God as a contingency plan. "Let's pray just in case," is their halfhearted mantra.

What I can say from my participation in the hospital community is that faith speeds up the recovery process. Moreover, faith heals. I feel no compunction in writing this because I have seen, with my own eyes, the preternatural power of faith. I have visited hospital patients who wholeheartedly professed that, during their darkest hour God pulled them up and out of the jaws of death. I have seen people I had given up on come back fighting because of their spiritual willpower. I have even heard doctors discuss the disparity between patients with faith and those without.

There is a story I know of that took place at Memorial Sloan-Kettering Cancer Center approximately a decade ago. A doctor operating on a prepubescent cancer patient came out to prepare the family for the worst toward the end of the surgery. He was certain the girl would die on the operating table and commissioned her deeply religious parents to pray because "that's all you can do now."

Her parents convened a prayer meeting in the patients' lounge with their relatives who had been pacing in the hospital corridors. They all entreated God to direct His loving kindness at this poor child. Now please understand that the parents, uncles, and aunts had been praying for months, but this time they invested their prayers with a greater intensity and maximal passion and aimed all their positive thoughts toward the operating room. This family genuinely perceived the parameters of medicine and the boundless, endless capacity of prayer. The doctor finally emerged from the OR and declared that a miracle had occurred. Not only had the girl survived surgery, but her vital signs were also good, and he expected her to make a full recovery with time.

This story has a happy ending. The girl is now a young woman with no recurrence of cancer. She will be able to experience everything other women her age can—career, family, etc. There are no lingering side effects, no repercussions to her illness. Should this be credited to faith or the skillfulness of the doctor? Well, the doctor himself had been certain death was imminent. At best he had prognosticated a bleak and pain-filled future for the girl. So how can we dismiss this incident as anything other than the power of faith? In fact, the doctor was not only astonished at her recovery but at the speed at which she recovered and was transferred from hospital to home care.

Why are we so swift to dismiss the strength, the solidity of faith? The medical community has long been a proponent of laughter as a panacea and perhaps instigator of recovery from cancer. Books have been written about the subject, patients' lives chronicled when they've synergized laughter into their medical regimen, and their convalescences documented. So if laughter, certainly no medicine or surgical procedure, can be deemed worthy of being absorbed into the vast cadre of complementary therapies, then why not faith?

When the unexpected occurs, when the hands of fate are tied behind their back in a stranglehold, we have to delve beneath the topography in search of answers. All I know is that there is "natural" and "supernatural." Natural is what is anticipated, predicated on the facts at hand. If a girl is dying, if her immune system is compromised, God forbid, death is the only natural conclusion. But if this girl is revivified and leads a normal life thereafter, then we have to look upwards for the origins of her rehabilitation.

Marianne Williamson, a famous non-sectarian minister, once said in an epilogue about a discussion of faith that "God can cure AIDS because God is above AIDS." Naturally, the Creator of the Universe is more powerful than anything in the universe; that's only uncommon sense. And I have been privy to an aural exposition of one man's fight and victory over AIDS using the efficacy of prayer and meditation. So do we remain on the left side of the fence even as the right side is filling up with those enlightened souls turned on to religion?

I say NO! The tightrope is still a precarious proposition, the high heels are still difficult to maneuver, and life is continuously changing in the wake of September 11, 2001, but with our faith in tow, we can manage to traverse it with our dignity, health, and happiness intact.

What I Don't See

By Mary Maynard
Monument, Colorado

I can see my wrinkles becoming the size of the Grand Canyon. This morning I noticed that the skin on my legs is loose and hangs in a funny way. My family laughs as I continuously forget almost every appointment I make to whatever doctor or orthodontist is next in line, although I never forget lunch appointments. I watch myself eat less and less each year just to maintain the same size. Although I do not feel sad, my sagging face is communicating something else. I notice the gray hair that seems to sprout overnight as if it got hold of some kind of fertilizer while I slept. It must be really sneaky, because I no longer sleep all that well or much. I see my face flush with the hot flashes that have become my new best friends. I see, but I do not see.

I see my teenage daughter becoming more sober. This might be a good thing, but the catalyst of her new responsible attitude is the reality of the harshness of life. I watch her struggle with what she wants to do when she grows up. I see her face as the truth of having to pay her own bills and live in an unfriendly world hits her, as friend after hormonally-challenged high school friend proves disloyal and juvenile. I see her come in from her job with a grave look of tiredness from the hard work of being a waitress. I watch her grow up. I watch, but I do not see.

I look at pictures in the paper and in magazines of hungry children. I try to keep this information in my head instead of my heart and tell myself that people are hungry because of repressive governments and that if we fly over to feed them, they will never rise up to overthrow the idiots that are posing as their leaders. I see their dirty faces and shabby clothing and want to wash both from my armchair several thousand miles away. I read the stories of the shame and degradation that some go through because of the jobs they must do or because they have no jobs at all. I stare at the black and white pictures and look at the hopelessness in their eyes. I look, but I do not see.

I watched a young wife sit up front at the memorial service for her husband this year at our church. I saw her hand reach out and touch each of her three children as if to empower them with her own strength to make it through that unfathomable and nightmarish experience. Just a few days before their lives had been about peanut butter sandwiches and hockey practice. I observed the look of shock on their faces as they tried to come into an understanding that their perfectly healthy father could die in a freak accident and that they would see him no more. I saw this young family sit surrounded by many and yet somehow alone in their pain. I saw, but I did not see.

I see the pain that this world provides for all in some way or another. As I have gotten older, I can even see great wisdom in pain. I now know that being poor when we were first married was good for me. It gave me the opportunity to discern between what was important and what wasn't. We got a chance to develop our characters in a way that would have been impossible had we suddenly come into a trust fund.

I know that the betrayal of growing older causes me to throw off stupid values. I am a person I like better because of all kinds of different pain that has come my way. Pain causes me to have to throw myself at God's feet as I never would if left to my own devices, since I tend to think I am pretty self-sufficient.

But even though I know that pain has real value in my life, I cannot like it. I can have joy in it, but it is a bittersweet joy that wishes I already lived in an eternity where pain was not necessary.

I see pain. I know that God is good. Between these two truths, there is a hidden world that consists of all that I cannot see. Faith lives there in the space that exists between what I can see and what I know about God.

My eyes look at all the world around me. Faith has different eyes that see on another level. Real faith uses both sets of eyes. It does not try to deny how awful life is. Faith sees the pain in all its horror. But then the inward eye shifts and looks at God. Just as clearly it sees His mercy and wisdom and goodness.

There is a gulf between these two truths. Faith bridges the gap. It chooses to believe everything it sees—pain and God. It trusts that there is a disconnect in the world and that the world that we see is not even the real world. Faith believes it cannot yet see everything going on where God lives.

I can see my friend's child in a wheelchair. She has had all manner of invasive tests and indignities that come with the reality of being 13 years old and handicapped. I can see that she must move herself around with her hands. Getting anywhere is hard for her. I have watched her lying in hospital beds for the myriad of special surgeries that will make her life more "livable." I have seen the look in her eyes as she watched her brother and sister run off down the street to be the first to arrive to play. I have observed the determination of her dad as he strives to do all he can to make her life as normal and as wonderful as possible. I have looked into her mother's face when she was working hard to come to some kind of peace with where her daughter must live, in a world of physical therapy and braces. I watch now as her family prepares for yet another two-day surgery that will leave scars both outward and inward. I have seen, but I do not see.

Today is my chance to have faith. In heaven, faith as I understand it here may not be necessary. Today I can choose to look at all that God says and has shown Himself to be and believe that He will reveal the unrevealed later. I can hand over to His wisdom all that I don't see.

Miracle Of Faith

By Micah Renae Torgrimson
Omaha, Nebraska

The Bible says in Hebrews 11:1 that *Faith is being sure of what you hope for and certain of what you do not see.* I've grown up in church. I knew all of the stories; I could sing all of the songs. At school I was always seen as the "good" girl, and my friends were the same. God was real; that I believed. I had faith that He had sent His Son to die on the cross for my sins. I trusted Him for my little problems, knowing that I'd always make it through somehow. But my faith in God was a quiet, surface faith. I was never bold enough to talk about my faith, and miracles were only in stories of long ago. God wasn't in the miracle business nowadays, at least not that I knew of. Until the summer between my junior and senior year of high school, I don't think I had ever seen how powerful or real faith in God could be.

The summer day was so hot that my clothes stuck to my skin and sweat dripped down the middle of my back. Even the slight breeze didn't help, because the wind was just as hot and humid as the air. Haiti is not the best place to be in the middle of June. But here I was, with 11 others from my church youth group. All week we had been working at a boys' shelter painting the walls, teaching Bible stories, and playing with the boys and some of the other neighborhood children. While we spent most of our time with the boys, we also had opportunities to see the city and meet many other people.

Before going to Haiti, I had never seen such poverty before. Garbage littered the streets. Houses made of cement bricks were half finished because people didn't have the money to finish them. I met families of six or seven who lived in one small room. Sometimes more than one family shared these rooms. I walked through an open market where dirt cakes were sold for a penny because at least it was something to take the edge off the hunger. The boys we worked with at least had the support needed to feed, clothe, shelter, and educate them. They had hope for a future. The others I met, talked with, and befriended didn't always know where their next meal would come from.

If anyone had reason to be hopeless, to be angry with the system, to be disappointed with a God who allows suffering and pain, those people did. *God,* I silently prayed so many times while I was there, *Why don't You do something?* But for a long time it seemed like God had no answer for me. I had a difficult time hoping, praying, having faith for a people I had come to know and love when their world seemed so hopeless, especially compared to the life I have in America.

About two weeks after we had been in Haiti, we were supposed to go to the boys' shelter again to paint. Unfortunately, about half of our team was sick. The two bathrooms we had were constantly occupied. After discussing our options, all of us decided to stay at the house, at least for the morning. Another morning of sitting around, sweating, playing cards, singing songs, and writing in our journals. Sitting on the porch, gazing up at the tops of the palm trees on the other side of the wall surrounding our house, I felt so helpless. Thinking about the people, how they needed to be loved and cared for just like me, I didn't see how I could do anything to make their lives any better. I still believed in God, but the faith that I had in Him seemed to be dwindling.

The sun was shining, and most of us were playing cards on the patio area, waiting for lunch, when there was a soft knock at the gate. Dan, our leader, peeked though the eyehole to see who it was before he let her in. She spoke rapidly to him in Creole. Her dirty, wrinkled flower dress hung down past her knees, and her smile showed her missing teeth. Her forehead glowed in perspiration. Her bare feet padded gently to the patio where we were, still talking to Dan. The prayer woman, as I called her, had come because God told her several of us were sick.

Our group stood in a circle around the patio, watching quietly as she washed her hands and feet. She didn't ask who was sick. She didn't need to. As she made her way around our circle, she stopped before each ill person and prayed for his or her healing. Her prayers were so passionate, so fervent, and although I couldn't understand what she said, I could tell that she believed in a God of miracles. She had faith that He would heal our team members. She listened to what God was saying and had faith that He would do what He said.

What amazed me most was that this woman trusted God with everything, and even her everyday actions revealed her deep love and faith in God. She didn't have a job. She had a family—children to take care of. She did what she needed to do and trusted God for His provision. Yet she still had hope enough to care about other people, to listen to and obey God when He told her what to do. Although I didn't see anyone healed or water changed to wine, I witnessed a miracle that day. I witnessed the miracle of faith in God. That woman, who had nothing, had everything.

I had always thought the people in the Bible—the Abrahams and the Peters—were the ones with strong faith. They were the ones who saw the wonders of God, not people today. In Haiti, I met a woman who had a faith that was everyday real. A woman who was sure of what she hoped for *today.* A woman who had the faith to see the glory of God, whether she actually saw His miracles or not. And, from seeing her example, my faith was strengthened. I, too, believed in a good, powerful God, and slowly I grew bolder in that faith.

I don't remember her name, but I wish I did. I don't even remember what her exact words were, because I don't speak her language. But the hope and the faith that radiated from her soul is something that I'll never forget.

7

A Bond Of Faith

An Uncommon Bond

By Dena Janan Dyer
Granbury, Texas

Sisters, we've heard, often share clothes, friends, rooms, cars, and dates. But Kathy Clenney and Nancy Dyer share something else—a bond they never expected.

In 1993, during a routine physical, Kathy heard shocking news. "Something is wrong with your kidneys," the doctor said.

At first she wasn't too worried. "I didn't have any symptoms," she says. But for three years her health deteriorated. Her charts passed from physician to confused physician, and she underwent a battery of tests. Finally a nephrologist (kidney specialist) got to the root of the problem.

"I had a biopsy, and it showed that I had less than 10 percent of my kidney function," Kathy relates.

During those traumatic years, she began to pray for strength, help, and hope. One night Kathy says she asked her husband, Travis, to pray that she'd die. "I hurt so bad, and I wasn't sleeping at all."

"A walk to the mailbox was a big deal," she says. "At night the leg cramps were severe. And food—just to smell it made me sick."

In February 1997 Kathy went on dialysis. Her specialist, Dr. Chary, recommended she consider becoming a kidney transplant recipient.

At first Kathy was adamant that no one give their life—or their kidney—to save her. "I thought I could live with dialysis, but after I went through the treatments for a while, I saw that my quality of life wasn't really better than what I already had. It wasn't much of a life at all. I just didn't know what to do."

Finally she consented to have close family members tested for a "match." But her son wasn't eligible, and her daughter was pregnant. Then her older sister, Nancy, offered to be tested.

"I said no," Kathy remembers. "I knew the surgery was dangerous and that the recovery time is much longer for the donor than the recipient. I didn't want her risking her life for me. I didn't feel that I deserved it."

So Nancy prayed and waited. And just as Kathy decided to have her name added to the transplant list, Nancy called her baby sister. "It could be a very long wait," she said. "Please, please, let me give you my kidney—I want to do it!"

Even now—five healthy years later—Kathy's voice breaks when she recalls how Nancy told her she needed to be the donor. "She said that our daddy had told her on his deathbed to 'take care of Kat,' and she wanted to keep her promise."

The sisters had grown up poor, and Kathy had contracted rheumatic fever as a child, so Nan had always felt protective of Kat—but even more so after her father pleaded with her to watch over Kat.

It was Nancy's insistence on keeping her word that convinced Kathy to relent. On April 25, 1997, the two sisters checked into a hospital in Memphis and began the arduous process of surgery and recovery.

"Once we made the decision to do it, I knew everything would be okay," Kathy says. "I felt like God was holding me up through the whole process. It was as if He was saying, 'You're both going to be fine. I have it all under control.' We've always been so much alike—the way we think, act, dress—that I knew her kidney would suit me just fine!"

Kathy even felt confident after initial blood tests immediately following the procedure showed that she might be rejecting her sister's organ.

Nancy recalled the terror she felt when she heard that bit of bad news: "I thought, 'She could die!' and I felt horrible that I hadn't helped her." They were both aware of a recent transplant patient whose body had rejected her new organ.

"I always knew there were risks," Nancy says. "My husband was really supportive—but my eldest son was pretty scared. And just a month after our surgeries, Kathy consoled a woman who had received her husband's kidney. He had died!" However, Kathy's faith was confirmed when her blood levels stabilized, and both sisters healed quite quickly.

In addition to similar genetic makeup, the duo share a sense of humor. Following the transplant, they were wheeled into the same recovery room and lay side by side on separate gurneys as they came out of anesthesia. "We got to laughing so hard about our pitiful conditions that it was painful!" Kathy remembers.

When Nancy had stomach troubles in 2002, Kathy jokingly offered her gallbladder to her older sis. "I feel like I owe her so much," she says.

But one thing that makes Nancy's sacrifice remarkable is her humility. "Kathy is so grateful. It's like she thinks I died for her," she says, shaking her head. "To me there was never a question about whether I'd donate my kidney. It was like she asked me for a loaf of bread, not an organ."

Kathy protests, "She saved my life! I'd lay down my life for her in a second."

"I always was good at giving, but I had to learn to receive. It was hard," she says. "My favorite Bible verse is one that says God's grace is sufficient for me, and His strength is made perfect in my weakness."

And so the two sisters who have shared so much—faith, a hard childhood, humor—now share good health, as well as a story of strength, help, and hope.

Faith At The Foot Of The Mountain

By Douglas Knox
Ashland, Ohio

"Though He slay me, yet will I trust in Him..."
Job 13:15

I always knew that God sometimes calls us to unusual faith requirements. They comprise some of the most exciting accounts in Scripture—Job's long vigil when God turned his face from him, Ezra and Nehemiah's work to restore the spiritual and civil life of the Israelites who had returned to Jerusalem from the Exile, Paul and Silas' midnight hymns of praise after they had been beaten and placed in stocks in a Philippian jail. They fueled my imagination and my zeal. I admired their radical faith in the midst of crisis.

Now He has called us. A mountain thrust up in front of us overnight, where a plain lent a wide view the day before. While ours may not have the epic significance of the Biblical accounts, it has left us gasping.

Last week my wife, Marie, woke up with abdominal pain so severe it doubled her over. I called work and told them I wouldn't be in and then took her to the emergency room at 6:30 a.m. The nurses, usually more concerned over insurance paperwork than the emergency at hand, brought out a chair and wheeled her away before the receptionist handed my card back to me. I waited in the lobby, trying to interest myself in back issues of *Newsweek* and *Good Housekeeping*. The clock crept past 7:00, then 8:00 and 9:00 and 10:00 without a word from anyone in the back.

I went home to look for something to do to mask the emptiness in my stomach. By 2:00 p.m. expectation prevailed over my self-control, and I called the hospital. "We were just going to call you," the person on the phone said. "You need to come in and talk to us."

The tone was too serious, too businesslike to be a billing question. I rushed back, wondering if they had been waiting for me to call.

A new receptionist, a lady in her late 50s, sat at the desk and didn't recognize me from the morning visit. With the wary tone of one who expected yet another healthy patient with psychosomatic symptoms, she asked if she could help me.

I introduced myself and said that my wife was in the back.

The drained expression on her face was almost palpable. She turned around and spoke to someone behind her, and within seconds a nurse came to the door. She was short with dark hair and looked altogether too young to be a full-fledged nurse. Where the receptionist was abrupt, the nurse was almost obsequious, falling all over herself to be pleasant. "Thank you for coming in so fast," she said with a smile that I could tell was forced. She led me to a room and pointed. "Your wife's in here."

I joined Marie who had an IV protruding from her arm. Bags of blood and saline hung from the stainless steel pole behind her. A minute later the attending physician joined us. He told us about the tests they had run, said that Marie's hemoglobin was two pints low, and then looked at Marie and said, "I'm afraid we have bad news. You have cancer."

The word cut a jagged slice through our hearts. The doctor explained that the CAT scan showed masses in her colon and ovaries that had metastasized to her liver and stomach.

Tears welled in Marie's eyes as she squeezed my hand. "Why didn't they catch it at the beginning of the year?"

He didn't know. The ultrasound they did then didn't show anything unusual, and the blood tests were negative. They had attributed her discharge to an active hemorrhoid.

I tried to be brave for her while she attempted to absorb the news.

The hospital transferred Marie to inpatient and then to the James Cancer Research Hospital on the OSU campus later that night. After a week of tests and joint consultation, the team there believes that they're dealing with colon cancer. They won't give us a definitive word. Tomorrow afternoon they'll perform surgery, and then they'll know more. The thought hasn't escaped me that tomorrow afternoon I may know how many months or weeks Marie has to live.

These men and women will hold her life in their hands. They don't strut, but they do walk with confidence. I need that right now. They're becoming my Team Hero, the elite combatants who will go in and extricate the silent enemy. Logically I know we're in for a long conflict, but I need to see it one step at a time. I'll be rooting for them while they're in surgery. Take every cell out. Do a biopsy on it if you have to, and then burn it. It's killing my wife, and I hate it.

Obviously I put a lot of stock in these men and women, and that's reasonable. But I'm also praying that God will spare her. Some may think this dualism between the temporal and the spiritual is a cop-out. One of my philosophy professors from my undergraduate days used to say that all faith is irrational, but she was wrong. All of us, whether we realize it or not, begin with something that we accept on no basis other than the truth of the thing itself.

Faith is not an irrational leap in an otherwise rational world. Nor is it a magic formula to get something that otherwise wouldn't be ours. Biblical faith recognizes that the beginning of our thinking is the all-wise God of creation. Solomon wrote in Proverbs 9:10, *"The fear of the Lord is the beginning of wisdom..."* Faith is the lens by which we understand the world around us, even when we don't get our own way. Sometimes it calls us to say with Job, *"Though He slay me, yet will I trust in Him."*

Both my wife and I love the Scripture, and we reach into it without thinking about it. I took solace in Job. Marie went to Daniel. The other day she told a friend over her room phone, "I guess this is going to be my lion's den." She's right in a way. Daniel faced the lions alone in a sealed pit, with only his God to protect him. As much as I'll be with her in my heart, I won't be able to go with her to the operating room. She's going to fight this one with her God at her side.

I try to sound confident for her sake, but I can't boast about how strong my faith is making me right now. Frankly, the way I beg God to spare the woman I've loved for 25 years makes my faith look pretty shaky, at least from where I stand. The thought that I might have to let her go terrifies me. I think about an empty house and bed and wonder if I'll be able to stand it.

Certain things are mine, however. God is faithful, and that gives me the freedom to continue to pray.

I can trust the surgical team because God's creation is still good, even though sin has brought things like cancer into the world. *"I will praise you,"* David wrote, *"because I am fearfully and wonderfully made."* The surgeons know the intricacies of the human body far better than I, but I know the God of the details. I know His creation won't let them down because His knowledge is infinite.

But that's as far as I can go, even at my present level of desperation. My fixed boundary is God's sovereignty. He is infinite, eternal and unchangeable, and that forbids plea-bargaining. Marie is His gift to me, and our times together are in His hands.

Right now our mountain looks impossible. The walls are sheer granite as high as we can see, with few hand or footholds. My fingers and toes are numb with the effort, and we have yet to clear the first escarpment. I don't even know whether we will finish the climb together or Marie go to Glory ahead of me. But this one thing I do know. Our God can be nothing but faithful.

Though He slay her, yet will I trust in Him.

Faith In Taylor

By Elizabeth Ann Fair
Midland, Pennsylvania

"Who are you talking to, baby?"

"I'm playing with Tyler," came her reply.

She's four now. They say time flies when you're having fun. I look at her every day, and I see Jesus in the flesh. No, not the virgin conception, but the embodiment of the Holy Ghost. If it had not been for Jesus, there would be no Taylor. Allow me to share my story...

We had gone to Kentucky that weekend, the weekend of Princess Diana's death. In spite of all of the drama surrounding the world events, we had a wonderful time—my parents, my three-year-old daughter, my husband, and I. We remember seeing the castle on the hill, a lot of horses, and realizing that there really *is* "blue grass" in Kentucky!

A few weeks later, I started to get very concerned about this sick feeling that I just could not shake. "What is wrong, God?"

"Nothing," was His answer. So I went on with life.

It didn't take long. I began to have the same symptoms of pregnancy that I had when I suspected my first. I knew in my spirit that God had chosen to bless us once more with a child. So off to the doctor I went.

"Yes, you are about five weeks pregnant!"

OK, I've been here before. I can handle this, I thought.

Then the hemorrhaging began.

"Oh, my God! What is wrong?"

"Nothing," came His reply.

"But, God, this is not right! This is not normal!"

"I am in control," was His reply.

But, God, I'm weak, I thought. *Physically exhausted, Lord. Spiritually weakening. I don't understand how You can say that something so wrong can be all right. God, please do not build me up to let me down. Not now...not with my children...*

I'm two months pregnant now, and the doctor wants to do a sonogram. As I lay there on that table and glance to my right, I can see some unexplainable things. Then I hear, "We have two sacs here."

Twins! This is history in the making. The last two generations have had twins. None of my cousins have had twins. Thank You, God!

"I want you to go home and keep your feet up as much as possible," says my doctor. "I don't want you to lift anything over 10 pounds. I will write a script for you to be on light duty at work. We want to take care of you, and we need to start now. I'll see you in two weeks, and we'll take another sonogram."

By now I had heard all the horror stories about what can happen if a sonogram is done too soon in the pregnancy. *But I have to trust this,* I think. *After all, I was thrown into this doctor's hands because of a change in insurance at the job, and I was so certain that this is where You told me to go, Lord. What is going on? I have been hemorrhaging for seven weeks now. Doctor knows this. What is wrong, God?*

"Nothing," comes His reply.

At the end of the two weeks I go back to my doctor. We exchange but a few words as I lay there on that table, my emotions running rampant. I pray; I cry; I glance; I wonder.

Once the procedure is over, the doctor says to me, "We may have a problem. You do understand that this pregnancy is also high risk, as was your first. What's happening here is that you are carrying twins, and one baby is not as strong as the other. We also have some concerns about your blood tests. It seems you have developed gestational diabetes. We will need to start you on insulin—just a shot a day for now—and I will need to see you every two weeks."

If ever a pregnant woman could feel a sense of weightlessness, I certainly did that day—not only from the "issue" I had been dealing with for the last nine weeks, but also from the feelings of helplessness, hopelessness, and despair that had gripped every fiber of my physical, emotional, and spiritual being. As the next two weeks went by, I questioned God *a lot*! I didn't understand, and sometimes I didn't want to. I just wanted out. This was certainly not good for the babies...

Once again I traveled back to the doctor's, this time with my mother as chauffeur. This time I am too weak to drive myself. This time I am too emotional to face the fate of my children alone. This time I cry.

"What we see here are the two sacs." My doctor continues, "This sac is healthy. This sac, as you can see, looks as if someone pinched it between their fingers and smashed it. You have been miscarrying a twin for the past three months, Mrs. Fair."

Oh, God! Oh, God! You said that everything was all right. You told me that nothing was wrong, God. This is not good, God! I'm on the edge, God! God, how could—

"Mrs. Fair," the doctor goes on. "I want you to stop work now. You need to keep your feet elevated as much as possible for the duration of this pregnancy. We will need to increase your insulin dosages to three per day, as well. I need you to monitor your blood sugar at least six times per day."

It was a good thing my mother was there with me, because at this point, my mind was in a total fog. I only half heard what the doctor was saying, and at this moment, God was not talking.

For the next six months I talk only to God about what has happened and only to my doctor about what could happen next. My mother and I talk about names. "If it's a girl, Taylor. If it's a boy, Tyler," is my decision.

My due date is so close now, and I am very excited. One more month to go—June 22 is the targeted date. It is now the third week of May, and I have a birthday party to plan. My three-year-old will be celebrating a birthday on June 3. My mother keeps telling me not to try to plan a party, that I don't really know how close I am to delivering. After much cajoling, I decide to postpone the party and have a celebration after we bring the baby home. Well, she knew what she was talking about...

On the morning of Friday, June 4, I begin hemorrhaging once more, and at 10:00 a.m. my husband is transporting me to the hospital. As soon as we reach the emergency room, there is a wheelchair waiting to take me to the maternity ward. Immediately the nurses hook me up to monitors, IV's, and more monitors. After five hours of monitoring, at approximately 3:00 p.m., I am told to go home—that these pains I am experiencing are not "real labor pains." I am told that I am not close enough to my due date to warrant a hospital stay right now and that the insurance would frown upon it—especially a weekend stay where there would be no one to release me until Monday should it be decided that this is truly a false alarm.

My husband, frantic by now, tells the nurses over and over, "My wife is going to have this baby tonight! You can't let her go home now! This is real!" All to no avail.

My doctor, whose hands are tied because of insurance loopholes, tells me on my way out of the room, "Call me immediately when your contractions get down to one minute apart. If you are still at home on Monday, call me at the office." Wow...

When we arrive home, the three of us—my husband, my now four-year-old, and I—make our beds in the living room. For the next seven hours I pace the floor, pad and pencil in hand. Every time I have a pain, I write down what time it occurred and how long it lasts. For seven full hours, I am an emotional wreck.

On June 5, at 1:00 a.m., my water breaks. Panicking unbelievably, my screams seem to shake the very foundation of our home. I am in the bathroom—me and God, God and me—when it happens. As my husband rounds the corner to come to my aid, he grabs the phone that sits on the phone table beside the refrigerator. Busting through the door, he grabs me and tries to get me onto the floor. I am in such pain that my entire body is as a stone figure. He leaves me, like the 911 operator instructs him, to find a blanket for me to lie on. At this point there is no more compromise. My husband grabs me with one arm and hoists me onto the blanket. The pain worsens, and I clutch the side of the bathtub. As instructed, my husband runs back to the living room to get a pillow for my head.

While he is gone, the baby's head crests. *This can't be happening, God. It's too soon—3½ weeks too early! Is everything all right, Lord?*

"I am in control," comes His answer.

Before my husband returns, all within a matter of about 20 seconds, my beautiful baby girl is lying on the blanket with me. Here is Taylor...

So now, looking back, it's funny to think that she would name her imaginary friend Tyler. How could she know? How could she understand? She's only four, and yet it seems she has the insight of an adult. She is so strong, but God knew she would be from the beginning.

How My Faith Has Grown Stronger

By Karen Kruse
Glenview, Illinois

As any author will tell you, getting published in today's market is a daunting task. It takes more than talent; it takes faith.

I am the author of *A Chicago Firehouse: Stories of Wrigleyville's Engine 78.* It is the story of the Chicago firehouse across the street from the ivy-covered walls of famed Wrigley Field. My dad served here for the first 14 years of his 30-year career. Growing up in the tightknit firefighting family, I had the knowledge to write an enjoyable and informative book, but I found I needed more; I needed faith.

This odyssey begins with *why* I wrote this book in the first place. Due to a friend's urging, I wrote a piece for a national magazine about visiting the firehouse as a little girl. Within months, it appeared on magazine pages around the country, much to my delight. The article met with applause from friends, and something special was at work here. Within two weeks, my destiny was decided, and I started on my way.

As the adventure played itself out, I realized the more faith I had in its outcome, the quicker it would come to fruition. While gathering facts for my epic, I started looking for a big-name personality to provide the foreword for the book. Perhaps this experience illustrates my faith more than any other.

Mike Ditka played football for the Chicago Bears at Wrigley Field and was known to visit the firehouse during those years. Being a Chicago icon, he was the perfect guy to help launch my project. I believed from the beginning I could get him to help. I asked a member of the local media, who I did not know, for an address to contact Mr. Ditka. The next day, I had the address of the New Orleans Saints coaching office where Mr. Ditka was then head coach. I immediately dashed off a letter to him asking for an interview.

Thirteen days later Mr. Ditka called my home. We had an animated chat, and he offered his help. He didn't have "firehouse stories" but would help any way he could. A month later, I called back asking if he would do my foreword. His assistant told me he agreed. I was on my way. The next month he got fired from the Saints organization. *Now what do I do?* I called the Saints office again. His assistant remembered me. Turns out, her husband was a New Orleans firefighter! She gave me the number to Mr. Ditka's personal secretary in Chicago. Perhaps she could help.

Undaunted, I made the call. Mary wasn't quite sure of me, but she never told me to go away. For months I kept in touch with her, never getting the meeting I would have liked, but not giving up either. I had faith. I *had* to keep going, despite my so-called "friends" warning me that I was fighting a losing battle and cautioning that I would never get Ditka to help.

But I didn't buy in to that kind of thinking. Eighteen months passed with me still making phone calls and keeping in touch, but still I didn't have the foreword. The book's draft was finished by that time, and I had found a publisher. Forging ahead, I called Mr. Ditka's office yet again and told Mary about the situation. I desperately needed Mr. Ditka's help—*now*!

Against all odds I received a fax. Coach Ditka sent the foreword I had dreamed about for over a year, and it was perfect. Faith and the will to succeed got me there.

The next day lightning struck yet again. Chicago's Fire Commissioner also offered his help. I had contacted him seven months earlier, but had heard nothing. Now, as if by magic, he stepped forward with the preface. It was yet another example of how all things are possible with faith.

All the while I was courting the big names for help, I had other battles to fight. The first publisher I contacted was all set to publish my book but changed her mind mid-stream. She loved the concept at first glance, but said I would have to rewrite it if she were to take it on. Numb, I left her office disappointed, but not devastated. I knew my faith was my strength and somehow, someway I would find the right publisher for my project. I prayed for guidance, having faith pieces would fall into place at the proper time. The very next month I found my publisher, and this one didn't change a word of my text! My book came out as I intended.

All the while I was working on this project, I felt the loving presence of firefighters who died many years ago guiding me along the way. As I wrote about them in my book, I could feel their help and love coming through. I was channeling their power. *They* would help me get this book published. I only had to *believe*. I had to have *faith*. They would take care of the timing and publisher. My own firefighting grandfather was among my fans "on the other side." Since starting this project, I like to say my angels wear fire helmets!

One thing about Chicago firehouses interested me since I was a kid: the red and green lights on each one. Since I was writing this book, I wanted to find out why they were there. I had faith I would find the answer, but I got more than I bargained for on the quest to enlightenment. A man I met only twice who owned a fire novelty store tipped me off to the name of the fire commissioner who ordered the red and green lights. I learned they are unique to Chicago and mean port and starboard. This particular commissioner had an interest in shipping and ordered the lights be installed just because he could.

I thought it was a great story and I had my answer, but the story wouldn't die. When that first publisher decided she didn't want my book, I left her office disappointed. To calm down, I ducked in to a local cemetery to "center" myself and pray for help from my firefighting guides. If they wanted this book done, I needed guidance! I had ultimate faith they would help but was frustrated at the time.

As I traveled through the cemetery, I came upon the gravestone of the commissioner who ordered those marvelous lights on Chicago firehouses. Tickled, I snapped a few photos and sent them to a website that features the gravesites of famous people. They are very good about giving me credit for writing biographies for the pictures I submit, so I wrote the piece and then forgot about it.

A few months later, I received the e-mail of a lifetime. The 87-year-old daughter-in-law of that commissioner saw my pictures of those graves and wrote to thank me. It touched me that I could touch her. I told her how important this book was to me and how those lights had captured my interest. It wouldn't surprise me if the commissioner was one of my special angels, helping with my epic. It's just one more example of my "friends in high places." They certainly make my life fun! During every lecture, I wear red and green angels on my lapel and tell this incredible story.

Finding a publisher and getting my words out there for the world to read was a monumental task, but getting it noticed by the public is even harder. My faith strengthened through the writing of the book, I had no reason to lose it now. I met people who wanted to help me when I needed them most.

While walking to the program for a memorial service for firefighters who died in the past year, I mentioned my project to a firefighter who immediately took me to meet the firefighter's union president. Months later a blurb appeared in the union newsletter plugging my book.

I sought publicity through newspapers and radio stations, and even though most offers were ignored, I persevered. I had faith that if I kept my name visible, somebody would bite. Sure enough, after three attempts at a prominent radio station, I was invited for an interview. I was nervous but confident I would be fine. Fate threw me a loop when I received more airtime than originally scheduled.

Faith that I will be in the right place at the right time has propelled me forward, eagerly awaiting the next adventure. Miraculously, my book was even nominated for a Pulitzer Prize in History. I inquired if local libraries would like to hear me speak on the book's subject and was elated when several took me up on my offer. Faith that I would survive public speaking gave me confidence and even more bookings and visibility.

When I step back and look at what I've accomplished and how, I'm amazed. My book hit store shelves in May 2001, long before the events of September 11. I state emphatically in my tome that firemen should be appreciated for what they do every day. In the 30 years my dad was on the fire department, he was thanked only *once* for saving a life. Since 9-11, it seems everybody is now on "my" bandwagon.

The timing of this book is unnerving. Why did I decide to do it now? Why was I pushed to get it written in four months? I feel I was used by powers greater than I to bring the book's message to the public. Now I see it had to be in print before the terrorist attacks of September 11. Even so, it was my faith to see it through and my feeling that I was doing the right thing, even when the odds said it would never work, that I credit for getting it done.

The past three years have been an incredible adventure. Due to the events that have transpired, my faith is stronger and unshakeable. I wouldn't have it any other way.

Love Thy Neighbor

By Kimberly Ripley
Portsmouth, New Hampshire

The Bible never defined the boundaries of neighborhoods, so when I decided to love a neighbor in Mississippi from my New Hampshire home, it might have seemed a bit strange to others. Pearlie Mae Maxwell* was elderly and poor. I received her name and biography from a group called The Box Project. It started as a meaningful way to share my family's blessings with someone less fortunate. It turned out to be love.

I had grown disillusioned with some of our community's means of helping others during the Christmas season. I knew it wasn't right to judge, but it didn't seem fair that families receiving assistance through the kindness of others should be out purchasing big screen TV's and video games. This was becoming more and more typical. Whatever agency was responsible for screening families to determine their holiday needs hadn't been particularly thorough. The Lord would help me handle this judgment business—but in the meantime I truly wanted to help someone. I wanted to help someone who genuinely needed our help—not someone who wanted to save his money for trivial things. When I first heard about The Box Project, I knew it was a gift. What I didn't know was that the gift would wind up being mine.

The Box Project asks donors to provide a monthly box for a person on their list. Their list was at that time comprised of elderly folks in rural Mississippi. I received a biography telling me all about Miss Pearlie. She was black. She was in her 60's. Her kidneys were failing and she was on dialysis weekly. She had little to no education and had been widowed for many years. She was a mother and a grandmother. And she had very little in the way of material things. At the suggestion of the program directors, I sent a letter of introduction and awaited a reply. In my letter, I asked her what she most needed or would like to have.

"Are you crazy?" my friends asked.

They naturally assumed I would be taken advantage of.

"What if she asks for things you just can't buy?"

I had faith in this project and faith in God's answer to my prayer. I wanted to find someone to help, and I wanted to correspond with that someone personally. Most programs didn't allow the donors to even know the family's name, let alone correspond with them.

My response from Pearlie Mae was delightful. Her handwriting, although legible, was filled with misspellings and incorrect grammar. Still I deciphered her words and loved their sincerity. She was a humble woman and asked for very little. She considered herself luckier than many of her neighbors.

"I am one of the lucky ones," she wrote. "I have hot water and electricity."

I was ashamed to think of the number of times I had complained recently. I complained about our home. I had complained about our yard needing work. And here was this lady feeling blessed for having hot water and electricity!

Her requests were humble, too.

"I'd like some cotton underpants, size ten," she wrote. "And I'd love to have some tinfoil."

My first box to Pearlie Mae was filled with kitchen and bathroom things. There were soaps, shampoo, new towels and face cloths. I bought dishtowels for her kitchen and lots of items she couldn't purchase with her food stamps—paper towels, dish soap, plastic wrap, and several large rolls of good quality tinfoil.

Each month brought new surprises—as many for me as for Pearlie. I learned a little more about her with each letter and was always astonished by her humble requests. Often she asked for something for one of her daughters rather than for herself.

"Rena needs some shoes," she said.

And she made certain to tell me that the items need not be new.

"We're not proud people," she wrote. "I am happy to have used things that you don't want anymore. You don't need to go out and buy new things."

Holidays became even more fun in our family as my children helped plan for and buy the goodies that filled Pearlie Mae's boxes. She loved stuffed animals, so we sent Easter bunnies, a black cat at Halloween, a turkey at Thanksgiving, and a beautiful calico cat at Christmas time.

When I lost my beloved grandmother in December of 1999, I wrote to Pearlie, sharing my sorrows. Having misplaced Pearlie's biography sheet after months of sending boxes, I knew she must have a birthday coming up. Hoping I hadn't already missed it, I also asked in this letter when she celebrated her birthday.

My reply came just a few weeks later. I was growing more and more fond of this lady and truly looked forward to her letters.

"I would love to have a granddaughter like you," she replied, in reference to my loss of my grandmother. "And my birthday is February 20."

I was stunned. That had been my own grandmother's birthday. I believed now, even more, that God had put Pearlie Mae Maxwell and me together for good reason.

I decided to lavish on Pearlie the little pleasures in life my grandmother had loved. I sent letters and cards more often. If I was shopping and saw a pretty blouse and thought, "Gram would have loved that," I'd buy it for Pearlie.

She was delighted when I found size eight extra-wide shoes.

"All mine fit too snug," she had said.

When the Mississippi wind grew chilly, I found cardigan sweaters that were soft and warm. To make time go by during Pearlie's kidney dialysis appointments, I sent her books on audiocassette and a cassette player.

When Pearlie could no longer stay in her apartment, she moved in with her daughter, Dorothy. And although Dorothy and her husband were taking care of her, I wanted to continue sending the boxes. Dorothy had access to a computer, and now we could correspond by e-mail.

"Mama spends a lot of time in bed," Dorothy would write. "Could you send her some night clothes?"

In time Pearlie's material needs became fewer and fewer, but it still thrilled me to find little things to send her—things that would have thrilled Gram, like flowers delivered from a florist, a porcelain Easter basket, or freshly-scented lotions and powders.

As Pearlie's health declined, I received updates from Dorothy.

"Mama's taken a turn for the worse," she'd write. "Please pray."

"Let Miss Pearlie know we're praying and we love her," I'd reply.

A few days later I'd rejoice when I received another e-mail.

"She's out of the hospital again."

I could feel God nudging me toward Dorothy. While her needs weren't the same as Pearlie's, I sensed she needed a friend. I sent some uplifting books and some soothing flavored tea. My grandmother had healed everything with prayers and tea.

Finally unable to meet her medical needs, Dorothy regretfully moved her mother into a local nursing home.

"She needs more care than I can give her," came her message—obviously riddled with guilt and sadness.

Now messages about Pearlie came weekly, as Dorothy was often gone visiting at the nursing home.

I sent more flowers.

Recently I was surprised to "hear" from Dorothy on a weeknight.

"Mama's not good. Her heart stopped and there's just a machine keeping her alive," she wrote.

I assured Dorothy once again of our prayers and love. The next day I e-mailed to check on Pearlie's condition.

"Mama left us last night at 11:00," Dorothy wrote. "Her heart stopped three more times, and we finally told them they'd done enough."

I never met Pearlie Mae Maxwell, but through the grace of God I knew her and loved her. She was a special part of my life. Her photo hangs today where it has hung for more than three years—on a bulletin board by my desk. Surrounded by pictures of my family, Pearlie looks right at home there. I know with certainty she's right at home with the Lord.

Do I regret that we never met in person? Maybe I do—just a little bit. I'd entertained dreams of arriving at Pearlie's doorstep and introducing myself amidst hugs and shrieks of surprise. But I have no regrets at all about the part of me I gave to her. I have no regrets about the modest gifts I provided. I know her best gifts are well provided now.

In a few weeks I'll contact the Box Project. I'll ask for another biography, and I'll send an introductory letter, just like I did with Pearlie more than three years ago. I have faith that God will send the perfect match.

I'll await a reply and a list from my brand new friend. I wonder if she'll need tinfoil?

*Last name changed for privacy.

I Am…

By Lydia Grace Goska Skidmore
Auburn, Washington

There are things of this world that were made to last forever. Mankind was created with a finite understanding of that which embodies our daily existence. Questions can be asked, but answers will not always be given. Doubts will surface, and it is in these often quiet streams of the subconscious that one must learn to trust and depend on the unseen.

For some of life's deepest struggles, the answer is not tangible. The foundation of the mind becomes the foundation of life. A time is indeed coming when our questions will be answered, our doubts will be destroyed, and all of mankind will acknowledge the truth of saving grace and sovereign deity.

It is for this time that we wait.

You know me.

And although you may not know that you know me, I know you.

I'm the steps in your house and the bubble gum that you chew. I'm the laces on your tennis shoes and the pen that you used at work yesterday. I'm water, I'm air, I'm land, and I'm ocean. I'm almost everywhere if you'll just take the time to find me.

Everyone has me, so don't think you're special or anything, because where I'm concerned, there are no favorites. You're the same as the person next to you in my eyes, and try as you might, your humanity will always find you out.

You see, I'm not destructible, and I'm anything but picky. I come in any shape you like, and I'll allow myself to be put almost anywhere. Sometimes I'm purposefully placed in something, like the insurance you pay every month, and sometimes I'll just formulate without conscious recognition like the chair that you're sitting in right now.

I'm really quite versatile.

If you hold onto me long enough, I'll become something valuable to you—like a treasure. If you knew my true worth, you'd sell all you have to claim me as your own. Of course, my worth in your eyes will not be found easily, so don't think it won't be without some toil and hard work on your part. But if you give me time, I can change you. I will push aside your doubts and show you to trust, and I will exile your fear and teach you to learn.

I have power.

I'm not powerful though. Sometimes I'm as strong as a lion, ready to take on the world, but sometimes I'm nearly as fragile as a daisy, easily broken in the wind. The strongholds that arise and the tears that fall are one and the same.

Some claim they lack me, but I am there, for I do not cease to be in one's life merely because of skilled articulations. The claim of my absence is the evidence of my existence. Sometimes words only prove to make me stronger.

I am there.

I'm the little girl's hand that holds onto her daddy's, and I'm the car that will drive you home tomorrow. I'm the telephone downstairs and the envelope you sealed last night. I'm the shirt on your back and the paycheck from work you sent in the mail.

And although many claim me, few really know me.

Some people deny me, as if their acknowledgment of my presence has anything to do with my existence. Some people cheat me. They keep me under lock and key unless convenience or a crisis makes my presence mandatory.

Some people hide me, afraid of what others will do if they learn that I'm there. Some change me, altering who I am to make me more appealing, less offensive, or easier to grasp.

And yet some people grab onto me, and they never let go. It is these that I'm here for.

Now don't get me wrong—I'm here for everyone.

But there are those who are different because I'm here. They are not the same as they were before they met me. I'm not a mere five-letter word in their vocabulary, and I'm not just a book they read once a week. I'm more than a facade they display for personal gain or another's benefit.

I am them.

They have let me in, and they have indeed been changed. Their life in the sunshine mirrors what I have taught them under the clouds. The words that they speak come from the inside—not their intellect, not their social class, not their earthly compatibility. Their daily lifestyle shows a greater calling than merely living life for the moment, oneself, or even others.

I am not me simply because I want to be. I could not have created myself as an all-important being capable of insurmountable courage. It's not because I said so that I am what I am.

I am what I am because of a man who was God 2,000 years ago.

It was through Him that I found the courage and the reason to teach you to love, to laugh, to cry, to enjoy, and quite plainly, to live. He was human deity, and through Him I was enabled to reach out to you.

Those who came before believed without seeing.

I was there.

Those who come after have God in the flesh to follow and a book to live by.

I am there.

Hold onto me, for I am priceless and eternal.

You may deny me someday. I forgive you. I will always be there, walking right beside you, waiting for you to turn toward me again. That whisper in the deepest part of your soul is me reminding you that I'm still here. I'm waiting. I will never force you to do anything. Where you choose to put me is your choice, and put me somewhere, you will.

I am there.

I always will be.

I am the wind's whisper at nighttime, and I am the leaves falling in autumn. I am the sweetest music you will ever hear, and I am brilliant colors as they splash across the horizon. I am the flower as it grows, and I am the baby as it forms. I am the changing of a human heart from rock solid marble to a moldable jar of clay.

Place me in time, money, or many, and disappointment will be yours in abundance.

Place me in One man, and I will never fail you.

Place me in the one true God, and I will never leave you.

As I said, I know you, and whether or not you think you know me, I'm still there.

I am faith.

8

Faith That Can't Be Broken

Faith: A Retrospective

By Audrey M. West
Brooklyn, New York

> "Human beings are not victims of trauma from birth to death; they can find fulfillment in experience that is hard to leave."
>
> —Jesse Taft

What does it take to survive numerous traumatic events in one's life? Luck? Tenacity? Good coping and survival skills? Support of family and friends? Drugs? Alcohol? Hope? Or faith? While many are born with silver spoons in their mouths, very few people have been spared any sort of trauma, family dysfunction, or crisis in their lives.

As for me, I am convinced that when I was born not, only did the doctor smack me, but everyone in the room must have followed suit considering the anguish I've endured since childhood. I cannot recall a time in my life when I wasn't involved in some traumatic event where I had to rely on blind faith to get me through the day.

I am constantly inundated with questions such as, "How do you manage?" "What keeps you going?" and "Why aren't you nuts?" (The latter being the most popular.) Basically, one needs good ole survival skills which can consist of all the above-mentioned attributes, the drugs and alcohol aside, but all of which could be defined in a single word: faith. Faith means a belief in one's self, in the system, in other people, and particularly in a higher being. Sometimes you don't even know what kept you going until you're encouraged to reflect.

For me, reflection alone can be traumatizing. I don't want to go into too many details, but a number of events transpired in my life that truly tested my faith.

At age seven, my five-year-old sister and I were placed or "sentenced" as I experienced it, into foster care at an orphanage run by priests and nuns. Life there was something like a torture camp. Abuse was rampant. I don't recall any sexual abuse, but there was plenty of physical, emotional, and psychological abuse. Being separated from my parents and siblings only added to the trauma.

I was "released" from the orphanage at the age of 13 and reunited with my mother and siblings. My parents had since separated. However, not long after returning home, I found myself in another situation that would again test my faith. I was assaulted and nearly raped (I ran for my life) by a family acquaintance that had also sexually abused me as child. Things couldn't have gotten any more desperate, or at least that's what I thought.

Returning home did not turn out as I hoped. It was a very dysfunctional environment characterized by drugs, alcohol, and violence. My sister ended up back in the foster care system, and I, unfortunately, married at age 16.

The marriage turned out to be just another abusive experience fraught with physical, emotional, and psychological trauma. My husband, who also abused drugs and alcohol, kept me isolated from family and friends and pretty much used me as a punching bag. Even though I managed to survive 25 years of mistreatment, I have always regretted putting my children through this experience. My faith was certainly tested during those years—my faith in God, in the courts, and in the justice system.

Four children were born of this union, two boys and two girls.

One day in 1988 my oldest son, at 21 years old, was shot and killed as he walked home from work. At this point, faith was the farthest thing from my mind. I felt like I was in limbo. Everything felt hopeless. Faith was no longer a belief that things would improve; it was more like desperation—a desperation to achieve something positive in my life. I couldn't accept the fact that I was put on this earth to live the life of Job. Once you begin to think of yourself as a victim, victimization prevails. I had to take control of my own destiny no matter what the obstacles. Nonetheless, I did not expect it to be easy.

In 1988, the same year of my son's murder, I finally separated from my husband and moved in with my mother. Her apartment was too small for my kids and me, so we had to camp out on the floor every night. Bearing in mind the torment I endured at the hands of my husband, I actually slept like a baby.

It was a very difficult transition. Many traumatic experiences occurred that continued to test my survival skills, including the untimely deaths of my father and all five of my siblings, all alcohol and drug related. In addition, my only surviving son was incarcerated and sentenced to 132 years for botched robbery. Ironically, my son's faith comforted me through this difficult time.

But in the years that followed, I obtained my GED, earned a BA from St. John's University, received my Masters in social work from Fordham University, and I earned my certification in social work this past year. I believe this was God's plan. If anyone had suggested this to me earlier in life, I would have spit in his or her eye. Yet, whether I was conscious of it or not, faith played a significant role in my life.

It was built on assurance, confidence, and conviction in my abilities and myself and in having the insight, tenacity, persistence, determination, and resilience to triumph over the obstacles placed before me. Maintaining a sense of humor was also beneficial to my survival, and that presently works to my advantage, as well. If I had to consider a second career, it would be as a comedy writer. Laughter beats Prozac any day.

Faith to me is a belief that you can find a positive in every negative and that bad beginnings *can* evolve into good endings, if you look for them. In retrospect, through my experiences I have acquired tremendous empathy—a prerequisite in social work. These experiences have given me insight and a connectedness to my clients.

As Eleanor Roosevelt once said, "…The purpose of life, after all, is to live it, to taste it and experience it to the utmost, to reach out eagerly and without fear for newer and richer experience…The experience can have meaning only if you understand it. You can understand it only if you have arrived at some knowledge of yourself…"

Faith, Hope, And Love

By Denise L. Schulz
Merrill, Wisconsin

When the words "in sickness and in health" were declared part of the weddings vows, I'm certain they were thinking of my grandparents. My grandparents are the most devoted people I know, not only to each other, but also to their family. My grandpa and grandma have been married for 62 years.

My grandma, Loretta, had a one-year-old daughter, DeElda, and was pregnant with her second one when Grandpa, Eugene, became awfully ill. DeElda also became ill. Grandma spent all day taking care of both of them. At night she rocked DeElda which left her with minimal sleep. Grandma did not want her husband to wake.

Finally, one day it was just too much for her body to handle and her legs gave out from under her. Grandpa took her to a hospital, but no one seemed to know what was wrong with her. In those days, I think it was pretty much trial and error. They gave her some vitamins, which later on they discovered actually made her worse. Eventually she was diagnosed with polio. This is also when they realized that my grandpa and DeElda had polio, as well, but they were only mildly affected.

Grandpa worked all week and then on the weekends drove to the hospital to be with Grandma. Grandpa's parents, Pa and Granny, kept DeElda while Grandpa went back and forth and during the day while he worked. Grandpa said she became awfully spoiled.

Many people today vaccinate their children from polio, but most don't realize how this disease could effect their family. My grandma was affected more seriously because of the vitamins they gave her.

Grandma was in so much pain they had to keep her in a special part of the hospital so no one could hear her scream. They wrapped her in wool with a special hot oil remedy (in hopes of not burning her). This special remedy kept her from getting worse. Still, she lost all muscle tone in her whole body except her neck and forearms. Yet she carried her second baby girl full-term.

I work in a nursing home and most people I've seen that had polio, have one stiff arm or one stiff leg as a result, which is very serious indeed. But my grandma cannot voluntarily move nearly any of her body.

Under the same circumstances, some people would give up living. Others would have put their spouse in an institution. But my grandparents are not some people! They are very special, and I'm proud to be their granddaughter.

I'm also proud they did not give up. You see, neither of those two daughters are my parent. If my grandparents had given up, I would not be here today to tell you their story. They had faith in each other, faith in their marriage and vows, faith in family, and most of all faith in GOD. Their love for each other demonstrates so much to me. It is more special than anything I can imagine. You see, my grandparents went on to have eight more children, to make that a total of eight living children, one miscarriage, and one stillborn child. My dad happens to be number 5 of the 10 children, so that makes me feel like a miracle of faith.

When Grandma came home, Granny helped out with the kids and housework and taking care of Grandma. When my grandparents moved to Crandon, the neighbor lady, Mrs. Trainer, took over that job. To my understanding, even though Granny and Mrs. Trainer assisted in the rearing of the kids and such, my grandma was still Mom and was respected as that. If Grandma initiated a discipline and the child continued to disobey, Grandma carried out the discipline. Granny or Mrs. Trainer might have had to assist in getting the child to Grandma, but my grandma carried out the deed.

My grandma was able to sit in a wheelchair for most of her younger life when her own kids were growing up. It is difficult for her to be up and about in a wheelchair these days. When I was very little, I remember her going for rides to look at Christmas tree lights. Grandma would sometimes get up if a family member were getting married in the church at the bottom of the hill from her house and for graduations and things like that. Of course, it always depended on how she was feeling that day. Even when I was a little older she would come outdoors during the summer picnic we'd have for their anniversary. Sometime in the early 1990's she had to stop even that. Now she is pretty much limited to trips to the doctor's office or the hospital.

My grandpa had a van that he took the seats out of and he would put Grandma in her wheelchair and strap her in. Then it changed to a hospital cart. In order to get Grandma from the bed to the chair they used a hoyier lift. To get her on the cart they just put her on a sheet and everyone grabs a side; then they count and slide, kind of like you see in emergency room shows. This must be done any time Grandma needs to go anywhere.

My grandma has never given up on life. She always finds something to keep herself busy. Grandma has crocheted rag rugs and many, many, many, afghans for her children, grandchildren, great grandchildren, and friends. Grandma does crossword puzzles and listens to her Bible on tape or others who read to her. Grandma enjoys listening to the birds sing and watching the squirrels run around on a big tree out her picture window. She can even sing like some of the birds. On occasion when she does this, they'll sing back to her. Grandma's bed is in the living area of the house so she is included in all the events. Her family is much too large for her to be in some bedroom off to the side. Telling old stories of the days gone by and being thankful for all that God has given her are things she also enjoys.

When I first moved away from home, I took great comfort in knowing that if I ever needed to hear a familiar voice, I could call and Grandma would be on the other end. Since Grandma is so reliable to be near the phone, the local rescue squad asked her to be a dispatcher for them. Because Grandma cannot reach and grab the phone like you or I can, Grandpa rigged up a phone for her to use. He wrapped a huge rubber band around the phone part, then another one hooked to that one that hung loose for her to grab. Grandma flops her arm over toward the phone, grabs the rubber band, bites the sleeve of her shirt, and pulls with her mouth to get the phone to her chest, then up to her ear. In a matter of seconds she can answer the person who needs help on the other end. This sounds like it would take an eternity for her to actually do, but it really takes her just seconds.

Grandpa and Grandma always figured out *how* Grandma could do stuff; they didn't sit around complaining that she couldn't do things. There are probably at least a thousand things I can do that my Grandma can no longer do. But I've never heard her ever complain about things she can't do. That within itself is awesome. I've never thought about that before now.

Faith has gotten my grandparents through the thick and the thin. For better or worse, for richer or poorer, in sickness and health 'til death do they part. I know they've dealt with many other challenges, other than just this bit of their life I've shared with you thus far.

Grandpa has not had help from Mrs. Trainer since he retired in his 50's. Grandma prefers her husband of 62 years now to be the one by her side. Grandpa has stayed very active in his retirement. Grandpa and Grandma have many children, grandchildren, and great grand children whom he supplies with things from his plentiful garden and his delicious homemade bread and bun dough. If you live within driving distance, it is a bonus because he will deliver the dough to you. It is wonderful to bake it for supper. As a bonus you get to smell the wonderful aroma of baking bread, as if you've spent the time making the dough yourself. When Grandpa describes how he starts his bread dough, he says, "I start with a gallon of milk," explaining how much dough he makes at one time.

He takes great pride in his accomplishments as a husband, father, and so on. Grandpa is also a veteran hunter. He still is going up in the deer stand this year. Grandpa shot two eight-point bucks a few years back, and he is 86 years old this year.

Often in my own life and my own marriage, I wonder what in the world will get me through the day. Then I think of the awesome example of faith and unconditional love my grandparents show me every day of their lives—how they have faith in themselves, their marriage, their family; how they've taught me to love God and have faith in Him. Through Him we can do all things. Then I know that I can make it through the day. So can everyone.

My life is nowhere near as hard as my grandparents had it. I can't imagine living one day confined to a bed and unable to move my knees by myself, or being responsible to move my husband's knees because he can't move them himself. This is what my grandparents do for each other. My grandma has been unable to move her body voluntarily and unable to get out of bed even with help most of my life. Her mind is fully intact, and Grandma is very wise. Grandma's caring and loving nature always reassures me. She loves all of us kids and prays for us, even though she's the one in need of our prayers. And I love the little things Grandma does—like how she nibbles the little ones' ears.

Grandma doesn't regret life. My grandpa takes care of Grandma in their home and enjoys taking care of the garden and making his bread dough. Most of the children live close by and visit weekly or more often. They help out with whatever needs to be done. When our family has get-togethers, the house is so full there's standing room only—and there's always food involved. I enjoy seeing everyone at these family functions, but I truly enjoy seeing these two marvelous individuals I'm lucky enough to call my grandpa and grandma the most.

Faith In A Dirty Shirt

By Jennifer Lynn Zolper
Modesto, California

I work in a cavernous kitchen with a man named Marty. He is a 47-year-old dishwasher, though it's not fair to stop at that since he also has two other jobs—cleaning the office of an auto parts store and detailing the used cars that are donated to our church now and then.

Marty is unmistakable. He is a triple-extra-big man whose shirt buttons threaten to pop. His wavy, light brown hair is graying and cut straight, jaw-length, and slightly greasy, topped by a "Jesus" baseball cap adorned with religious pins. He is missing his right front tooth. He shuffles everywhere in his favorite red and black flipflops. His clothes on any given day are visibly dirty. Without a liberal dollop of God's grace, Marty can be hard to look at.

When I first noticed Marty, I worked the coffee ministry for our Saturday night congregation of 800. He and his "thirsty mug" stood out. I set out mountains of 8-ounce Styrofoam cups with matching lids, but Marty shuffled up with his red, 52-ounce insulated mug, smiley-face nametags from previous weeks neatly lined up around the circumference, and filled it up with visible pleasure. The beverages were provided free. There was no limit, and most weeks I didn't mind his taking an extra-large helping of iced tea. What troubles me now are the memories of how I used that image to create eye-rolling, tongue-clicking entertainment during a few lagging conversations. It was easy to sin against a person I had chosen not to know.

A few months passed after I started my new job as a caterer in the church kitchen. My boss took her well-deserved vacation days, and I catered a few events in her absence. The church staff found an eager assistant for me during those three days—Marty. He helped set up the buffet and wash the dishes. I knew he needed the work, but Marty was more eager than we realized. He apparently didn't realize it was a three-day gig. He kept asking when he was going to be needed again. Did we need him on Tuesdays for the large, early breakfast? Could he take those dirty dishes off our hands on Monday afternoons? Before long, charity, need, and naked naïveté had clasped hands to create our tiny staff of three.

Usually my boss and I worked alone. To drown the quiet, much of the time I told her stories from my past. Inevitably, though, we wondered together about Marty. I knew that he might have been living under the bridge on the south end of town, had it not been for the grace of God and a friend who helped him a year ago. But that was nearly all we knew beyond his character: He is a cheerful, smiling, unsinkable testament to finding joy in Christ despite life's circumstances. We wondered if he had family to help him, where he had worked before, if he had any skills, and how he had ended up in poverty. It was clear that in order to find out, one of us would have to ask him.

As a general rule, I like to talk. I especially like to find out about people's histories, and I love to read interesting biographies. So it was no surprise to me that I could not keep myself from digging into Marty's past. Luckily, I am also the kind of person who does not flinch when asking personal questions. The rewards usually outweigh any momentary discomfort, and for me, a faux pas is a fair price to pay for a good story.

I knew where to find Marty. I had recruited him to take over the Saturday night coffee ministry when I burned out.

He always greets me warmly and with a smile, despite his missing tooth. His eyes crinkle. That night I got the answers to my questions and more. We talked as friends, and Marty got the opportunity to reveal himself. He got to tell his story.

I discovered that he has a sister who cuts his hair and a son who, at the time, was just getting married. A former wife from long ago. A good job at a well-known diner chain until all of their restaurants closed. And a difficult time finding work after that. I learned about his dependence on the will of God in his seeking provision, traveling with people he had helped, and starting a new little life each time. As his stories swirled within me, I was changed. Knowing the causes helped to soften the effect of his appearance.

I also found out why he doesn't wash his hair. The question unraveled into a story that has changed the way I will see Marty for the rest of my life.

You see, it's because of the scabs.

Marty explained to me that the scabs covering parts of his head need to stay dry or they soften and try to come loose. Combing his hair is also tricky, because he can't let the comb touch his scalp, so he doesn't do much of that either. These facts don't challenge the mind until you know that the scabs are five years old and very thick. They are like plugs that can loosen and leave holes deep in his scalp.

On a night five years ago, some teenage boys got tired of his persistent street evangelism, and they beat his head in with baseball bats. They beat a huge, gentle man until he was bleeding on the ground. One visit to the doctor, and he has been healing on his own ever since. He just wants to leave those scabs alone.

I believe I graduated to friend status that night. Not because only his friends know that story, but because it thawed a compassion in me which I had deftly kept numb. Something unreal became real. Puzzle pieces snapped into a panorama of complete faith. When Marty takes Evangelism Explosion classes and goes out into the night to visit people in their homes, sharing Christ, he is not just being obedient; his love and faith in God take him to a place where he could be suffering flashbacks from post-traumatic stress. He is misunderstood and discriminated against because few know his lost tooth is the result of violence, not neglect. He continues to dream big dreams and believe big things for God's glory. My favorite is his plan to evangelize the future colonists living on Mars.

I know that Marty doesn't change lives wherever he goes. Many still walk right by him, shifting glances toward, then away from, his stained shirts and holey grin. They are moved, but not in a way that nudges their hearts or pleases God. I'm sure some pray for him.

But I know that God chose to put Marty near the center of my life. I am familiar now with his unusual habits and his simple approach to this life. I am amazed at his giving heart. I have hugged him and wondered at the things he has taught me—lessons I thought I had already learned. When I see Marty today, I still see the imperfections, but they are only camouflage hiding a portrait of radical faith.

Faith In God

By Victoria Molta
East Haven, Connecticut

My concept of and faith in God didn't truly change until I was a young adult struggling with a mental illness and feeling very alone with no one to turn to. I kept journals on a regular basis, and each entry was like a prayer to God. It was my way of communicating with a Higher Power that I knew in my heart existed.

Even as a young child of nine years old, I had my own concept of God. My cousin was teasing me mercilessly one day, and I remember saying to her, "God doesn't like it when you say mean things."

When I was growing up, I attended church with my family. It was one of the few rituals we did together. There it was instilled in me that Jesus Christ was the Son of God. Above the altar was a life-size figure of Him with hands spread out and nailed to the cross and one foot crossed over the other nailed at the base of it. His head was bent over, a crown of thorns plastered to his head and drops of blood emerging from underneath it.

I enjoyed attending church mostly because I had the opportunity to wear pretty, colorful, crisp dresses and shiny black, patent leather shoes. I was accustomed to the rituals of church. I squirmed restlessly in the pew while the minister delivered his sermon. Toward the end of the service, we filed in line to receive communion, kneeling down at the altar with our hands cupped to receive the wafers, the body of Christ, and sip from a silver chalice containing grape juice, blood of Christ. After church our family often went down the street to a restaurant called Woody and Eddy's for a buffet brunch of eggs benedict, blueberry pancakes, crisp bacon, raisin toast, and links of sausage among other sumptuous edibles.

When I was 14 years old, my parents divorced, our family split up, and my mother moved us—her four children—3,000 miles away from my dad in California to Connecticut. The structure of organized religion fell away just as the structure of our family fell apart.

Tumultuous teenage years passed along with my mother's rocky second marriage and me having to attend three different high schools in three years. I didn't think about God or religion or Jesus Christ. I just wanted to hide from life. A dark cloud obscured the sun and its radiant light.

I started college in 1979 and embarked on a rite of passage, separating from my family and on the brink of starting a life of my own. College wasn't exactly the real world, though. It was a bridge that I crossed leaving behind my childhood and family of origin and facing a life of my own where I would make my own decisions, choose the direction I wanted to go in, the work I wanted to do, and the people I wanted to love. But the bridge I traversed across was like a rickety suspension bridge, and halfway across, the bridge collapsed, and my world fell apart.

I fell great depths, desperate to grasp onto anything. Through falling, I found myself beginning to pray.

I was 20 years old and suffering from depression and psychosis, struggling to function in my third year of college. The mental disorders followed a series of illnesses that had nearly killed me the previous summer. During that time I was very sick with a high fever and couldn't keep even fluids like soup down without vomiting, and I constantly fell down while attempting to walk, thereby bruising myself. My speech was also slurred. My mother had rushed me to the hospital, and after extensive tests, I was diagnosed with encephalitis, hepatitis, and mononucleosis.

I was hospitalized for a week, and when I was released, I couldn't care for myself, and it took the rest of the summer to recover.

But I didn't ever fully recover, and I was never the same person again. I turned to God while I was in the pit of despair. I just wanted Him to be with me throughout the turmoil in my life because I felt so very alone.

I had been taught formalized prayers recited from the Bible and had memorized the Lord's Prayer but was not aware that my simple cries to God for help were prayers, as well, and just as valid as the beautifully stylized Biblical psalms and passages.

During this third year of college, I began to keep journals. My poems and passages were prayers to God, as well, though at the time I didn't know it.

God didn't make everything magically right in my life. I suffered through an abusive relationship and a mental breakdown and subsequent hospitalization in the months that followed. But despite the ordeals, by the grace of God, I managed to graduate from college.

Finishing college was not only the completion of my formal education, it signified crossing that bridge to adulthood. Though the bridge I was on collapsed and I fell into what felt like the pit of hell, I was able to climb out of it and get to the other side.

I truly knew what hell was like, and I didn't want to stay there, succumbing to agony, suffering, and isolation. I also didn't want to remain in the perpetual state between childhood and adulthood, forever dependent on my parents' help in order to live.

I began my ascent up the craggy cliff to a land above me that I imagined to be filled with other people who had made it to the other side. It was faith that kept me going. I didn't really know where my life would take me, but I truly believed that if I climbed one step at a time, I would be led to a place far away from the pit.

At 24 years old, I was diagnosed with a mental illness, began taking medication regularly, attended a psychiatric day hospital, and applied for social security disability after suffering another breakdown and hospitalization. Once again it felt like a slip and fall into the pit. But I never gave up. Something was pushing me forward, and it was God.

I was never taught about this kind of faith as a child. Faith and hope came from within the depths of my heart, and it was then when I discovered that God was not only above me watching me, but also within me guiding me along and loving me as no one has ever loved me.

Years have passed and I am 41 years old. I have lived through the trials and the joys of life like everyone. But I have not been in the pit of despair in a long time, and I finally found the other side—a place of peace that I cherish. On my journey to recovery 15 years ago, God gifted me with a man in my life who would become my loving husband, partner, soulmate, and best friend.

I think of my husband as the manifestation of love and all the love that God feels for me. The love is wholly felt and given. At the core is great peace.

For the love I am given, I give my expression of love back to my husband and my eternal gratitude to God. My concept of God has changed. I feel Him complete me like flesh filling out a skeleton or lush green leaves filling out the bare branches of a tree.

True Faith

By David Doyle
Westlock, Alberta, Canada

It was September 13, 2000, and something tragic was about to happen in Edmonton, Alberta. I was doing everything that I could to stop this tragedy, but I knew it wouldn't be enough. The only one who could stop it was God.

When my daughter, Faith, was born on August 19, we thought she was perfectly healthy. But in the next 25 days, she deteriorated to the point that the doctors wouldn't be able to keep her alive much longer. The ventilator that was pumping almost pure oxygen into her lungs so she could breathe was also destroying her lungs. Oxygen that pure is toxic, and lungs aren't designed to have air forced into them with that much pressure. It became a catch 22—more oxygen and pressure so she can breathe or less so it doesn't kill her.

The doctors told us it was only a matter of time and not much of that. What comfort did they have for us? The odds of it happening to another of our babies were less than us winning the lottery, but that didn't do anything to help baby Faith. Despite their words, we had a plan and a prayer. God would heal her tonight. It would be such a powerful witness to those around us. Who could deny the power of God when He raised an infant girl from her deathbed?

We prayed for her. Our church prayed for her. Our town prayed for her. At least two international ministries prayed for her. One sent a healing cloth and oil to anoint her. With all these prayers of faith going up to God, we were sure her healing was secure.

We took Faith off the ventilator on a Wednesday evening. I fully expected her to recover right away. It wasn't long before I noticed that her feet and fingers felt cool and were turning blue. I prayed harder. I didn't want to let doubt enter my soul. About 30 minutes later, in her mother's arms, my baby breathed her last and died.

Grief doesn't set in right away. It comes slowly, and with it comes the questions. First you ask them in your heart. When you get braver, you ask them in your mind. Sometimes you may ask a few of them with your mouth, but that is rare. Why had God let her die? Did we do something wrong? Did we not have enough faith? What if I had kept praying through the night even though she was dead? Would God have honored my faith or just given in because of my stubbornness?

Other people asked questions, too. How were we doing? Was there anything they could do? One of the most interesting questions was asked of my wife, Jeanna. One of her ex-boyfriends asked if she and I were still together.

When I heard about it, that question struck me as really strange. Why wouldn't we be together? I had never thought that "until death do us part" could mean the death of our child. I always thought it just meant her or I, but that is what happens to many families. The pain is just too much, and a few months after the death of a child, the parents go their separate ways. The thought hadn't even crossed my mind. I guess I trusted in Jeanna's love for me. I figured that it was the same as my love for her. When the storm struck, we held on to each other for support.

It was the same with God. I still had a lot of "why" questions rolling through my brain, but I knew one thing. God loves me. My faith in Him and His love never wavered. It never even came into question. I knew that God is faithful and His promises are sure—even His promise to heal the sick.

So here I had two faiths. I had faith that God would heal my daughter, and I had faith that God is love and loves me personally. The one failed, because my daughter died. The other succeeded, because it upheld me thought this dark time. What was the difference between these two faiths?

The one faith was based on God's promises. I had read about them for years, but I didn't really know them. My dad had often taught us about the covenant that God had with Abraham and how it applies today. I believed all of it in my mind. And when my daughter became sick, I studied it. I watched videos by famous evangelists who talked about God's healing for everyone. I read Scriptures that promised the same thing.

I prayed those Scriptures. I stood on the Word, and 25 days later, my daughter died. What was my problem? I tried to build my faith in the midst of my crisis and put my trust in that faith. When the storm peaked, my faith collapsed.

The other faith was based on God. I had known Him since before I could even read. I had talked with Him and sensed His presence more times than I can remember. His existence and His love are the central pillars in my life.

When the storm hit, my faith, my God, held me secure. My faith was not shaken even though it appeared that God had lied about His ability to heal us. The strange thing is that I didn't know that it was upholding me. I didn't pray extra hard that my marriage would last through this storm. I didn't ask God to reveal His love to me so that I wouldn't fall into doubt. That faith is such a part of me that it worked without any effort on my part. It had been a part of me for so long that when the storm came, I wasn't swept away.

I think that is the true nature of faith. If we have to force it or study up for it, then it isn't true faith. If it is based on a result that we are hoping for, then it isn't true faith. And if it is dependent on what someone else has told you, then it isn't true faith. If it isn't true faith, it will fail you when it is tested.

True faith, on the other hand, will pass the test. It happens naturally, almost by accident. True faith is based on a person, not an event. Faith in God is based on who He is, not on what He has done or will do. True faith is independent of other people; that is, it doesn't need other people saying that God is love for you to believe that He is. You believe it because that is who God is, period.

True faith comes as you meet with God. Faith is often compared to a seed, and like a seed, it takes time to grow. The more we meet with Him, the more we get to know Him. Then our faith is based on a person that we know, not a law that we read.

So often our faith is a paradox. I said that true faith is not based on a law I read. But I read the Scriptures and met God there. I said that true faith is not based on what someone said, but I have met God many times in the words of others. Both of these resulted in true faith. I have also met Him during worship and prayer. All of these helped my seed of faith to grow. It grew into a true faith in the God that I kept meeting.

True faith is like the trust I have in my wife. I don't need someone to tell me she will remain faithful to me. I know her, and I know her love and her commitment to me will pass the test. Oh, and that ex-boyfriend who asked if we were still together—we almost never see him anymore. He just doesn't come around. True faith passes the test.

The trial, the hardship, the storm, comes only to test your faith, and it shows you the difference between true faith and wishful thinking. Before the storm hit, I thought my faith was a fortress. But half of that fortress fell under harsh winds. The foundation, however, was secure. Now I can begin to rebuild my faith. I will build it on the God that I continue to meet.

What Is Faith?

By Jarrod D. Schrunk
Bellbrook, Ohio

What is faith? Why do we need it? What purpose does it have in my life? How much do I have? How much do I need to be safe? So many questions, but not enough answers. Maybe that's not the case. Perhaps we're looking too hard when all the answers are at our fingertips.

In my years as a Christian, I've heard a lot about faith. I've heard sermons preached on it, I've heard songs sung about it, and I've read books written about it. But all those things did were enable me to know about faith. I knew everything there was to know about faith, but that was all. I didn't really know what faith truly *was*.

To be honest, I didn't learn what faith really was until last year when my faith was put to the ultimate test. Up until then, my faith had never really been tested. Maybe a few pop quizzes here and there, but no major tests. My head knowledge of faith wasn't going to get me through this. It was time to see if I really had what I claimed to have and know a lot about.

My test started with one word. That word was cancer. My test came when my health was attacked. Most 21-year-olds only have to worry about getting a bad cold, the flu, or if they have a stressful life, a mild ulcer. I wasn't faced with any of those. I was faced with the possibility of cancer and the possibility of a serious kidney infection.

Facing the possibility of cancer is tough enough. But when your father died of cancer at age 43, the word cancer gets your attention very quickly. I'll admit I was nervous when the doctor ordered a series of tests for cancer. Many, many thoughts and questions went through my mind, and I wanted answers right away.

During this time I had two choices. Choice number one involved me getting down on everything and assuming the worst. It basically involved me failing this test of faith. Choice number two involved me enduring the test. Even though I didn't know what the outcome was going to be, I had to stand strong and endure this faith test.

The first part of the test came when the doctor told me to prepare for the worst. Without even thinking, I told them to do the tests; but I also told them I believed that the results would come back negative. Most would probably call my response denial. Now that I look back on it, I call it faith. I passed the first part, but I knew this test was far from over.

The second part of the test came during the waiting period. The blood had been drawn, and the tests were being done. Now I had to wait for the results. I remember that entire week being bombarded with negative thoughts. Most just bounced off of me, but a few got into my mind. That's when all of the "what ifs" would start, and that's when the test really started to get tough.

I compare this test to the tests I took in high school. Those tests usually consisted of two parts—a multiple-choice part and an essay part. Most of the time the multiple-choice part of the test was the easiest. Then came the essay part, which I always considered the most difficult part of the test.

The first part of my faith test was no problem, but now I was facing the essay part of the faith test. This is where my faith was put on the spot. Either I was going to pass the test or I was going to fail it. There was no middle ground.

There were many verses I clung to during this test, but the one I clung to the most was Hebrews 11:1. Up until then, it had been just another verse, but during this time it became real to me. It answered my question about what faith really is. What is faith? It is the confident assurance that what we hope for is going to happen. It is the evidence of things we cannot yet see.

Here's an illustration. Imagine that you're on the roof of a very tall building. Extending off of the building is a board that is connected to a building on the other side of the street. Faith is stepping out on to that board knowing that it won't hold you up, but you step out anyway.

That's exactly what I had to do in my situation. I didn't have the assurance from the doctors that everything was going to be okay. Had they told me the tests would more than likely come back negative, it would have been easy to pass this test. But I had to step out in faith and go against the odds. When they said I might have cancer, I told them I didn't, and that I never would.

I had to keep telling myself that everything was going to be okay because once just wasn't enough. There were times I would be up all night in so much pain that I was about to give in and admit that the tests were going to come back positive. There were times during the day that I would be so weak and worn out that I didn't know if I would ever get my strength back. But it was all part of the test I was going through.

I could have easily given up, but there was no way I was going to let the devil be victorious. That's why I clung to Hebrews11: 1, especially the part where it talks about hoping for things that we can't see. I remember when I would pray telling God that I didn't know what the results were going to be, but I believed everything was going to be okay. In the midst of my pain and weakness, I still believed that with every part of my heart.

I even remember telling God at one point that I didn't care what the results were, because regardless, it was going to let Him show off just how awesome He is. If the tests came back negative, it would show that He is bigger than any doctor's opinion. If the tests came back positive, He could demonstrate His healing power and take away all of the sickness. Regardless of the outcome, I knew I was going to be the winner.

The tests were finally complete, and I found myself back at the hospital awaiting the result. Most people in my situation probably would have had a huge knot in their stomach, but that wasn't me. I walked into the waiting room with a smile on my face while quietly humming a song of praise. The receptionist looked at me really funny, because she knew why I was there. I guess she was expecting me to walk in all down and nervous, but I was at peace, and my faith was stronger than ever.

I remember sitting in the doctor's office literally bored out of my mind. I didn't see the point of going there in person, because regardless of the results, I knew everything was going to be okay. After about 10 minutes of waiting, the doctor came in to tell me all of the test results came back negative. No cancer, no disease, and no kidney infection! The devil's attack failed, and I passed my faith test.

I'm going to be honest; it wasn't an easy test. As I said earlier, there were times during the waiting period that I allowed negative thoughts to stick in my mind. But my faith in my Heavenly Father was strong enough to cancel out every one of those negative thoughts. Because of my faith and my willingness to worship in my darkest hour, I was able to pass my faith test.

I have no idea how many different definitions there are to the word faith, nor do I think there can only be one. What the word faith means to me might mean something totally different to another believer. But if I were to give my definition of the word faith, this is what it would be. Faith is when in your darkest hour, you know that things are going to be okay. When things look hopeless and you can still say, "God, whatever the outcome is, You are still my Jehovah God and I'm going to still love, honor, worship, and serve You." That is what faith is to me.

There is something awesome about faith. The more you have, and the more you truly know what it is, the closer it will bring you to your Heavenly Father. After my battle with my health, I can honestly say that I have grown so much closer to my Heavenly Father. Because of my faith being tested, He is now more real to me than I ever thought possible!

Faith. We need it, and we need to be willing to have it tested. I can honestly say that my faith is Jesus Christ has made me into the man of God I am today.

9

Faith Is My Companion

A Simple Piece Of Wood

By Robin Gomez
Albuquerque, New Mexico

I was nine years old when I realized I had a magic wand. Okay, so it was only a stick. But it was still magic. Other kids had imaginary friends. I had a stick. I think it all began after I watched an old black and white western on television. The frontier town was suffering a terrible drought, and a stranger rode into town on a beautiful Appaloosa and announced that he could find water with a forked stick. *And I thought I had a good imagination.* The town's people and I were both skeptical. But the stranger walked around on the cracked earth holding the forked stick out in front of him until he found the right spot. The town's people began to dig, and sure enough, the water bubbled like oil to the surface. *Wow! That guy was really something. If it could work for him, it could work for me.* Suddenly the stick in my hand had magical powers. I instantly became the luckiest kid on the block.

Of course, I may have been the only one to think that. I was trying to survive incest and abuse. My parents were divorcing. My mother, eventually followed by all my siblings, left. My father was drinking more than ever. Actually, I have no memory of a time when he did not drink, when he did not beat, when he did not rage. As luck would have it, he was a not a happy drunk. Alcohol unlocked the door to all his ghosts and transformed him. A cruel and physically abusive, raging bull emerged. I used to take my imaginary wand and circle it over my head three times to protect myself from my father's wrath. Heck, once I even used it to give myself the super powers necessary to scramble out a window and into the dark. Doesn't sound like such a big deal now, but I was a chubby kid with no coordination. I had faith in the wand, so out the window I escaped just seconds before my father could beat me in another drunken rage. I had faith, so I was not afraid of the dark. I was not afraid of being alone. I was not afraid.

When I was 11 years old, my father told me that love was a figment of my imagination and that the sooner I accepted that truth, the easier my life would be. The sooner I segregated the reality from the fantasy, the less pain I would suffer. The sooner I faced the inevitable, the quicker I would be prepared to face the world and life with my soul safely encased in emotionless armor. He used to wake me up in the middle of the night, sit me up in the bed and make me repeat his truth over and over. When he was satisfied that I was earnest in my belief, he would shut off the light and stumble back down the hall. I circled the wand over his head five or six times. What could it hurt?

Well, it never really helped either. My father's will to be unhappy was stronger than my magic wand. Of course, it didn't save him because it wasn't real. But my faith was. It took faith, not magic, for me to continue to love him through all the years of abuse. It took faith and a profound belief in God. I had faith in my father's heart, in his soul—the one that was buried under decades of pain. I tried to infuse him with my faith, give him my strength. It didn't work. He didn't want faith. His faith rested in alcohol and the places it took him. No matter. I had faith in him until the day he passed from this life.

Like every person on the planet, I have been blessed with wondrous and tragic events. The wondrous events make me cry. I don't have as much experience with them, so I am always humbled by the inventive ways in which goodness finds it way to the surface. When it happens, I can feel the doors of my heart being thrown wide open, and the intimacy scares me. The tragic events, however, are familiar territory. I have my feet on solid ground and know my way around. Either event allows me to draw on the faith that has sustained my life and allows me endless conversation with God.

My magic wand has undergone quite a few changes over the years. Now I rely on it more like a measuring stick. I use my childhood as the template against which I measure the other events of my life. When something overwhelming happens, I measure the current problem against my childhood. What I recognize every time is that if I was able to survive my childhood, I can survive anything. A current challenge may be inconvenient or uncomfortable, even painful, but it is nothing compared to my childhood. What I remember is that I am resourceful and strong and capable. What I remember is that I am a woman of great faith and that faith has been a constant and enduring companion in my life. What I remember is that God walks with me always, and I feel myself swell with faith.

We have all been tested again and again during this life. We have been injured and deceived and broken. And yet, we find our way, guided by our faith in each other, in love, in whatever we each believe God to be. No matter how much we deplete the supply, it seems to restore itself and is always abundant.

Dear friends of mine passed away recently. One from breast cancer, the other from complications related to diabetes. My step-father struggles daily with cancer. And there are others. So many others. Every day seems to be a struggle. There are days when I fear I will lose my way. It's during these times that my faith is almost visible, like warm breath on a cold night. Magical swirls of faith that are inhaled and exhaled by my mind and heart. It sustains me as surely as food and water and air.

An invisible wand gave me courage as a child to survive and endure. An imaginary measuring stick gives me strength and temperance as an adult. A simple piece of wood acted as a tuning fork that pointed me in the direction of God and anchored my life in faith.

An Angel Named Frank

By Michael Shafer
Stanfordville, New York

Knowing that the worst time is half an hour after snow begins, I went for those deserted back roads as if I really needed to have that lunch. As I slid toward a sharp curve at the bottom of a steep hill, my stomach registered an all too familiar shock of recognition—no way to stay on the road. Our family car, the neat little VW square back we could barely afford, landed with its wheel hooked over the bottom rung of a fence.

At times like this some people choose hysterics. My characteristic defense is to lapse into a passive, trance-like state, so as I stepped out into that dark, raw morning and wandered up onto the road, I was numb. Strange as it might seem, my only thought right then was, *God, I'm really sorry. I've wrecked your car.* It was only a moment.

Then out of the snow came an old Chevy. It crept down toward me, stopped, and out jumped this heavy-set, unshaven, middle-aged guy, all business. I think he told me at some point that his name was Frank, but I'm not sure I ever knew anything about him. He certainly wasn't interested in who I was; he was just there, looking through me toward the car, surveying the scene. He began muttering as if at nobody in particular about the laws of physics—which made sense to me when he picked up (I swear I don't know where it came from) a two-by-four and told me to help him lift the car off the fence. It was so easy. The tire was still inflated. Though the axle was bent, the car was drivable; you could go straight by pulling the steering wheel a quarter turn to the left. Seeing all this, Frank became detached, if not disinterested, and began another sentence about the laws of physics, punctuated it with, "I guess that damn degree was worth something after all," and then he just left. Both of us were on our way—he to God knows where and I to Mt. Kisco for a clergy luncheon via the VW service center right down the block. I caught a ride home from the rector of a parish next to mine, borrowed a car from Mary, a parishioner wintering with her son, and got a decent insurance settlement; the whole event was charmed.

I wish I could tell you more about Frank, but don't angels always defy description? They simply appear, do their thing, and then disappear. The saying that goes "Fools go where angels fear to tread" needs revision, however. God sent fearless Frank to salvage a fool's errand. I'm sure that there have been many other times, but this one was unmistakable. Frank's appearance, if you will, was the centerpiece of an experience controlled and surrounded by a loving God who finds us even in our craziest spaces. He moves in our hearts and then lavishes blessings in response to the prayers He inspires: e.g. "Dad, I'm sorry I wrecked your car."—"It's O.K. son, here's Frank."

You may have heard other stories of people like Frank who find themselves employed as God's agents. I heard one about a man who, down to his last penny, sat with his wife at a dinner table empty of food—there wasn't even milk for their two small children. They prayed for God's mercy, and there was a knock at the door. A stranger appeared with two bottles of milk in his hands, "I was in prayer and this idea came that I'd better bring this here." I believe it. After all, I once was standing around praying in a snowstorm.

And besides, my wife and I have been enlisted. A few years ago on a May evening around midnight on the Taconic Parkway, we ended up spending a great weekend (which just happened to be completely free) with a family whose refrigerated van had broken down. We ended up driving together in my rented van to their appointed food concession.

Not all angels come as people with two-by-fours or milk bottles or credit cards. Some, we've heard at Christmas, appear supernaturally with messages like Gabriel's. Others simply appear, and the glory speaks for itself.

I know a woman who saw a light outside her kitchen window at a time when she desperately needed to see one. I believe her when she says it was an angel, because her life changed. She feels that she is deeply loved, and the joy that brings becomes infectious. Everyone is blessed by her.

But whether dressed in overalls or supernatural brilliance, angels do come. They come to people with deep needs in response to faith in a loving God. Their appearances are unforgettable, and we learn from them. I, for one, have learned some humility. I used to take pride in my capacity for faith. Parishioners have sometimes complained to me about their lack of personal experience with God, as if they were "one down." Now I know better, and I tell them so. I didn't meet Frank because I was a great spiritual person. I met him because I was on a fool's errand.

I am glad, though, that I have been gifted with a good instinct, one I have jealously guarded ever since. This instinct was employed by St. Peter when he said to Jesus that he could not leave Him because he had nowhere else to go. *Simon Peter answered Him, "Lord, to whom shall we go? You have the words of eternal life."* John 6:68 I went to God that day because God inspired it. I still do, and God still deserves the credit.

I relearned something that day, something that has nothing to do with any virtue peculiar to me and that applies equally to all of us: We are very important. Not because of who we are but because of *Whose* we are. God was the rightful owner of that VW because He owns me. When we allow it, He takes great pride of ownership. *He* has never wrecked anything or anybody.

I was reminded in the hush of a new snowfall that God reigns.

And Not By Sight

By Naomi Rose
San Francisco, California

For we live by faith, not by sight. 2 Corinthians 5:7

I am trying to step as cautiously as I can, but every dozen paces or so my foot catches on something, and I stumble a bit. Hiking downhill has always been much more of a challenge for me. My thigh muscles ache from the strain of steadying myself. Perspiration is dampening the back of my shirt, and as the late afternoon wind blows, I shiver a little. The two most difficult things for me right now are keeping up with the rest of the group and keeping up the pretense that I am enjoying myself completely, that this is fun, that I am just like everyone else.

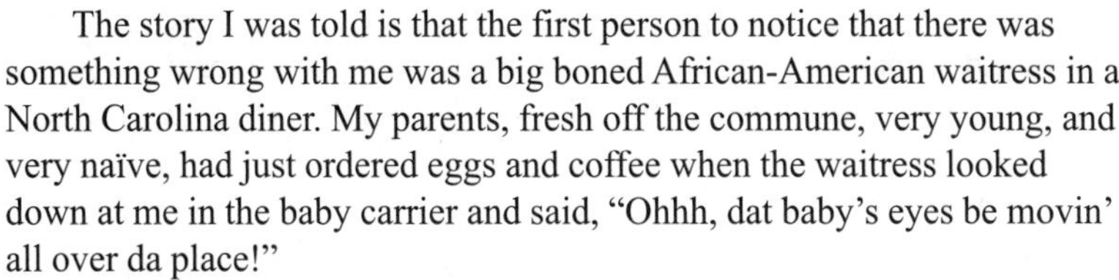

The story I was told is that the first person to notice that there was something wrong with me was a big boned African-American waitress in a North Carolina diner. My parents, fresh off the commune, very young, and very naïve, had just ordered eggs and coffee when the waitress looked down at me in the baby carrier and said, "Ohhh, dat baby's eyes be movin' all over da place!"

As soon as I was old enough to think about such things, it seemed to me that I spent a good portion of my childhood in the waiting room of Children's Medical Center anxiously anticipating the moment when they would call my name. Surrounding me in the waiting room were other kids with eye disorders, some of them much more severe than mine. Some of their faces mirrored nervousness; many just looked tired. In either case their expressions strongly contrasted the waiting room walls that were painted with a cheerful mural of a tropical rainforest. I could make out the shapes of waterfalls and birds and trees, but I knew that some of the other children were unable to see any of these images or these bright colors. Even as a child, I found that mural's existence strangely ironic. Most of us children could see these vibrantly painted rainforest animals about as well as they could see us.

I hated going to the eye doctor more than most anything. Each time it was the same routine. My name was called, and I would walk past a phalanx of grinning nurses who greeted me by my first name without having to look at their charts. I was in there so much I probably could have walked up to the counter and said, "I'll have they usual," and they would have responded, "OK, Naomi, you've got it: some poking, some prodding, the usual eye tests you can't pass, topped off with some stinging eye drops and an excruciatingly bright light shone into your face."

The eye drops were the worst. It must have been so hard for my mother to watch her little girl being held down by two nurses (apparently I was a bit of a squirmer) while another nurse propped my eye open with her thumb and forefinger and dispensed four types of stinging liquid into it. My mom always struck a deal with me: If I could manage to behave during the torture, she'd buy me a milkshake on the way home. To this day, I can't get a Frosty from Wendy's without my eyes watering a bit at those memories.

I was diagnosed with a condition called…OK, so nobody wants to know the specifics of that or why it's untreatable with lenses or surgery. I know this because I've sensed the stifled yawns of people when I respond to their questions: "So what exactly is um, well, um, *wrong* with your eyes?"

It suffices to say that after tests, tests, and more tests, one of my ophthalmologists sat down with my parents and me. I must have been around five years old at the time. Most of the words he used were too big for me (and probably my parents) to understand, but one sentence leapt out at me like one of those tigers in the fake tropical jungle on the walls—lifelike, yet unreal:

"I'm afraid she'll never be able to do some things—for instance, she'll never be able to ride a bike."

That day we rode home in silence. And my mom forgot to buy me a milkshake. I chose not to remind her.

Growing up, I wavered between wanting to keep my handicap a secret and wanting everyone I knew to understand what I was going through. I was frustrated both when somebody would notice and point out (as if I didn't know) that my eyes shake ever so slightly and when I had to remind one of my friends to read me the prices on the menu at Burger King (which, incidentally, is posted way too high). Eventually I became adjusted to ambivalence.

Now faith is being sure of what we hope for
and certain of what we do not see.
Hebrews 11:1

I always knew that driving a car was going to be something I would not experience. I wasn't given much of an opportunity to forget this fact. There are few things that are important in Texas: God, football, and what kind of car you drive. I come from a die-hard Ford Mustang-loving family. I could have brought home any type of guy—he could be too old, too young, a Gentile, a vegetarian—as long as he didn't drive a Chevy. Cars were in our blood, and I am still fascinated by them. But as my brothers oohed and ahhed over car magazines featuring the latest, greatest, and fastest models, I could not wholeheartedly join in, for the sting of reality invaded my enjoyment and reminded me that I would never really be normal.

As each of my friends in turn took driver's education and received their little pieces of freedom-granting paper, I grew more and more resentful. I clung tightly to the idea that there must be a reason—there must be some explanation—why I could not have something I wanted so desperately.

When I was 10 years old, my family rented a cabin out on a remote lake in East Texas. In the middle of the night, the silence woke me. I crept outside hoping to get a peek at the vast lake. I noticed that it was shiny, illuminated. Instinctively I looked up at the sky, and for the first time ever, I saw them. Stars.

It seemed to me that I had entered another world. I no longer heard the crickets or felt the evening breeze. All was still and quiet, and the sky was lit up with millions of Christmas lights.

I can remember only one other moment in my life when I was filled with a similar sense of incredulity. It was the first time a man told me my eyes were beautiful.

"You're kidding me."

"No, I'm not. Go ahead."

"But Ari…" I protested. "I can't drive your car."

"I'm telling you, you can," he said and placed the keys in my hand. Then he opened the driver's side door and motioned for me to get in.

I couldn't believe he was serious. Even as he went around to the passenger's side and got in the car next to me, I felt that any minute he'd change his mind. I was almost hoping he would.

I ran my thumb along the inside of the steering wheel. "I'm scared," I whispered.

"Most people are the first time they drive," Ari replied.

"Aren't you afraid that I'm going to crash into a wall or something?" I asked him.

"Nah," he answered. "Just remember: The brake is your friend. The brake is your friend."

I laughed. I put the key in the ignition and jumped a bit as the engine awoke. I marveled at the fact that I was making a noise that I'd heard millions of times before but never personally created.

It was only a few revolutions around an empty parking lot (and I admit I did almost hit a dumpster). It was just me, a friend, and a 1987 Honda. But I don't think anyone anywhere has ever had a better 22nd birthday.

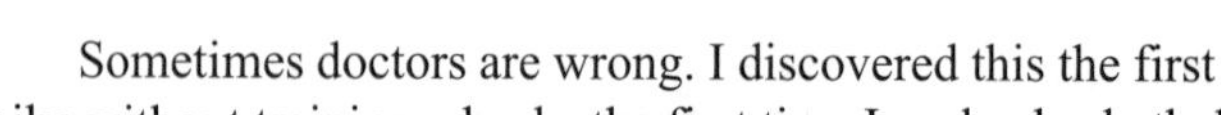

Sometimes doctors are wrong. I discovered this the first time I rode my bike without training wheels, the first time I sank a basketball into a hoop, and of course, the first time I (illegally) drove a car. So when someone says to me, "Don't lose faith. Maybe someday they will find a cure," it makes me smile. Because maybe they will. And maybe they won't.

In the meantime, I continue to step carefully…but still forward, feeling my way along…by faith.

Faith In Healing

By Vanessa A. Johnson
Ama, Louisiana

I can still see the look on the doctor's face, his eyebrows creased so tightly they appeared as though they'd touch. My attention was suddenly drawn back to his mouth as I heard him say, "Mrs. Johnson, the results came back positive, and they confirm that your husband has a tumor on the pancreas." That was in February 2002.

As I heard the words, I had this sinking feeling in the pit of my stomach. Suddenly I recalled that everyone I'd known who'd had the dreaded disease of pancreatic cancer had died, and I immediately feared the worst. There were two things I knew about pancreatic cancer: one is that there's no cure for it, especially if it isn't detected early; and two, that the life expectancy is short—usually less than a year—because this disease rarely displays symptoms until the advanced stages.

Tears began to fall from my eyes, for these are words you never want to hear about anyone, let alone someone you love. But this is how our ordeal began.

I say began because now the things that were happening to my husband, Welton—prior symptoms that included diabetes, rapid weight loss, itching, diarrhea, and jaundice—had a name. Before this we knew something wasn't right. We just didn't know what.

The symptoms started presenting themselves in May 2001 when my husband was diagnosed with type 2 diabetes. Deciding to change his eating habits because he was overweight, Welton followed the *Sugar Buster* diet and lost one to two pounds per week. The doctor prescribed Amaryl for the diabetes, but it didn't lower his blood sugar. Glocophage was then prescribed, but it didn't help either, so insulin was prescribed next.

The dosage started at 10 units daily with instruction to increase it until the desired level was obtained. Within weeks the dosage had increased to 50 units and other symptoms presented themselves. By the end of January, Welton began itching severely. Allegra was prescribed for this, to no avail. Various blood tests were performed with negative results, and the weight loss began increasing rapidly.

By mid-February Welton developed severe jaundice, and the doctor became concerned and referred him to a surgeon because he thought that gallstones might be causing the bile duct to be blocked, thus causing the jaundice. The following week an x-ray of the abdomen was scheduled and the results were inconclusive for gallstones. The test did reveal an enlarged liver, but the surgeon concluded it was fatty tissue because prior bloodwork had negative results.

Because of the rapid weight loss—now 80 pounds, the severe itching, and the jaundice, it was confirmed Welton's bile duct was blocked, thus causing the itch. The doctor prescribed Questran, but it provided little relief, and an upper GI was scheduled the following week in the hope that it would provide a clearer view of the abdomen. The result confirmed the diagnosis of the tumor on the pancreas.

An appointment was scheduled with a renowned cancer surgeon who explained the surgery that was necessary—a pancreatoduodenectomy, which is a procedure that involves removing part of the pancreas, stomach, and small intestine.

Through all of this, our faith remained strong. We felt that if we truly believed, everything would be okay—because that's what we'd prayed for—then through faith our prayers had already been answered. Because of other circumstances we'd experienced in recent years—my pregnancy with my son, Jalen; his premature birth and extended stay in the neonatal intensive care unit; his malrotation surgery followed by hospitalization for pneumonia; and his succumbing to it 12 days later—we'd had frequent contact with doctors.

But rarely have any of them used God and faith in their healing process. We were pleasantly surprised when this doctor encouraged us to rely on our faith to bring us through this ordeal. He asked if we believed in God, and naturally we replied, "Yes." Then he said he wanted us to continue having a positive outlook, explaining that according to the Bible, if we constantly speak of sickness and death in terms of having it and letting it get the best of us, then that's what would happen, but if we speak of health and healing, as God promised, then surely that's what we'd get and that we truly had to believe it for it to happen.

"I'm a doctor, not God. I can't do what I do without His guidance. I owe all that I am to God. Nothing is impossible with Him, and that's what's going to carry you through this," he said.

The doctor ordered a lung biopsy before the surgery, explaining that he wanted to be sure a mass he'd noticed on the x-rays wasn't cancerous. Because of our faith, we knew the result from the biopsy wouldn't be positive. We also believed that even though there was a tumor, it would be okay, too.

The Bible says, *"Ask and it will be given to you; seek and you shall find; knock and the door will be opened to you."* Matthew 7:7 I remembered Welton telling me he had contracted pneumonia years ago, so I knew this was the reason for the mass on the lung prior to the biopsy, and my assumptions were validated when the results revealed the mass was scar tissue. The surgery was next.

Welton and I are both spiritual and prayerful. We feel our faith in God has carried us this far, and when we left the surgeon's office, we were both thankful that this spiritual person had been sent to us. We were in union in our prayer request for healing and felt our prayers had been answered with the early detection of the tumor. I felt the cancer was in the early stages based on some research I'd done. I also remembered both surgeons were surprised to learn my husband hadn't had abdominal pain, as pain is one of the major symptoms of advanced stage pancreatic cancer.

The only thing left to do was take care of the evil (the tumor) that Satan had planted—this would be done through the surgery—and then follow up with treatment to further eradicate the disease.

Finally the day arrived for the pancreaoduodenectomy. We arrived at the medical center at 5:30 a.m., and at 7:45 a.m. Welton was taken to pre-op where a catheter was inserted in his neck. The procedure took 1½ hours, but during this time I assumed he had been taken to surgery following pre-op. My son and I learned otherwise when we were called to the reception desk. We assumed we were about to receive the first update from the surgery. It turned out to be our opportunity for one last visit with Welton before he went into surgery. It was a little unsettling to see blood spattered on the bed, pillow, and floor from the procedure, and I could see the pain on my husband's face. But faith wouldn't allow the hurt at seeing his pain show on my face. Besides, I didn't want Welton to sense that anything was wrong or that I was holding anything back from him. We visited briefly and were assured we'd be given frequent updates throughout the surgery.

Around the five-hour mark, just as I was beginning to get a little antsy, the receptionist again summoned us to the desk. There the anesthesiologist told us the surgery was nearly complete and he needed my authorization to do an epidural. He explained that because of the size of the incision, my husband would be in severe pain and the surgeon wanted to be sure adequate pain medications could be continually administered. He assured us that after the surgery the surgeon would also come out to explain how the surgery had gone and to provide another update on my husband's status.

Thereafter we started receiving phone calls from family and friends who were anxiously awaiting news. The surgeon came out and advised us that the surgery had gone well and that he didn't have to remove any of the stomach as previously thought because the tumor was small and contained and it was being sent to pathology for testing. He explained that Welton's vital signs remained stable through the surgery and that he was being moved to the post-operative intensive care unit (PICU) for the weekend.

The first few hours in PICU were painful for my husband, but he told me the surgeon had asked him if he minded if he prayed with him as they were going into the operating room. He said they had prayed all the way to the operating room. Welton said at that point he knew he was in God's hands and everything would be okay.

The following morning when I arrived at the medical center, I found Welton sitting in a chair watching television. He had stopped taking the pain medications because they numbed his entire midsection which made him uncomfortable, and he felt the medications would prolong his recovery.

The cancer surgeon remained positive on his visits, and his positive outlook reinforced ours. I have witnessed many occasions where medically trained professionals put themselves on pedestals and never once mention God playing a part in what they do. I'm not saying they're not spiritual or they don't believe in God. What I'm saying is you rarely hear it from them. This surgeon was a refreshing inspiration.

Welton remained in PICU throughout the weekend. On Monday night he was transferred to a private room where he remained until his release date the following Friday. The pathology results came back positive for cancer, but the surgeon felt the cancer had been contained and hadn't spread to other organs. He also said he felt my husband's prognosis was good and that if he continued with the positive outlook, he'd beat the cancer.

The doctor outlined the treatment plan, but he warned us that the chemotherapist and the radiation specialist wouldn't put a positive spin on their treatments, and the most important thing was for us to remain positive. He strongly suggested Welton receive treatments of chemotherapy and radiation because that would eliminate any cells left behind that couldn't be removed by surgical procedures.

Three weeks after the surgery, chemo and radiation therapy began. The chemotherapist and radiation specialist suggested an aggressive approach to treatment consisting of administering chemotherapy drugs and radiation therapy simultaneously through the Hohn catheter inserted in Welton's chest. The catheter would also make it easier to draw blood as needed.

After the surgery, Welton gained some of the weight back. He said he purposely did so just to see if he could.

His digestive system, which sustained the largest impact of the surgery from the small intestines being cut, appeared to work properly, and the dosage was reduced significantly on many of his medications.

Prior to finishing the second phase of chemotherapy drugs, my husband returned to work full time. His appetite had returned, and he was consuming lots of fruits and vegetables and taking vitamins to help build up his strength to help fight the negative effects of the treatments. He received chemo on two Mondays consecutively and then was off for a week. On the off week, he attended church services.

Ironically, Welton's last dose of chemo was September 30, 2002, the anniversary of our son's death. Since then we have had a time of waiting and praying. We just celebrated Christmas and are two days before the New Year, 2003. With our faith in God, we feel Welton's health has been restored.

If you truly believe in God and believe that He is true in His word, then you can overcome any obstacle Satan throws your way, but you must have faith and you must believe.

Hebrews 11:1 states, *Now faith is being sure of what we hope for and certain of what we do not see.* 2 Corinthians 5:7 says, *We live by faith, not by sight.*

We believe we are blessed. God is an awesome God, isn't He?

Faith Or Fear: The Choice Of A Trucker's Wife

By Samantha Winchester
Brattleboro, Vermont

Each morning I rise to the sound of the roosters dutifully crowing from their perches in the barn. The sun coming over the horizon stretches its illuminating fingers through a stand of pine trees beckoning me to begin my day. My children scurry from their warm beds to mine, all three of them snuggling under my Indian print comforter to lovingly wish me a good morning. Outside the sun may or may not be shining; the rain could be falling; it's all the same to me. I am grateful to be given one more day in my hectic but blessed existence.

The luscious smell of oatmeal drenched in maple syrup fills every room of the house. Sitting on the table before us is a frosty pitcher of sweet cream freshly collected from the jerseys and holsteins grazing in the green field outside my window. After chores and breakfast, we begin our home schooling day with songs of praise and a time for devotions. Finishing off-tuned bars of *My Country 'Tis of Thee, Jesus Loves the Little Children,* and other songs, I ask the children, "What prayer requests or thanks do you have today?" They've made a game of this, trying to be the first to spurt it out. "Please keep Daddy safe today." This is, without a doubt, the most oft-repeated prayer in our lives.

You see, my husband, Robert, has a job that is considerably adventurous and could definitely be deemed hazardous. He is a long distance truck driver, traveling to and from Massachusetts and Los Angeles. Wanderlust courses through his veins. The open road, the deserts, and the crisp mountain air call his name and entice him to keep his 18 wheels rolling down the long and lonely highways of America. Since he was a child, he dreamed of driving the big rigs and seeing this expansive country. Over the years, the children and I have had the glorious privilege of traveling with him quite frequently, as I have my class A license and try (and I emphasize *try*) to do my share of the driving when I'm with him.

It takes a tough breed to handle the job, though. The hours are long and exhausting. Tension permeates your body, beginning in your shoulders and traveling down your arms reaching into your stiff fingers. When I'm asked if it is difficult to drive a tractor-trailer truck, my usual response is, "I'd rather give birth again." This usually draws a chuckle, and I assume my point has hit its mark. I drive mostly for the pleasure of being with my husband and to help support his business. Don't get me wrong, I thoroughly enjoy the perks of traveling to various locations, but I am always relieved to return and stand once again on the steps of my home in Vermont. We have been sweetly rewarded for our miles traveled living and seeing for ourselves diverse geography, people, history, and the great panorama that God created for us.

Both my children and I have witnessed firsthand the dangers Rob deals with being out on the highways weaving his way through the miles and miles of roads before him. He is an experienced and levelheaded driver, and it is not with him that danger typically lies. Formidable weather, wandering wildlife, deviant traffic, and perilous road conditions all threaten his well being numerous times a day. Covering the number of miles we have traveled in our truck—our old purple Freightliner has almost a million miles under her belt—we have seen more than our air share of horrific accidents strewn across this nation's roadways.

One such incident stands out in my mind. It happened not long ago, but I'm sure the sheer horror of the experience will be branded in my memory for many years to come. We were traveling south through Missouri in the early morning dusk. The sun had yet to come up behind us. The air outside was quite chilly, making the windows cold to the touch. I was wrapped in the thermal sleeping bag in the bunk with the children, and Rob was trying to make it to Oklahoma before daybreak.

Coming around a bend in the road, he spotted a huge mass of bright yellow and orange flames licking at the darkness. The object appeared to be parked on the shoulder of the opposite side of the highway. In the haze of the early morning hours, that illusion proved to be incorrect. Hurdling across the median and into our lane of traffic not a hundred yards before us, the advancing fireball awaited our arrival. Deep sleep is usually not something that comes easily while cruising down the highways at 65 miles an hour and the bumpy Missouri roads make it even harder. I heard Rob yell from the other side of the black curtain, felt the urgency in his voice and the quick braking of the truck. I jumped up and lurched into the cab just as he brought us to a stop.

Sitting before us, finally coming to rest, was a tractor-trailer truck fully engulfed in flames. Pulling his air brakes swiftly, Rob yanked open his door and ran toward the fiery beacon. Other trucks pulled to a stop beside us, each driver hopping out of their rig and running toward the truck. The commotion woke the children, each one of them peeking their heads from behind the curtain to find out what was wrong. Three loud explosions sent numerous bodies running from the blazing truck. The tires had lost their battle to stay inflated as the heat reduced them to melting rubber. Within minutes, all that was left of the truck was a pile of red hot metal.

The driver had amazingly escaped from the wreckage, limping about with only one shoe. A witness from the other side told of seeing a car that had flipped and lay dark in the roadway, unbeknownst to the truck driver. He had come upon it within seconds and did not have time to avoid crashing through it. The gasoline from the car had presumably ignited the fuel from his ruptured tanks, setting the truck ablaze immediately. The people in the car had not survived the blow.

For a somber four and a half hours, we sat watching the various emergency crews clean up. Over and over, I repeated a prayer of thanks and praise to the God who had kept us under His wing and protected us, for if we had been only a second or two farther ahead, the results could have been tragic for us.

I knew of these dangers long before this accident happened. I've seen many accidents before this, and I'm sure I'll see plenty more. Without faith, I would feel overwhelmed with worry every moment my thoughts drifted to my husband and to what conditions he might be facing. There are many times when that worry wart wiggles his way in and I let my guard down and neglect to have faith that God will keep him safe.

This morning ritual of praying for his safety, for me, is echoed time and time again during the day. There are moments when I am driven to say a short prayer for him and I wonder, did God lead me to do this because Rob was in danger? Each instance these dynamic emotions consume me, I thank Him for instilling such conviction within me. Without faith, I would live in constant fear for my husband's life, that the next road trip he took could be his final earthly journey, and I just could not live that way.

When I sat down at my cluttered desk surrounded by invoices, stuffed expense envelopes, and colorful school papers to write this story, I assumed it would be easy. With all the experiences I've had and the tales I have to tell, I thought the words would just come gushing out in torrents, flooding this essay with well thought emotion. I came; I sat; I was stumped. How could I have nothing to say about a subject that I felt so passionately about?

After days of reflection, it finally hit me. I live on faith; I eat, drink, and breathe faith. Without faith I would quaver before taking that first toe-chilling step into the vestibule of the day. I would want to hide under the shadow of my covers and yearn to revel in its cocoon of darkness. Each moment I would tremble in anticipation of what this ruthless world would dish out next. Thankfully, I am not afraid, and I know through my ever-growing faith that these words will stay with me and bolster me up when I waiver and need them most:

"For I am the Lord, your God, Who takes hold of your right hand and says to you, Do not fear; I will help you." Isaiah 41:13

Starting Over

By Richelle Putnam
Meridian, Mississippi

I am discouraged. Not with the world, but with myself as a Christian. Every Sunday and Wednesday night I sit on a hard pew taking in God's Word. Again.

And again.

And again.

Days, weeks, months, years pass by and every Sunday and Wednesday night I'm still sitting on a hard pew taking in God's Word. Again.

And again.

And again.

I've listened to the stories of Abraham, Isaac, Jacob, the twelve tribes, Elijah, Elisha, Hannah and Samuel, Kings Saul, David, and Solomon, the prophets, the division and fall of Israel, Mary, Elizabeth, John the Baptist, the birth of Christ, the calling of the disciples, the parables of Christ, the death of Christ, Paul's conversion, John's revelation—all of them over and over again.

And again.

And again.

I've completed Bible studies on almost every book in the Bible—Old and New Testament—and taken accredited Bible courses. I've debated with non-believers and believers revealing proudly *my* impressive knowledge obtained through diligent study. I've signed petitions concerning moral and political issues and written senators, advertisers, and whomever I needed to in order to make *my* Christian views known. Some might say I've accomplished a lot as a Christian. But I am writing this to confess that indeed I haven't.

When I turned *my* life over to Christ, changed *my* lifestyle, *my* attitudes, and reared *my* children in the church, I thought I was doing *my* job. As a family, we read Bible stories and learned Bible verses taped to our refrigerator. I discussed the downward spiral of the world with my children, thanking God that one day we would be together in heaven and I wouldn't have to worry about the effects on my children and loved ones any longer.

God would have His justice and we, His children and chosen ones, would be set free forever. We would be eternally separated from all the wretched sinners and their atrocious acts. Now here I am with grown children, grandchildren, and years flowing past under life's bridge, realizing that I sought *my* salvation all those years through self-centered motives—the assurance of eternal life. I used *my* Christian walk to be an example to *my* family and friends to keep them from the world. I longed for their salvation so they could dwell with *me* in eternity where we'd all live happily ever after and escape the fiery abyss of hell.

I now face some hard, cold facts about *my* long Christian walk.

It hasn't been about Christ at all. It's all been about *me.*

Inside the walls of my elegant hundred-year-old church, magnificent stained glass windows portray the life of Christ. The exterior is no less grand than a king's castle with heavy mahogany doors along the front. The landscape is meticulously trimmed and formed into perfect leafy structures.

I have led the children waving palm branches on Palm Sunday down the aisles to the altar where a wooden cross hangs above the pulpit. My family has walked together to light the Christmas advent candle. Visiting friends and family members have sat beside my family on our usual pew.

There I sat wholeheartedly taking Christ's love, grace, mercy, and forgiveness that I didn't deserve and not even giving half-heartedly back the love, honor, and obedience He deserved. I shunned the children He was grieving over—the lost, the sinners—like the prodigal's brother had.

My God, my God, how I have forsaken You.

Every action I've taken as a Christian, every word spoken by me has been in vain, senseless, of no value, without sharing the love Christ gave freely to me. The knowledge I so earnestly sought is useless without giving myself to those *outside my* family and friends, sharing Christ's love through kindness and concern, not holier than thou words, debates, and petitions.

Without love, my time perched on hard pews was as futile as tilling rock and clay and expecting a great harvest. If I couldn't love others, how could I say that I love Christ? As a child, I had learned John 3:16. But as an adult, He drew me to 1 John 3:16. *This is how we know what love is: Jesus Christ laid down his life for us. And we ought to lay down our lives for our brothers.*

Verses 17 and 18 go on to say: *If anyone has material possessions and sees his brother in need but has no pity on him, how can the love of God be in him? Dear children, let us not love with words or tongue but with actions and in truth.*

His Word never stops teaching, no matter how many times I've read and studied it. So after years of Biblical history and reading the Bible many times through, I must now return to where I began. On my knees. Head bowed. Arms lifted. A child again, humbly petitioning forgiveness for arrogance, pride, and self-righteousness, for hoarding His free gift of grace, mercy, and salvation like a greedy, selfish child, and sharing it only with those I deemed worthy.

My eyes closed, my ears finally open to hear *His* desires for *my* walk with Him, He says, "Where are the needy families your church adopted and bought gifts for at Christmas? And the children at Boys and Girls Club your Women's Ministry helped to buy toys for as a Christmas Project? And the residents of a halfway house that you provided refreshments, a devotion, and activity for two hours once a week for a month? Remember the kitchen help you hired to help with your church's Open House? Why did you not fellowship with them rather than the other ladies in the church? Why did you not break the shell around your comfort zone and ask about *their* families, *their* lives, and fellowship with *them* while doing the dishes? Why did you not build relationships with *them*? Sit at the table with *them*, like I sat at yours? Why did you not invite *them* into my house for Sunday service? Why did you not leave the safe comfort of your church, venture out into the community to search for my lost children? And when they started their journey home to Me, why didn't you rush out to meet them, arms and heart open to receive them, and walk with them the rest of the way?

Why?

But the answers were cream pies that had already pelted me in the face. I'd been comfortable in *my* usual pew, with *my* usual family, among *my* usual friends, tithing as little as I could, not financially, but spiritually and physically. I'd invested in church programs, buildings, and charitable organizations rather than people and held my head high like I'd really accomplished something in God's Kingdom. I'd attended all the church functions, helped prepare meals while wearing an apron with my church's logo, and decorated the sanctuary for Christmas, all the while feeling satisfied that my family, friends, and I were saved and convincing myself that family and friends always come first.

But where was my Savior in all this?

What about the Son who wanted me to feel so comfortable and secure with Him that He chose to be born among the stench of animals in soiled, molded hay in the cold of night, no roof over his head, with only the poorest of the poor to see to His needs? What about the Teacher who sat at my table to teach me and drank from my cup even though He would be chastised for doing so? What about the Physician who met me at the well to heal me, accepting the ladle of water I dipped for Him while society shunned me and ridiculed Him? What about the Father who, with arms extended, tears flowing down His flushed cheeks, dashed down the dusty road to meet me, a straying child making her way home, and welcomed me with a feast celebration?

He loved me enough to not only leave His comfort zone, but also sacrifice His life, be beaten, spat upon, and nailed to a cross. And all He wanted in return was for me to love Him and His other children, to bring them home. The ones I called "sinners of the world." The outcasts. The prodigals. Yet, I wouldn't leave my social, cultural, ethnic, and religious comfort zones, using the excuse of protecting my loved ones from the world, keeping them behind the closed doors of the church. I taught them to separate themselves so they could stay pure, clean, holy, instead of working alongside them, teaching them how to love and help the unlovable, being an example of Christ, rather than a religious snob, a Pharisee. I cared more about the reactions of others than the lost children He grieved for. I cared more about my place in the church than His place.

Standing with the congregation, hymns filled the sanctuary like thousands of melodious birds. I wondered how Christ could look at me without shaking His head in disappointment. How out of tune I must've sounded to Him when His word so clearly says: *What good is it, my brothers, if a man claims to have faith but has no deeds? Can such faith save him? Suppose a brother or sister is without clothes and daily food. If one of you says to him, "Go, I wish you well; keep warm and well fed," but does nothing about his physical needs, what good is it? In the same way, faith by itself, if it is not accompanied by action, is dead.* James 2:14-17

Dead. My faith was dead. As hard and cold as the brick and mortar used to build the church.

So what now? What could I do after all these years? Convince myself that it's a hopeless cause and that I'm a hopeless case? Become a recovering Christian like so many others have done?

But how could I give up when Christ never gave up on me? How could I, after reading and believing His word throughout the life He breathed into me, place His Word upon a shelf and act like it never meant anything, that it had no power, and my life could go on without it.

The wonderful thing about being a Christian is that I have a Savior who can raise the dead. And if He can raise the physically dead, He can raise the spiritually dead—even the dead faith of a believer. I have a loving Father who not only allows me to start over, but grants me a new life with no penalties, no probation, no parole, no strings attached. He says to me exactly what I would say to *my* prodigal child who returned home dirty, hungry, and humbled. *I forgive you.*

I can simply lift my eyes and hands toward heaven and thank Him again for His undying love, compassion, and forgiveness. I can start over, as a little child upon His knee, with a much stronger faith in Him and even in myself as a Christian.

And I will keep Matthew 25:35-36,40 always in my heart—*'For I was hungry and you gave me something to eat, I was thirsty and you gave me something to drink, I was a stranger and you invited me in, I needed clothes and you clothed me, I was sick and you looked after me, I was in prison and you came to visit me.' "The King will reply, 'I tell you the truth, whatever you did for one of the least of these brothers of mine, you did for me.'"*

When I find myself failing as I so many times do, I'll return to His Word for hope, to strengthen and restore my faith in the author and finisher of faith—Jesus Christ.

A Tap On The Shoulder

By Margo Lynn Dill
St. Charles, MO

Canceling my wedding was heartbreaking. Love remained, but my fiancé and I had problems we couldn't resolve. Together, we returned shoes and dresses, called the florist and reception hall, and threw away our beautiful invitations with the quote, "Today I marry my best friend." I'll never forget watching my fiancé read those words with tears streaming down his cheeks.

Telling friends and family proved equally difficult. But trying to explain the situation to his six-year old son was almost impossible. Looking into his innocent eyes, I said, "I'm going to move to St. Louis in one month."

"Where's that?" he asked.

"It's a long drive, Sweetie. About four hours."

In a soft voice, he said, "But then you'll never get to see me." He left me speechless. I thought nothing could feel worse, but I was wrong.

Returning home, happy memories followed me everywhere. While fishing with friends, my stomach fluttered as I remembered my fiancé's son catching his first fish, and I yearned to be back in that time. When decorating my new apartment for Halloween, I found his Spiderman costume and pieces of straw for our scarecrow mixed in with my decorations.

These reminiscences created dread and anxiety over the approaching Christmas season, once my favorite. I questioned God. How could He make me feel this way? Hadn't I been through enough? I did nothing to deserve this!

Even before Thanksgiving, remembrance of Christmas past filled my mind: attending a candlelight service with my fiancé on Christmas Eve or buying toys for his son and watching him rip open action figures and miniature cars. The memories of chopping down our Christmas tree and stringing fresh popcorn haunted my thoughts.

How could God expect me to be joyful over the birth of His son when I was alone? I burst into tears at the sight of commercials for *Charlie Brown's Christmas Special* or *Rudolph's Shiny New Year*, shows we had watched together. Decorating my apartment took longer than I planned because I often had to stop and wipe my eyes, especially when hanging a lone stocking.

I tired to convince Mom to do something different. "Let's go to Florida or have a chili cook-off," I said.

"Why?" she asked.

"No reason," I lied, "Just something different." I didn't want to admit my unending sadness. *Shouldn't I be over him by now?* But a tape of past celebrations played in my head, constantly rewinding and showing again.

"It wouldn't feel like Christmas," she said.

So I relented, knowing I would spend this Christmas hiding the hole in my heart with a fake smile on my face.

Talking to others, I discovered many people felt the same way about the joyous season. Perhaps their mother had died during the year; she wouldn't be around to make her traditional dinner. Or maybe a childhood home had burned to the ground, no longer to be enjoyed during the holidays.

I was surprised there wasn't a group: Christmas Haters Anonymous. Special memories disturbed many people, not just me—people who would do almost anything to have those good times back again, almost anything except put faith in God.

To escape lingering thoughts, I involved myself in as many activities as I could: bunco, book club, dinner club, and a singles group. In spite of my anger toward God, I attended my old church and served on a contemporary worship planning committee. I'd do almost anything not to be alone.

During a committee meeting, my minister passed out a theme list for December services. My job, as well as that of the other members, was to brainstorm non-traditional ways to reach people who didn't connect with a regular church service. We split into groups and each worked on one service for the month. He assigned me the one I most dreaded—Christmas Eve. But the strangest part was the theme: How To Celebrate Christmas When Your Heart Isn't In It. My heart pounded as I listened to my minister explain his ideas.

He said, "I want to reach out to people stuck in the past. Teach them how to cherish memories of loved ones and to be happy that God once blessed them with these people. Hopefully, we'll provide faith that there'll be good times again."

I broke out in a cold sweat and thought, *It's as if he's talking directly to me.* How could I plan a service to help people like this when I was a person like this?

"It's our job," he said. "To help each other enjoy Christmas in the present."

It was almost as if God Himself had tapped me on the shoulder and said, "Hey, look! People need you. Stop feeling sorry for yourself and do something."

Several ideas popped into my head—songs, poems, and short stories fitting the theme and ideas for a dramatic performance. I even suggested reading *The Grinch Who Stole Christmas* by Dr. Seuss.

To prepare for this service, I read heart-wrenching stories and listened to inspirational music. My anger toward God dissipated. Focusing on the birth of Jesus Christ filled my heart with joy. The dread I had experienced the last month made it easier to help others with the same problem. Thoughts of giving to people who had less than me occupied my time. I became excited about Christmas coming and waited with anticipation for church on December 24.

During those weeks, when I remembered my fiancé and his son, I sometimes felt a tightness in my chest, but I said a prayer of thanks each time I thought of us sitting quietly in the glow from the lights of our tree or baking sugar cookies.

On Christmas Eve many people, including Mom and Grandma, attended the service. My eyes brimmed with tears as I listened to a record of the song, *Christmas Shoes*, relaying the story of a little boy without enough money to buy his dying mother a pair of shoes. Smiles warmed the faces of children and adults and especially my 86-year-old grandma as the Grinch learned the true meaning of the season. At the end of the service, goosebumps covered my arms when everyone in the congregation stood in a circle, holding candles with the lights dimmed. We sang *Silent Night* and passed the light of peace to one another. Mom's voice rose above the rest. Soon the sanctuary filled with a glow, just as my heart had while I planned this service.

The holiday was not awful. One of my favorite parts had been buying gifts for my fiancé's son. I missed shopping for a child, so I adopted a young girl from the giving tree at the local library. While enjoying Christmas Day with my parents, Grandma, and boxer puppy, I allowed myself to remember my fiancé and even to laugh about some funny times: our tree falling to the floor weighed down by too many ornaments and our dog eating bird feathers and getting sick on Christmas morning. And I created new memories to share: attending church, opening gifts, watching funny movies, and eating too much!

I believe God spoke to me through this experience. He had not forgotten me as I once thought. I thanked Him for helping me through my pain and especially for giving me the opportunity to help others. If I had not experienced my loss, I wouldn't have known how to touch other lonely people. God renewed my faith in spite of my anger. Now I lean on Him during difficult times.

10

A Child's Simple Faith

April Showers

By Bonnie Compton Hanson
Santa Ana, California

"Winter storm on the way!" the radio blared. I glanced out the window. Already dark clouds were forming above our small new subdivision in rural Illinois.

Just then, "Mom! Mom!" In blew my three bundled-up boys and a crisp October wind.

"Mom!" cried five-year-old Robin. "There's a cat down in the ground!"

"Oh. You mean someone's cat's been buried?"

"No, Mom! Please! Come see! She needs help!"

Six eager hands pulled me outside to the curb. "Can't you hear it?"

Yes, I could—a very faint meow. Floating right up from the storm drain!

Chat, almost four, squinted down into the darkness. "Maybe we could drop her a rope."

Two-and-a-half-year-old Jay started calling, "Here kitty, kitty, kitty!"

By now a crowd of neighborhood children had gathered around. "This storm sewer drains across the street," one of the older boys explained. "If we go down to the opening and call, maybe she'll come out."

At the culvert opening the children took turns shouting, "Kitty! Kitty!" Finally when Jay called, out she came. Muddy, wet, bone-thin, with a woefully deformed tail. But alive.

"Whose cat is she?" I asked.

"No one's," piped up one of the girls. "Her old owners kicked her down there to get rid of her."

"Well, she's ours now," Robin announced. "'Cause Jay's the one she came out for."

Back at the house we wiped the pathetic creature off the best we could. Then, looking around for something to feed her, I filled a bowl of milk.

But ignoring the bowl completely, the cat sat and washed herself all over. Now we could see that she was a longhair with striking black and white markings. Only when she was immaculate did she turn to the milk.

Even then, instead of gulping it down, she sipped daintily, stopping to clean her whiskers from time to time.

"Look at that!" my husband, Don, exclaimed. "A real lady!"

And that's how Ladycat came to be with us.

Just in time too. For all night long we were hit with wave after wave of pounding rain. By morning it had changed to snow.

But inside our home glowed with the joy of a new playmate. For hours on end Ladycat would play balls, blocks, and cars with three enchanted boys. She blossomed under this love. But two things about her sad past remained: her deformed tail (perhaps broken in that kick down the storm drain) and her need to go outside and hunt for at least an hour every night.

Frozen days rolled into frozen weeks of 10, 20, and 30 degrees below zero.

Then on Valentine's Day all three boys got the chicken pox—Chat so severely that he went into a coma and had to be hospitalized. His brothers begged me not to let Ladycat out that night in case something happened to her, as well.

But the air that evening was spring-like with just a little drizzle. "Don't worry. She'll be right back," I assured them.

Quickly, though, that drizzle whipped itself up into a wild rainstorm. And for the very first time, Ladycat did not come back. All night long, as I cared for Jay and Robin, I kept listening for her discreet call. But I only heard the rain—until it stopped and everything froze.

The next morning Don's car slid all over the glass-slick road as he headed off on his long commute to work. But I couldn't call him to see if he got there okay. I couldn't even call the hospital 15 miles away to check on Chat. Or turn on the radio. Or lights. Or the heater.

For under the weight of all that ice, power and phone lines had snapped. Our furnace and water heater were inoperable. In fact, nothing worked but our gas stove. Soon it was so cold inside that the boys had to be bundled up in their snowsuits all day long—complete misery with those itching pox!

By evening both boys had bronchitis. But sick as they were, they kept going to the window, looking and calling for their missing pet.

In the middle of the night, Don woke up in excruciating pain with a grossly swollen abdomen. Even though the house was freezing cold (it was 20 degrees below outside and not much warmer inside), his whole body was afire.

"Don!" I gasped. "I think you have appendicitis!"

Normally I would have called the doctor or 911. But with the lines down, I couldn't even call my neighbors next door. Don needed to go to the hospital right away. But Robin and Jay were far too sick to take out into that frigid air. Don would have to go alone.

As quickly as possible, I packed him in ice, covered that with towels, threw a winter coat over his pajamas, and sent him out into the bitter night—praying he'd be able to make it to the hospital without passing out—or ending up in a wreck.

By the next day, Robin, Jay, and I all had pneumonia. But so did almost everyone else for miles around. Only the most critically ill could be admitted to the hospital. In fact, Don had to sit up in a waiting room all that night—with ruptured appendix, peritonitis, and double pneumonia—before they could even find a cot for him.

Finally after a week power and phones returned. After two weeks, so did Don. And after three weeks, Chat did too. But not our missing cat.

February blurred into March, one storm following another. The same with illnesses: measles, German measles, several strep infections. Finally Chat came down with rheumatic fever—in such pain he couldn't be touched without screaming.

"It's all because Ladycat left," Robin sobbed one day. "Why doesn't she come back? Doesn't she love us anymore? Doesn't God love us anymore?"

Yes, God, why are you letting this happen to these innocent children? Don't You love us anymore?

"God knows where Ladycat is," Chat replied weakly. "I'm going to pray and ask Him to bring her back home to us for Jay's birthday!"

On April second, just a few days away? What an impossible prayer!

The last day of March was as white, cold, and dreary as ever. But the wind shifted. And on April first, the skies opened up.

"Look, children!" I cried. "April showers! It's raining cats and dogs!

"Cats?" Jay cried. "Is Ladycat here?"

"She will be," Chat assured him. "For your birthday. God will bring her back."

Changing the subject, I asked, "So what *do* you want for your birthday tomorrow, Jay?"

"Ladycat. Just Ladycat."

That evening the rain finally let up. Then at the dinner table Robin suddenly asked, "Who's at the front door?"

"Ladycat!" Jay shouted.

All three boys ran to the door, flinging it open wide. A biting wind roared in—followed by a tiny, mud-covered creature barely able to move.

Don jumped up. "Quick! Get her some food!"

But as feeble as she was, the cat slowly, painfully cleaned herself all over. Only then would she eat. Ladycat was back.

The next morning we retraced her tiny footsteps in the mud—all the way to the culvert where we had first found her. Ever since the ice storm—that night she had disappeared—the opening had been completely frozen over. She had been down there the entire time, subsisting on mice and snow—until freed finally by the previous day's warm April showers.

Arriving home just in time for Jay's birthday.

Just as three little boys and God knew she would.

Balloons

By Caroline J. Zepp
Lemoyne, Pennsylvania

As a child of neglect, I became an attentive student of deprivation. I studied well my own worthlessness, as my father taught long...vigorous...relentless lessons. Himself a child of poverty, Dad created a wasteland of a homelife for all of us. My mother watched, having given so much of her power to him, as so many women believed they were relegated to do in those days. He rarely bought good food for us to eat. I recall eating fried bread as a treat.

Since my father paid for heating only occasionally, the house was often cold and damp. I hold one particular memory clearly in my mind. My sisters, Margie and Nini, and I fell quickly, one after another, into the same bed. Because I was the youngest, I was sandwiched in the middle. My mother hoped that there I would be somewhat warmer. How horribe for her—to feel the need to attempt to preserve one child at the expense of the others! As we all gasped our final sighs before resting, small clouds rose about our mouths. The chill of the bedroom air bit my nose. And so, on another routine evening, the lightswitch clicked off...and we slept.

The furniture, walls, and floor were colored with a dismal glow. They were even more deeply blackened further by the depression that wept across the rooms. With no bathtub, hygiene was, at best, minimal. There was an old washing machine that could only be used during the summer because it was outdoors. We had no indoor toilet, and the outdoor one was filthy.

Even in the midst of all this mistreatment at his hands, I still pursued the attention and affection of the primary man in my life. From time to time my eyes hesitated toward his, apologetically seeking connection. When met only with the punch of his anger and disinterest, they would scurry away, my body obediently following. My father held an absent presence. He was always preoccupied...distant...even mysterious. I know now that there is no mystery to being depressed and angry and filled with rage.

He did not even recognize my needs and certainly did not desire to place presents in my hands...or in my eyes...or in my soul...for Christmas or birthday or just because. He orchestrated our relationship so that I would never ask for anything. It may seem impossible to close the open hand of a child. However, he knew that if he ignored that open hand long enough, I would close it myself. Without voicing the question, I knew the inarguable answer...No! No to everything I needed. No to everything I wanted. No to the cry of my heart just to be loved. That cold, angry, and brutal "no" carried with it an unspoken admonition to "sit down, shut up, and get out of the way." I walked among landmines of verbal abuse and neglect. Not wanting to detonate those mines, I reconciled within myself begging, "I won't ask for anything. Just don't scream at me."

Grandma and Aunt Jean were the lights of my life. Aware of the desperation of the situation, they were sure to provide yearly Christmas presents—for each child a toy and a piece of clothing. They intuitively knew how important it is that a child receive the fulfillment of her needs *and* even desires. They mailed food to us periodically throughout the year—lots of pasta and pasta sauce. Periodically I remember my mother opening a box with lots of red and glass chips all over the inside of it. She would clean up the remnants of the broken jar, and we would gratefully receive the rest. You may wonder, like I have recently, why they did not just send money. I believe at one time they did simply send the funds. However, somehow the dollars always managed to disappear in my father's hand. Like his paycheck, those gifts would slip through our hands and be gone before we ever saw them.

For their yearly vacation, Grandma and Aunt Jean visited me, my siblings, and my mother in the agony of our world. They came to this filthy, angry place of extreme deprivation to meet my eyes, talk closely with me, play with me, and attend to some of my physical needs. They used to bring boiled ham and sweet rolls to the farm on which we lived. Never—before or since—have I tasted such a feast.

With the exception of my father, all of us relished their visits. Once, after they had fed, clothed, and nurtured us (having done this since the birth of my oldest sibling), Dad screamed at them, even hurling names at them...names usually reserved for the harshest of enemies! My oldest sister, Nini, said she remembers thinking, "What is going to happen to us if they decide they cannot take care of us anymore?" Her comment on a birthday card to Aunt Jean was telling. As a 13-year-old, Nini wrote, "Thank you very much for all that you have done. I appreciate it very much—Believe me."

As an adult, the realization of how much they gave up for us has fallen on my heart and shoulders. They were 50- to 60-year-old women working in the 1960's. Their paychecks could not have been large. They gave away what people dream of...plan for...build for...just so we could survive. Aunt Jean sold a prized Blue Boy painting in order to buy food for us one year. She spoke of this without bitterness or hatred...yet through tears.

Controlled by his anger, I obeyed my father's silent command to not ask for my needs to be met. I was hushed, in large part, by fear. However, quite honestly, the thought of asking for anything never crossed my mind until I was about seven years old. At that time and for some unknown reason, I decided I wanted a bag of balloons. With great intensity, I scribed a letter to my grandmother and aunt requesting this present.

After sending this letter, I received the granting of my wish in the mail—a bag of balloons. I remember feeling a mixture of happiness and guilt. However, more prominently, I recall how foreign it felt to make a request and have it fulfilled. It was as if this place inside—which seemed to be the size of a small inner tube—swelled inside my body. I struggled with shallow breaths and was left happily light-headed. I believe it was excitement. But it was an emotion I had not exercised very often—at least not at any time other than when Grandma and Aunt Jean were visiting.

The balloons brought joy, laughter, color, and distraction to our house. My mother laughed heartily when her false teeth moved as she tried to blow one up. When one of the children reached up to retrieve it from her hand, she objected, "No, let me try again!" She was apparently enjoying her wrestling match with the balloon.

A few months later, with great hesitation and substantially greater guilt, I made a second request...again for balloons. This time, however, I felt more in control, more powerful, and more expectant that I would be heard. In a week, I had the second bag of balloons. Though still amazed, I was starting to make a real emotional connection between voicing my desires and having some trust that I would be listened to and that someone would do something about it.

I recently bought a CD player. My mind paced back and forth over this decision. As I pored over this object, I felt transformed to this place of wishing where children go. I relished thoughts of how I love to listen to beautiful spiritual music—over and over. I permitted myself to hope...to dream...and to expect. In short, I now have a very expensive bag of balloons.

I am learning to bring my requests for balloons to my Father God. In doing so, I dance inside. Occasionally I feel that sense of swelling inside that captures my breath and leaves me dizzy. I am finally starting to gain an understanding that when I ask Him for balloons, He stops, looks in my eyes, and holding my face in His hands, He says, "What colors do you want?" I tell Him. Then I walk away, truly knowing that they are in the mail. A moment later, I hear His voice speak my name. I return attentively to His gaze. Once again, He gently holds my face in His hands and says, "Is that all you *really* want—a bag of balloons?"

My eyes bubble with tears. "Tell me what you really want." He wraps His arms around me, my body now throbbing with the effort of all my tears. "No, that's not all I want. I want You to love me and pay attention to me and tell me I am okay." There are tears, many tears...in my eyes...and...tears in the eyes of my Daddy.

Then He sits me on His lap. Turning around, I am brave. I gasp, thinking He will show me again where I came from and that the Lord will give me the emotional fortitude to deal with all that deprivation. But it is so much better than that...and this is who *my Jesus* is...as I turn around, all I can see, as far as I can see, are *balloons*!

There are inflated balloons of all shapes and colors, beautifully grouped and arranged, as if on a vast hillside. So many of these flood around me that my eyes cannot gather them all. I see three heart balloons in the front. I am utterly amazed!

I look at Daddy in surprise. He has a huge smile on His face which says to me, "I have loved you with an everlasting love. I have kept your tears in a bottle. I have heard *all* your requests for balloons. And I am able to do exceedingly, abundantly, above all you are even able to ask or think. And you...my precious, beautiful child...can have *all the balloons you want*!"

For All I Trust Him

By Melva Cooper
Jonesboro, Arkansas

We were going to be grandparents! Our older daughter was pregnant with her first child and our first grandchild. *You created my inmost being; you knit me together in my mother's womb,* from Psalm 139:13 became alive as the ultrasound showed those delicate inner parts being formed. We watched in awe as we identified eyes, nose, mouth, toes, fingers, and a tiny heart beating fast. A smile crossed our faces when a hand was raised as if waving to the family. Gymnastics were performed right before our eyes. After a few minutes that little one settled down, put a hand beside the face and went to sleep. What an introduction to a first grandchild! Yet after all that time with the ultrasound, the doctors and nurses still could not tell us if the baby growing so rapidly in its mother's womb was a boy or girl.

A baby boy's name was selected quickly. But what if it was a girl? Books with baby's names were purchased and family and friends offered advice, but mother and father could not agree on a girl's name. One Sunday a few weeks before this little one was to be born our pastor preached a message on FAITH. He used the acrostic:

For
All
I
Trust
Him

As the grandmother my spirit was quickened that this was to be the name of our first grandchild if indeed she was a little girl. I knew our daughter and son-in-law were coming to our house for lunch after the services, and I could hardly wait to suggest to them the name Faith. I never got the chance. The first words out of my daughter's mouth when she and her husband came through the door that day were, "Mother, if we have a baby girl, we are going to name her Faith." God had spoken to her at the same time and said *name your baby Faith.* It was settled. If a girl was born, she would be Faith. Little did we know that her life would become one big faith journey, trusting Him for everything.

On March 14, 1989, Faith Ann Williams was born by c-section. Every finger and every toe was perfect in detail. As a bonus she had beautiful red hair that would soon become ringlets of curls around her head. So that her mother's body could heal quickly, I stayed with them day and night for the first week. It was a precious time. A special bond formed between us as I spent the wee hours of the night, feeding, cuddling and loving her. Faith soon learned her grandmother's voice, as I talked to her while doing all the necessary things that keep a tiny baby happy. I loved those midnight hours when everyone had gone to bed and it was just the two of us. Faith would look up at me as if to say, "Thank you, Grandma, for being here to feed me again tonight."

That beautiful first granddaughter became my constant companion. Her mother worked part-time at night, and Faith spent a lot of time at our house. She was a model child. My prayer partner. Often, we unloaded the dishwasher together, singing her "helper song" and praying for missionaries around the world. Some days she called me just to say, "I love you, Grandma."

At the tender age of five, Faith watched *The Easter Story* on video several times, and she could pray every word of *The Lord's Prayer*. Faith would open her Bible to Luke and "tell" the story of our Lord's birth. She hardly missed a word as it is written in God's Holy Word. Even though she hadn't learned sounds and couldn't read words, she spoke that Christmas story as if she was reading it word for word. So we were not surprised one night when she would not go to sleep until her mother had walked her through the steps of praying to receive Jesus in her heart.

The day she started kindergarten her mother and I wanted, several times, to call and just see how she was doing. We needn't have worried. When she came home from school, she was excited. She had made new friends, she loved her teacher, and with joy in her voice she told me, "Oh, Grandma, today we pledged allegiance to the American Flag, the Christian Flag, and the Bible." I prayed her allegiance would always be to those things.

Our family didn't take a vacation during the summer between Faith's kindergarten and first grade years, so my husband and I decided to take our daughter and granddaughters with us on a business trip. Excitement mounted as Faith counted the days until time to go with Granddaddy and Grandma. Immediately upon arriving at the hotel, they donned their bathing suits and headed for the swimming pool. Imagine their delight to find an indoor and an outdoor pool side by side. There were also a whirlpool and a sauna. They really had a hard time deciding where to swim first, so we let them try all four. They were having a wonderful time when spontaneously Faith, with that head full of red, natural curls swirling around, said to me, "Grandma, if I had any money, I would give it all for this one day." With much happiness, I knew God had allowed Faith to express from her heart what the Bible calls perfect praise.

The next school season soon passed and I found myself at Faith's end-of-the-school-year award's program. When her teacher began giving out the awards, Faith's name was called for Spelling, Phonics, Reading, Math, Writing, and a special award for being a straight "A" student all year. But the award that ministered to this grandmother the most was the Bible award. When she walked, once again, to the tiny stage in that school cafeteria to pick up her Bible award, her teacher said, "Faith, has known her Bible verse every week all year long."

The world seemed so perfect those days. A loving husband, a caring church family, and precious granddaughters to enjoy.

But then in just a few hours that world literally fell apart.

Our family was suddenly thrust into a time of suffering. We grasped for that faith that we thought we knew so much about. It definitely was time to trust *Him* for everything.

Faith's father came home from work and told the family he did not want to be married to their mother anymore. He would no longer accept the responsibilities of being a full time husband and dad. In one seemingly big swoosh, he helped pack their suitcases, buckled them in their seatbelts, and told our daughter to bring them all to our house.

Pain such as our family did not know existed echoed over and over for many days and nights to come. Then seven-year-old Faith, who had never known anything but the perfect family, became the child without her home and her dad. Many nights those first few weeks I went to bed with their crying stabbing at my heart.

We prayed God would get us through those traumatic transition days. Daily we asked God to be a father, tender and compassionate, to the girls (Psalm 103:13). As grandparents we could love them, feed them, and shelter them, but we could not fill in the gaps in their hearts from their earthly father leaving them. We learned together that God binds up wounds and heals broken hearts just as He promises in Psalm 147:3.

Holidays were most difficult. As the first Christmas season approached, we made a conscious effort to keep Christ before them as the real reason we celebrate that day. Christmas Day arrived, and I could see our daughter plunge, once again, into the depths of despair because her family was torn apart by divorce. I could also see from the sparkling eyes and smiling faces that the girls were having a wonderful time. In the midst of opening gifts and taking pictures seven-year-old Faith startled us all by exclaiming in her happy voice, "This is the best Christmas I have ever had." My husband looked at me. I looked at our daughter. We all looked at one another to see if we had heard her correctly. And then without realizing the Lord was prompting her, Faith said one more time, "This is the best Christmas I have ever had." It was music to our ears, sent from our Heavenly Father through the mouth of the very one we had been concerned about.

Gradually we settled in as a family. My husband and I committed ourselves to taking care of them and sacrificing the comfort that comes with retirement and being "just grandparents." It was not always easy, but God confirmed to us that we were in His will. He often reminded me through my granddaughters what it means to be more like Jesus.

After the girls had been living with us about 14 months, Faith brought me a picture she had drawn of a heart broken from top to bottom.

She said, "Grandma, God has healed my broken heart. Last year my heart was broken, but God has healed it."

And then she drew a picture of a heart wholly complete, without any breaks. I held her tightly in my arms and thanked God for being faithful with His promise He had given me soon after they moved in with us.

I was grateful that Faith knew that is was our great and wonderful Lord who healed her. We loved and cared for her during those troublesome days, but only God could heal her broken heart.

Weeks turned into months and months made years. They seemed to go quickly as we all adjusted to the new lifestyle that we were tossed into so turbulently. The smiling face of our granddaughter came from a deep faith that was all about trusting Him.

When Faith was 10 years old, I found a page in her Bible that she had written at church the Sunday night before. It read:

"I love my mom, dad, sister, Grandma and Granddaddy, Aunt Julia, Uncle Alan, Levi, Brooke, Uncle Roger, Aunt Lori, Jordan, Tanner, Grandma Cooper, Robin, Dana, Aunt Bettie, Becky, Karissa, Holly, Heather, and Michael. But

Most of All
JESUS
GOD
HOLY SPIRIT

Amidst the tragedy that would have broken the spirit of many, Faith was once again trusting her Heavenly Father who had carried her through the many heartaches in her young life.

Faith is now a young teenager. She is a cheerleader at a small Christian school in our town. Her friends call her often. With her beautiful red hair, she already has that carved, graceful look that would beautify any home. Inside her there is an integrity that God cries out for all of us to have. For All I Trust Him is a way of life for this young girl we named Faith those many years ago. She has an earthly father who has not been around a lot of the time—but a Heavenly Father who has proven He will never leave her nor forsake her. Some in this world would call her family dysfunctional. Because Faith has learned to trust Him for everything, she knows the reality of God's love and care.

Letters To Heaven

By Judith A. Connor
Butler, Pennsylvania

"Dying and going to heaven is a reward for living the best life you can live. Since I believe this with all my heart, I rarely cry when I think about my sister...my parents think this but do not truly believe it. I find myself helping them instead of them helping me."

To Carrie,

Your brother was only 12 years old when he wrote those words. Imagine—12 years old, and his faith was strong.

When you died so unexpectedly, I tried to believe that life doesn't end with death—but a kernel of doubt lodged in my heart. I voiced the words, "We'll see Carrie again." But they were empty words, spoken as much to assure me as to comfort Josh. And Josh, it seems, needed less comforting than I.

During and after the funeral, I received countless testaments of your selflessness, easing my doubt, but never erasing it. I listened to personal accounts from friends and relatives, stories that swelled my heart with pride. At the funeral home, Dawn's mother clasped my cold hands between her warm ones and told me, "Carrie tutored my Dawn. You know, Dawn never had many friends, but Carrie was kind to her—took care of her." And I recalled Billy and Johnny talking about Dawn while we were all sitting in your grandma's kitchen. As your cousins described Dawn, in a way that young kids do, for a good laugh, not out of meanness, you sat quietly in the background, refusing to join in just to fit in. Rather than shame them into silence with your tutoring account, you spoke not a word.

That story, along with many others, should have reinforced my faith. Such kindness and charity must by rewarded, if not during this life, then surely the next. But the doubt still lingered.

When the stories dwindled and people drifted away, leaving me alone with my grief, I was drawn to your bedroom like a moth to a flame. I wanted to know you better, to find a reason for my loss in the pages of your journals. In search of those spiral notebooks that were once off limits to prying eyes, I was both afraid and compelled to look. What if I discovered a facet of your life better left unknown? My fears were groundless. I read English essays that tugged at my heart and pored over journal passages that stirred my soul. As I read, I could hear your voice as if you were beside me reading the words.

"Dear Mr. Bunny, In the light of the world's present situation, all of the injustice and strife, I feel that I cannot with good conscience accept any presents from you this year... just take my share of gifts and give it to an orphanage or a shelter for abused children, those without real homes..." You went on to offer Josh's presents to charity, as well, assuring Mr. Bunny that your brother wouldn't mind, that he was wise for his years. You received an "A" from Mr. Hartle. If I didn't know you as only a mother knows her child, the skeptic in me might have sensed a ploy for a good grade. But I believed in your sincerity, and Mr. Hartle, who wasn't a sucker for ploys, must have believed in it also.

That Easter Bunny essay, dated March 27, 1990, was written exactly seven days before your death. Was that when God said, "Okay, she's 'heavenly material.' Let's take her." Was "seven" a significant number of days to wait before rewarding such purity of heart with life after death? How could I continue to doubt? But still, my faith was weak.

Your journals, full of insight and wisdom, captivated me with your kindness—but it was your final entry, dated January 18, that raised the hair on the back of my neck. *"I'm feeling restless, on the edge of discovery. I've been feeling that a lot lately. As if I'm going to reach this major conclusion about my life. And then suddenly it slips away..."*

I should have needed no other sign, and yet, I questioned. By taking you from me, was God punishing me for my sins? After I so neglected your spiritual life, would God accept you into heaven? Is there a heaven? Oh, I spoke the right words to all who would listen, but my thoughts negated those words.

"Dying and going to heaven is a reward for living the best life you can live. Since I believe this with all my heart, I rarely cry when I think about my sister... my parents think this but do not truly believe it. I find myself helping them instead of them helping me."

To Joshua,

I read your journals shortly after you wrote them and then again nearly a decade later. Where did you acquire such faith at such a young age? Why couldn't I feel it, too? After Carrie's death, I struggled to believe. And then, 10 years later, you left us, too, Josh—you, who had no fear, who promised to always be here. My faith, a small seed that needed nurturing, withered from neglect. There was little room for faith to grow when choked with weeds of bitterness.

Unlike your sister, who kept a diary from age 5 until she died at age 16, you left behind only two notebooks, writing assignments from your sixth grade teacher. I wish there were more so that I could learn your heart as well as I had learned Carrie's. But just as that one passage revealed a faith that was strong, your actions showed a heart that was kind. I needed no written words to demonstrate your decency. You pretended a callousness to mask the sensitivity within, but your closest friends soon discovered a soft center.

There was Aaron, the lonely boy who lived beside us. You befriended Aaron, bringing him into our home when he had nowhere to run, including him in your plans with your other friends. And he followed you like a stray that's been rescued, forever after loyal to his rescuer. Aaron—with all the wild hairdos—became a hair stylist, and he now sports a tattoo—a cross on his forearm with your name beneath it.

There was Jen, the sister of one of your best friends. You defended Jen to her brother and other friends; they delighted in tormenting her—made a sport of picking on the kid sister. You came to her rescue, always and often. You took pride in talking her out of depression and persuading her out of bad relationships, spending hours on the phone. Once I thought you were sweethearts; later, I discovered you shared a friendship few teens ever find. Jen, who worshipped you as her hero, closeted herself in her house for weeks after the funeral, barely eating, rarely talking. Finally she came to see me, and we talked for hours, a healing process for us both. She opened up to me, teaching me about a Josh I didn't know, and she managed to laugh again. Jen, the aspiring writer, later wrote an essay for her college English class entitled, "My Best Friend, Josh."

When I think of the mark you made with Aaron and Jen and so many others, how could my faith still falter? When I recall Carrie's kindness to those less fortunate, how could I continue to wonder? Surely, two such meaningful lives didn't end with the finality of death. There must be more. Joshua, help me to believe that there's more.

Ten days before your death, when a deer sought shelter under a pine tree outside our dining room door, you didn't talk of getting a gun. Instead, you watched the deer from the doorway, careful not to frighten her away. And you cautioned me against trying to feed her. You believed God's creatures must fend for themselves in order to survive. And she stayed for three days, knowing she was safe from harm. Seven days later, you died in a fire while rescuing a friend.

What more proof did I need of life after death? The deer must have appeared to let us know you'd be okay before she took you away. And seven days later you died a hero's death. But saying it must be so doesn't make it so. Everybody can't be as innately self-assured as you were. For most of us, faith needs to be nurtured from a seedling into a sprout before it can mature and blossom.

Finally I joined the church, that same church I talked about joining when Carrie died. And I'm trying to develop a personal relationship with God. It might bring me closer to you and to Carrie; it might keep you alive in my heart until I see you again. And I've got to believe that I'll see you again. After losing it all, that's all I have left.

My dearest Joshua, so young and so sure. In the face of my doubts, your faith never faltered. And despite those doubts, your faith gives me hope.

Prayers For The Faith Of A Child

By Mark L. Redmond
South Bend, Indiana

Driving down the street that cold, snowy day, I knew that something was terribly wrong. I let my thoughts wander into the past. Life had once been going smoothly for me.

At the age of five, I had accepted Christ as my Savior. I had rarely missed Sunday school, church, or the after-school Bible club my mother led at the public school I attended. In high school I was a leader in our youth group. After high school I graduated from a Christian college with a Bachelor of Science degree in secondary education and married my lovely young wife.

We taught at a Christian school that first year in Tennessee, and life was good. Later we moved to a different ministry halfway across the state and our son, Benjamin, was born. He only increased our happiness.

When God led us to Indiana a little over a year later and put me back into teaching, we were delighted, and just short of a year after our move, Melody was born. We purchased a small house, did extensive remodeling ourselves, and settled in. Life was about as good as it could be.

But less than two years later, my wife Susi was hospitalized for two months and diagnosed with acute rheumatoid arthritis that left her practically bedridden. During the next five years, she did not respond to any of the usual treatments. Once she nearly died from toxic shock syndrome.

Then Susi's condition improved enough that she could walk short distances with a walker. She could still drive a car, but not our 1979 Volkswagen Rabbit with its standard transmission and no power steering. We needed to buy a different car.

We were just scraping by on my meager salary, supplemented by occasional help from our parents and whatever I could earn at part-time jobs. We had no extra money—no savings account. Still, I went to several local used-car lots, hoping to find something with power steering, automatic transmission, and a monthly payment we could afford. No such vehicle existed.

We were raising our children to believe, as we believe, in the power of prayer, and both fourth-grade Ben and second-grade Melody had accepted Christ as their Savior. Both had seen answers to prayers for groceries, winter boots, and money to pay bills. Both had seen answers to prayers for missionaries, sick people, and church-related needs. Both understood that prayers are not always answered with "Yes," and both knew we needed a different car.

"Dad, are we praying for a new car or a used car?" Ben asked from the passenger's seat.

"A good used car," I replied, forcing a smile. His next question nearly made me run off the road.

"Can't God give us a new car?"

In the moment of silence that followed, I pictured my Heavenly Father with His arms folded across His chest and a smile on His face as He challenged me, *Well, can't I?*

I glanced at the skinny little 10-year-old bundle of faith sitting beside me and swallowed the lump in my throat. "Yes," I said.

When we got home, I changed our prayer list. We began to pray daily for a *new* car, and I began to think of ways to explain to my children why we hadn't received one. We prayed for months with no visible results, but the faith of my children never faltered.

On Easter Sunday in 1987, our church gave us a brand new Pontiac 6000 during the morning service. As Susi and I stood beside the car, crying, I saw Ben and Melody coming toward us in the crowd. When they stopped in front of the car, I said, "Look what the church gave us—a brand new car!"

Their faces glowed with delight but showed no trace of surprise. Looking up at me, Ben queried, "Isn't this what we asked for?"

This Easter will mark the 18th anniversary of the gift car. It had over 120,000 miles on it when we finally traded it in. Ben is a happily married father of two, serving God as a youth pastor in Minnesota. Melody, still living with us, is a graduate of IUSB and has just finished her first year of teaching second grade in our Christian school. Susi, still faithful to the Lord, although she is a semi-invalid, now battles not only arthritis but also intractable migraine headaches. I am still teaching high-school English in the same school.

Since that special day, we have covered a lot of rough road as a family. Ben faced two surgeries and missed one semester of his junior year in high school because of sinusitis. Several times we nearly lost Susi, and at least two of those times, Melody was the one who found her and initiated the action that saved Susi's life. We have either called 911 or rushed to the emergency room on numerous occasions. We still barely scrape by on my teacher's salary with help from both sets of parents and my working several part-time jobs. Daily we battle discouragement over health concerns and medical bills.

Susi and I, grandparents now, are past 50. We are tired—emotionally as well as physically—but we are still here. We may have slowed somewhat, but we are still moving forward.

Susi relies on me for spiritual leadership, but I sometimes fail her. At those times I return in my mind to the driver's seat of a 1979 Volkswagen Rabbit and listen to a child's voice, asking, "Can't God…?" I grip the steering wheel and once again see my loving Heavenly Father, arms folded across His chest, asking, *Well, can't I?*

Grateful for the lesson God taught me through my children, I know that we can overcome our circumstances. We have matured through the trials we faced in the past. Nevertheless, as we encounter new trials, our daily prayers are requests for the faith of a child.

The Lifeline Of Faith

By David Vickery
Croydon, London, England

When I was a little child, God was real to me. I remember being moved to tears by some of the words in hymns. At that time in England, it was customary to have a religious service each day at school before lessons began. At our Christmas carol service, when I was no more than seven years old, I was gripped by the truth of the carols in the candlelit darkness. The mysteries swirled about me, timeless and uncompromising. The world was changed and the realities revealed. I was a child of God.

Then, imperceptibly, as I grew older, my faith seemed to fade away. It was as though it was a flower that dried up from lack of watering. The water was there, of course, but I chose not to use it—or to use just the merest drop on rare occasions.

During my high school years, several of my schoolmates confessed their faith publicly. I remember feeling uncomfortable about this. I even joined those mocking their obvious sincerity which, being sincere, was uncool.

But I didn't need them. I didn't need God. As a close relative who was an atheist said to me once years later, "I just want to live my life." That's how I felt then. I was enjoying life fine as it was, and the last thing I wanted was to stop having fun and submit to a lot of strictures. I remember reading somewhere about a child who was asked how he saw God. The child said that to him God was an old man who sat around watching people enjoying themselves and tried to put a stop to it. Although I didn't put it exactly like that, something similar to that was in the back of my mind. I accepted the idea of God *intellectually.* But I didn't accept Jesus as *my God.*

One night, some years after I'd left school, I was lying in bed reading a book, as was my habit. I was lying there with my shriveled, almost dead faith. Then it happened.

I don't know how it happened—perhaps there was a line in the book I was reading or some leap of imagination. Maybe it was my stunted flower of faith crying out for water. But suddenly I knew I was worthless. I was without identity. I was in hell.

Since that time I've heard many church sermons, but I've never heard one about hell. As C.S. Lewis says in *The Screwtape Letters*, it is no longer a fashionable topic. Where the Victorians thought much about death, hell, and damnation, we seem to think of all that as faintly ridiculous. We're too earthly minded to be of heavenly use, to reverse a popular saying. Demons are joke figures in tights, wearing horns, and carrying pitchforks. And who can believe in that, in this day and age?

Who can believe in the classic picture of hell with its souls shrieking in agony, suffering endless torments at the hands of cackling demons, burning forever in a fire that never consumes?

I'd read English literature. In particular, I'd been impressed by the sermon that James Joyce describes in *A Portrait of the Artist as a Young Man*. I'd been impressed by his word power. But I hadn't believed what the sermon was saying.

But what is hell? Hell is separation from God. It is living for all eternity and being separate from God—and knowing it. Surely the gothic fantasies of demons and hellfire would be almost incidental in the face of that realization.

I sat up at the time, sweat pouring from me. I was in a state of panic—more than I had ever experienced in my life. The room confined me. The world confined me. It was all true. God was true. God was truth, not an intellectual reality.

And suddenly calm descended. I was drowning, and faith had thrown me a lifeline. I was God's child once again, and nothing could separate us. I was not worthless. I was a glorious child of God. Even the reflection of a billionth part of His glory made me glorious, too. Because I had accepted Jesus' sacrifice instead of disdaining it or—even worse, perhaps—ignoring it, hell had no fury. Death had lost its sting.

Shortly afterwards I sought out a friend—one of those who had so publicly announced his commitment at school and whom I'd mocked—and asked him to recommend a Bible to me. He did so, I bought it, and I proceeded to read it from cover to cover.

In doing so, I discovered that the third person of the Trinity was real, too, and not some intellectual concept. He was sent as a helper to us to help bring us into union with God until Jesus comes again.

I believe that the Holy Spirit is real. I believe that He threw me a lifeline and brought me back to life. That lifeline was my faith, suddenly watered and bursting into glorious bloom like one of those flowers that lie dormant for years in the desert waiting for that once-in-a-lifetime rainstorm.

Years later I met a lady on the Internet from far-off Georgia. I had never found the right girl and (almost but not quite) believed that I would never get married. I used to lie awake at night and say to myself, "Is this all there is, Lord?"

He did not let me down. Ask, and you shall receive. I asked, and I received a lifeline a second time. We were married a year later.

One of the things my new wife insisted on was that we go to church regularly. I had avoided this in my solitary life. I had prided myself on being a "mere Christian," drawing on C.S. Lewis' book title, *Mere Christianity*. If you believe and put Christian precepts into practice, why go to church?

I now know that while it may be possible to be a non-church-going Christian, it is infinitely better to be a church-going one. The fellowship of those who believe is just one of the many benefits. I know that we can do more for Him united than divided.

I have received the lifeline of faith. And now I, like any other believer, can throw that lifeline out to others—perhaps through this very story. And if so, it is not I alone throwing that lifeline, but the Holy Spirit guiding my hands.

11

Trust In Him

Faith To Praise

By Angela Nicole Baughman
Carbondale, Illinois

I suffer occasionally from insomnia. It used to really frustrate me, but over the years I have learned to take advantage of the nighttime hours. I do a little bit of everything when I'm awake: pay bills, do housework, read. I have learned to trust that sleep will eventually come. My periods of sleeplessness usually only last a few days, and then weeks will pass and I will sleep normally.

In the fall of 2001, I experienced an unusually long period of sleepless nights. I was struggling with the idea of a job change, and I spent a lot of time in those dark hours praying and asking for guidance.

I had been asked to give a devotion to a monthly women's group that met through our church. One night I spent praying and seeking direction on what to share with them. Someone suggested I bring something on dramatic interpretation "interp" ministry. I had written and shared a few interps at my church and had taught a couple of simple things to the children and youth, and now the women's group was interested in learning something, as well.

As I thought about a song that would be appropriate, I was led to consider Sandi Patty's *Safe Harbour* off her *Find It On The Wings* CD, so I began to work on it when I was up at night. I would play the song over and over—softly so as not to disturb my sleeping husband. Motions and movements came, and a confidence began to build that this was the right thing to share.

But then I began to sleep better again, work and life got busy, and I didn't complete the song. I wished I had because something just felt like it was the right message to share, but I knew I could always just teach them something I already knew and it would be so much easier for me. The date was quickly approaching anyway. I was to present my devotion on Thursday, September 13, 2001. As it turned out, that was two days after the terrible terrorist attacks on our nation.

As I stood in the Student Center of the university where I worked and watched the horrible images unfolding on the television on September 11,

2001, I could think of nothing but the words to Sandi Patty's song. "They'll know a place where they can come in from the darkness." So much hurting. So much sorrow. Who but the church as God's messenger could shed any hope at all in the midst of this tragedy?

Problem was, I no longer had enough time to prepare this song and finish it in time for the women's group. There was barely enough time in my schedule to eat between now and then, so how could I possibly find time to pray and work and rework and perfect something like this? Yet I knew it was right. It's why I had been led to it so much earlier. *Why didn't I finish it when I could have?*

Five minutes before I needed to leave that day I found myself alone in my kitchen, still uncertain of what to do. Two CDs sat on the counter in front of me. One was a song unfinished that carried the message I needed to give. The other, a song with little relevance to what we were all feeling, that I knew well and could teach with confidence. I lifted my face heavenward, and with tears spilling over I said, "Okay, but You have to go with me." I picked up the CD with the unfinished song, grabbed my Bible and headed out the door.

On the way over, I thought, "Maybe no one will show. It's been such a devastating two days—maybe everyone will just stay in with their families and this won't be an issue." I also prayed to God, "Lord, You know this isn't done. You know I need Your help to do this."

To date we had the biggest group of ladies we had ever had at our monthly gathering. I almost laughed out loud as I pulled up and saw all the cars. I just stood outside for a moment. It was cool enough that I could see my breath, but I hadn't bothered with a jacket. Then I clutched my Bible and the CD close to me and headed into the meeting.

We ate a bit, talked, and laughed, and there was a sense of community. As I started the devotion, I read from the third chapter of Ecclesiastes. A time to…a time to…a time to… We prayed together, and then I began to share the story of the song. No one had ever heard the song before, which to me was almost better. It was linked now, in my mind and in theirs, to this event as an example of what we're called to be in the midst of a hurting people.

As we worked through the interp that evening, God met me in a very real and personal way. He finished spots where there were holes. He opened the hearts of the group. We worshiped Him. We lifted our hands to Him in praise and surrender and felt our hearts soften as a result.

After that night, I went to the leadership of our church and proposed a new ministry. It is called Lifted Hands. *Lift up your hands in the sanctuary and praise the Lord* from Psalm 134:2. Many of the ladies that were there that evening at our women's meeting now come to monthly Lifted Hands practices. We share God's message of love through a creative ministry that somehow bridges generations, denominations, and worship style preferences. We have led services at churches, camps, and community events. We are servants of our Lord.

I don't have that hectic job that allowed me little time for God anymore. I recommitted my life to Christ and vowed to serve Him wherever He would lead. For this time, I lead this group of beautiful women in praise through interpreting song. I have faith that I will know what to do tomorrow when tomorrow comes.

Safe Harbour, Words and music by Bob Farrell & Greg Nelson, © 1994 Word, Incorporated

Home for Christmas

By Jules Lentz
Naperville, Illinois

"I'm not ready to die," my dad tearfully said.

"It's not fair. You're full of life. I need you!" I shouted angrily.

In June 1988 my dad was diagnosed with terminal stomach cancer. The doctors expected him to live only two months. Just the day before, we had been planning some details for my younger brother's wedding in August. Now we wondered whether Dad would still be with us. Until this time my dad was making the most of his life. He loved his home and his children. He took much pride in getting older, looking forward to turning 80. I doubted God's timing.

In the days that followed, Dad always tried to seem happy. He smiled and joked whenever anyone was around him. He started reading the Bible daily, saying he had to make up for lost time. Dad dared to ask the Lord for many things—to be at his son's wedding and to spend quality time with his children. In exchange, Dad devoted the rest of his life to Jesus. He prayed continually and told us how much he loved the Lord. The Lord granted Dad's wishes.

Our time together was special. We talked about the past; he felt his life was truly blessed. I tried to get as many insights as possible into his life before I was born. It seemed important for me to ask all those questions that had been irrelevant before. I wanted to learn as much as I could about one of the greatest men in my life. Dad loved answering my questions and sharing his stories.

But as the holidays approached, he grew weaker and spent more time sleeping. My mother, sister-in-law, and I shared caring for him. We learned how to be his nurses: controlling the machine that checked his vital signs, administering medications, and supplying nourishment. My dad wished to spend his last hours at home. With the aid of hospice, his wish was granted.

As in past years, we decorated for the holidays. Christmas had always been our favorite time of the year. This holiday season was different; we just went through the motions. My thoughts troubled me. *What gift could I give Dad to treasure in his last moments?* I tried to think of things to give him great comfort. I couldn't bear for Christmas to come and not have something special for him. *Would he even be here for Christmas?*

I prayed daily asking God to guide my decision. I wandered through malls in tears and left disappointed. Nothing seemed appropriate or made sense. Standing by my faith, I prayed that God would direct me to the right gift. One morning while I was driving, my answer came—a Christmas service at home. I visited our priest and asked him to perform a service on Christmas Day at my parents' home. Reluctantly, the priest responded that day was the busiest of the year for him. I stressed that the service was truly the only gift that would comfort Dad and suggested doing the service early Christmas Eve day. The priest agreed to have the service at 2:00 p.m. on Christmas Eve. I was delighted and felt ready for Christmas. I had peace of mind; I knew it was the right gift. My dad was pleased to hear about having his own special Christmas service. He thought it was wonderful.

On December 24 at 4:00 a.m. my phone rang. My mother called to tell me to hurry to their home; my dad was dying. We lived an hour away; my husband and I raced to put on our clothes and headed out. On the way we picked up my brother, Jamie. When we arrived at their home, Dad was propped up in bed going in and out of a trance. He was having a deep conversation with an invisible someone and speaking in an unknown language. We had never experienced anything like it. With my arms around him in a tight embrace, I told him how much I loved him. He shook his head, came out of the trance, and muttered "I love you, too."

"Thanks for waiting for me, Dad," I cried as tears flooded my eyes.

Sternly he said, "There was no need to hurry. I'm not ready yet." It was as though he knew exactly when the right time would be. Tears rolled down my cheeks as I sat on the bed next to my dad, hugging him tightly as though I could prevent him from leaving me. I never left my dad's side that day. Christmas music was playing in the background as we read the Bible together.

At 2:00 p.m. the priest arrived along with a nun. My mother informed the priest that my dad was near death. As the priest entered the bedroom, Dad's eyes sparkled. He smiled and held the priest's hands; Dad had been waiting for him. The priest began Mass with all of us crowded around Dad. My brother, husband, and I sat on his bed. Other family members, including my mom and my dad's brother, stood in the small room. We all held hands. Throughout most of the service Dad was speaking in tongues again. Then when the priest began Our Lord's Prayer, Dad joined in and recited the prayer out loud. After we all received Communion, the last rites were given. When the service was over, my dad smiled and nodded to say thank you. Some family members left the bedroom. My mother walked the priest and nun out of the house. We turned the Christmas music back on softly. Moments after the priest had left, Dad stared at the top of the dresser directly in front of his bed. He shouted "Mom!"

We called my mother to come into the room because we thought he was calling her. After a long pause, he said, "I'm ready." Dad raised his hands up to reach for someone. His eyes stayed focused on his vision. His body shook until his soul left. We realized he had called out to his mother who had passed away many years ago. She had come to meet him for his journey to heaven. We had experienced a miracle and knew that he had gone to a better place. The Lord asked Dad to spend Christmas with Him. God's timing was perfect; Dad had received the perfect Christmas gift.

When Dad died, *The Little Drummer Boy* was playing on the radio. How ironic that the song talks about the finest gifts we bring. The service had comforted everyone in our darkest hour. The Christmas gift wasn't just for Dad; it was for all of us.

Lessons From Dixie Lee's Faith

By Raelene E. Phillips
St. Paris, Ohio

My best friend and I were shopping and stopped just inside the mall to laugh at the antics of bulldog puppies wrestling in the shredded newspaper of the window display at First Pets. "Let's go in," she suggested.

My eyes filled with tears when I saw the darling little bundle of gray fur sitting atop her pillow in the fifth cage. She look so much like Rebel, the schnauzer we had lost to some strange disease two years before. But the tag said she was a schnoodle. Before long the clerk brought her to us, opening up one of the play rooms. We sat awkwardly on the little stools while the little puppy ran back and forth between us chasing a ball.

At first we tried to be mature saying, "It is too much money. She is not full blooded. Who knows what a mixture between a schnauzer and poodle will eventually look like." But those words soon turned to, "Look how smart she is. And she certainly looks exactly like a schnauzer now."

Later I wondered if God ever thought about my pedigree (or lack thereof) before sending Jesus to buy me with His blood.

Within three days the puppy was home with me and my husband. "What should we name her?" we asked. Our grown children both live below the Mason Dixon line. We love visiting them and hope to retire in Tennessee or North Carolina. Our last dogs had been named Shiloh and Rebel, for obvious reasons. Our daughter suggested, "Why not Dixie?" And so it was decided. My husband, the civil war fanatic, soon added a middle name—"Lee"—as in Robert E.

It must have been scary for little Dixie Lee to come into our home. She wanted to come, but her little memory must have gone back a few weeks to when she had been with her first family, all of whom looked just like her and with whom she could snuggle.

And it was then that I began to mentally compare her journey to that of myself as a newborn Christian. Yes, she wanted to be with us—like I wanted to become a Christian—but sometimes the memory of her first family seemed to haunt her, like the memories of the worldly lifestyle sometimes haunted me. I needed to be taught and nurtured by older believers. I needed fellowship. *Aha,* I thought. *Dixie needs fellowship!*

And so, by the hour, we played with her. She brought delight to our hearts and laughter to our throats as she fell over her own feet and wrestled with the toys we gave her. Certainly God must have smiled at me as I stumbled over the words in the Bible and wrestled with the phrasing so familiar to older saints. But in much the same way that Dixie brought joy to our lives, I think it brought delight to His heart to watch me grow.

A large part of Dixie's early days with us involved training. She was so tiny that she could not maneuver the steps to our back deck when we took her in and out to "do her business." For a while we carried her (which brought to mind the famous poem, *Footprints,* in which the Lord is said to carry us). But eventually we decided she needed to learn to go up and down the steps herself.

I sat her down at the bottom of the five open wooden steps to the deck and walked up them, calling her name on each step. She sat there looking so forlorn, head cocked to one side, as if to say, "It's too high. I can't do it. Please help me."

I wondered how I would feel if someone were asking me to scale something six times my height. But I kept calling and, one step at a time, she maneuvered her way up. How I bragged on her! Sometimes it feels as if God brags on me when I learn something one step at a time, too.

But then came the harder part—going down. She just sat and stared. I smiled to myself as I said, "C'mon, Dixie. Have faith in me. I won't let you fall." It was as if God was saying to me, "I have said those same words to you many times." And I knew that just as I have learned that God keeps His word, Dixie would eventually learn that I would not let her fall.

While Dixie has brought lots of joy into our home, there have also been moments when discipline was required. I collect teddy bears, so there are plush toys all over the house. I knew these would be too much temptation for her, so we gave her one of her own. One bear out of the many is hers and hers alone! She is truly a smart puppy. We only had to tell her a few times which bear she could wrestle and chew. From the Garden of Eden forward, God has been telling His children which toys are good for us and which are not. Sometimes I am not as smart as the pup.

Sometimes now that Dixie is older, it is hard for my husband and me to remember to give her food and water every day. She seems so self-sufficient that we truly forget that without us her daily needs would not be met. Sometimes she will just sit at our feet and whine. After we have told her to "Go play!" or asked her "Do you want out?" we will sheepishly look at each other and say, "Does she have food and water?"

We are embarrassed by the empty bowls that await us. But Dixie does not reprimand us or act hateful. She just gratefully sits down and eats and drinks. Thankfully, our Heavenly Father does *not* forget to meet our daily needs.

But the Bible also tells us in Ezekial 34:26 that God will cause special showers of blessings to come to us *in their season*. Oh, that I could learn like Dixie to just accept them gratefully when they come and not whine and cry when God chooses for whatever reason to withhold the special blessings for a season.

Dixie stays in a cage when we go away. It has become a place of refuge for her. It is her private place where she waits for us to return. When she was a small puppy, I taught her to like going into this cage by giving her a doggy biscuit each time she went in willingly. Now our one-year-old Dixie runs immediately to the cage every time she hears us getting the dog biscuits from the box.

God taught me early in my Christian walk that He will meet me in a private place if I will go to it willingly. My devotional life would be so much better if, like Dixie, I would *run* to meet Him there. And if I would learn in my heart of hearts, like she has, that even though sometimes I have to wait, my Master will always return to spend time with me.

Dixie and I go for almost daily walks on our long country road. I have taught her to walk right beside me on a leash, not tugging to get ahead of me or dragging along behind as she did when she was a new puppy. I tell her what a good dog she is and that she should "Walk nice!" and she looks up at me, wagging her nub of a tail and smiling that doggy smile of hers. This always makes me think of how much better off I would be in my walk of faith if I did not try to get ahead of my Master or lag behind Him. Why don't I learn to "walk nice?"

On our walks we go past a farm where two big labrador mix dogs greet Dixie with snarls and barks. I have noticed that if she is right beside me, she just smugly looks them in the eye as if to say, "My master would not let you hurt me." But if she has gotten ahead of me or behind me, she whines in terror and comes running to me for protection.

When I encounter the equivalent of a big dog in my life, it is certainly easier to believe that God will protect me if I am walking close at His side.

Dixie also teaches me on these walks to "seize the day." Every little diversion is an adventure to her. When a grasshopper jumps, she tries to follow it. When a butterfly crosses our path, she tries to catch it in her mouth. A caterpillar is cause for a delay while she investigates. Her little tail wags wildly, and she trembles with excitement. "Carpe diem!" she seems to shout. This makes me think of how I deal with interruptions in my life. Why can't I learn that every little diversion could be an adventure, perhaps even a God-given opportunity?

Sometimes when we go away in the car, instead of shaking the box of dog biscuits that triggers a run to her cage, we will ask Dixie, "Do you want to go along?" She turns into a whirlwind, racing to the door and back to our feet continually until we are ready. She jumps into the car and eagerly watches the road, never asking where we are going, just happy to be along for the ride. I am certain that I would be a much happier Christian if I could learn to stop asking God where we are going and just be happy to be along for the ride.

One evening my husband had put Dixie outside, as always, leaving her out for about 10 minutes. When he went to call her in, she was outside the chain link fence looking into the cornfield. Someone had left the gate open. My heart was immediately in my throat, and I wondered what I would have done if she had seen a squirrel or rabbit and been lost in the corn. Immediately, I knew—we would have searched and searched until we found her. Not unlike God, Who allowed me to have free will even after I was saved. When I wander away, He searches until He finds me. The three parables of the lost (the sheep, the coin, and the son) in Luke 15 teach us that our Heavenly Master could never let us wander away from Him any more than I could let Dixie be lost in the corn.

Perhaps the way that Dixie's faith in me reminds me most of my faith in God is what she does every evening when she gets tired. She has a pillow that is all hers on the floor, but somehow that is not good enough. She sits at my feet and places one paw on my knee as if to say, "Can I come up?" When I pat my lap, she is on it in a heartbeat.

But even that is not good enough. Putting her paws on my chest, she lays down looking me straight in the eye. Then she snuggles her head under my chin. And I hold her. No matter how ornery she has been that day, I always say, "You are the best little dog in the whole world, Dixie Lee."

It is then that I am reminded of my goal. Some day from this earth I will look up to heaven and see Jesus eye to eye. I'll say, "Can I come up?" and He will pat His lap. I want to climb up into His lap and snuggle under His chin and hear Him say, "Well done, thou good and faithful servant."

Not A Matter Of Faith

By JoAnna Lynn Oblander
Great Falls, Montana

"You must have an incredible amount of faith," they say. Their words communicate to me their misunderstanding of the word faith. I did not search six and a half years for my son because I had great faith. The search for my son was the search of a desperate mother—a mother who had never seen, held, or even touched this son she loved so dearly. A mother to whom God had communicated so strongly her ownership that every fiber of my being knew without question that I could not give up until he was found.

Faith had nothing to do with the anguished days and nights that I spent searching Internet adoption sites. Faith had nothing to do with praying for a golden contact that would enable me to find Andrew and bring him home. It had nothing to do with my pleas to God to please watch over my son and make sure that somebody loved him.

If I had great faith, I would have been content to let God run the show. However, the honest truth was that instead of allowing Him to speak peace to my soul, my soul was always screaming out orders, always screaming in anguish, always screaming how unfair it was that God knew where Andrew was and I didn't.

I can imagine now, in retrospect, one of many scenes of frustration that must have played out between God and His angels:

Angel: "I understand you have a very difficult assignment for me?"

God: "Yes. We have a screamer on our hands who will not listen. However, the message that I have for her is important, and we cannot give up."

Angel: "What would you like for me to do?"

God: "We will not be able to communicate to her as long as she keeps screaming. Let her scream until exhaustion overwhelms her. Then she will fall asleep. When she falls asleep, give her this dream that I have prepared for her. After she receives the dream, she will know that I have provided someone to love and care for her son, Andrew. It is essential that we get her to stop screaming and start listening. I have much to communicate to her."

God: "Were you able to give her the dream last night?"

Angel: "Yes, she screamed most of the night, but as You predicted, she eventually fell asleep. I wasted no time in giving her the dream. She woke up as soon as the dream was over, and it was evident that the dream had a profound effect on her."

God: "That is wonderful. Now hopefully she will be a better listener."

The dream did bring peace to my soul. For months I had desperately prayed that God would make sure that Andrew was loved and taken care of. Then God stepped in, laughed at my feeble ideas of how to create a loving atmosphere for my son, and showed me His superior ways.

In the dream several things were communicated to me. The most important revelation was that a little girl was with Andrew. I was told that she was four years old, that her name was Diana, that she took good care of Andrew, and that she loved him very much.

I had directed God to find an adult, female caretaker who had room to make a special place in her heart for my Andrew. Instead God had provided a four-year-old angel who could give him attention all day every day. I was humbled. Both of my daughters were past the age of four. Neither would have matched the standards set by the National Day Care Association, but both of them would have been wildly successful at making a baby feel wanted and loved.

My search now took on an addition. I was now looking for Andrew and the little girl, Diana, who loved him. Adoption agencies continued to tell me that I was trying to find a needle in a haystack. All were willing to let me pursue the adoption of some child that they already had information on. All but a few did a good job of waiting to laugh until I hung up the phone. A man from a Christian agency let me know that he would not be able to help me in my search until I found Andrew. I let him have it with both barrels (figuratively). I reminded the man that I had not dreamed up this adoption. I already had four wonderful, healthy children. I had no need to fantasize about one more mouth to feed, one more body to clothe, one more child to nurture, care for, and worry about. God had initiated this search and He better know that if anyone were capable of helping me find this child or guide my search, it would be God. He sighed and told me that he could not help me. I kept on searching and making phone calls.

When I found Octavian, I knew he was my big break. I was certain that he was my golden contact. He had helped several other couples adopt. He was Romanian and had had several spiritual promptings while helping other couples. His promptings had led him to individuals and documents that had been necessary in finalizing those adoptions. I knew that God had helped Octavian before, and I felt confident that God would help Octavian again.

Once again I was certain I had the answers. Once again I tested God's patience. Octavian was indeed a golden contact, but he was not the contact that would ultimately find Andrew and Diana for me. He searched for several months and then let me know that I shouldn't call him in Romania anymore. He directed me to call his friends in the United States if I needed to get any information to him. Later I was informed that Octavian had given up and decided that finding Andrew and Diana was a lost cause. I am grateful I never knew this until after I found them.

Whether Andrew and Diana actually existed was never a matter of faith for me. I knew they were real. I knew they were just as real as the green grass in my yard, sunsets at the end of the day, or hunger when I didn't eat. What did become a matter of faith to me was the question of whether I would ever find them. When I was given motherly feelings for Andrew, I never realized the implications involved. No loving, nurturing mother can give up on her child. It was no different for me with Andrew.

Four years after God revealed Diana to me and six years after He told me to find Andrew, I was back screaming at God. I let Him know how unfair He was to me. How could He do this to me? Why wouldn't He let me have my son? What had I done to deserve this? After all, I was not only willing to take Diana—I wanted to have Diana.

Then in one of my rare moments of unquestioning contemplation it occurred to me that maybe, due to all my impatience, God had chosen to give Andrew and Diana to someone else. My heart broke. I had wanted Andrew and the little girl for so long. I never knew if Diana was a sister, an orphanage friend, or just what.

If I had to, I could manage without the little girl—God had not given me the feelings of a mother for her. However, Andrew was another story. I didn't know how I could go on without him. I loved that little boy as though he were my own flesh and blood. If I had to lose him, I knew that I would grieve for his loss the rest of my life.

Finally I became submissive. While previously I prayed in every way I could think of for help in finding Andrew, now I prayed that no matter what God had decided that He would just let me know and that He would help me deal with His decision, whatever it was.

Only days later, I found Mickey Elmer. Mickey was a part of the same adoption agency as Octavian's friends here in the United States. I did not know if Mickey could help, but I knew right away that she wouldn't give up on me. She laid out a course of action for us to follow. I was only too glad to follow her lead.

She felt comfortable that Octavian had exhausted the leads in Romania. She suggested we search in Moldova. I agreed with her suggestion.

When that turned up no results, she suggested we search Hungary. We did but with no results. She then asked me if I would mind if she opened the search to all of the countries her agency serviced. I was convinced that Romania was the place, but I gave her the go ahead. I was losing hope.

Within days a contact with their Russian division called me for some information. She directed me to some secure Internet sites. I did not find the children there, but I continued to search other Internet adoption sites on my own. I began to worry that maybe somehow I had passed by them—that somehow I had missed the children. The Russian representative soon called me again. She asked me if I had found anything that looked promising on the Internet site she had directed me to, and I told her that I hadn't. She then mentioned that a little boy and his sister had just showed up on their available listing. The little boy's name was Andre, and would I be interested in looking at them?

God's spirit washed over me like an ocean breeze. I instantly knew that my prayers were finally being answered. I knew that God had not given Andrew to someone else. I knew that I got to be the lucky one to take him home.

The day they emailed pictures of Andre and his sister to us, our family raced home to watch the picture download together. All six of us cried as we watched the picture of Andre and Dina download line after line. The picture had no more than downloaded to their eyes when I knew that it was them. We all knew. I called Mickey to let her know that our search was finally over.

A few months later as we met Andrew and Dina (translated Diana in English) for the first time in the Russian orphanage, our translator leaned over to me and asked me, "Did you know that the children are very close? Dina has taken care of Andre since he was a baby. In fact, he does not call her Dina—he calls her Mama Dina." I nodded my head that I was aware, but I did not explain that I had known this for several years.

My search for Andrew and then for Andrew and Diana had nothing to do with faith. Faith has to do with not knowing something for sure but believing it anyway. I knew with surety of their existence.

My life today has everything to do with faith. Every day requires me to use that faith. Some days I am better at it than others, but my Heavenly Father consistently provides me with opportunities to practice it. And every time Andrew calls me Mom or gives me one of his big hugs or looks at me with one of his impish smiles, I am reminded how important it is to put my faith in God and let Him lead the way.

Part In The Lord

By Brenda Lachman
Houston, Texas

I met Grandpa on a rainy day. I noticed he hardly said a word before or during the creamed corn, fried chicken, and mustard potato salad that Big Mama and her daughter, Frances, my mother-in-law to be, prepared so well. As the apple pie was being served, his voice sounded melodious, with a trembling softness, almost like a whisper, when he sang one of the old cowboy songs remembered from his youth—just a few phrases—and then stopped to delight in the ice cream melting with caramelized sugar and cinnamon.

It wasn't until we cleaned the table that I came to realize how much his hands said—hands that spoke about good old Texas soil. A lifetime of hard country livin', working long hot hours facing the sun, hoeing crops. Just doing his part in the cotton fields. I noticed the muscles so perfectly marked; they spoke of strength and not turning back on anything as they also whispered of gently milking the dairy cow each morning or embracing Big Mama.

I remembered then all the vivid narratives I had heard from Bill when we were dating—the adventurous summers he and his brother spent at the farm. Charlie, older than Bill by several years and experiences, was a constant companion for him and a friend during those hot summers spent on the farm in the early 70's. Bill spoke often about his recollection of the warmth and love his grandparents shared—those daily rituals that were as reliable as daybreak itself.

Big Mama would start their breakfast while Grandpa milked the cows. Then they would drink fresh brewed coffee while Grandpa read to Big Mama from the Good Book. Thoughts were exchanged and prayers whispered as they discussed the Scripture and its wisdom. After breakfast, as Big Mama turned out the dogs and saw to the chickens and other assorted animals, Grandpa would begin working the garden soil, removing weeds, and cultivating the plants that would feed them and that they enjoyed so much. He would spend most of the day's light in that garden, repairing fences, or tending to any of the other hundred jobs a farm requires.

Grandpa had a horse named Misty. Big Mama had purchased him with the money she saved by breeding dog hounds. Grandpa loved horses. Near the turn of the century, Grandpa was only a boy named Leo riding his favorite horse to and from school each morning. That was one of the many things he longed for with old age. He had spent many years riding horses as transportation in his youth; most of his early life he lived in the country at a time when horses were a necessity in farming areas. Later in life he would still rather ride than drive the old red truck—except for Sundays when he would take Big Mama to the big brick Baptist Church. Then he would drive the narrow road to town.

One day Big Mama decided she did not want to arrive to church in a truck, so Grandpa sold the old faithful truck and bought a Road Runner.

Many years later when he could drive no more, it was sold, and they watched services on the TV. Though they may have been busy at the farm and unable to attend, they never forgot God or His word nor took for granted the many blessings they shared in their life together.

Grandpa's eyes held the same confidence his hands did. They were the blue of cool, crisp mountain air, and their peaceful glow spoke to me about faith. Rather than waiting for the turn-of-a-friendly-card kind of faith, he had the faith to follow the path appointed to him. That kind of faith only comes from knowing where you come from and where you are going. The kind of faith that comes from the trust a son has in his Father.

His Father called Grandpa home eight days after Bill and I got married. Big Mama invited me to sit next to her, close to the window on a sunny afternoon two days after the funeral. She told me how years ago he had laid the floor and built most of the rooms in the house with his hands—every day a section more, a nail here, a dowel there, until he finished the two bedroom house where they moved after Frances, Bobby, and Sharon, their three southern daughters, married and moved away.

As she talked, I looked at the impeccable floor—not a gap or a gouge, not a single splinter—revealing the patience of his work… the faith in the gifts granted. Big Mama looked too. Her eyes glowed with the memories.

I looked at my hands and saw motherhood.

Then I searched my own past, and there, in the farthest corner of my heart, I saw my father's hands, not in soil but in water as he taught me how to swim—big strong hands that, even though not those of a fisherman, would masterfully open dozens of oysters every morning and make them for us to eat for breakfast. Irving, my brother, enjoyed the salty taste mixed with squeezed lemon. I enjoyed the expectation of it all. I enjoyed just being with them both.

I smiled to think of the amazing miracles that exist in the baker's hands, the virtuoso's, the mid-wife's, and the power of hands in prayer. I ached in sorrow for the hands that beg, humble and defeated, challenging our faith. Hands all doing their part. Hands that help the unborn, hands that cover your grave, hands that make you suffer, and hands that bring you joy.

And then there are the hands of our Lord Who taught us obedience and forgiveness on the cross.

I looked at Big Mama doing her part—being there for all of us. Her hands rested in her lap—always ready to serve, to heal, to comfort, and to love.

Praying Rain

By Karen Sue Campbell
Brooklyn, Michigan

It is without a doubt the greatest of all gifts…faith...that decision to trust in God, a God so wonderful, so loving, so giving as to know with absolute certainty that ***Thy will*** is ***the way*** and ***my will*** is ***no way*** to have peace.

Another new year begins and everything is fresh, especially our ideas about all that we must accomplish over the course of this next year. We are given another new opportunity to finally do it…to finally have it…to finally accomplish the one feat that we have not yet accomplished. And we begin our hurry one more time, because the world is in a hurry and our minds are in a flurry, a flurry of "must" and "need," a flurry of "should" and "want." But it is never enough; we are never enough, or so we believe—

Yet all the while we are sitting in the lap of promised abundance:

Ask the Lord for rain in the springtime; it is the Lord who makes the storm clouds. He gives showers of rain to men, and plants of the field to everyone. Zechariah 10:1

He has promised us rain—not only rain, but plants and grass for everyone…fields of grass. I shall stand in the grass and wiggle my toes and shine my face into the droplets of rain that mix with my tears of gratitude, for I am blessed. He has promised these blessings, but now I wonder, when will they arrive? I am worried. I see strife all around me, and I feel tremendous pain. My hope is drained, and my heart aches from all that I see.

Our world sits precariously this New Year on the edge of chaos. Fear runs rampant. We fear war. We fear the Middle East. Worse yet, we fear each other. Fear is running our lives. Just ask the driver that curses you as he passes your car on a double yellow because you are driving the speed limit and he needs to get to the stoplight one car length ahead of you. Or ask the lady tapping her foot and frowning your way because you questioned the price your milk rang up at the grocery checkout and she has one more important thing to do. Just ask any of them, and they will eek out for you fear through their impatience and unkind utterances of obscene language.

Where there is fear, there can be no faith, and without faith, there can be no peace.

The dictionary defines faith as: unquestioning belief that does not require proof or evidence.

Are we to spend one more year running in the direction of our past and our own fear, or are we to spend this New Year and our newest opportunity sitting with His promise of abundance, praying for rain?

The Native American Indian tradition understands what it means to pray for rain. To pray for rain is to sit on the dry, parched earth and to smell it even before it arrives. Praying rain in the Native American Indian tradition means seeing rain, feeling rain, and knowing rain exists now in this dry, parched moment of time. Praying rain is about knowing that God is here for us at all times and understanding that His promise of rain is here even before we ask for it.

In a world that is driven by fear, can we muster this kind of faith? Is it within our own tradition to smell rain? To see peace? To feel love? To know abundance? Do we remember His promise? Will we ask? Do we have faith big enough to hold our unquestioning belief in rain?

"Also, seek the peace and prosperity of the city to which I have carried you into exile. Pray to the Lord for it, because if it prospers, you too will prosper." Jeremiah 29:7

Our modern world is always in a hurry. Higher tech means faster speed. But should we go faster? Perhaps it is time for us to stop running. Perhaps it is time for us to do less and pray more. Perhaps it is time to make light. Yes, light. It is time to shine on the world and each other our kindness, our patience, and our peace.

It may be that our world is beginning to recognize this. I had an experience recently that hints at this possibility. I wanted to give a gift to a little boy, but he told me that he didn't like toys. In fact, he said he didn't collect anything, and he reported that he really didn't want anything because there was very little that he enjoyed.

I tried to give a child a gift for the holidays, yet this small child had no interest in receiving it. It stumped me at first, but after I thought about it, I understood. This kid was a member of the new generation, not yet even one decade old and already bored with the world of man's creation. This is the child of our New Year.

We need to remember we do have something to give—all of us—something we old folks (over 10) are forgetting to share with one another each and every day.

Faith.

I can tell this small child about our Lord's promise. I can teach him about love and patience. I can remind him to know peace, to see peace, and to feel peace. When I drive my car everyday, I will bless those that curse me. When I shop, I will ask the impatient shoppers behind me to go ahead of me. When I see fear, I will hold faith. I will remember to know in my heart with absolute certainty that ***Thy will*** is ***the way*** and ***my will*** is ***no way*** to have peace.

"He will turn the hearts of the fathers to their children, and the hearts of the children to their fathers; or else I will come and strike the land with a curse." Malachi 4:6

May we spend this New Year smelling rain.

Restoration Of Faith

By Shaila M. Abdullah
Austin, Texas

I looked about groggily like a woman in a drunken state of suspended sensibility. Through half opened eyes I saw the nurse scribble away at something on a desk directly in my line of vision. After only a moment of disorientation, I realized where I was. I passed a hand lightly over my stomach in desolation and mild panic. The little bulge was still there, but the contents had been emptied. I felt a wave of nausea pass over me, and then a sharp pain shot up my belly and traveled quickly up my spine. I writhed in pain and called out to the nurse. She rushed in and with skilled precision injected some fluid into the IV; the pain ebbed away in seconds.

And then I saw him. He had the same half panicked look he had worn when they wheeled me off to the operating room, only this time it was followed by a grateful smile at seeing me awake, his wife of seven years. Gently he helped me with my clothes. Downstairs his family waited for me in the car. They all stole glances at me periodically without staring. I had gone in a pregnant woman and come out exactly what I was three months ago—an infertile woman!

At home we dodged around the inevitable. He brought me nabiyeki udon, my favorite Japanese dish, on a tray to eat in bed. We never ate inside the bedroom. That had been the cardinal rule when we moved into our very first home three months ago. Today was an exception. I slurped hungrily but felt groggy after only three mouthfuls. He laid me gently down on the bed, and his warmth touched me deeply. His eyes were large with unspoken sorrow. Perhaps he felt partly to blame. The girl he had loved so dearly had been broken by events of their union. His lips moved in kind utterances—utterly meaningless conversations that went nowhere. He talked about our beautiful house, the fish aquarium we hoped to have one day, his upcoming promotion at work, and I concentrated not on his words, but on how his jaw moved, the rhythm of his soothing voice. Childlike, I let sleep take over.

I dreamed of unicorns and green expansive land; I dreamed of sheep and dog that stole into our backyard, only it wasn't our backyard. It was a strange field that ended in an arched gate, and however hard I tried to lock the gate, the animals would trot right back in. Then he came in, bringing me a crate of garden mums of all colors—fiery amber, ivy white, passionate purple—with a big smile on his face, and that's when I see my childhood friend, and I rush up to her with two tubs of the mums that I want to give her. But I can't, because that's when I wake up.

The house is strangely quiet. It's the kind of silence that whirls around you over and over like a white, thick, suffocating fog until you give in to the whiteness. It's the quietness that gives the ticking of the clock a surreal quality. It forces the questions I have silenced inside me to suddenly find a voice. *Why me? Why me? Why now?*

I ponder over those questions. Why was my baby snatched away from me when I had never even questioned God for all those unproductive years of my life? I craved a child, but I always felt that when the good Lord felt I was up to the task, He would surely bless me with an offspring. So when we found out that we were going to be parents finally, it was a long awaited happiness. Only our joy was short lived. The baby that we saw on the ultrasounds was part of my body for only a short while—the little peanut with the flickering heart on the monitor screen that in our mind's eyes was already a child playing in our yard. My very faith was shaken the moment the doctor walked into the room and pronounced that the little life inside me had passed away.

I am angry—I am fierce at Him! How could He do this to me? Later when he brings me some dinner, he finds me in tears—a pitiful spectacle in my jammies with my runny red nose. He tweaks my tear-streaked nose playfully, a nervous habit of his that he indulges in when words fail him. I collapse in his arms, and together we wallow in the grief that we don't talk about but that overnight became a vital part of our lives, just like breathing—or even eating.

On Sunday I refuse to go to church and instead curl up on the bed with a book that a friend brought me. I have moved no more than 10 feet from my bed in six days, and during that time, I kept myself deliberately drugged with painkillers, but the pain I wanted to evade was not a physical one.

Around noon I am restless. I think of him in the church sitting in the pew wondering about the wife he had before—the bright-eyed, witty woman he loved who made him feel secure. I feel his sadness. Like a stormy ocean, it passes over me in dark waves and envelopes me in its gloomy cloak. I turn the radio on to drown the feeling. It is set to his favorite radio program—the one he listens to on Sundays.

"Asaph was a God fearing man who fell into the trap of thinking that

God was treating him unfairly."

I listened absently, my book still open in my lap. The heroine was seeking vengeance on her beloved who had cheated on her. Disgusted, I shut the book. The program continued, and I turned the volume up and leaned against the pillow.

"It seemed to Asaph that God was favoring the unbelievers more, while he was left to face trials and tribulations. Asaph felt that God's blessings were never directed toward him."

I nodded almost mechanically. That's exactly how I felt. I was hooked. This was a good station.

"However, Asaph finally realizes that he had been wrong in his analysis and that his thinking had been shortsighted, even shallow. He discovered that our life on earth is only a short passage to eternity and that any bounty we receive from God, including our offspring, are handed to us, completely undeserved, in His divine mercy. And if God—for reasons best known to Him—decides to recall that largess, who are we to question Him?"

I realize I am crying.

"And so Asaph declared: *Yet, I am always with you; you hold me by my right hand. You guide me with your counsel, and afterward you will take me into glory.* " (Psalm 73:23-24)

The program ended, but I couldn't move, not even to turn the radio off. During the commercial I tried to collect my jumbled thoughts. So many of my questions were answered through just a few words. Was this God's way of showing me the love He has for His children? With the realization that it was, I got out of the bed with renewed energy and drew open the drapes. Sunshine tumbled in, covering the room in a promising glow. I thanked God for the restoration of my faith, for the rebirth of my soul, and for the ability to thank Him for a precious gift, though of short duration. And above all, for the strength it had instilled in me to face adversity.

The Weaver

By Julie Anne Daubé
Colorado Springs, Colorado

My heart was pounding as I shook my husband awake. "Alex, get up. Dad wants to talk to you."

Puzzled and disoriented, he rubbed his eyes. "Can't it wait?"

I had told my father that Alex went to bed just four hours earlier, having worked storm duty for the electric company until 5:30 a.m., but Dad still insisted on talking to him. My throat was dry and hoarse. "No," I said. "He said it's really important. He called last night, too." Now I was beginning to understand my father's cryptic phone call at 9:00 p.m. Something was terribly wrong.

Shaking, I followed Alex into the kitchen. I listened to his end of the conversation, hoping against hope that my fears were unfounded. Since our wedding the previous month, Alex and I had been praying for my mother's deteriorating health. Her symptoms indicated nothing more serious than osteoporosis, though a recent dizzy spell had intensified our concern. Alex's voice, calm and steady, reassured me. *She's just in the hospital*, I told myself. *She'll be all right.*

Alex hung up, and I looked at him expectantly. His face was grim.

"What happened?"

He appeared to be choosing his words carefully. His expression softened. "You know how we're always saying it's going to be wonderful when we finally get to heaven?"

I nodded, unable to speak.

Tears filled his eyes. "Well, it looks like your mom beat us to it. She's very happy now with Jesus."

I was desolate. How could she be dead? Just six months ago my parents had retired to a beautiful piece of lakefront property in the Pocono Mountains where they had built my mother's dream home. They had never been happier. Now my father would be alone. I let out a choked sob. "Why? Why *now*?"

Alex held me as I wept, wondering how a loving God could have taken my father's beloved wife from him. Within a few hours, we were driving to be with my dad in Pennsylvania. During the three-hour trip, I sang my favorite hymns—"Amazing Grace," "Be Not Afraid," and "On Eagle's Wings." Despite my anger at God's timing, my faith in Him sustained me. I could feel the Lord's arms around me, blanketing me with peace. Still, the question persisted: Why hadn't He answered our prayers for healing?

When we arrived, I could hardly bear to listen as Dad explained what had happened. He came home the night before to find my mother's lifeless body beside their bed. She had died of a heart attack.

My mom had been the center of my father's world. How would he cope? As a Christian, I was supposed to believe that all things work for good for those who love the Lord. But how could any good possibly come from this?

During my search for a sympathy card, I found one with a poem called "The Weaver," describing our lives as a tapestry of colors chosen by God to accomplish His purposes:

> "Oft times He weaveth sorrow, and I in foolish pride
> Forget He sees the upper, and I the underside.
> Not till the loom is silent, and the shuttles cease to fly
> Shall God unroll the canvas and explain the reason why."

The poem went on to say that the dark threads are as needful as those of gold and silver in the pattern the Lord has planned for us. I understood then that God was under no obligation to explain why He chose to take my mom home when He did. I only knew that He could be trusted to do what was best.

As the years passed, I began to see glimpses of the finished tapestry in my dad's life. One of the threads was a woman named Dolores whose abusive husband had committed suicide. She and my father dated for several months before he realized she was struggling with alcoholism. Again and again, she promised to stop drinking. When it became clear that she couldn't quit, Dad ended their relationship. But the friendship Alex and I had developed with Dolores opened the door for us to share the gospel with her. One evening as we sat in her living room, Alex asked her if she wanted to receive Christ's gift of eternal life. "You have nothing to lose," he said when she hesitated.

In a dull voice she replied, "You're right. I've already lost everything."

The three of us joined hands as she half-heartedly invited Jesus to be her Savior. Before we left, she hugged us. "I love you guys!" she exclaimed. A seed of faith was planted.

In the next few months, we saw Dolores' faith blossom as she gave her alcoholism to Jesus. When she survived a major car accident without a scratch, she told us, "I wasn't alone. Someone was in the car with me." We knew she meant the Lord.

In time, Dolores and my father resumed their relationship and began to talk of marriage. Then one morning a message on our answering machine shocked me awake. "Dolores had a stroke," my dad said.

I felt numb as the truth sank in. All my father's plans, hopes, and dreams...gone, for the second time in two years. But he refused to give up. Since Dolores had no family, Dad took her into his home and took care of her after her release from the hospital. Once again Alex and I prayed for a healing that never came. Through physical therapy Dolores learned to walk again, but she never regained her speech or ability to function independently. That Christmas my father gave her an engagement ring. "We'll get married as soon as you're better," he promised. But before Easter she died of an accidental prescription drug overdose.

"I don't know what God wants from me anymore," my father confided in me after the memorial service. Despite his grief, he continued to attend church faithfully, even volunteering to teach Sunday school. Once again I reminded myself that someday we would see the finished tapestry.

Today my dad is married to a wonderful woman named Betty who has helped him connect with God like never before. Their faith in Christ is the cord that binds them together. "Thank God we have Jesus," Dad told me recently.

My own faith has been strengthened as I came to understand some of the reasons for these dark threads in my father's life. Dolores, who had never known love until she met my father, now lives with Christ in everlasting glory. If God had healed my mother, instead of taking her home, Dolores never would have come into our lives. Who knows where she would be spending eternity.

Seeing God work in my father's life helps me to face the hard times in my own. Although I won't always know why God weaves dark threads into my tapestry, I will trust Him until the darkness is no more.

"Thy Will, Not Mine"

By D. Henley
Charlestown, Rhode Island

I had been sitting at my living room window at precisely 11:28 nearly every night for the last several months waiting for Judy's Bronco to drive by as she headed home from second shift. It wasn't much, but it was the only contact I could have since she left me. I knew it would have been unfair of me to ask her to come back, but losing her left a painful void inside of me that I thought might never be filled.

Hearing her voice on the phone that day in May stopped my heart, and then what she said chilled it.

"David, I need help," she said, her voice quivering as if from some terrible exertion. "I think I'm dying, and I think I might be glad."

"I can't tell what's real anymore," she continued. "I took a bunch of my antidepressants and some anti-anxiety pills and some other stuff—I don't know what. I look at my face in the mirror, and it seems like the skin is just running right off. I tried to steady myself on the doorframe, and I swear my hand went right through it. I was in the bathroom playing with the razor blades. I want to hurt myself."

My heart started beating again, only now in triple time. I needed to go to her, but I looked down at the electronic home confinement device the court had ordered strapped to my ankle and suddenly knew what powerlessness was.

I hadn't spoken to Judy in nearly half a year, since the day two weeks before Christmas when I came home to find her sitting in the darkened living room in the little cottage where we lived. She was supposed to be at work. Judy and I had been together for nearly three years at that point, and for most of that time I had been trying unsuccessfully to quit drinking. I had been to treatment centers, to a halfway house, even to prison for a short time, and still I was struggling.

For months I had been drifting into occasional AA meetings only to find myself in some sleazy bar or another afterward. Pulling into my own driveway after getting off of work required a battle within myself that I was frequently incapable of fighting. And I spent a great deal of energy trying to figure out how to get this woman who had been standing by me through so many trials *out* of my life so I could drink again the way I wanted to.

When I woke up that cold December morning, I knew in my heart I was going to be drunk by the end of the day. When I found her sitting there that evening with no lights on in the house despite the sun having set, I had just returned from a trip into Providence, the capital city of my home state of Rhode Island, where I had spent the day running errands and resisting the urge to stop off at the downtown honkytonks. I figured I'd better get closer to home before I got started to lessen the chance of yet another drunk driving arrest. Even that was taking all of my concentration and willpower; the last thing I wanted to deal with was her being home from work.

"I need to ask," she said as the gloom gathered in the room. "Are we ever getting engaged, or am I wasting my time?"

I was stunned. I laughed right out loud, right in her face. Engaged? What, and get married? Plan a future together? How was I supposed to make those kinds of decisions when it was all I could do to come up with a reasonable plan for getting me a drink or two or four?

She left then, as I laughed and babbled, and I had only seen her once more, when she pulled into the driveway late at night on Christmas Eve. I had opened the presents she had left for me—a zoom lens, flash, and tripod for my camera, a hobby I had tried to pit, pitifully, against my drinking. The cottage door was open, the weather having turned warm and wet. Needless to say, I had just returned from a night's carousing, trying to forget the tragic joke my life had become. As I saw her get out of her truck, I stood and lurched for the door, tripping over the brand new tripod and crashing head first into the clutter on the floor. As I struggled to get to my feet again, I looked to the door, and she was gone.

Now after all these months there was her voice at the other end of the line, and she was in trouble. She needed me. I knew immediately what was happening. Although I had not talked with her in months, I had kept tabs on her through mutual friends and acquaintances where we worked. I knew she had taken an apartment just about a mile down the street from my place and she was spending a lot of time at a country western bar nearby. I knew she was drinking—a lot—and that she was popping pills and abusing prescriptions and bringing men home after closing time. As it turned out, she had some pretty serious issues of her own that had been hidden in the tumult my alcoholism had created.

And I knew why she thought I could help her. She had been keeping track of me, too. She knew about the death of my sister's daughter over the holidays. In fact, that was why she had stopped by on Christmas Eve—with the thought that I might need a friend. And she knew that I had, in fact, gotten that "yet another" drunk driving arrest that led to my home confinement. But most importantly, she knew that now, months later, I was still not drinking and was attending AA meetings regularly.

What she couldn't know was the true extent of the changes I had gone through since she left—in part because she had left, in fact. By the end of that holiday season—actually on December 31, after getting released from court to await a hearing on my latest fiasco—I had finally given up. I had been beaten too badly, too often. This time I was ready to surrender. I crawled back into the AA meetings as soon as my damaged body would allow, starting the new year off with a whimper.

For the first time ever, I began to let somebody else take over the decisions in my life. I handed myself over to the AA members to do with as they would. In the language of the Twelve Steps, I admitted I was powerless over alcohol and came to at least hope that a power greater than me could restore me to sanity. I had some difficulty with the third step. Although I was willing to turn my life and my will over to AA, I did not have a God of my own understanding. As a lapsed Catholic, I had ignored the whole "God thing" for years. Now as I sat in the meetings in the very church basement that had served in my childhood as the parish elementary school where I had received my first spiritual instruction, I found it necessary to face my ideas of God all over again.

"David, I need you to come. I think I might kill myself if you don't."

Step Three: Make a decision to turn your will and your life over to the care of God as I understand Him.

"If you do not abide by these rules, or if you break the terms of your home confinement, you will be found and taken immediately to the state prison to serve out your entire term," the judge's voice echoed in my mind.

"Judy, listen to me," I said, terrified. "Don't do anything, okay? Just fix yourself a cup of tea or another drink or whatever you need and wait. I know what to do."

In my meetings list book I had collected a number of phone numbers for AA contacts. One of the first was for Betty M., a nurse who worked at the same facility where Judy and I worked. Betty and her husband were both very active program members with many years behind them. I called her, left a message on her machine, and started to pray. I got down on my knees for the first time since I was a child. I squeezed my hands together until the knuckles turned purple. I sobbed into the blankets on my bed. I raised my head and my voice to the God I was not even sure I believed in.

"God, please help her!" I said, and only days later someone pointed out to me that that was probably the first time I had ever prayed in the name of someone else rather than my own selfish needs. After what seemed hours the pain and fear began to lift, ever so slightly, and I was able to crawl up from the floor and into my bed. Some time later, I slept.

It has been 12 years since the day that Judy called me, unsure if she was going to let herself live through the day. Betty got to her, convinced her to go to the emergency room, stayed with her through the night, and then brought her to the same treatment center I had been to myself years earlier. I visited her there a few weeks later.

It has been 12 years now, and neither of us has picked up a drink, a drug, or a razor blade. I ask God each morning now for guidance through my day, and when the day is done, I thank Him for His gifts. Those gifts are abundant in my life, as I know they are in Judy's. We are both married now, though not to each other, and both very much in love with our spouses, both of whom are also members of AA.

We both returned to college to finish up degrees left floating in the alcoholic haze, and each of us is working and successful in the jobs we only fantasized about when we were drinking. While I lost several siblings to alcoholism, I also saw several members of the next generation of my family come into AA and find measures of peace and happiness. And Judy reconciled with the children who were taken from her long before we ever even met. We run into each other frequently at meetings and events.

To this day I learned that the best way for me to know peace in my world, whether troubled by tragedy or stressed out by everyday occurrences, is to close my eyes, take a few breaths, look for that still, small voice inside, and accept that it is all going according to plan.

"Thy will, Lord, not mine, be done."

Finding The Right Church

By Julia Horst Schuster
Destin, Florida

When we first moved to Florida a few months ago, the first thing on our agenda was to find a church home. We had never needed to "shop around" for a church before. We'd attended the same one in North Carolina for years and were perfectly happy there, so this was a new experience for us. We had already decided we wouldn't feel comfortable at "the beach church"—you know, the church closest to the beach where all the "tourists" flock in their flip-flops and tastelessly disguised "beach attire." That would not be the proper atmosphere in which to bring up our darling little daughter. So no need to even visit there, even though it was located less than a half a mile from our home.

Instead, we drove eight miles down the highway to "the other church." And, oh, what a beautiful church it is. Massive beams support dark wooden rafters, and padded pews and kneelers face a formal altar with a bank of windows opening to all God's nature beyond. *It is a magnificent place. And the perfect place,* I thought. *This is the church for us,* I was certain. So the next day I called the church office and registered our little darling for faith formation classes. We were set. Now we just needed to get involved and meet some people to help make us feel at home, right?

I had never before realized that churches have personalities. I never knew that a building could breathe, could communicate, could speak to me, but this building did. Oh, and the parishioners we met were such lovely people, friendly and welcoming. The priest was a warm and jolly Irishman who had wonderful homilies and always got us out of there on time. *What more could a person ask of a church*, I wondered?

But something wasn't quite right. As much as I liked the building and the people in it, as much as I tried to make this church "work" for me, it lacked something—I just wasn't sure what. It lacked that intangible something that I couldn't grasp at first. I would sit in Mass waiting for that feeling. You know the feeling. That *aha* feeling you get when you know you are at home. As moving as the homilies were, as dynamic and fulfilling as communion was, I didn't feel that spiritual connection that I had grown so accustomed to in the church we'd left behind before our move. What was wrong? I started to doubt my connectedness with God. Was I not participating in the Mass the way I should? Was I not "into it" the way I should be? I vowed to try harder. I would make this church "work."

Then it happened.

We ran late one Sunday morning. We didn't have time to drive the eight miles from our home and get to Mass on time. What were we to do? Did we dare visit "the beach church?" It looked like we had no choice.

We piled into the car and arrived within two minutes at "the beach church," not knowing what to expect, but dreading it just the same. We couldn't see the church from the parking lot and were surprised to find a labyrinth of pathways leading from all directions through a natural wooded area and intersecting at the sanctuary entrance. Statues and meditation alcoves nestled among the trees along the paths, and a large bricked area lay before the great doors leading into the foyer. I was impressed, but of course, I didn't let on. This wasn't our church. We were just visiting out of necessity.

We entered a large foyer and were greeted by a multitude of "welcomers" and the priest himself, a 40-something ex-surfer bum wearing Birkenstocks, rimless glasses, and a buzz cut. *Interesting,* I thought with a sneer. Six-foot tall urns in rustic shades of golds, greens, and copper stood sentry outside and inside the space. We passed through tall doors into the sanctuary where the slate tile floor vanished before us into a huge baptismal pool. People knelt to dip their fingers in the waters and bless themselves, or they paused at a raised font gurgling softly and flowing down into the larger pool. Glass surrounded us on all sides, giving the sensation of a natural amphitheater surrounded by woods. Pews encircled the altar, positioned squarely at the heart of the grand circular room. I glanced up. A faceted crystal and wooden cross hung above the altar, with a kaleidoscope of light and color reflecting through it, spilling the morning sun into the room. I didn't realize I had stopped and was gawking until another astonished visitor bumped into me from behind.

We shuffled to an un-upholstered pew. I genuflected toward the center of the room, unable to decipher exactly where they had hidden the tabernacle. *Strike one,* I thought. The tabernacle should be in full view. I was looking for a box, a gold box with doors like the one we had in North Carolina, and I didn't take the time to notice the candles around what I had thought to be the altar. It was the tabernacle. They had placed Christ exactly where He should be at the heart of the room.

We sat down, and I couldn't stop myself from gazing around the space to see what else there was to see. "Not exactly my taste. Too contemporary, too cold," I whispered to my husband, unwilling to acknowledge that this place was really pretty neat.

The priest processed in, proceeded by all the Eucharistic ministers. A small choir, accompanied by stringed instruments and horns, led the congregation in the opening hymn. That's when I noticed it—no missals, no hymnals. Everyone sang along from the bulletins that the flock of welcomers had handed out when we first arrived. *Strike two,* I thought. *They are too cheap to buy missals. What will everyone do without pages upon pages of text to shuffle though during Mass?*

The priest stood beside his chair during all the readings, with his arms crossed over his chest and his chin raised like an approving (or disapproving, depending on your perspective) schoolmaster overseeing his adolescent flock. Latecomers filed in, dressed in garb ranging from tacky to flat out tasteless and most of which wouldn't be appropriate attire for a rock concert. *How could anyone wear such clothes to church? Strike three,* I thought, at which time I decided just to suck it up, suffer through it, and not worry about it because we were never coming back.

That's when it happened again.

The priest began his homily. He was intelligent, funny, and engaging. In spite of my negative attitude, his words reached out and grabbed me, touching on something significant that had happened to me that very week. This bothered me. I hadn't counted on feeling anything. I hadn't counted on this. *Visitors luck,* I told myself.

I glared at my watch; the priest was running long, very long. I patted my foot. *This won't do. This won't do at all. We'll see what he can do with the celebration of the Eucharist. If I don't get goosebumps, he's toast.*

How arrogant I was. I positioned myself to make it impossible for the priest or for God to get through. I closed my stance, made no eye contact, offered and gave nothing whatsoever of myself. I was determined not to like this church or this priest. I was determined not to acknowledge the tug at my heart.

The priest lifted the host. "Take this and eat it. This is my body, which will be given up for you."

What's this? I wondered. The priest held a loaf of real unleavened bread—not those pasty wafers, but real bread. I glanced around the sanctuary, counting heads. There were 700 people present—easy. I multiplied that by the number of Masses given on a weekend. Some angelic parishioner had been very busy making bread. I had never experienced this before.

The hairs on my arms were the first to react. A lump wiggled its way up my throat. I swallowed hard but couldn't force it down. My eyes stung, and tears rolled. My fingers tingled and goosebumps exploded across my skin like happy poison ivy on steroids. Goosebumps! Blessed goosebumps. They were back in full force. Oh, where had they been?

I quaked through the remainder of the celebration, riveted by every aspect and nuance. When the Mass ended, I staggered to my feet and shuffled out of the sanctuary, still reeling from a spiritual experience these words struggle and fail to express. I pushed through the massive doors leading into the outer courtyard and stopped dead as if my feet had been glued to the concrete.

Before me stood a huge crucifix, the most magnificent depiction of Christ's suffering and His love for us I had ever seen. How had I missed this when we first arrived? Now that I had seen it, how could I leave? I stared up at this work of art, awestruck by its beauty, stabbed by its power and meaning. This was the place. This was the church. This was where my family was supposed to be.

Now, you may be asking yourself…is this woman crazy? She chooses her church by how many goosebumps it generates, how many tears flow, or how beautiful the surroundings? Well, no, not exactly, but I can't say you're all wrong. I believe that when God wants us to be somewhere, when He wants us to do something and we refuse to listen or to cooperate, He uses personality specific ways to help us along. For me, He used goosebumps and most certainly tears. My priest back home used to say that my bladder was located behind my eyeballs and, at the slightest provocation, it had a great tendency to leak.

We all know the feeling of God's finger on our back, the little signals He uses to help us along our path. We don't always acknowledge them, but we usually know when we're doing what's right or when we're doing what's wrong. What I learned, once again, from my refusal to listen to God's wishes, is that He's always there for us, regardless. Even when we put up obstacles and attitudes that the most patient of family members wouldn't tolerate, God doesn't mind. God is different. His living water is fresh and clean and pure no matter where on our path we happen to be.

But in those wondrous moments when we feel Him, when we find that right place or that right thing, His water is so irresistible, so sweet. Our faith comes alive. There is no question that it is God talking. There is no way we can shake it off, disregard it as a coincidence or luck—it is God. He is speaking directly to us. And we listened! We actually listened, but more importantly, we heard!

We now attend "the beach church," and I fathom to say we always will. I'm not sure exactly why He wanted us there. It's convenient—that's nice, and we are getting involved. All I know is that when I am there, I am home. Our little darling manages the long Masses without incident, which is a miracle in itself. And the vacation crowds don't affect me. Standing room only must be pleasing to God, don't you think? I look at them all as innocents who haven't a clue what they've walked into, and I pray that God will zing them the way He did me.

And every time I enter the vestibule, a little saying goes through my head as I walk down the aisle to my seat…

There's no place like home. There's no place like home.

12

One Day At A Time

God's Faithful Timing

By Karen Jo McTague
Anderson, Indiana

I couldn't believe the words I heard on the phone. "My mother had a stroke, and she is dying," said my ex-husband. With a hesitant, cracking voice he said, "Please tell Pamela that I don't know how long her Grandma is going to live."

I was shocked. I never had to tell someone that a loved one was dying. That same night I told my daughter the painful news. She started to softly weep, and she tearfully said, "This means that I will never hear her call me her 'sugar pie' anymore. I want to go see my grandma."

By the time I called to make travel arrangements for a visit, her grandmother had passed away. Now Pamela was even more determined to actually see her to say goodbye. In order to give her closure, I immediately made plane reservations to Virginia from Indiana.

As a young, single mother, I have to admit I was scared to take a 10-year-old child to a place I had not even visited myself. However, I knew God would supply our needs. He knew how important it was for my daughter to attend her grandma's funeral and how important it was for me to "step out" in faith and let Him take control of this distressing event. "Please help me, dear God," I prayed.

Unfortunately, there were no direct flights to our destination. Our itinerary included a layover in Pittsburgh and a change of planes. I said a prayer while we were getting off the plane in Pittsburgh.

"Dear Father, please show me someone who can help me find the gate on the other side of the airport." It was one thing to find the gate myself; it was another to find the gate while keeping an eye on an energetic little redhead by my side. My daughter was skipping beside me down a long corridor as I focused on the succession of gate numbers before me. Suddenly, I heard voices calling, "Pamela, is that you?"

I couldn't believe it! My ex-husband's brother and his wife from Houston, Texas, had noticed us walking down the main corridor. They invited us to sit with them. I had only seen them once in my life, and that was when I was pregnant with Pamela. Career choices had separated my ex-husband's family members so they were dispersed across the country.

"How did you know it was us?" I asked. With a slight look of apprehension, they said that they weren't sure it was me, but they both recognized Pamela because I had faithfully included her picture in the Christmas card I sent them each year. Talk about reaping the benefits of the Biblical Scripture Matthew 5:39 about turning the other cheek! I always knew that even though I was not a part of their family anymore, I wanted to maintain a Christian attitude, and I made sure all family members received correspondence about Pamela. It was not going to make a difference that her father and I were divorced.

"Thank you, God," I whispered. "You answered my prayer!" I felt so relieved to be in somewhat familiar company.

"We don't know why the airline routed us here to Pittsburgh at the last minute. We were supposed to have a layover in Atlanta," they told me. "In fact, we have never been in this airport in our lives!"

I knew. God had answered my prayers. And He added a special blessing to my plea. When we checked our tickets, we realized all of us were on the same flight to Virginia.

When our flight arrived at our final destination, they had a rental car waiting and asked us if we would like a ride to the hotel. What a blessing! I knew taxis would be scarce at such a small airport. In fact, I thought I was probably going to have to make special arrangements and call the taxi company. Then I remembered that I had committed everything about this trip to God and put it in His hands.

At first, I was really uncomfortable at the funeral home during the calling hours. I knew my ex-husband did not want me there. But I was there for Pamela, and by putting my trust in God, I knew it was the right thing to do.

The hardest part was enduring a funeral home visitation without an actual body and trying to explain to Pamela why her grandmother wasn't there. You see, Pamela's grandmother had passed away in Amarillo, so her body had to be shipped to the funeral home. Unfortunately, the flight was delayed due to a horrifying ice storm that hit the Texas panhandle, and to make matters worse, her body had to be transferred to another plane in Dallas, and government regulations kept her body from being transferred immediately. Her body finally arrived at the funeral home for the last 15 minutes of calling hours.

Once I gave Pamela a detailed explanation, however, she seemed content to sit and wait for her to arrive. After all, that's why we were there. During our wait, a longtime friend of her grandma's said, "You know, Honey, your grandma was late for her own wedding, and when I questioned her about her tardiness then, she told me that when she died, she would be late for her own funeral. So I guess she meant what she said!"

For over two hours I sat in the same room with my ex-husband's family trying my best to make conversation. This long wait gave Pamela an opportunity to talk with relatives neither she nor I had ever seen before. They were very interested in her school and her activities, and it gave her insight into her father's roots and an opportunity to know a bit about where he had been born and raised as a child.

I was so glad that God had answered my prayers. I was a young single mother who put the situation in God's hands because I knew how much it meant for my daughter to see her grandma one more time on this earth. God showed me His miraculous power by supplying our needs.

Today I am still amazed at God's timing for miracles, whether it is a matter of days, hours, or minutes.

There are times when unfortunate situations arise and I start to doubt in God's timing, but then I think back to "the trip to see Grandma." That changes my focus and reminds me that my faith in God is the anchor I hold onto to be the best single parent I can be. This faith has sustained me throughout the years when I am uncertain about single parent situations.

For instance, when Pamela was a bit older, the thought of sending her by herself on a plane to visit her father frightened me, especially when it was 2,000 miles away. But my prayers gave way to the peace that only God can give through His Holy Spirit. I realized that if I can't trust God with my child, then whom can I trust? That put it in perspective for me.

Trusting God became a daily routine when it comes to my daughter. She is now 21 years old and a senior at a private Christian college majoring in economics and business management. I know that God has wonderful plans for her life. The most important thing I can do as a parent is to trust in God for miracles and answered prayers and remind her to have faith. He shows His ultimate power by using friends, and even the people we would least expect, to be the answer to miracles. Whether His timing is in a matter of days, hours, or minutes, He is always faithful to His promises.

I Have Endured Because of Faith

By Karen Seelenbinder
Lima, Ohio

I sat alone on a wooden bench that sunny fall day. Shaking with fear, I envisioned my upcoming failure performing my first solo for the college of music. I pleaded with God to take away the terrifying, crippling fear. I prayed and I pleaded. People walked by oblivious to my torment. The time had come. I picked up my music and clarinet and trudged heavily toward the music building.

Ever since I can remember, I have always believed in God, in Jesus Christ, and in the Holy Spirit. They were three entities I had never seen, heard, touch, felt, or smelled. I knew they existed because every minister, Sunday school teacher, and Bible spoke them into existence. Who else was I to call upon in my hour of intense fear? So I prayed to the unknown three and approached the stage of disaster.

I stood before the audience of students and teachers in the large auditorium listening to the introduction from the piano. I felt cold fear creep into every limb of my being. I took a deep breath and attempted to begin my solo. The sound of the notes shook and vibrated like an animal crying in misery. For 12 minutes I endured, moving my fingers mechanically, wondering when it all would end.

My mind cried out asking God where He was. What happened to my prayers and my beliefs in His great and awesome power? *Get me out of here!* my mind pleaded as I played measure after measure. My hands shook; my legs shook; my tongue could barely touch the reed it was such a vibrating mess of muscle.

Finally, I played the last note to a sympathetic round of applause. I flew off the stage, grabbed my case, and ran outside. I sat beneath a low lying tree crying uncontrollably, knowing I had failed. My heart began to harden, and my mind started to play tricks on me. I thought God had failed me.

As I got up and walked away, my faith began to diminish. I wanted to toss away the uselessness of a faith that didn't work. This faith in an almighty, caring, and loving God. But God would have no part of it. He kept bothering me. Nudging me. Continue reading My word He seemed to say. The faith I had in God continued within me, but because of my disappointment, it became a stagnant faith. No growth. No climbing. Just a plateau. *God exists, but He doesn't intervene,* I thought.

Four years passed, and it was time for my final group of solos. My senior recital. I felt the fear bubbling, and I wondered how I could possibly play five songs. I practiced; I prayed; I believed in God and prayed once again about taking away the fear. Four years of uncontrollable fear in the school of music. I couldn't shake it. It had consumed me like a debilitating cancer.

My family came. My friends came. The professors came. Some had driven many miles to hear me play. The introduction of the first piece filled the room, and I began to shake. Once again I focused on the fear and not on the beauty of the music God had given me to play. Where was my faith in the talent He had given me to perform? What did I really believe in? Faith? Or fear and failure? The first piece ended. A soft round of applause greeted me.

I looked out at the faces realizing, finally, how far everyone had traveled—how much this recital meant to them because they cared about me. *Shake off the fear,* God seemed to say to me. *Quit looking at yourself! Be a part of the music—music created in heaven without words, given to you as a gift, to play for these people.*

Always the faith, the inner strength. And I did. I shook it off. The applause was louder after each piece. The uncomfortable feeling of a performer failing began to disappear. By the end of the recital I was walking on the water of music with Jesus. What a miracle that day was! I had broken out of the grip of stagnation, for a moment.

But life continued, and I fell backwards into fear and failure, soon abandoning anything that was challenging in a career. I cowered once more under a low lying tree for shelter, except this time I didn't emerge for several years.

Always there was the rhythm of faith beating within my soul—something I couldn't define or understand—but I knew God was with me. It's just something I knew without words.

But still I wondered, wasn't there more to this life than walking in circles and hiding from anything that might cause an element of fear? I looked upward. Once again, I prayed to the three. In my faith, I believed there had to be more to living than wallowing in my present stagnation of failure.

God took me to the nursing home where my Grandma lay 95 percent immobile. I stared at her, hardly able to comprehend how she looked. Old age was a cruel joke. Her white hair was straight and matted, and her cheeks were deeply sunken, drawing her mouth open. Her immobile body lay sideways and the sadness of it pierced my heart, and I wondered about this loving God once again. I sat holding her hand. Her eyes seemed to search for something. Looking, looking, darting back and forth. A restlessness seemed to consume her as she moved one arm up and down, rearranging things on her eating tray. Music from a portable radio played in the background. I asked if she would like me to read something to her, and she said yes, she would like to hear from the Bible. I asked if she would like to hear about Nicodemus. Yes, she would. As I read, I felt her eyes looking at me, and when I had finished, I noticed she was looking beyond me. Suddenly, it struck me. Here was someone so close to seeing Jesus. She had climbed her mountain of life, the mountain God had set before her, and now she was at the peak ever looking, looking for the One whom she had based her life on. Soon she would see the doors of heaven open and Jesus welcoming her into His home called heaven. She had climbed her mountain because of faith in the three she could not see. I had never known someone so close to the ultimate reward for her life of faith.

This place called heaven would soon become her reality and no longer a reflection of thoughts. Soon her present reality would fade and a new reality would welcome her spirit.

I closed the Bible, and my grandmother held my face with her weak hand, and I realized faith is an ongoing journey. It is about stepping out when there is nothing visible to support me. Faith isn't about results and expectations of God. Instead, it is a belief built upon a rock. It is an underlying foundation supporting me with hope, love, peace, and strength. Faith is believing God is who He says He is. Believing is my choice. He gives to me the gift of life, a musical solo only I can play. My walk joins with His, creating a beautiful harmony void of fear and failure. Suddenly I found the strength. Yes, I would continue walking this musical journey of faith in the hope that one day Jesus will say "well done" in the midst of a hearty round of applause.

Journey To Faith

By Linda S. Dupie
Fredericksburg, Virginia

I thought I knew what faith was and what it meant—until the day my father died. When I saw the peace on my father's face and felt the strength of his faith, I realized the cracks in my own foundation of faith. I had long sought what I saw in him, but it eluded me.

For me faith meant believing in others. While that is faith on some level, the truth I sought was deeper. Getting to a truer, deeper faith was my struggle. My faith in others led me to believe that all was right and I had no right to question the inconsistencies in my life. I couldn't question my happiness, because I had a loving supportive husband and children who were healthy and happy. How could someone who has all that question her happiness? With such a full life, how could I question my role in life? Putting others before me was expected—that was the way life was supposed to be. To question life's order would put others out.

Perhaps my perception of faith was born from the feeling that I never quite lived up to the expectations of others. I led myself to believe that faith lies in people's acceptance and praise of me. Once I learned that I would never be exactly the person they wanted, I became a pretender in life—giving a falsehood to the way that my life "should" be but wasn't. I surrendered *me* to conform to others' beliefs. I made a home others would enjoy. I raised my children the way I was taught, not the way I felt was right for them. I repeated patterns from my childhood and created a cycle that was familiar. There was no joy in my day, no attempt to live a life.

No matter what I tried, it wasn't good enough. I searched for faith in every imaginable place. I couldn't find it in my family and friends. It wasn't in my work, and it wasn't in raising my children. I no longer had the passion to write. There was no excitement when I finished writing an article. And when something I wrote was accepted, I chalked it up to being a fluke. Raising my children became a chore. I felt shame for wanting to run away and be alone. Every time I shouted or put them off, my faith in failure grew. My successes in writing and other facets of my life looked like failure in my own eyes. Despairing, I believed in my failures. This feeling overwhelmed me and caused me to withdraw.

Whatever this was, it wasn't faith. Faith that draws its breath from despair isn't faith, but I knew faith no other way. Yet how could someone like me, who came from a mostly happy, loving family, believe that was where faith lay?

In my father I saw a glimpse of the faith I wanted. He exuded an inner strength I'd never known in another man. He made no pretense when it came to what he said or believed. He made no excuses for his actions and words, because he believed them to be right. He had faith in himself and the life he led.

The day my father died I started a new journey. I began looking for my faith in a place that I never thought to look before—I began with me. I took a small step inside me. It was the beginning of an awakening to the faith within me. I felt a sort of peacefulness and wanted to feel it more. I never thought examining my life and the paths I had taken would rip a hole as wide as the sky in my heart and soul, but it did. But if I wanted to have the serenity and the faith I had seen in my father, I had to tear away the false layers of me.

Slowly I put aside the things I thought brought me comfort and satisfaction. I shut off the computer, put aside my business, and concentrated on what I saw in me. I didn't like the images I saw. I saw a person going through the motions of living but not living life to her potential. She was a mother to her children. She loved them and took care of their every need. She was a wife. She took care of and loved her husband. She cleaned the house and cooked the meals. She did what was expected.

But looking deeper, I saw a sad woman—a woman who really had no idea how to be happy. She had forgotten the simple joys of cuddling with her husband and seeing hot chocolate rings on her children's mouths as they drank cocoa from oversized mugs. Worst of all, she had left herself behind, pushed her dreams aside, and given her entire self to family and home. The simple pleasures had become chores. I didn't like her.

Beyond the woman, I saw the child who learned to have faith in despair and saw that the despair was not faith but the child's attempt to try to do the impossible—trying to please everyone but herself. I watched as the young girl tried to run faster or hit the softball further, all to get a parent's approval. I saw the same young girl struggle to be thin and pretty. I saw the constant failure build until she believed it was her faith. I looked at that child and told her, "What you have is not faith. Faith is not a burden. Faith is freedom. Faith is the willingness to look at yourself and know you are the person God intended and made you to be."

My journey into myself is leading me to a truer faith in me. Though the journey continues, I have found the courage to say aloud, "This is who I am supposed to be. I do love and will have faith in myself as I am, for that is how God loves me."

Matthew 7:7

By Lee E. Scanlon
Grass Valley, California

A few years ago I found myself nurturing an unexpected seedling—a seedling that had sprouted twice before in my life, and here I was again in the quiet, hidden corner of my garden, nursing it again. The seedling? Love. Not the adolescent daydream of falling in love nor the hormonal falling in lust: The simple, unexpected act of "falling in love." That romance-hued happening that strikes once, (I would hope,) at least once in a lifetime, for it blossoms into that wonderful experience when two individuals begin to explore the mystery of their being with each other and find contentment in that exploration to the exclusion of other social activities. This falling in love or romance may be as a giant Sequoia to one or as a rainbow-petaled bush to another or even as a small budding flower to someone else, but there is—in the human experience—nothing like it.

My first encounter with post-adolescent love and romance came at the age of 21. I had just completed three years in the U.S. Army, most of which I spent in Japan. There I had learned more about life than I really wanted to know. I returned to America and civilian life at college, and at first the social life was uncomfortable. Too many people were too concerned about pop music, the "right" clothes or their own and other people's looks, and what crowd or clique or circle they did or did not fit into. I began to question what I perceived as their view of reality.

But fortunately a seed was planted when I met a young woman at college. We dated on and off for several years. She was my first real experience at this highly intense, interpersonal relationship. I had been relatively girl-shy in high school and with so much to do in those days: sports, drama, and public speaking, who had time for girls? (Well, we're all entitled to at least one oversight in a lifetime!)

Anyway, as this woman and I dated, I learned a great deal from her, but in spite of the fact that she flew across the country to spend a week with me at one point in our relationship, I could not bring myself to share my true feelings…to "open up" those deepfelt emotions. She flew back home after that week, and I never saw her again. Our relationship evaporated rather than ended, and I never told her that I loved her. I hold no regrets for that lost relationship, though I have often thought back to that time with her and wondered what might have happened if I had been more able to express myself. Nevertheless, I enjoyed what I could of the relationship and learned more about this difficult process of intimacy.

My second experience came four years later at age 25, helped along by a healthy influx of hormonal influence. This time I shared my feelings, and within eight months we married. The marriage lasted for nearly 31 years, and in that time, two children came into our home, and I thought I was finally beginning to understand a little bit more about this "love." I had also learned more about the process of nurturing. In one way or another I told my wife—every day—that I loved her and how grateful I was that she was part of my life. Each year my love continued to grow, and at one point I marveled at how much I had learned above love and what I had thought was love when our relationship began.

This blossoming ended when my wife told me she did not love me anymore. I discovered she had developed a relationship with another man and had been involved with him for several years. I had been totally ignorant of the situation. Thus, what I thought I had learned above love, romance, and intimacy disappeared into an abyss of pain. For the first and only time in my life, I contemplated suicide…very briefly, but it crossed my mind. My recovery from this unexpected end to such a long-term relationship took nearly a year. I felt it was an area of my life that should best be abandoned. Then for the third time, love and romance entered my life.

This rather cheerful bud caught me unawares. Having lived some 3/5 of a century, my life story would fill a lot of pages, though I might prefer that some of them be left blank. This, my living book, has recorded world changes as empires disappeared overnight and men walked casually on the moon while great and small lived their allotted span. Time, as we all discover, passes, taking with it faded dreams, lost joys, remembered friends, blossoms, and weeds. But for me it is now clear—time will never end one part of my life, even when all rational thought tells me that that part of life is over. For me this one enduring aspect of life is romance, even into a sixth decade of changing social values, morés, and relationships. Romance is the ninth wonder of the world.

This rumination came about because of this third woman that I came to love. This blossoming came very late in life and at a time I thought all such dreams of blossoming were just that—dreams. Having lived these six decades (and half of that time in a now-failed marriage), I had forsaken such youthful dreams, locking them away (I thought) forever—those dreams of inexperienced youth that believe tomorrow stretches on forever and have the courage to pursue their dream. *Only the young,* I thought, *can handle the pangs of romance and the onset of love and still recover from its loss, should that occur.* It was, I thought, a garden best untilled. Well, it isn't true. At least for me it isn't true. At any age what really changes is not the ability but the courage to plant and nurture.

Fate or chance or even inspiration led this woman back into my life. We had known each other in balmier and indeed, less arthritic days. She was and remains—to me—one of the most striking women I have ever known. Though older and harried by arthritis, she is still beautiful in the fullest meaning of the word. A beauty of body, mind, and spirit. Over the past years, as we began seeing each other and working together, what had long been admiration on my part, bloomed into love.

Having struggled through rebuilding a life alone, I neither sought this romance nor even expected it. But as my feelings began to sort themselves out, I finally found the courage to tell this woman of my love and what that meant to me. And for me an unusual addendum. Whatever her answer or response, I wanted to remain her friend. This was something I had never said to any other woman in my life. I felt that if a woman I loved could not love me, it would be too painful to continue any kind of a relationship. But this is not the case. In some way I hoped and continue to hope that I will always be part of her life. This is what I told her.

She, too, wanted to remain friends. But at the same time I was told in as gentle and kind a way as possible that my feelings were not reciprocated. "I cannot return your love and affection, and that is my loss," were her exact words. While I was saddened by the response, what truly made my heart ache was a phrase she used in describing her own feelings: "I do not have romantic feelings anymore. I gave up those fantasies a long time ago." How sad a phrase that seemed then and even now as I write these words. Are feelings then mere fantasies? Unreal illusions that have no place in life? Are all relationships merely fantasies? I don't believe so.

Feelings, for me, are the strongest reminder that I am human and alive. But the ultimate sadness comes in contemplating a harvest that will never be. Pruning the experiences of life is important. That is how we make decisions and move forward. Pruning is one thing. Rooting out the plant seems an overreaction.

Having lost again, I turned at last to the place I should have turned first and on my knees sought His help. It didn't come right away nor for several years. But an assurance came that there was a companion for me, so I continued my search. It came when He knew that I and my companion were ready for the love that was His gift to us. The search took almost 12 years, but I found my love in what I thought a most unlikely place—the Internet! Our emails became phone calls and finally the actual meeting, face to face. (Which took some planning as she lived in California and I lived in New Mexico!) That was Memorial Day 2001. We were engaged in August and have been married since March 2002. Neither of us has ever been happier.

I cannot imagine living life without my Ginger and the romance and love that is her gift to me. This aspect of living in which there are those feelings toward someone whose presence (whether in one's mind or in one's space) quickens the heartbeat or brings a smile or even just a moment of heady, heightened, awareness; someone whose voice you cherish; someone, who regardless of the inroads of time, remains beautiful in mind and spirit. It is the harvest of remembered conversation, looks, and smiles; the joy of sharing. It is the shared intimacy that comes from two against the world; the deepest conversations from the heart and hearing the unfearing heart speak—not the shallow conversation of friends passing through another day that looks so much like the preceding and following days that even the conversation never changes—unafraid to share dreams, hopes, desires, and even passing fancies. For in those intimacies there is no fear of judgment to preclude the dream; no fear of lost communication. It is the joy of being…together. But romance and love, I have also discovered begin and continue with faith.

Romance should blossom in every soul. Each of us has need of it to dress this sometime desert of existence. We need the hope of romance and love as well as the reality. For as Shakespeare said, "We are such stuff as dreams are made on." And in those dreams, time—the ultimate enemy—disappears, leaving two in suspension between heaven and earth, forging their own reality within the gift of a divinely given and sanctioned union.

The beauty of any hope or dream is how fresh it first appears and then remains to brighten one's heart and soul in those hours of each day in the quiet corners of our life. I have found someone who makes love blossom and sends its fragrance to the heart of my soul. And so love through faith is mine again and I dream and look and hope, today, tomorrow and to whatever lies in the garden beyond the gates of time.

No Permanent Solutions

By Terry W. Burns
Amarillo, Texas

The gun lay on the table, its flat black surface malevolent in the twilight darkness. We'd been staring at each other for hours, it with its one black eye of death.

I hadn't come to this cheap motel room with a sense of purpose—more out of a lack of direction. Clinical depression...real...physical...the terms generally used didn't do the job. No mere word could remotely explain what happened in the pit of my stomach, the tightness in my chest, the lump in my throat that wouldn't go away.

The head was the worst. Not pain...more like...fuzzy...disoriented. My little metal friend was there to take advantage of this helplessness.

The breaks...that's what they called it...just bad breaks. Losing my job, my father and brother dead within months of each other, car trouble. More? Does it matter? No, it doesn't. Nothing mattered, that was the problem.

Nobody understood, nobody but my little friend. The friend understood, and he waited. Infinite patience.

I picked up my friend. Cool to the touch, almost cold. Yes, that's him, cold and detached. Professional. Knew his business. Like an ice cube pressed to my temple. Eyes closed, a light scent of oil told me it was there. Absolute patience.

A knock. *Are you kidding me? Now?* My friend went back to the table, hidden under a towel. So patient.

"Terry?"

Recognition seeped through my brain. The swirling fog in my mind obscured it but begrudgingly allowed it through. "Saundra? What are you doing here?"

"Your cousin told me you were staying here. I'm sorry about your brother."

Sorry. Yes, well-meaning people lined up to express sorrow over and over. Daddy's funeral had drained me. I couldn't do it again. "Thanks. It was somewhat unexpected. Have a seat. You haven't changed a bit."

She laughed and tossed her long brown hair. Her laugh was a ray of sunlight, cutting through the fog. "Not true, of course, but nice of you to say."

"Actually it was true. I'd have known you anywhere. How do you do it?"

"Just one day at a time. How are you holding up?"

Tendrils of fog started to creep back in. "I'm fine." The oldest line of them all.

"Everybody says that. How are you really? We always could tell each other everything. But I know you. It's hard, isn't it? Hard to say what you feel?"

I expelled a long breath of air and broke eye contact. "I don't like to burden other people with my problems."

"It's not a burden. Problems and pain are meant to be shared. The more we share our heartaches, the smaller the piece we have left to bear. If enough people share, it almost disappears."

Was that how it worked? All these people and their meaningless words—were they just trying to take a little piece of my pain on themselves? "It's hard."

"I know. Oh, how I know. When I lost Momma nobody would talk about it. Everybody said to put it behind me, not to dwell on it." The smile disappeared. "They said I had to move on. I still haven't. There's no closure." She looked up and found my eyes. "I still need to talk about it. And you need to talk. We can't go on keeping these things inside of us." She brushed at the corner of her eyes.

"I'm sorry about your mother. I liked her a lot."

"See what I mean? You just took a little piece of my pain yourself, and I immediately feel better knowing you care."

I did care, down deep in the dead spot where my heart used to be. Isn't that remarkable? I had given up on my own pain but couldn't stand for her to hurt, even after all these years.

I said it aloud. She smiled. "I knew we could still talk. One thing that helped me was where I read in the Scriptures that God promised He wouldn't give us more than we could bear and always gave us a way out."

A way out! Yes, my little friend under the towel. I looked across the table. Saundra was beautiful, breathtaking, and she was caring. Maybe there was another way. I liked this one better.

Reduced to working in a convenience store. What a downer after years of making good money. All these people knew me when I was on top. Now I saw the pity in their eyes when I asked if they wanted paper or plastic. They could keep their pity; there was no shame in a man doing what he had to do.

Why does God want me to do this? I've always felt everything in life happens for a reason. I still do. What reason? What am I supposed to be learning?

The reason walked in about 3:00 a.m. A pretty young lady who seemed strangely disoriented, as if she didn't know why she was there. She was reading the backs of the boxes in the medical section. Then I noticed her over in the cleaning products reading labels, and I knew.

I said, "I had a gun."

"What?" She spun on me with confusion in her eyes. "What did you say?"

"When I tried to commit suicide, I had a gun."

"I'm not...I mean...you're mistaken."

"Am I? You didn't find anything in the medical stuff that looked like it'd do the job, so now you're reading the back of a drain cleaner jug?"

"It's none of your business."

"I think you're wrong. It is exactly my business. For months I've been sitting in this nowhere job wondering why. Now I know God put me here to wait for you. I've been where you are. He put me here for you."

"I don't believe in God."

"Why not?"

"If there were a God, He'd make life better."

"God doesn't promise life will be good, but He promises to help His children when the tough times come. He got me through mine. He sent somebody to me at the exact moment I needed it."

"And you think He sent you to me?"

"I was here first. Who was sent to whom?"

"He didn't send me anywhere."

"Why are you here? Don't you have drain cleaners at home?"

"No, I have a two-year-old girl. Too dangerous."

"She's not alone?"

"I dropped her with a neighbor."

"My name is Terry, by the way." I held out my hand. She offered me a cold, damp, wet fish of a hand.

Not looking at me, she said, "My name is Carol Ann." She looked up. "You're gonna lose your job."

"Trust me. This isn't much of a job."

"It's more than I have."

"Is that the problem? You out of work?"

"That's part of it. I have so many problems."

"Is your little girl healthy?"

"Yes."

"Don't you realize what a blessing that is? My kids played such a large part in my turning away from killing myself." She jerked her hand away and started to turn. "Oh, you don't like that! Sounds different, doesn't it? Killing myself. Permanent. Nasty. Not clean and neat like maybe some medicine that would let you just quietly resign from the human race, is that it?"

"You don't know...you don't have...you can't...oh, why can't you leave me alone!"

"We discussed that. Sit down. You drink coffee?"

She nodded.

I talked to her about how I still had problems and told her the only way I was able to cope was with the help of God.

"Are you sure it isn't Him that's doing it to you?"

"God is my father. You think He loves me any less than your father loved you? He disciplines His children. Not because He likes to punish them, but because they need to learn something."

"You think He's punishing me?"

"Probably not. Life can just be hard sometimes, but in my case it doesn't matter whether He is or isn't, He's the one who can help me through it. I can't imagine getting through life's problems without His help."

"Oh, I don't know. It just doesn't seem worth it."

"I know—believe me I know. Are you prepared to never see that little girl again? What's her name, by the way?"

"Hattie. No...I guess I hadn't thought about that."

"What would Hattie do without you?"

"Somebody would take care of her. They always do. She'd be better off."

"Somebody will take care of both of you. You need a church home."

"They wouldn't accept me. I'm just white trash."

"No such thing. Our church has all kinds. Hey, I just had to take bankruptcy, and I'm working in a convenience store. You gotta know I don't have two nickels to rub together."

"I don't understand. What is it that helps you so?"

My heart leaped in my chest. There it is...the opening.... "It isn't a thing—it's a Who. You ever hear of Jesus?"

"Sure, everybody has. Some religious dude."

"No, He's *THE* religious dude. Carol Ann, He already knows you, knows all about you. He sacrificed everything He had to die on the cross for your sins. How could anybody do more for you than that?"

"I've heard about the cross thing. Sounds dumb."

"I can see how it'd look that way. What's smart about giving up your life to pay the toll for a whole world full of people that don't care anything about you? But He loved us...all of us and gave all He had."

"I still don't get it."

"The Bible says no sinner is going to get into heaven, and we are all sinners."

"That sounds like a no-win deal."

"It is a no-win deal, unless somebody pays the price for us. That's what the cross was all about. That's the only way we can get into heaven—through Him."

"So if I go home and...you know...do it...I wouldn't go to heaven?"

"Have you ever accepted Jesus as your Savior?"

"No."

"Not a chance then. If you don't make the trip to Heaven, you think you'll ever see that daughter again?"

"It's not as easy as I thought."

"Put as simply as possible, it's nothing but a permanent solution to a temporary problem. Where does this leave us now?"

"I'm not making any promises."

"I didn't ask for any. I'm not making you any promises on my situation either. I'm just fighting it a day at a time. Will you promise me that much?"

"Yes." She got up. "I've gotta go get Hattie."

"You aren't going to do anything?"

"No, you've given me a lot to think about. I'm not going to do anything stupid."

Suddenly her arms were around my neck. I heard her whisper, "Thank you," in my ear. We stood that way for a long time, crying together. She stopped in the door on the way out. "Maybe your God did put you here for me. I have to go to church and find out for myself." Then she turned and was gone.

I was exhausted. I went to my knees and prayed I had truly helped. I'd be off soon. Then it occurred to me that in a normally busy store there had been no customers for over two hours. God had not only sent her in, but He had given me the time to talk with her.

Therapy

By Chaun Archer
Hollywood, Florida

"Get up and write!"

This was the resounding command I heard as I lay in bed counting butterflies because the sheep got tired and took a break. It was almost as if someone was lurking in the dark watching me. I tried to ignore it and to pass it off as my inner self reacting to night after night of sleep deprivation. Driving myself into a madman's state of mind, thinking about my past, present, and the frightening possibility of a not-so-bright future, a bone chilling fear overtook me.

A presence filled the room and left me immobile. I could hear an inexplicable rush of anxiety that froze my tears and constricted my lungs. When the blood began circulating through my body again, I had the strength to sit up and survey my surroundings.

I knew I would find no one, but I had to make sure that this was what I thought it was, an answer from God. Still feeling this presence around me, I managed to squeak past my lips, "Write what?"

There was no response, and I began to think it was just my imagination. I lay down again and drew the covers up to my neck, clenching them tightly, not wanting to let go. I tried to make myself believe that as a result of poor sleeping habits, I was driving myself insane.

Then, just as I relaxed again, I heard it. "Get up and write!"

This time I jumped to my feet, bumping into things in the darkness, and flicked on the lights. Just as I suspected, there was no one there but me, and I knew I had not gone far enough over the edge to hallucinate.

I claimed to be a writer, so the thought of me writing was not far fetched. However, with not one published piece and after months of constant writer's block, I was beginning to think my confidence had overtaken my reality and that what I thought was a passion was really only a little girl afraid to grow up and get a real job.

Now, after dedicating a few days to God through prayer and fasting to find out my purpose and calling, He was answering. But the answer had put my feelings in a blender and liquidized them. I could taste this strange ooze seeping into my blood and flooding my mind with feelings of fear, anxiety, joy, confusion, and emotions that have no names. This is where I decided to step out in faith and put my trust in Him.

A few months earlier I was going through severe mental anguish. My body, mind, and soul were all disconnected. I was looking for completion and continuity, something with substance that would last. I was distracted, and I felt like my life was worth nothing. Fresh out of a long and drawn out, abusive relationship from which God had rescued me, feelings of loneliness began to haunt me. Depression embraced me and became so familiar that I did not want to release its comforting presence.

I was not where I had set out to be, and years of trying to live up to everyone else's expectations and failing were almost more than I could bear. I was the product of an unwanted teenage pregnancy and grew up in a home of drug, alcohol, physical, sexual, mental, and verbal abuse, violence, promiscuity, and hate. You name the demon, and it was there. This environment left me angry and afraid. My mother died when I was 12, my father was never really there, and spiritually I was burning out.

God had blessed me in many ways. I had the opportunity to go to college; I had a job, a car, and an apartment; and I was very grateful. Like many others, I thought I knew Him and loved Him, and He loved me. But I discovered this was a delusion when, on my way to my 21st birthday party, I got into an accident and thought, *If you were to die right now, where would you be?* Speechless and in tears, I couldn't answer, and it was at that moment that I knew I did not really know Him at all, and my quest began.

I started to get closer to God and began developing a more personal relationship with Him. It got to a point where I could feel His presence, and I wanted to be closer still. I switched jobs for financial security, and things were beginning to look great. I began to get comfortable, and I believed nothing could go wrong and trouble was far from me.

Then my world started to move faster, spinning so fast I could hardly hold on. My half brother, who was also my roommate at the time, left without warning and left me with a lot of debt and headache. Lies he told were revealed, and I realized he was not coming back. Again, another person I trusted and loved had let me down, and the familiar heartache returned.

Two months behind on the rent and faced with an eviction notice, I sought God's help. It was then that I turned on the television to watch a Christian channel, and He spoke to me once again.

One of the speakers said, "The Bible says, 'Many are called but few are chosen.' I believe that the difference between the called and the chosen are those who are willing to suffer." That had never been an option for me.

When things got bad, I begged for God to get me out, never considering His will. I thought being a Christian made me exempt from suffering. Now He was trying to get me to another level by strengthening me. That very night I cried out to God and told Him I was willing to suffer and go through the fire because I knew He was purifying me. I stepped out in faith. He spoke to me that night and told me not to move out of that apartment.

The next day during my daily devotions before work, I read James 1:2-4: *Consider it pure joy, my brothers, whenever you face trials of many kinds, because you know that the testing of your faith develops perseverance. Perseverance must finish its work so that you may be mature and complete, not lacking anything.* With a renewed confidence I stepped out the door, and there it was. They had put a sticker on my door that said "FINAL NOTICE OF EVICTION" and that I had to be out by the following day at midnight.

Yet for the first time in my life, I was not afraid. Fear had no power over me; instead there was joy. I was reminded that this was just a testing of my faith, and He told me not to run away from this one. When asked what I was going to do, I told friends that came to help that I was not moving. I told them I knew what the sticker said, but that was not my final notice—God is, and until He tells me to go, I will stay.

That night my boyfriend stayed, and we prayed through the night and gave God praise and thanks. Sure enough, God delivered me, and my faith and trust were once again renewed.

The next week I went in to work and got fired. Yet God had prepared me through the day so I knew something was coming. Despite the news, I was singing a new song, and I was happy. My life was beginning to have a purpose, and I saw God's will being developed. I did not know why or what He wanted me to do, but I trusted Him. I now had no obligations but to the Lord, and I had the opportunity to go to a women's conference not far from where I stayed. There He spoke to me again, and I realized that there were still some things I was holding onto and did not trust Him with, like my finances. He was right. I began to listen to Him more about what to do with my money and how to spend it.

When I got back home, I kept getting this notion to buy a desk. I knew that without a job, I had to save every little penny I had, and I questioned and prayed about this feeling. I ignored it for a while and then finally I gave in with hesitation. I put restrictions on the purchase of this desk and said that if it cost more than $50, I would not buy it. Then I found a consignment store with a huge L-shaped desk and they said they would sell it to me for $25. I could not argue with that and took the desk home. Confused with such a purchase, I did nothing with it until I could be sure why God wanted me to buy this desk.

I decided that I would take some time out with God—well, quite honestly, God decided—I only agreed. I unplugged the telephone, television, radio, any type of distraction, and prayed and fasted. I had never had this type of alone time with myself or God, and it was driving me insane. My mind jumped into the driver's seat and went full throttle on a joy ride through my painful past, present, and future. Having left behind common sense and any logical emotion, I was out of control. The distractions were gone, the curtains opened, and I stood face to face with reality.

I did not have a job and had very little money, I had an education I was not using, and I now owned a huge desk I felt I had no use for. Depressed, at times I would laugh out loud, then cry in the same breath. I began to question God and my existence, trying to understand it all. At night I had trouble getting to sleep because I could not relinquish myself from the tiresome burden of thought. I was losing focus and all sanity.

Then on the third day, in the wee hours of the morning, as I lay there traveling this rugged journey, I heard it. "Get up and write!"

Certain it was not just the horror of an intruder or, worse still, my mind, I went to my newly acquired, used, $25 desk, turned on my computer, and wrote.

My purpose revealed itself with each stroke on the keyboard. I began to write, and therapy was initiated. I began typing like a maniac, and I loved it. Never had I been so sure of what my calling was. I was in love. A new and unique kind of love. While working, I did not have the time to focus on my writing. I was too busy trying to make ends meet. Now I was focused and trusting in God to use my talents.

Three months went by and finally God told me to leave the apartment. Working on my writing and freelance web design, I still had no stable job, but I left, not knowing where He was sending me. He provided for me and comforted me through the hard times. I am still trusting in Him and His word, keeping the faith and knowing that everything is okay. I believe that God keeps His promises, and He promised that He would never leave us or forsake us.

There are some things we have no control over, and realizing that we cannot do it all by ourselves makes trusting Him easier. Constant faith and trust in God allows me to be happy in the good times as well as the bad, knowing that better times will come. My journey is not over. As a matter of fact, it has just begun. Through faith, I have chosen to suffer for Christ, knowing that He will take care of me and will never leave my side.

13

Blessed Are The Faithful

The following stories were selected as the two grand prize winning entries from among all the entries received in our 2002 Obadiah Press Annual Writer's Contest. The theme of the contest was "Faith" and these two entries, among others, moved us to tears. I pray reading them will touch your heart and soul and strengthen your faith, as well. Just as God's promise of eternal life is fulfilled at the end of our journey here on earth, so, too, we have saved these stories until the end—saving the best for last.

Tina L. Miller
Editor & Publisher
Obadiah Press

Death, Life, And Faith

By Cheryl Abrams Collier
Greer, South Carolina

The day my oldest brother died was, perhaps, the worst day of my life. But it was also one of the most meaningful. For it was on this horrible day that God put all of my declarations about having faith in Him to the test and taught me a valuable lesson about the true meaning of totally trusting Him with my life. As Larry took his final breaths, I cried out to God for help, and He answered my plea, not in the way I expected, or even wanted, but in the way that I needed, in the way that would prove to me forever that my Father is, indeed, in control and faithful to His promises.

I remember clearly the day that my sister-in-law called my mother and me with the news that would change all of our lives forever. Larry had had a kidney transplant—my other brother (I'm the youngest of three children) had donated the kidney—and Larry's body was in rejection. But this is not the beginning of my story. For that, I must travel back to the day of my salvation.

Two of my best friends had been witnessing to me for years. Not only did they tell me about Jesus and His love for me, but their lives were also radically different from mine. They had a peace that I knew nothing about. They had joy while I was growing increasingly depressed with each day that passed. But most importantly, my friends had a deep faith in someone beyond themselves. I realized one day that I wanted what they had. I wanted it desperately. I could no longer live without it. So one Sunday morning in my best friend's church, I received the One my soul had been longing for.

Though I fell deeply in love with Jesus, I had many obstacles to overcome. Fear, worry, anxiety—these were just a handful of the negative emotions that had plagued me for my entire life, and they continued to be a huge problem in spite of this newly found love relationship with the Lord. My inability to trust Him, my lack of faith, threatened to destroy me spiritually. A constant battle raged in my mind. Was I truly saved? Could I really trust that God would save me if I prayed a simple prayer repenting of my sins and asking Jesus into my life? Could I live for the Lord, or would I fail Him miserably, doing more detriment to His kingdom than good?

Worry plagued me daily. Doubt assaulted me at every turn. At times I was convinced that I must be losing my mind. While I knew that it was typical for newborn babes in Christ to experience some fear after conversion, I also knew that my doubt was abnormal, for it had lasted well beyond the early days of my salvation. Five years after coming to Christ, I still struggled just to trust the Lord for the smallest things in my life. I knew that my doubt could not possibly be pleasing to God, but I could not seem to help myself. I wanted to believe Him for everything, but somehow I just couldn't do it. At age 21, I was almost as desperate to be able to rest in the assurance of faith in God as I had been to receive Christ as my savior.

It was out of this sense of overwhelming need that I began to cry out to God for deliverance from unbelief, for a faith in Him that would transcend all of my doubt and empower me to trust Him like never before. Little did I know how God would use my brother's illness to teach me, one painstaking step at a time, what it truly means to place all of my faith in Him.

When Larry developed kidney failure at the very young age of 32, I began to pray to the Lord for his healing. The sicker he grew and the more obvious his need of a transplant became, the more earnest my prayers grew. I fought with the doubts that flooded my mind and struggled to believe that God would be faithful and answer my prayers. I read Scripture on healing, committing it to memory and telling myself that Larry's healing was right around the corner. When his specialist finally said that a transplant was inevitable, I doubled my efforts. If I prayed hard enough and believed with all my heart, I told myself, God would perform a miracle. He had to. Didn't His word promise that God would answer the "effectual, fervent prayers" (James 5:16) of His children? Didn't Jesus Himself say that if we are persistent in going to the Father in prayer, He will answer us and grant us that which we desire from Him (Matthew 7:7-8)?

On the day of Larry's transplant, I was away from my family for the first time. While I lamented the fact that I could not be at the hospital, both my brother and mother assured me that everything would be all right. It was my first day of graduate school orientation, and there was no way to get out of the mandatory meetings.

"We'll be fine," Larry assured me, "and you can come see me over the weekend. You don't need to be here. Everything will turn out okay—you'll see."

What could I do? I had no choice but to do as my brother asked, and oddly, I felt a strange peace that I had not ever really experienced before. Though I was a bit afraid to admit it to myself, let alone to anyone else, I felt that God had assured me that everything would, indeed, be fine.

"I am in control," it seemed the Lord was saying to me. "Trust Me."

For once, I did not worry. An overwhelming peace came over me and I was able to focus my attention on the new information I was being given about life at the University of Georgia and what would be expected of me as a graduate student. Before I knew it, the day was over, and I was able to make contact with my family. Both my brothers had made it successfully through the surgery. Larry's body was not rejecting the new kidney. His prognosis was good.

Eventually, first Reggie, who had donated the kidney, and finally Larry were released from the hospital. Both my brothers were doing well, and I was able to rest in the faith that God could, and would, answer my prayers…as long as I sought Him hard enough and did my part to prove to Him, by my earnestness and perseverance, that I truly deserved to have the need met.

Five days after his release Larry was back in the hospital, his body determined to reject the foreign organ. But I wasn't worried. God had answered my prayers because I had been diligent and worked hard to believe. Surely everything would be okay. It had to be. There simply were no other options. Even after we were told that my brother had been given an overdose of anti-injection medicine, was in a coma, and had unexplained internal bleeding, I still held tenaciously to faith. I had prayed fervently as the book of James implores believers to do. I had memorized Scripture on healing and the character of God. I had worked with all my might to be the best daughter God could ever have. In spite of the doctor's horrible report, God had to heal Larry. He would be faithful because I had done all I could to rid my mind of the sinful doubt that had plagued me; I believed, so God was obligated to meet the need...wasn't He?

When, four weeks later, the doctor removed Larry from the ventilator that had been keeping him alive, I experienced doubt, and yes, even anger to a degree that I had not allowed myself to acknowledge since the beginning of this ordeal with my brother's health. What had gone wrong? Hadn't God promised? Where was His faithfulness? What of my newfound faith in Him?

Where are You, Lord? Don't you know how much I need You? my spirit cried out in desperation.

As tears began to flow down my face, before my sobs could reach the uncontrollable stream for which I knew they were destined, I sprinted from the hospital room where Larry's life was slowly ebbing away. The only place I could think to go was the bathroom. Thankfully, no one was there to witness my gut-wrenching sobbing or to hear my agonizing pleading with the Lord.

"Where are You, Father?" I cried. "Are You even really my Father? I've done everything I know to do to build my faith in You. I've done all I know to do to make myself worthy of Your grace, Lord. Please! Please! Please, God, please don't let Larry die. You can touch him, Lord! Please!"

My cries were met with silence. Utter, lonely, heartbreaking silence. Sitting on the bathroom floor, I felt hopelessly alone. Where was God now? Where was my faith now?

As I continued to weep, and as guilt over my outburst assaulted me, too overcome to pray, I began to hear that still, small voice of God, that same voice that spoke so profoundly to the prophet Elijah during a time of great desperation in his life. God's amazing, unfathomable peace flooded my soul and brought calm to my spirit. What the Lord imparted to me as I huddled on that bathroom floor truly changed my life forever.

The Lord taught me that faith is more than simply believing; it is knowing that He will meet our needs in the right way, and at the right time, because He is sovereign. Moreover, faith is not dependent on our goodness or how much or little we think we merit a touch from God; it is contingent upon the reality that we serve One who knows all things, can do all things, and loves with a magnitude that the human heart will never fully comprehend.

As I pulled myself up from the floor, I truly knew I was not alone and never would be. While I didn't understand why the Lord did not choose to spare my brother's life, already I knew that I had been forever changed. For God had shown me that faith isn't derived from my fickle efforts to believe but from entering into His rest (Hebrews Chapter 4) and accepting that He knows what is best, even when I don't understand His ways.

I wish I could say that I have never experienced a moment of doubt since God touched me on a cold hospital bathroom floor, but that is simply not true. However, I do know deep in my being, despite temporary bouts of unbelief, that I can put my faith in the One who is always faithful. I trust Him today because He gave me the assurance on the dreary October day of my brother's death that He would meet all of my needs, even in the darkest moments of my life. I trust Him today because He has been faithful to that promise over the last 16 years.

A Rare Kind Of Faith

By Edison McDaniels II, M.D.
Virginia Beach, Virginia

I knew there was nothing I could do as soon as I saw those films. It was one o'clock in the morning, raining, and I looked at those damn images and knew there was nothing I could do to help her. It was worse than that, though. I knew there was nothing anyone could do to help her.

She was going to die.

Not right there, not even that night. But as I looked at the two-dimensional images of her brain, my brain reassembled them in the three-dimensional space of my mind, and I knew she was never going to see four years old. I hated myself for knowing that just then.

I flipped the switches on the light boxes, darkening the images. I stood there for a long moment, my right hand rubbing a new crease onto my forehead. I had a headache just thinking about what was coming. It's hard enough to tell somebody they're dying. It's another thing to tell someone that their future is dying—that all their hopes and aspirations have met a dead end.

Literally.

I was in no hurry to impart the secret I alone knew. The hospital corridor was dim as I slowly walked the hundred or so feet from radiology to the ER. Half the lights had been turned off—to conserve energy, I guess. It leant the place a surrealistic look, though, and in the darkness of that moment, I felt the long, cold fingers of death nearby.

But a neurosurgeon—that would be me—comes to know that death is always nearby, never more than a heartbeat or two away in either the day or the night—it just seems closer in the dark.

My footsteps echoing in the emptiness didn't help. I imagined the grim reaper and those hands—oh, God, those hands: big, brutish, calloused, almost a foot from base of the palm to the tips of those menacing fingers with their unmerciful touch. I saw the face of death, too, obscured not by an executioner's hood, but by a mask, the kind we wear in the operating room, where the eyes alone speak for the rest of the face. As I imagined it, the reaper's eyes were dark, sunken, lurking things that I couldn't quite look at. Some things are better left unseen, even unimagined.

Walking down that corridor, death looked like a clumsy, ungainly shadow—the boogeyman, the closet monster from my childhood, the eater of souls. Me.

I wasn't the grim reaper, of course—just the messenger. I would deliver the news, they would fall apart, we would call somebody from the clergy to help out, she would be admitted, and the futile suffering that was the battle to save her young life would begin. I say futile because this was a disease from which nobody ever recovered—not when the definition of recovery included survival and cure anyway.

I had seen it all before.

I stopped by the desk for the medical record. I had gone directly over to radiology upon my arrival and hadn't needed the girl's name then. There aren't many brain tumors lurking about the ER in the middle of the night. My first thought, upon glancing at the record, was that she had my birthday—an odd but perfectly normal coincidence that I could have done without at that moment.

I'm not a superstitious person, but I've always been fascinated by birthdays for reasons I can't really explain. Everybody has to be born sometime, I suppose. It's just that sometimes the coincidences that stack up around birthdays seem a little stunning, even eerie. Take my birthday, for instance, May 12. My wife's birthday is August 1. Nothing too interesting there, except that both of her sisters were born on May 12. See what I mean?

So she's born on May 12, and her name is Sidney Berry. Sidney, like my little sister, the one who died on my ninth birthday after a long and mostly futile battle with brain cancer.

Like I said—stunning, even eerie—coincidences.

The curtain was closed around the cubicle, and I stopped a moment to draw a last ounce of strength from the air before entering. When I finally opened it, I found a black man of about 40 sitting on the single chair beside the gurney. On the gurney itself was the cutest little girl. She had olive brown skin and thick black hair that was combed back into a single ponytail with a wide pink ribbon around it. She wore pink pajamas to match, a one piece sort that included booties and a long zipper down one leg.

She was lying on her side facing her father, and when I entered, she sat up and smiled at me in a way that no patient before or since ever has. Her lips curled back with a pleasant grin, her cheeks dimpled, and she batted a pair of big, soulful eyes at me. From that first moment, I had the impression that I already knew her—and that she knew me.

There was something else about that smile, though—something intensely disturbing, and it was probably the reason I had been called so quickly that night. It was uneven, a subtle asymmetry between the two sides that became a glaring chasm of difference to my trained eye. She was still beautiful, but the left side of her mouth lagged, and the dimple there was mostly just a suggestion. I suspected it had only been like that a day or two at most; otherwise somebody would have brought it to her parents' attention. Parents are often the last to notice things like that.

Mr. Berry was a big man—not fat, but big boned. He, too, smiled and immediately rose from his chair, putting his hand out to shake mine. I introduced myself and asked if Mrs. Berry was about. He said yes, that she had gone to the bathroom and would be back presently. "Okay," I replied, then began to ask a few questions to gather a history. It wasn't terribly important—that history—but I wanted and needed to establish a rapport with them. You can't just blurt out something like, "I've seen the images of your daughter's brain and you might as well start looking for a coffin now." Although, truth be told, I've met physicians who would do just that.

We talked a while. When Sidney's mother returned, I introduced myself to her, leaving out—for the moment—the fact that I was a neurosurgeon, just as I had done in introducing myself to her husband. Nobody's ever happy to see a neurosurgeon, especially when their child—their future—is concerned. I wanted to work the field on my terms just then, bring them up to speed slowly and compassionately.

So we talked. They were remarkable people with a soft, easygoing manner. I liked them both immediately. They were obviously well educated—I found out later that he was a Navy Captain and she was a college professor—but there was nothing pretentious about them at all. They were every bit the concerned parents.

Sidney had been diagnosed with an ear infection, and I asked about that. "That's right," Mrs. Berry said. "She's been pulling at her ear a lot lately—keeps rubbing the side of her head, as well."

"I see," I said. *She's probably had a headache,* I thought. *Kids will do odd things with headaches—just about everything except say they have a headache.*

I had been leaning against the gurney all this time, and now, as Sidney's mother spoke, the girl stood up and put her arms around me from behind. She laid her head on my shoulder as naturally as my own daughter would. She, too, was just three, and the similarity between the two spooked me as I felt Sidney's small arms embracing me. For just a moment I found it hard to concentrate on what her mom was saying. "Any vomiting or problems eating?" I finally asked, knowing the answer.

"Hasn't been eating well—just picking at her food. I thought it was the flu at first." She looked at me, and I saw the concern in her eyes.

"And vomiting?"

"No vomiting, but—and this is the reason we came in tonight—she's been gagging a bit," Mrs. Berry said.

"Can you tell me about that?"

We talked some more, and I tried not to appear overly concerned, but I was never very good at lying.

"Do you know what the problem is?" Mrs. Berry finally asked.

"Well, let me examine Sid, and then we'll talk, okay?"

Sidney still had her arms around me from behind. Her father picked her up, and she immediately kissed him and offered an enormous, though lopsided, smile. Pound for pound, I've not seen a bigger smile since, and it made my heart glad. He gently set her back on the gurney.

"Sidney, can you close your eyes tight, Sweetie?"

She did, and I saw immediately that her left eyeball rolled upward until only the white was visible. That's called a Bell's phenomenon, and it always looks a little eerie, especially in a three-year-old. It's not abnormal, though; the eye is supposed to roll up like that. But the eyelid is supposed to cover it, and Sidney's eyelid stayed put. That was the abnormality.

Next I had her stick her tongue out, and instead of jutting straight out, it pointed off to the left. *Damn,* I thought, ticking off a list in my head. Each abnormality not only confirmed the diagnosis on her films, they also suggested a relatively advanced stage of disease.

When I finished the exam, Sidney lay down and closed her eyes. Looking at her, I couldn't help but think of my Sidney, my precious little sister, and of the lingering torment her death became. It always seemed to me that she had spent her last few weeks and months dying when she should have been living. I put the image of Sidney—both of them—out of my head and turned to her parents. I couldn't put off what I knew any longer.

They looked at me and I at them. I can't say that I fumbled for words; I had been a neurosurgeon a half dozen years by then, and finding the words wasn't the problem. It was the sentiment that I struggled with—trying to keep my voice from breaking. In less than an hour, this little girl had turned me inside out. She had that kind of force of personality.

Some people live 70 years and never make an impact on another person. Sidney Berry was three and had an impact on every person she met.

"I'm sorry," I said. "There's a tumor." And just like that, they knew.

We spent some time, quite a while really, discussing it. I remember telling them they should get another opinion but that it was inoperable.

When we finished, I told them I'd make arrangements to have her admitted.

"Why?" Mrs. Berry asked. "What can you do for her tonight that we can't do for her at home in her own bed?"

The answer, of course, was…nothing. What better place could there be for a little girl with an inoperable brain tumor than home in her own bed? And just that quick, I knew.

They got those other opinions, but so far as I know, she never spent a night in a hospital. She died in her own bed three months later, her family at her side.

She might have lingered a bit longer with chemotherapy, but that wouldn't have been living, her parents said. They had faith she was going to a better place, and what they wanted to remember was the way she lived, not the way she died.

A rare kind of selfless faith that was—letting a child live in the midst of dying. It made my heart glad.

Finding Faith In Your Life

Think you don't have enough faith? Did you know you can pray for faith? *"Ask and it will be given to you; seek and you will find; knock and the door will be opened to you."* Matthew 7:7 All you have to do is ask...

Pray with me now:

Dear Lord,

Sometimes I feel so weak when I want to be strong. I don't always understand Your ways, and it troubles me. I want to be good and faithful to You, but I have a hard time trusting that You have a greater plan and that everything happens for a reason—especially when I am hurting and I feel all alone. I know You will never leave me or forsake me. I know this in my head. Help me to feel it in my heart. Wrap Your loving arms around me now, and let me feel Your presence in my life. Comfort me, and give me peace. Strengthen my faith that I may carry on to do what You would have me do and fulfill Your will for my life. Help me to find joy in You and the blessings You have given me. This I ask in the name of Your beloved Son, Jesus, who gave His very life that I might have the promise of eternal life with You in heaven.

Amen.

I hope this book of faith and this prayer has blessed you today and will continue to do so. Please share it with others who need to read this message of faith.

Tina L. Miller

Tina L. Miller is the author of *When A Woman Prays*. If you would like to learn more about prayer and how it can strengthen your faith, read *When A Woman Prays* and be blessed!

Contributing Authors

Shaila M. Abdullah was born in Karachi, Pakistan. She has written for local magazines like *Women's Own, Fashion Collections,* and a magazine of the *Daily Dawn* called *Tuesday Review*. She lives with her husband in Austin, Texas.

Chaun Archer was raised in the Bahamas and attended Northwood University in West Palm Beach and Florida Computer College in Pembroke Pines, Florida. She enjoys reading, writing, and poetry and is currently working on her first novel.

Annette Argabright has always wanted to write, but only started getting ideas for stories a few years ago. Since that time she has written several stories and has begun the process of searching God's path for them.

Nathanael Vincent Armstrong is a children's church minister at Solid Rock Church in Loshodon where he also plays drums on the worship team. He met his wife, Hayley, there when they were preteens, and they have been in love ever since.

Angela Nicole Baughman holds a Master of Business Administration degree from Southern Illinois University, Carbondale. She manages two home-based businesses and lives with her husband and son in southern Illinois.

Trent Lee Brandt targets his writing to Christians who are lacking faith. He writes for newspapers and has a devotional website called The Christian Letter. His favorite verse and life motto is found in Proverbs 27:17.

Marguerite A. Brown is a native New Yorker currently living in Las Vegas, Nevada. She enjoys both reading and writing immensely and dreams of becoming a published fiction author someday.

Rhonda Buck is a wife and mother of four from Winnipeg, Manitoba. Instead of using her BEd., she is taking a stab at writing. "The coffee is good and the dress code is casual," she says.

Terry W. Burns has published inspirational fiction, *To Keep a Promise* and *Don't I Know You?* and will release a new series of Christian western novels beginning in the spring from River Oak Publishing. www.terryburns.net

Karen Sue Campbell completed a dissertation for a Doctorate of Science in holistic theology. Her interests are writing, healing arts, and her lifestyle education practice, heARTworks, a partnership with artist and teacher, Robin Wellman.

Hugh Chapman and his family live in Horseshoe Bend, Arkansas. He and his wife, Julie, continue their careers as educators within the Izard County School System in Brockwell.

Nancy M. Chapman is a freelance writer and editor based in Norfolk, Virginia.

Cheryl Abrams Collier teaches English at North Greenville College, a Christian liberal arts college in South Carolina. She and her husband attend Park Place Church of God where she also teaches Sunday school and discipleship training.

Michelle Christine Conkey is a novice writer living in Louisville, Colorado. She journals regularly and aspires to share with her daughter the life lessons she has learned and to share God's grace and love with hurting women.

Judith A. Connor has lived in Butler, Pennsylvania, her entire life. She and her husband, Pete, had two remarkable children, Carrie and Joshua, who both died at a young age. Judith works in a steel mill and also sells real estate with her husband.

Melva Cooper is a freelance writer from Jonesboro, Arkansas. She writes for *Christian Motorsports Illustrated, Just-A-Minute Devotions,* and *GospeLines.* She has been published in numerous magazines and ezines. www.melvacooper.com

Julie Anne Daubé is the author of *The Shadows of Babylon*, an end-times thriller published by PublishAmerica. A former college instructor, Julie lives in Colorado Springs, Colorado, and works as a staff writer for a missions organization.

Michael John Demchsak is a freelance writer and serves on a church planting team for the Christian & Missionary Alliance, planting a church for postmoderns in Austin, Texas, where he lives with his wife and three children.

Sharon Dexter is a retired elementary school teacher now working as a freelance writer. She serves as an elder at her church and feels blessed to have a supportive husband and a loving son.

Marie E. DisBrow writes poetry, articles, and devotionals that have been published in the ezines, *This Christian Life* and *Simple Joy*. Her work has also appeared in *Progress*, *Cross & Quill*, and Marlene Bagnull's devotional, *For Better, For Worse.*

Margo Lynn Dill, an elementary writing teacher in Boonville, Missouri, has published short stories, articles, poetry, lesson plans, and essays. Her essay, "Finding Strength," appeared in the anthology, *God Allows U-Turns, Vol. 4.*

David Doyle has lived in the small town of Westlock, Alberta, his entire life. He now lives with his wife and son, Josiah, and writes in his spare time.

Vicki Goodfellow Duke is an instructor of public speaking, speech arts, and drama at Mount Royal College in Calgary, Alberta. She is a mother of four.

Linda S. Dupie is a freelance writer from Virginia, continuing her journey to finding her true self. When she is not pursuing her dreams, she is spending time with her husband and two daughters.

Dena Janan Dyer is a wife, mom, writer, performer, and speaker who has had pieces published in over 125 magazines including *Woman's World, Today's Christian Woman, Writer's Digest,* and *Discipleship Journal*. www.denadyer.com

Elizabeth Ann Fair actively serves as minister, Sunday school teacher, and assistant to the youth pastor at her church. She is also a Girl Scout troop leader, an officer of her school district's P.A.L.S. organization, and a veteran.

Elisabeth (Lisa) Ann Freeman is the award-winning author of *The Pictures That Destroy The Mind* and *Coming Out of Sexual Addiction*. Her stories have been in magazines, and she speaks to groups about faith and healing. www.atime2heal.org

Cindy Ruth Garcia has been a missionary in Mexico for 20+ years with Operation Grace World Missions, Inc. She and her husband have four children and are on sabbatical to minister to them and to broaden their educational opportunities.

Maria Garriott has been published in *The Christian Century, The Baltimore Sun, The New York Quarterly, Our Sunday Visitor,* and others. She has a Master's in writing and lives in Baltimore with her husband who pastors an inner city church.

Robert L. Giron has had five collections of poetry published including *Songs for the Spirit*. He writes in English, Spanish, and French and is a professor of English at Montgomery College in Takoma Park, Maryland. He lives in Arlington, Virginia.

Robin Gomez has written several children's books she hopes to publish someday. She writes for pleasure and possible publication and belongs to the Southwest Writers and Blue Mesa Critique Group. She lives in Albuquerque, New Mexico.

Dorothy M. Gundlach has had two stories published in *Obadiah Magazine* and writes prayers as a *Guideposts* prayer volunteer. She lives in Hot Springs Village, Arkansas.

Bonnie Compton Hanson is the author of several books including the *Ponytail Girls* series, poems, stories, and articles (including stories in three *Chicken Soup* and two Obadiah Press books). She resides in Santa Ana, California.

Arthur Harley is a previously unpublished author who lives in Parkland, Florida, with his wife and two children. He is also the finance manager for a real estate development firm.

Julie Bonn Heath lives in Washington state where she is working on a non-fiction book about her spiritual, life-changing adventures. Previous works include a story, "Wait Awhile" in the anthology, *Nudges From God* (Obadiah Press, 2002).

D. Henley is a writer living in Charlestown, Rhode Island.

Gloria P. Humes is a wife, mother, and grandmother, an educational specialist, and a member of New Way Fellowship International Church. She is also a certified Christian counselor and author of *Divorced: Marriage Over!...But God!*

Faith Jaudon, wife of deWayne Jaudon, dedicates this first published work to her parents, Rev. Will and Margie Griffith. She attends Liberty Christian Fellowship and resides in Rincon, Georgia.

Lisa K. Johnson lives in Jonesboro, Arkansas, and is a wife and mother of two teenagers. She is a registered nurse and writes as a hobby. This is the first time her work is being published. Lisa desires that her writing be a tool to glorify God.

Vanessa A. Johnson has been writing since 1994 and has completed a nonfiction book, *When Death Comes A Knockin'* that deals with the death of a loved one and the grief process and is working on a fiction novel, *Sacrifices In The Name of Love.*

Heide AW Kaminski writes for a local newspaper, *The Good News*; a monthly newsletter, *The Interfaith Inspirer*; and several anthologies. Learn more about her new book, *Get Smart Through Art,* at www.thewriterslife.net/Kaminski.html

Douglas Knox lives in Ashland, Ohio; is employed as locksmith for Ashland University' and leads a local mission outreach Bible study. He has three daughters and four grandchildren. His wife, Marie, went to live with the Lord in April 2003.

Jonathan Louis Kotulski was adopted into a family that brought him much hope throughout his life. He is studying piano at Moody Bible Institute and desires to share in God's glory through music.

Chave P. Kreger has a freelance writing/copywriting business and an affinity for words. She enjoys aligning them on the page and manipulating and ordering them around for public relations/advertising campaigns or personally for prose/poetry.

Karen Kruse is the author of *A Chicago Firehouse: Stories of Wrigleyville's Engine 78*, a Pulitzer nominee in history for 2001. Karen is also a regular contributor to *Working Writer*. www.achicagofirehouse.com

Brenda Lachman, an English and drama teacher, has written school plays, lyrics for CDs, and a social political novel, *Only For A Year*, which she recently rewrote as a movie script. A native of Acapulco, Mexico, she now lives in Houston, Texas.

Catherine B. Laska is a beginning writer from Wausau, Wisconsin, who aspires to be a freelance writer. She enjoys writing inspirational poetry and is presently working on essays and articles involving her mission trip to Africa.

Jules Lentz is a writer, public speaker, and wish granter for the Make-A-Wish Foundation. She teaches Journaling for Teens and Journaling for Women, writes children's and humorous gift books, and lives with her husband, Ron.

Rochelle Griffis Lyon is a long-time writer who finds the process to be a continuous source of joy and discovery. She and her husband live in the country—the perfect place for inspiration.

Wendy Ann Mattox is a Christian freelance writer. She resides in Caldwell, Idaho, with her husband and four busy daughters.

Mary Maynard is a wife and mother of two children. Along with her Grand Canyon wrinkles, getting older is causing her to lose her once perfect eyesight, which is making the list of "what she does not see" even longer!

Edison McDaniels II, M.D., is a graduate of Stanford Medical School, a former commander in the U.S. Navy, and a board certified neurosurgeon. He now lives in North Dakota where he spends a good deal of time writing.

Karen Jo McTague is the grants and research officer at Anderson University, Anderson, Indiana; former president of the Indiana chapter of the Association of Professional Researchers for Advancement; and the mother of a grown daughter.

Victoria Molta is a mental health advocate who currently works as a peer support warmline operator, counseling the mentally ill by telephone. Her writing has appeared in a number of print and online publications.

Suzanne Murrell was blessed with a Southern upbringing and now considers herself a friend and teacher of children and a mentor of parents. She is a mother of three and previously worked with Head Start and Salvation Army Child Services.

JoAnna Lynn Oblander writes from her home in Great Falls, Montana.

Marilyn Phillips, a teacher, has written three books: *A Cheerleader for Life, Cheering for Eternity*, and *God Speaks to Cheerleaders* (www.cheercca.com). She has had many articles published in magazines and has contributed to several books.

Raelene E. Phillips, a pastor's wife, is a graduate of CLASServices who enjoys motivational speaking to groups. She has written five books including *The Freedom Trilogy, Where is Your Pineapple,* and *Puppy in the Pulpit.* www.raelenephillips.us

Tina Pinson lives in Grand Junction, Colorado, with her husband, Danny. They have three grown sons. Other than writing, Tina likes to draw and sing and has been known to lend a hand in mechanics and construction.

Richelle Putnam is a writing instructor and speaker, has won writing competitions, and has been published in *World Wide Writers, The Copperfield Review, Cayuse Press, Writer's Journal*, and more. http://www.authorsden.com/richellemputnam

Mark L. Redmond, a high school English teacher and a freelance writer, has had more than 25 short stories and articles published and is currently writing volume five of a middle-grade series of western fiction, *The Adventures of Arty Anderson.*

Carolyn T. Reeves is a wife, mother, grandmother, and retired science teacher. She is the author of *Understanding Science While Believing the Bible,* published in 2004 by Master Design. She and her husband, Jim, live in Oxford, Mississippi.

Kimberly Ripley is a freelance writer from Portsmouth, New Hampshire. A wife, mother of five, and home-schooler, she derives writing topics from her family's many hilarious antics. www.kimberlyripley.writergazette.com

Julie A. Rocheleau works part-time as a home care nurse. She, her husband, and her stepdaughter, Renee, reside in Michigan and are adopting a child from China. Julie enjoys fly fishing with her family and singing in the community choir.

Naomi Rose is a writer who lives in San Francisco, California.

Susan Rose is a freelance writer who encourages readers with inspirational articles. "Many Christians are discouraged, not knowing how much God loves them and wants to help them. I simply tell what the Lord has done for me," she says.

Lee E. Scanlon is a fifth generation Californian and is a retired college professor. He has two children, two stepchildren, and four grandchildren. He is a published poet, the author of several scholarly articles, and an award-winning playwright.

Carolyn R. Scheidies' credits include over a dozen published books, several booklets, and contributions to several books. She writes for various publications and has a column in a regional paper. http://welcome.to/crscheidies

Donna Schlachter has been writing ever since she can remember. She is happily married to Patrick and has two daughters and four grandchildren. www.livebytheword.com

Jenni Schoneman is a school librarian who lives in Merrill, Wisconsin, with her husband and two boys. She has written freelance articles and served as editor of a pro-life newsletter.

Todd Christopher Schroeder is an attorney at Schroeder, Blankemeyer & Schroeder and an aspiring writer. He lives in Ottawa, Ohio.

Jarrod D. Schrunk is a seminary student and is pursuing a full-time writing, youth, and worship ministry. He attends Solid Rock Church and Lamplighter's Open Bible.

Denise L. Schulz is a daycare provider, Creative Memories® consultant, and mother of three children—Jordan, Alyssa, and Kurtis. She lives with her family in Merrill, Wisconsin.

Julia Horst Schuster writes Southern fiction sprinkled with ghosts and laced with crazy women suffering from generational dysfunction. She writes a newspaper column, short fiction and nonfiction, essays, and freelances for a major web portal.

Michael Shafer is an Episcopal priest, the pastor of The Episcopal Church of the Regeneration, Pine Plains, New York. At the time of the story, he lived in Westchester County, New York.

Karen Seelenbinder is an aspiring freelance writer of children's books and middle grade novels. She has worked full time in retail management and commission sales for 25 years.

Lydia Grace Goska Skidmore is a young woman with a passion for Jesus and a fetish for words. She is studying to become an American Sign Language interpreter.

Diana L. Smith is a stay-at-home mom of three small children and stepmom to two teenagers. She lives in Upstate New York, runs an Internet business, writes theater and manuscript reviews, Sunday school lessons, and is writing a novel.

Abigail Susan Steidley is a freelance writer in Virginia Beach, Virginia. She has written for magazines, anthologies, and websites. http://abigailsteidley.tripod.com/writing.

Abigail M. Tatem lives in Neptune Beach, Florida, and is studying public relations at the University of North Florida. She is also a full-time employee at AOL and plans to continue her writing career at the *Folio* based out of Jacksonville, Florida.

Marie Thomas is a nutritionist and freelance writer from Massachusetts. She is a published author, health writer, and former senior technical writer for Prime Computer, MIT Lincoln Laboratories, and Raytheon Company.

Micah Renae Torgrimson is a student at the University of Nebraska at Kearney where she is majoring in English with a minor in journalism.

Tonya Aldena Townsend is a graduate and employee at Anderson University. She is married, has two stepdaughters and a son, and is an active member of her community and the Middletown Church of the Nazarene.

David Vickery was born in 1958 in London, England. He is married to Angie who was born in South Carolina. He works as a freelance marketing consultant in Southern England.

Claude Bert Victory received his B.S. degree from Cal-State University in Los Angeles, California. He is a published poet, and his 55-word short story, "The Wedding Day" received national acclaim.

Niambi Walker grew up in Louisville, Kentucky. She is currently working on her PhD at Birkbeck College, University of London, in policity and sociology.

Lisa Landen Watkins lives in Mechanicsville, Virginia, and is a stay-on-the-go mom of three active sons. In addition to several areas of ministry in her church, she is also an event speaker and author. She attends Mechanicsville Christian Center.

Audrey M. West was born in Brooklyn, New York. She is widowed with four children, three surviving, and six grandchildren.

Nadine Coretta White is an Army veteran who is pursuing a health care services degree at the Univeristy of Phoenix. Her husband is still in the military, but she is enjoying being a stay-at-home mom for her daughter.

Nancy Arant Williams has authored many inspirational women's fiction novels, including *Coming Home to Mercy Street* and *In The Company of Angels,* with many more contracted for publication. www.nancyarantwilliams.com

Samantha Winchester has always loved to write. Between trucking, farming, and raising her children, she has many stories to tell. She recently completed an online writing course that "lit a fire" under her, and she hasn't put her pen down since.

Jan Yonke is an aspiring writer who lives in Wausau, Wisconsin, with her husband, Gary. They have a daughter, Shanna, and two sons, Nate and Josh. She has had essays published in various local newspapers and Christian publications.

Caroline J. Zepp is a Christian writer who lives in Pennsylvania. She has written creatively since her teenage years and particularly enjoys using her poetry and prose to communicate God's fatherly love for His children.

Jennifer Lynn Zolper writes from her home in central California. She focuses on Christian poetry and has been published by the Utmost Christian Writers Foundation and *The Penwood Review.*

To purchase additional copies of this book, go to **www.obadiahpress.com** or call toll-free: **1-866-536-3167**
$24.95 + $3.00 shipping/handling per copy

Or send check or money order to:

Obadiah Press
Living By Faith Orders
607 N. Cleveland Street
Merrill, WI 54452

Be sure to specify how many copies you would like, include the proper payment, and provide an address for shipping your books.

MasterCard, VISA, and American Express are accepted.

If ordering by credit card, you MUST include your billing address (as it appears on your credit card statement), your credit card number and expiration date, AND the three-digit security code on the back of your card at the far right side of your signature area. Your order cannot be processed without this information.